mediatization

PETER LANG
New York • Washington, D.C./Baltimore • Bern
Frankfurt am Main • Berlin • Brussels • Vienna • Oxford

mediatization

concept, changes, consequences

EDITED BY
Knut Lundby

PETER LANG
New York • Washington, D.C./Baltimore • Bern
Frankfurt am Main • Berlin • Brussels • Vienna • Oxford

Library of Congress Cataloging-in-Publication Data
Mediatization: concept, changes, consequences / edited by Knut Lundby.
p. cm.
Includes bibliographical references and index.
1. Social change. 2. Mass media—Social aspects.
3. Social interaction. I. Lundby, Knut.
HM831.M43 303.48'33—dc22 2009012795
ISBN 978-1-4331-0562-3

Bibliographic information published by **Die Deutsche Bibliothek.**
Die Deutsche Bibliothek lists this publication in the "Deutsche
Nationalbibliografie"; detailed bibliographic data is available
on the Internet at http://dnb.ddb.de/.

Cover design by Sophie Appel

The paper in this book meets the guidelines for permanence and durability
of the Committee on Production Guidelines for Book Longevity
of the Council of Library Resources.

© 2009 Peter Lang Publishing, Inc., New York
29 Broadway, 18th floor, New York, NY 10006
www.peterlang.com

Printed in the United States of America

Contents

List of Tables and Figures   vii

Foreword: Coming to Terms With 'Mediatization'   ix
Sonia Livingstone

Acknowledgements   xiii

Contributors   xv

Introduction: 'Mediatization' as Key   1
Knut Lundby

Concept

1. Mediatization: A Concept With Which to
   Grasp Media and Societal Change   21
   Friedrich Krotz

2. Dimensions: Catch-All Label or Technical Term   41
   Andrea Schrott

3. The Mediatic Turn: Exploring Concepts for Media Pedagogy   63
   Norm Friesen and Theo Hug

4. Theories: Mediatization and Media Ecology   85
    Lynn Schofield Clark

5. Media Logic: Looking for Social Interaction   101
    Knut Lundby

Changes

6. Complexities: The Case of Religious Cultures   123
    Stewart M. Hoover

7. Differentiation: Mediatization and Cultural Change   139
    Andreas Hepp

8. Soft Individualism: Media and the Changing Social Character   159
    Stig Hjarvard

9. Dressing Up: The Mediatization of Fashion Online   179
    Synne Skjulstad

Consequences

10. Shaping Politics: Mediatization and Media Interventionism   205
    Jesper Strömbäck and Frank Esser

11. Everyday: Domestication of
    Mediatization or Mediatized Domestication?   225
    Maren Hartmann

12. Mobile Belongings: Texturation and
    Stratification in Mediatization Processes   243
    André Jansson

13. Social Inequalities: (Re)production through
    Mediatized Individualism   263
    Tanja Thomas

14. Continuities: Communicative Form and Institutionalization   277
    Eric W. Rothenbuhler

Conclusion: Consensus and Conflict   293
Knut Lundby

Index   305

List of Tables and Figures

TABLES

1 "The characteristic space" of the mechanism of mediatization   54
2 "The characteristic space" of the mechanism of
  mediatization with examples   56

FIGURES

Chapter 1

1 Face-to-face-communication, mediated communication, and
  the mediatized conditions and forms of life   24

Chapter 2

1 Mediatization on macro and micro level (following Coleman 1990)   50
2 Dimensions of the mechanism of mediatization   53

Chapter 3

1 Student academic learning model. © M. Molenda   72

Chapter 7

1   Tendencies of mediatization and cultural change   146

Chapter 9

1   Drawing based on the website of Miu Miu   179
2   Drawing based on the website of Miu Miu   186
3   Drawing based on the website of Miu Miu   191
4   Drawing based on the website of Miu Miu   192
5   Screengrab from the website of Bruuns Bazaar   194
6   Screengrab from the website of Bruuns Bazaar   195
7   Screengrab from the website of Bruuns Bazaar   195
8   Drawing based on the website of Patrizia Pepe   197

Chapter 10

1   A four-dimensional conceptualization of the mediatization of politics   216

Chapter 12

1   The process of texturation as the production of spaces of belonging   248

Foreword: Coming TO Terms With 'Mediatization'

SONIA LIVINGSTONE[1]

Society is witnessing a historic shift from a dualistic communication environment in which mass mediated communication variously gradually came to complement or undermine the traditional reliance on interpersonal communication. We are moving towards an environment characterized by diverse, intersecting, and still-evolving forms of multimodal, interactive, networked forms of communication. The academic world is grappling with competing concepts and frameworks by which to understand these changes. Although we seem gripped by new communicative forms—digitally convergent, hybridized, remediated, intertexual—it is the analysis of the entire communication environment that matters. This in turn rests on a critical understanding of the socio-historical processes that shape and are shaped by that environment—globalization, individualization, commercialisation, and (the object of this volume) mediatization.

Both society in general and scholars in particular have yet to come to terms with the growing importance of media power. This book examines the idea that, in order to do so, scholars must also come to terms with, indeed to embrace, the notion of 'mediatization.' Although an awkward word in the English language, scholarship is now conducted within a global, and therefore multilingual, dialogue. Distinct from, though overlapping with, the notion of 'mediation,' which exists in most languages to refer to processes of conciliation, intervention, or negotiation among separated, often conflicted, parties, in the Germanic and Scandinavian languages, 'mediatization' refers to the meta process by which everyday practices and social relations are historically shaped by mediating technologies and media organizations.

Such distinctions are all too easily lost in translation. But the argument here is that the media do more than mediate in the sense of 'getting in between'— whether to generate mutual understanding by reconciling adversaries or whether to promote (and naturalise the effects of) powerful interests, as insightfully analysed by Raymond Williams' *Keywords: A Vocabulary of Culture and Society*. Rather, they also alter the historical possibilities for human communication by reshaping relations not just among media organizations and their publics but among all social institutions—government, commerce, family, church, and so forth.

This claim is implicitly marked even in how we label our work. Several decades ago, research in this field was published in books entitled 'Mass Communication and…' or 'Television and…' Now, our books are retitled 'Mediated Politics' or 'Mediated Health' or 'Mediated Family'. This linguistic shift signals an analytic refocusing from a social analysis in which the mass media constitute one among many influential but independent institutions whose relations with the media can be usefully analysed, to one in which everything is mediated, the claim being that all influential institutions in society have themselves been transformed through the history of mediation. According to the earlier model, media and communication studies analyse the relationship between media and politics, say, while in other disciplines they analyse the relation between politics and the health, or society and the family. But in a heavily mediated world, one cannot analyse the relationship between politics and the health, or society and the family, without also recognizing the importance of the media. All these spheres and their intersections have become mediated—or mediatized.

It seems that, for a growing body of European theorists, several of them represented in this volume, 'mediation' is too broad a term, referring not only to the socially constitutive importance of media but also to other mediations—transport, money, narrative, and, the paradigmatic case, language. On the one hand, the claim that the media are now as powerful in shaping society as are these other mediations is in itself exciting, challenging. On the other hand, we must not lose sight of the distinctiveness of media institutions, of their forms and devices, and of the associated activities and practices by which they are becoming embedded in every sphere of life—work, leisure, learning, culture, politics, health, and even our intimate understanding of ourselves. Mediatization retains this distinctiveness and also, usefully, encompasses the very multiplicity of today's media (including and replacing separate discussions of print, radio, television, internet, etc.), recognizing changes in the media themselves, as new and diverse technological and symbolic forms emerge to complicate established theories of communication.

Thus the concept allows us to rethink questions of media power in terms of richly contextualized, strongly historical processes that reject narrowly linear assumptions about media effects or impacts.

These are grand claims we are making—first, that the media mediate everything, entering into and shaping the mundane yet significant relations among individuals and between individuals and society; and second, *as a result*, that the media mediate more than ever before, ushering in historical changes that may be judged more or less critically. The first is a claim about meaning, process, connection; the second is a claim about the gradual transformation of power relations among institutions and publics; these claims are, of course, mutually interdependent. Consider a striking parallel. In the early nineteenth century, Napoleon mediatized the states of the Holy Roman Empire by interposing an intermediate level of territorial authorities between the miscellany of independent cities, the princes and the archbishops and the Emperor, as legitimized by the German Laws of Mediatization. As Wikipedia explains, 'Mediatization, defined broadly, is the subsumation of one monarchy into another monarchy in such a way that the ruler of the annexed state keeps his or her sovereign title and, sometimes, a measure of local power.'

It appears today that, with scarcely less audacity, Rupert Murdoch and the other media moguls of this world are interposing their global capitalist media institutions between publics and governments (and other religious, educational, or cultural authorities). Just how far the power of both publics and their traditional authorities has in fact been 'annexed' by the media is as yet unresolved. But it makes a fascinating agenda for the chapters that follow.

NOTE

1. An article-length development of these ideas is published as Livingstone (2009), On the mediation of everything, *Journal of Communication*, 59(1), 1–18.

Acknowledgements

The *idea* for this book came up during a breakfast meeting between Andreas Hepp, Eric Rothenbuhler, and myself on the last day of the International Communication Association (ICA) conference in Montreal, May 2008. The actual book, however, has been initiated in discussions in several academic constituencies—among them panels on mediatization at ICA in San Francisco 2007 and Montreal 2008, as well as International Association for Media and Communication Research (IAMCR) in Stockholm 2008. Some of the authors are also linked to European Communication Research and Education Association (ECREA), and to German and Nordic media studies organizations. The NordForsk network on 'Mediatization of Religion and Culture' has provided a workshop setting for discussions on mediatization. Thanks to the contributors of this book for all the inspiration they have shared throughout this project.

The editor has worked on mediatization in the international research project he directs, on 'Mediatized Stories. Mediation perspectives on digital storytelling among youth' www.intermedia.uio.no/mediatized/. The Research Council of Norway, through this project, has contributed funding for some of the costs of this book.

Discussions with participants in the Mediatized Stories project have inspired the present volume. I want especially to mention Nick Couldry, Stig Hjarvard, Kirsten Drotner, and Sonia Livingstone. Further discussions on mediatization (versus 'mediation') are gathered in the book, *Digital Storytelling, Mediatized Stories: Self-representations in New Media* (Peter Lang 2008, edited by Knut Lundby).

I am grateful to Göran Bolin who made me aware that Jean Baudrillard already in 1976 introduced the concept of mediatization ('l'information médiatisée'), as noted in the Introduction to this book. I am also grateful to Andreas Thieme for research assistance into German texts and distinctions on *Mediatisiering* and *Medialisiering*.

Thanks for the publication rights that have been granted here:

Wiley-Blackwell gave Sonia Livingstone permission to use material from her article 'On the mediation of everything' in *Journal of Communication*, issue 1, 2009, as a basis for her Foreword in this book.

For Chapter 3 Dr. Michael H. Molenda granted Norm Friesen and Theo Hug permission to use the illustration in their Figure 1.

Stig Hjarvard for his Chapter 8 acquired the right to publish this revised version of chapter six in his book *En verden af medier. Medialiseringen af politik, sprog, religion og leg* ["A World of Media. The Mediatization of Politics, Language, Religion, and Play"], Copenhagen: Samfundslitteratur, 2008.

Charlotte Mehder at Bruuns Bazaar gave the right to reprint the screengrabs from the website of Bruuns Bazaar (Figures 5, 6 and 7) in Synne Skjulstad's Chapter 9.

Thanks also go to Mary Savigar and Bernadette Shade and their teams at Peter Lang Publishing in New York for all encouragement and excellent follow-up through this production process. The anonymous reviewers helped to make the book more readable—thanks for the advice. Heather Owen gave superb language revision service to most of the authors who are not native users of English. As will be clear from the various chapters, authors have been free to apply US English or UK English as they preferred.

Knut Lundby
Oslo, April 2, 2009

Contributors

Lynn Schofield Clark Associate Professor and Director of the Estlow International Center for Journalism and New Media at the University of Denver, U.S.A., where she directs several research projects on digital media and young people, families, intercultural relations, and world religions. She is the author, editor, or coauthor/coeditor of four books and is currently completing a book on how U.S. teens and their parents negotiate digital media in their busy daily lives, which is tentatively titled, *Media Rich and Time Poor: Digital Dilemmas of the American Family.* She was a Visiting Professor at the University of Copenhagen studying mediatization in 2009. E-mail: Lynn.Clark@du.edu.

Frank Esser Professor and Chair of International & Comparative Media Research in the Department of Mass Communication and Media Research at the University of Zurich, Switzerland. Previously he taught at the University of Mainz, University of Missouri-Columbia, University of Oklahoma, and the University of Texas-Austin. His research focuses on cross-national studies of news journalism and political communication. He has published five books and sixty book chapters and journal articles. In Zurich, he is Deputy Director of the "NCCR Democracy," the Swiss Research Center on Challenges to Democracy in the 21st Century, which studies the impact of globalization and mediatization on societies. E-mail: f.esser@ipmz.uzh.ch.

Norm Friesen Canada Research Chair in E-Learning Practices at Thompson Rivers University, Kamloops, British Columbia, Canada. He has been developing and studying Web technologies in educational contexts since 1995 and is the author of several editions of books on the effective implementation of online learning resource collections and course management software. He is also author of *Re-Thinking E-Learning Research: Foundations, Methods and Practices* (Peter Lang), coeditor of the journal *Phenomenology & Practice* (www.phandpr. org), and is a member of the Canadian delegation to the International Standards Organization (ISO) subcommittee for Standards in Learning, Education and Training. E-mail: nfriesen@tru.ca.

Maren Hartmann Assistant Professor for media and communication sociology at the University of the Arts (UdK) Berlin, Germany. Her main fields of research include media in everyday life, appropriation concepts (especially domestication), nonuse, cyberculture, youth, and media. Among her publications are *Technologies and Utopias: The Cyberflaneur and the Experience of Being Online* (Reinhard Fischer, 2004) as well as the coedited *Domestication of Media and Technologies* (Open University Press, 2005) and *After the Mobile Phone?* (Frank and Timme, 2008). She is the vice-chair of the DGPuK media sociology section and member of the Executive Board of ECREA. E-mail: hartmann@udk-berlin.de.

Andreas Hepp Professor of Communications and Head of the Institute for Media, Communication and Information (IMKI) at the Faculty of Cultural Studies, University of Bremen, Germany. He is author, coauthor, and editor of various books and journal articles on media, communication and cultural theory, media sociology, inter- and transcultural communication, cultural studies, media change, methods of qualitative media research, and audience studies. Recent books include the coedited volumes *Connectivity, Networks and Flows. Conceptualizing Contemporary Communications* (Hampton Press, 2008) and *Media Events in a Global Age* (Routledge, 2009). E-mail: andreas.hepp@uni-bremen.de.

Stig Hjarvard Professor at the Department of Media, Cognition and Communication, Section for Film and Media Studies, University of Copenhagen, Denmark. He has published books and articles on television history, journalism, globalization, and mediatization theory. Research on mediatization includes studies of politics, religion, play, and language. He is coeditor of the journal *Northern Lights* and head of the national research programme *News and Journalism in Transition*. Publications in English include *News in a Globalized Society* (editor, 2001), *Media in a Globalized Society* (editor, 2003), and *The Mediatization of Religion: Enchantment, Media and Popular Culture* (editor, 2008). E-mail: stig@ hum.ku.dk.

Stewart M. Hoover Professor of Media Studies and Director of the Center for Media, Religion, and Culture at the University of Colorado at Boulder, U.S.A. His research in audience and reception studies is rooted in cultural studies, anthropology, and qualitative sociology, where he has concentrated on studies of media and religion. His most recent books are *Religion in the Media Age* (Routledge, 2006), (with Lynn Schofield Clark and Diane Alters) *Media, Home and Family* (Routledge, 2004), and the edited volume (with Nadia Kaneva) *Fundamentalisms and the Media* (Continuum, 2009). He currently studies the contribution of religion and media to masculine identity and the implications of the media for religious authority. E-mail: Hoover@colorado.edu.

Theo Hug Associate Professor of educational sciences at the University of Innsbruck, Austria, and coordinator of the Innsbruck Media Studies research group. His areas of interest are media education and media literacy, e-education and microlearning, theory of knowledge, and philosophy of science. He is particularly interested in interfaces of medialization and knowledge dynamics as well as learning processes. Some of his recent work is focusing on media communities, instant knowledge, bricolage, and didactics of microlearning. E-mail: theo.hug@uibk.ac.at.

André Jansson Professor of Media and Communication Studies at Karlstad University, Sweden. He is the editor of *Geographies of Communication: The Spatial Turn in Media Studies* (with Jesper Falkheimer, Nordicom, 2006) and *Strange Spaces: Explorations into Mediated Obscurity* (with Amanda Lagerkvist, Ashgate, 2009). He has published articles in, for example, *Journal of Visual Culture*, *European Journal of Cultural Studies*, *Space and Culture*, and *European Journal of Communication*. He currently leads a research project studying mediatization, participatory culture and civic communities in the Swedish countryside. E-mail: andre.jansson@kau.se.

Friedrich Krotz Professor of Communication and Media Research at the University of Erfurt, Germany, and Head of the research centre Communication and Digital Media. He cooperated in numerous research projects on media use and reception with European, U.S.-American, and Japanese colleagues. Currently, his main areas of research are digital and interactive media, the social and cultural change induced by media development, theory of communication, and methodology of communication research. He is editor of *Communications—The European Journal of Communication Research*. To his recent books belong *Mediatisierung: Fallstudien zum Wandel von Kommunikation* [Mediatization: Case Studies about the Change of Communication], (Wiesbaden, 2007), and *Neue Theorien Entwickeln* [How to Develop New Theories] (Koeln, 2005). E-mail: friedrich.krotz@uni-erfurt.de.

Sonia Livingstone Professor in the Department of Media and Communications at the London School of Economics and Political Science. She is author or editor of twelve books and more than a hundred academic articles and chapters on media audiences, children and the Internet, domestic contexts of media use, and media literacy. Recent books include *Audiences and Publics* (2005), *The Handbook of New Media* (edited, with Leah Lievrouw, Sage, 2006), *Media Consumption and Public Engagement* (with Nick Couldry and Tim Markham, Palgrave, 2007), and *The International Handbook of Children, Media and Culture* (edited, with Kirsten Drotner, Sage, 2008). She was President of the International Communication Association 2007–8. E-mail: s.livingstone@lse.ac.uk.

Knut Lundby Professor of media studies at the Department of Media and Communication, University of Oslo, Norway. He holds a doctoral degree in sociology of religion and has a research interest in the relationship between media, religion, and culture. He was the founding director of InterMedia, University of Oslo, an interdisciplinary centre researching design, communication, and learning in digital environments. Lundby is the director of the international project Mediatized Stories: Mediation Perspectives on Digital Storytelling Among Youth.' He is the editor of *Digital Storytelling, Mediatized Stories: Self-representations in New Media* (Peter Lang, 2008). E-mail: knut.lundby@media.uio.no.

Eric W. Rothenbuhler Professor of Communication at Texas A&M University, coeditor of *Media Anthropology* (2005), author of *Ritual Communication: From Everyday Conversation to Mediated Ceremony* (1998), coeditor of *Communication and Community* (2001), and author or coauthor of more than fifty articles, chapters, essays, and reviews on media, ritual, community, media industries, popular music, and communication theory. He was formerly director of the Media Studies MA Program at the New School University (2001–2004) and faculty member at University of Iowa (1985–2001). E-mail: Rothenbuhler@tamu.edu.

Andrea Schrott Andrea Schrott worked as research assistant of Prof. Frank Marcinkowski at the Department of Mass Communication and Media Research at the University of Zurich, Switzerland, in the fields of Political and Scientific Communication. In her doctoral thesis, she dealt with 'mediatization' and its implications. She is now working at the Swiss Federal Institute of Technology Zurich as Didactic Manager. E-mail: andrea.schrott@mat.ethz.ch.

Synne Skjulstad Postdoc scholar at the Department of Media and Communication, University of Oslo, working on a research project on cross-mediated and aestheticized advertising and branding in digital domains, labelled *BRANDO*. Skjulstad has a background in media studies. She has previously been working with practice-based research relating to digital media expressions, spanning from hypervideo, experimental online research mediation, to digital media in dance performance. Skjulstad's Ph.D. thesis 'Mediational Sites: A Communication design Perspective on Websites' investigates dynamic web interfaces as textual constructs. In the thesis, she develops a communication design perspective to design and communication. E-mail: synne.skjulstad@media.uio.no.

Jesper Strömbäck Ludvig Nordström Professor in Journalism at the Department of Media and Communication, Mid Sweden University, and Research Director at the Centre for Political Communication Research, Mid Sweden University. His work has been published in journals such as the *International Journal of Press/Politics*, *European Journal of Communication* and *Journal of Elections, Public Opinion and Parties*. His most recent books are *Handbook of Election News Coverage Around the World*, coedited with Lynda Lee Kaid (Routledge, 2008), and *Communicating Politics: Political Communication in the Nordic Countries*, coedited with Mark Ørsten and Toril Aalberg (Nordicom, 2008). E-mail: Jesper@jesperstromback.com.

Tanja Thomas Assistant Professor of Communication Studies and Media Culture at The University of Lueneburg, Germany. Her research in Media Studies focuses on Critical Media Theory, Cultural Studies, Gender Studies, and Governmentality Studies. She has published widely on Media and Cultural Studies, on Media and Racism, Nationalism, War, and Popular Culture as a mode of socialization in neoliberal societies.

Her most recent publications include anthologies on Media Culture and Social Acting (*Medienkultur und soziales Handeln*, 2008), Media and Social Inequalities (*Medien—Diversität—Ungleichheit*, 2008). She is coeditor of *War Isn't Hell, It's Entertainment: Essays on Visual Media and the Representation of Conflict* (McFarland, 2009). E-mail: thomas@uni-lueneburg.de.

Introduction: 'Mediatization' AS Key

KNUT LUNDBY

1 -18

'Mediatization' points to societal changes in contemporary high modern societies and the role of media and mediated communication in these transformations. Processes of mediatization affect almost all areas of social and cultural life in late modernity.

ALL-EMBRACING MEDIA

The day-to-day activities of individuals, families, networks, organizations, companies, and institutions in high modern settings involve a repertoire of technical media. Everyday life and the operations of society depend on mediated communication. Who could manage without a cell phone, e-mail, favourite social networking site, or whatever means of communication one chooses to stay connected? How could one relate, interpret, and act in one's small or big world without access to news in suitable media? As the internet has become commonplace, literally a World Wide Web, it's difficult to imagine information exchange, banking, or travel planning without it. The emerging generations may not be able to imagine life without mediated gaming, online or playing with their own console. Contemporary entertainment relies heavily on the media. Cultural industries, artists, and publics go 'mediated' more often than 'live.' People fill their leisure time with images and sound from films, television series, radio, and recorded music. And still people read newspapers, magazines, and books.

The media are everywhere, all-embracing. High modern societies are media-saturated societies. Lash argues that there are two modernities and that the second modernity or post-modernity is one of generalised mediatization. 'The second modernity is one in which the media spread like a disease. The first modernity describes a process of rationalization. And the second modernity describes one of mediatization' (Lash 2005). The contemporary complex conditions could not be handled without mediated communication. What would politics be without the media? What would trade, finances, and commerce be without information and communication technologies? How could companies manage without internal mediated communication in their intranets? The new media and communication technologies are everywhere. Social interaction 'offline' merges with social interaction online. Media environments and mediated communication are part of the contemporary high modern condition.

This situation, sketched in an impressionistic way above, involves ongoing social and cultural changes. The media themselves are changing. This involves the technologies, the media organizations and their output, as well as media consumption. New media practices play back and (re)shape the technologies and the social and cultural contexts where the media are embedded. The media institutions are themselves transformed. Other institutions in society, like politics, sports, or religion, also change as they include new forms of mediated communication. People's lives are shaped as they relate to their media environments and include a variety of media in their daily practices.

GRASPING THE SITUATION

How can we get to grips with the contemporary media-saturated situation as well as the changes of the all-embracing media? This is a challenge to scholars and students as well as to citizens, institutions, and companies trying to navigate the media environment. Which concepts and approaches to use? Let us point out a few milestones.

The Canadian 'medium theorists' made early attempts. Harold Innis argued in the very early 1950s that the communication media play a major role in the shaping of modern societies (Heyer 2003). In the 1960s, his student, the visionary Marshall McLuhan, pointed to the 'implosion' driven by the electronic media following the 'explosion' of the print media. This transformed people, social relations, and societies (McLuhan 1962; 1964). 'Medium theory' explores the influences of communication technologies that go beyond the specific content they bring. Although criticized for a mechanistic or deterministic view, medium theory has more nuanced arguments about interactions between media and society rather than simple statements about media wholly shaping society (Meyrowitz 2008). In the version of 'media ecology' theories, the focus is on media as environments (Newton 2008). (See further discussions in the chapters by Norm Friesen and Theo Hug, and by Lynn Schofield Clark, in this volume.)

Out of the political conflicts and cultural resistance in Latin America in the 1970s and 1980s, Jesús Martín-Barbero (1993) inscribed the popular mass media in matrices of communication and hegemony. He understood the transforming role of the mass media through the negotiations they invited in a variety of cultural contexts. He shifted focus from 'the media' to the processes of 'mediations.' This was a shift to the places and processes where the media are consumed and given meaning. In the Latin American context, he observed the mediations within popular social movements. In the articulations between communication practices and social movements that go on in a plurality of cultural matrices (Martín-Barbero 1993, p. 187), the transforming mediations are to be found.

John B. Thompson (1995) made a general argument about the media and modernity. He focused on symbolic forms and their modes of production and circulation. This made him aware of the systematic cultural transformation that has followed the symbol-handling modern media. He claims they began to change patterns of communication and interaction in profound and irreversible ways. These changes Thompson termed the 'mediazation of culture' (Thompson 1995, p. 46)—without the 'ti,' but close to the processes of mediatization as described in this book.

Roger Silverstone picked up from Martín-Barbero and Thompson. Although his British countryman had introduced 'mediazation,' Silverstone kept 'mediation' as the conceptual tool to grasp the transformations of society and culture. He regards 'mediation' as a fundamentally dialectical notion, different from but at the same time complementary to the concept of communication. Silverstone pointed out that the concept of mediation requires scholars to address communication processes 'as both institutionally and technologically driven and embedded' (Silverstone 2005, p. 189):

> Mediation, as a result, requires us to understand how processes of communication change the social and cultural environments that support them as well as the relationships that participants, both individual and institutional, have to that environment and to each other. (Silverstone 2005, p. 189)

Thus, while Silverstone applies the concept of mediation, this book argues that the changes and transformation he points to are better grasped with the concept of mediatization. 'Mediation' is too general a term, with a different connotation of conflict-resolution alongside processes and changes within the modern media.

'Mediatization' goes more specifically to the transformations in society and every-day life that are shaped by the modern media and the processes of mediation, as laid out by Silverstone.

Mediatization takes place within matrices of communication, culture, and hegemony (Martín-Barbero). It shapes society and culture as well as the relationship that individual and institutional participants have to their environment and to each other (Silverstone).

What Silverstone claims for 'mediation' is, in this book, valid for 'mediatization.' Processes of mediatization have roots in the technologies of the modern media, as would also be claimed by media theorists. However, social processes also shape mediatization. With Silverstone again, 'Institutions and technologies as well as the meanings that are delivered by them are mediated in the social processes of reception and consumption' (Silverstone 2005, p. 189). 'Mediatization' is the key to these processes.

HOW GENERAL OR SPECIFIC?

How encompassing are the processes of mediatization? Gianpietro Mazzoleni provides an answer in *The International Encyclopedia of Communication:* 'From a very general point of view, "mediatization of society" is a concept that indicates the extension of the influence of the media (considered both as a cultural technology and as an organization) into all spheres of society and social life' (Mazzoleni 2008c). For him, mediatization of society involves all spheres of society.

Is it fruitful to apply such a general concept? It may be, as a reminder of how involved late modern societies have become with the media. However, a workable analysis has to be more specific. Mazzoleni so indicates as he, on the one hand, points out the main processes of change behind the mediatization of society and, on the other hand, discusses mediatization *in* society, that is, in the main domains or institutions where mediatization processes could be observed.

An even wider approach to mediatization is taken by Juergen Habermas. He tailors his general *Theory of Communicative Action* to the lifeworld concept of society and to the differentiation of lifeworld structures. The socially integrated lifeworld where people experience patterns of belonging is becoming more and more rationalized. This is part of the modernization processes. The lifeworld is, at the same time, both uncoupled from and made dependent upon the big systems in the economy and state administration. This dependency results from the *mediatization* of the lifeworld by system imperatives, Habermas claims. This mediatization depends on Habermas' very general definition of 'media,' as, for example, money and power. Such 'media' may 'colonize' the lifeworld (Habermas 1987, p. 305).

These are major transformations of society, however, beyond the scope of mediatization as defined in this book. A more specific definition of 'media' is applied here, as modern (mass and interactive) media of communication. Hence, we look for social transformations and cultural changes that relate to the modern communication media as cultural technologies and as social institutions. (See Theo Hug and Norm Friesen's chapter for a further discussion.)

Friedrich Krotz follows this path, although he makes big claims: mediatization is one of the meta-processes shaping modernity, alongside individualization, commercialization, and globalization. 'The specific relevance of mediatization lies in the fact that it is a meta-process that changes communication and so the core of human action', says Krotz (2008, p. 24). The mediatization meta-process, then, 'in particular makes it clear that lifeworld-specific communication remains the basis of communication and meaning in general' (Krotz 2008, p. 28).

However, there has to be an institutional perspective on mediatization as well. Stig Hjarvard (2008b) takes this approach. This implies an analysis of the interplay between media and other social spheres or institutions. Hjarvard reviews the scholarly literature on the topic and outlines the uses of 'mediatization' in media studies or, to be more specific, in media sociology. He defines the mediatization of society as

> ...the process whereby society to an increasing degree is submitted to, or becomes dependent on, the media and their logic. This process is characterized by a duality in that the media have become *integrated* into the operations of other social institutions, while they also have acquired the status of social institutions *in their own right*. As a consequence, social interaction—within the respective institutions, between institutions, and in society at large—takes place via the media. (Hjarvard 2008b, p. 113, emphases in original)

Hjarvard distinguishes between a direct (strong) and an indirect (weak) form of mediatization. In direct mediatization, formerly non-mediated activity converts to a mediated form, for example, in online banking. Indirect mediatization is when the media and their symbolic world in terms of form, content, or organization increasingly influence an existing activity. The example is a burger chain where a visit involves exposure to film characters and cartoon animations along with the eating of a hamburger (Hjarvard 2004).

Besides involving themselves in other institutions, the media during mediatization appear more and more as an independent institution within society. This duality exactly characterizes mediatization. On the one hand, mediatization 'intervenes in human interaction in many different contexts, while it also institutionalizes the media as an autonomous entity with its own logic,' Hjarvard (2008b, p. 116) notes. The *ways* in which mediatization affects and shapes society and social life is fundamentally a question of the media intervening into the social interaction between individuals *within* a given institution, *between* institutions, and *in society at large,* he explains (Hjarvard 2008b, p. 120).

This brings the phenomenon down to concrete processes that could be analysed empirically. The amount of mediatized interactions at all levels brings about changes or transformations of everyday life, institutions, and society of such scale that big claims have to be made. Still, as Kirsten Drotner (2008, p. 71) remarks, there is a need for middle-range explorations of actual media forms to understand media's both material and immaterial aspects in processes of mediatization.

The contributors to this book are all within the scope outlined above. They aim to understand how and to what extent social interaction, with its symbolic or cultural expressions, institutions, and societies, is shaped in processes of mediatization with modern media. However, the authors emphasize different aspects.

MEDIATIZATION IN VARIOUS FIELDS OF ACTIVITY

So far, the discussion has been on the mediatization of society at large. Specifications may be given in terms of the *level* of analysis, from micro interactions to macro patterns of society, as indicated above. However, studies of mediatization are also made in relation to specific fields of activity: these activities are either routinized into institutions with strong structures or kept more fluid.

The first social scientific works on mediatization were in the field of *politics.* How the media interfere and transform politics is a continued and visible part of mediatization research. Mazzoleni summarizes the main effects of mediatization on politics: first, their agenda-setting capacity; second, that the media in general and television and the 'tabloid press' in particular make politics spectacular and personalized. The third effect is the fragmentation of politics; the fourth, the selection of political elites through the imposition of media-driven mechanisms on the political communication (Mazzoleni 2008b). The mediatization of politics may be a challenge for democracy (Mazzoleni and Schultz 1999). Different phases in the increasing influence of mediatization in political communication can be identified (Strömbäck and Nord 2008). Jesper Strömbäck and Frank Esser develop this in their chapter here. The mediatization of politics is usually discussed on a theoretical basis. From time to time, a 'reality check' is performed; Tom Moring and Juri Mykkänen (2008), for example, show through long-term Finnish election data that mediatization of politics is not necessarily a continuously expanding phenomenon. On various indicators, the degree of mediatization may vary. 'Mediatization of politics may not be a one-way road, after all,' the Finnish researchers conclude.

Distinctions between aspects of mediatization are also made when Stig Hjarvard (2008c) discusses mediatization of *religion.* With reference to Joshua

Meyrowitz, he looks at communication media as conduits, as languages, and as environments. The metaphor of conduits draws attention to how the media transport content or messages. In Western countries, religious issues are depicted by the media themselves in mixes of institutionalized religion and other spiritual elements, Hjarvard claims. Considering media as languages gives focus to the variety of media formats that frame the messages and the relations between sender, content, and receiver. In Europe and America, it becomes visible that religion in the media is extensively formatted according to the genres of popular culture. When analyzed by the metaphor of media as environment, one observes the ways media systems and institutions facilitate social interaction and communication. From a long-term perspective, the printing press weakened the church's control of religious texts and stimulated alternative thinking, thus stimulating processes of individualization. Taken together, the media as conduits, languages, and environments make up the mediatization of religion—as they would do in other fields where the core elements of activity assume media form (Hjarvard 2008c).

Mediatization has been discussed by scholars in a wide range of fields or institutional areas, or in general processes across fields or institutions. Such studies and considerations include the growing media presence in identity constructions, especially among the young (Fornäs 1995, p. 210); in gender relations (Meyrowitz 1985; Mazzoleni 2008c); the mediatization of consumption (Jansson 2002b); the tourist experience (Jansson 2002a); the mediatization of play (Hjarvard 2004; 2008a); of knowledge and learning (Ludes 2008, pp. 111–115); and of language (Hjarvard 2007; 2008a). Philip Auslander (2008) discusses performance in a mediatized culture. 'Media events,' the live broadcasting of history described by Daniel Dayan and Elihu Katz (1992), could be understood as mediatization (Mazzoleni 2008c). Simon Cottle (2006a) digs into mediatized conflicts, and Denis McQuail (2006) into writings on the mediatization of war. (See also the conclusion to this book.)

'MEDIA LOGIC'

Contemporary scholars of mediatization point to a certain 'media logic' as a driving mechanism behind and within the processes of mediatization. When, in these transformations, core elements of a social or cultural activity assume media form, Hjarvard holds, 'the activity is, to a greater or lesser degree, performed through interaction with a medium, and the symbolic content and the structure of the social and cultural activity are influenced by media environments and a media logic, upon which they gradually become more dependent' (Hjarvard 2008c, p. 13). Mediatization is the process of social change that to some extent subsumes other social or cultural fields into the logic of the media, Hjarvard (2008c, p. 14) proposes. In an article explicating an institutional approach, Hjarvard explains that:

> Mediatization is to be considered a double-sided process of high modernity in which the media on the one hand emerge as an independent institution with a logic of its own that other social institutions have to accommodate to. On the other hand, media simultaneously become an integrated part of other institutions like politics, work, family, and religion as more and more of these institutional activities are performed through both interactive and mass media. The logic of the media refers to the institutional and technological modus operandi of the media, including the ways in which media distribute material and symbolic resources and make use of formal and informal rules. (Hjarvard 2008b, p. 105)

It's not just the media that operate according to their own 'logic.' Agents and actors in other institutions accommodate it as well. If political actors begin to *adapt* to the notion of newsworthiness inherent in the logic of the media institutions, they will come to *adopt* the same media logic and standards of newsworthiness (Strömbäck and Nord 2008, pp. 103–104).

'Media logic,' then, plays an important role in the understandings of 'the processes that shape the nature of the changes brought by mediatization,' Mazzoleni (2008c) holds. He regards media logic as the combination of a commercial logic, a technological logic, and a cultural logic. He does not explain the latter. He mainly finds the logics of the mediatization processes in the commercial and technological aspects. The commercial logic involves the commercialization of both the media institutions and society as a whole, followed by the industrial logic of the media or cultural industries. The technological logic refers to how the applied technologies shape content in production and reproduction processes (Mazzoleni 2008c).

The term 'media logic' was introduced by David Altheide and Robert Snow (1979). They focus on media formats. The characteristics of format are 'how material is organized, the style in which it is presented, the focus or emphasis on particular characteristics of behaviour, and the grammar of media communication' (Altheide and Snow 1991, p. 9). The underlying idea, Mazzoleni explains (2008a), is 'that of a dominant form, a representation of reality, and content definitions to which media producers conform.' By identifying these 'formats,' Mazzoleni maintains, it is possible to better understand what lies behind the processes of media production. These production processes are complex. They usually imply certain standardizations and specifications in order to keep a profile, adapt to audiences, and maintain efficiency. 'The term "media logic" captures the whole of such processes that eventually shape and frame media content' (Mazzoleni 2008a).

The 'media logic' of mediatization processes is further explicated—and questioned—in Knut Lundby's chapter in this book.

NEW EYES ON MEDIA INFLUENCE

The concept of mediatization may help see 'old' questions in communication studies and media sociology in new and more striking and relevant ways. This particularly applies to questions of media effect and influence.

When the media were few, one could ask, for instance, about the 'effects' on social life of the introduction of radio. With the all-embracing media, questions of the media's influence have to be posed in new ways. The media-saturated environment calls for approaches other than thinking in terms of cause and effect. The concept of mediatization helps to grasp the influence of mediated communication in contemporary late modern complex societies. 'Mediatization' offers a conceptual context for specific processes of agenda setting (McCombs 2004), and of how news media influence and shape messages through 'framing,' that is, by selecting some aspects of a perceived reality and making them more salient in a communicating text (Entman 1993; Pan 2008).

A distinction has to be made between media influence, as outlined above, and power structures. Mediatization is not an even process, affecting and involving all actors in the same manner or to the same extent. Some actors or agents have more power than others, in Max Weber's sense of 'the probability that one actor within a social relationship will be in a position to carry out his own will despite resistance…' (Weber 1978, p. 53). Although power in the media field is more about symbolic power (Bourdieu 1991; Couldry 2000), media producers and users have different capabilities and positions to taking part in the media's construction of reality (Couldry 2000, p. 4). Among the variety of producers and consumers, there is further differentiation: there is an 'uneven landscape of power in which the media process is founded' (Couldry 2003, p. 19). Hence, it is an uneven landscape of power in which the mediatization processes take place. Different actors (people as well as organizations, companies, and institutions), have unequal power to interfere in the mediatization processes. Mediatization also splits and differentiates.

'Mediatization' gives media scholars a different agenda and a different set of priorities and guiding ideas about what to study and how to study it. It also addresses a key role for the media in larger processes of social change. This should also be of interest to other scholars and students in the social sciences and humanities. So, what are the changes following mediatization?

CHANGES AND TRANSFORMATIONS

A historical perspective on mediatization sets contemporary society in contrast and helps us to understand the specific role of new media as cultural technologies in the transforming processes.

Mediatization follows modernity. Friedrich Krotz lays out the big picture when he characterizes mediatization as one of the meta-processes behind modernity, together with individualization, commercialization, and globalization (Krotz 2007, 2008). This could be observed from a long-term, general historical perspective and in a shorter, more recent span of history, where the mediatization processes are more complex, encompassing. In Western societies, the former takes us back to around 1450, while the latter could be observed some 500 years later, well after 1950.

John B. Thompson, in *The Media and Modernity*, takes the origins of mediatization (or 'mediazation of culture,' in his wording) back to Gutenberg and the media organizations that were established from the second half of the fifteenth century following his invention of the printing press (Thompson 1995, p. 46). In her study of *The Printing Press as an Agent of Change*, Elizabeth Eisenstein (1979) actually describes a long-term story of mediatization.

The recent historical period of mediatization is the context of Hjarvard's analysis. This development has accelerated in the last decades of the twentieth century in high modern, mostly Western or westernized, societies like Europe, the United States and Canada, Australia, and Japan—with other countries emerging. This is the historical situation 'in which the media *at once* have attained autonomy as a social institution and are crucially interwoven with the functioning of other institutions' (Hjarvard 2008b, p. 110, emphasis in original). This is the recent historical phase where there is a growing surplus of mediated information and entertainment and a following deficit of attention. The media have to struggle for their share of people's attention, and hence take various mediatizing techniques into use. This was observed by the sociologist Gudmund Hernes in 1977, with reference to Herbert Simon's and James Coleman's notes on 'media rich' versus 'media poor' societies and social situations (both in Greenberger 1971).

The year before, in 1976, Jean Baudrillard had introduced the concept of mediatization ('l'information médiatisée') in *L'échange symbolique et la mort* (p. 98). Here he discusses modes of media presentation in relation to Walter Benjamin on photography and film and Marshall McLuhan on television. In the English translation in this chapter on 'the order of simulacra' it reads that today's objects 'no longer has anything to do with yesterday's objects, any more than "mediatized" information has with the "reality" of facts' (Baudrillard 1993, p. 63).

Winfried Schulz (2004) argues for the reconstruction of mediatization as an analytical concept. He relates mediatization to changes associated with communication media and their development. Schulz points to four processes of social change where the media play a key role: first, in *extension* of the natural human communication capacities; second, in partial or complete *substitution* of social interaction and social institutions when non-media activities assume media form, or new media substitute traditional forms of communication; third, in the *amalgamation* where boundaries between mediated and non-mediated activities are dissolved; and finally, *accommodation*—the changes induced by the mere fact that communication media exist, and so people and institutions have to adapt to them. Schulz regards these four processes of change as components of a complex process of transition. 'As the concept emphasizes interaction and transaction processes in a dynamic perspective, mediatization goes beyond a simple causal logic dividing the world into dependent and independent variables. Thus, mediatization as a concept both transcends and includes media effects' (Schulz 2004, p. 90).

Mediatization involves processes of social *changes*. These changes may have the character of *transformations*, as the changes incurred by the media may change the direction, the form, or character of the actual social or cultural activities. As Schulz concludes, 'The concept of mediatization has heuristic value if it precisely defines the role of mass media in a transforming society and if it stimulates an adequate analysis of the transformation processes' (Schulz 2004, p. 98).

LOST IN TRANSLATION?

Sonia Livingstone (2009) in her essay, 'On the mediation of everything,' documents how the meaning of terms like *mediation, mediazation, medialization,* and *mediatization* may easily be lost in translation as they appear from different language contexts. This book chooses and focuses 'mediatization' as the keyword. It is necessary to argue for this in relation to uses in various language areas. This discussion will be limited to the German- and English-speaking countries in Europe and Northern Europe, with Scandinavia as an in-between case where linguistic roots are near German, but language use is closer to English.

The old Germanic use of 'mediatization' was related to the early nineteenth century, when the states of the former Roman Empire were 'mediatized' by Napoleon. Mediatization is, then, the subsumation of one monarchy into another in such a way that the ruler of the annexed state keeps his title and maybe some power. Livingstone (2009) makes the link to present media empires or conglomerates, and to Hjarvard's definition of mediatization (cf. above). Today, 'the media not only get between any and all participants in society but also, crucially, annex a sizeable part of their power by mediatizing—subordinating—the previously powerful authorities of government, education, the church, the family, etc.' (Livingstone 2009).

Contemporary German-speaking media scholars distinguish between 'Medialisierung' and 'Mediatisierung.' They may be used interchangeably, but usually there is a significant difference in whether there is an 'l' or a 't' in the word.

Krotz (2007) explains that 'Medialisierung' focuses the status of society as a media society and its consequences (e.g., Imhof 2006), while 'Mediatisierung' observes the ongoing processes of change with focus on the processes. 'Mediatisierung' describes the horizons of social change in relation to media change. It points to the interdependence between the media and other societal subsystems; the development is open and the processes not yet finished. Krotz looks at the mediatizing potential of digitalization and digital media in particular. They lead to an even more complex media environment and further differentiation of communication and mediatization processes. Whether digitalization radically changes the phenomenon of mediatization is discussed in Lundby's chapter on media logic.

Following the Norwegian Gudmund Hernes' early observations on the mediatizing processes in the 'media twisted society' (cf. above), the Swedish media scholar Kent Asp in 1986 introduced a concept of 'medialization' in a study of the power and influence of the media in political processes (Asp 1990). Jesper Strömbäck moves the terminology to 'mediatization' (Strömbäck and Nord 2008). Stig Hjarvard brings in a significant Danish contribution to the Scandinavian research with his recent publications on mediatization (Hjarvard 2004; 2008a; 2008b; 2008c).

In English, 'mediatization' has sounded a rather awkward term (Livingstone 2009). North American scholars have been writing on the phenomenon of mediatization without using that word. This is the case with the Canadian initiators of Medium Theory (Innis, McLuhan) as well as the U.S. theorists of 'media logic' (Altheide and Snow), to mention a few significant contributors. In Britain, John B. Thompson (1995) tried 'mediazation of culture,' and Simon Cottle has looked for 'mediatized' phenomena (Cottle 2006a; 2006b). However, British scholars have preferred the term 'mediation' to denote the same kind of transforming processes that this book discusses as 'mediatization.' Roger Silverstone's argument for 'mediation' is noted above (Silverstone 1999; 2002; 2005; 2007). Several of his colleagues have followed suit, sticking to 'mediation' as the key term for tensions and transformations (e.g., Chouliaraki 2006; Couldry 2008b; Thumim 2008).

MEDIATIZATION, MEDIATION, AND REMEDIATION

Nick Couldry makes an explicit discussion of 'mediation' in relation to 'mediatization,' applied to the study of digital storytelling and its democratic potential (Couldry 2008a; 2008b). He acknowledges that mediatization, as developed by Schulz, Krotz, and Hjarvard, aims to understand a wider transformation of social and cultural life. He regards this 'a useful attempt to concentrate our focus on a particular transformative logic or mechanism that is understood to do something distinctive to (i.e., to "mediatize") particular processes, objects, and fields' (Couldry 2008b, p. 376). He finds this fruitful as long as this claim is specific and directed towards *forms* or *formats* suitable for media representation.

Couldry's objection comes when larger societal and cultural transformations are seen to operate from a single source and in a common direction, by a coherent 'media logic.' He characterizes this as a linear dynamic; 'an essentially linear transformation from "pre-media" (before the intervention of specific media) to "mediatized" social states.' Couldry then rather turns to Silverstone's concept of mediation, which he finds 'emphasize[s] the heterogeneity of the transformations to which media give rise across a complex and divided social space rather than a single "media logic" that is simultaneously transforming the whole of social space at once' (Couldry 2008b, p. 375).

Couldry brings valid objections to a simplified application of an overall 'media logic.' Such uses will be further questioned in Lundby's chapter. Although he aims at a kind of division of labour between the two concepts of mediation and mediatization, Couldry's criticism appears one-sided in favour of 'mediation.' As noted, in this volume, the general understanding of 'mediatization' is fairly close to Silverstone's use of 'mediation,' which Couldry supports. He holds that the concept of mediation is best fit to grasp the social transformation in which the media are involved. However, the authors in this book argue that such changes should rather be analyzed as 'mediatization.'

'Mediation' is here a broader and more general concept applied to acts and processes of communication with technical media. 'Mediation,' then, comes close to the German 'Vermittlung.' Mediation in this sense may, as Hjarvard (2008b, p. 114) notes, affects both the message and the relationship between sender and receiver. However, it will not, in the long term, transform institutional practices or modes of social interaction.

'Mediatization,' however, may incorporate the concept and processes of *remediation* (Bolter and Grusin 1998). Remediation is the representation of one medium in another. Bolter and Grusin see this as a defining characteristic of the new digital media. Through the same binary code in digital media (Bratteteig 2008), there is an expansion in multimodality (Kress 2003, p. 5), playing out text, images, sounds, and graphics in new combinations (Kress and van Leeuwen 2001, p. 2). Multimodality may foster changes in practices that are part of mediatization processes. In multimodal practices, semiotic transformations take place (Kress 2003). In mediatization processes, semiotic transformations occur along narrative and institutional transformations (Lundby 2008).

Fredric Jameson, following in the footsteps of Jean Baudrillard, sees the postmodern condition as an expression of 'mediatization.' He describes the spatialization of post-modern culture as 'the process whereby the traditional fine arts are *mediatized:* that is, they now come to consciousness of themselves as various media within a mediatic system in which their own internal production also constitutes a symbolic message and the taking of a position on the status of the medium in question' (Jameson 1991, p. 162, emphasis in original). Bolter and Grusin (1998, p. 56) consider Jameson's mediatization of traditional fine art a process of remediation. However, as Hjarvard holds, the post-modern concept of mediatization—especially as laid out by Jean Baudrillard (1994)—is too grand, as it proclaims the disappearance of reality. It is also too simple, as mediated reality replaces experiential reality. Rather, mediatization should be conceived of as 'an *expansion* of the opportunities for interaction in virtual spaces and a *differentiation* of what people perceive to be real' (Hjarvard 2008b, p. 111, emphases in original).

THE AIM AND CONTENT OF THIS BOOK

This book puts the existing body of literature on 'mediatization' under critical examination. The above introduction has focused the main, recent contributions to the scholarly debate on mediatization. The following contributions aim to take the debate on mediatization in media and communication studies to a critical edge; to make a contribution in ongoing discussions in the field in academic constituencies across North America and Europe and throughout the world. It aims at theoretical depth. It intends theoretical dialogue across traditions. It covers empirically a range of social and cultural fields and activities where the changes of mediatization come to the fore. The approach is mainly media sociological, although it also relates to other scholarly communities of discourse.

The book has three sections. The first looks at the *concept* of mediatization, and the second at major *changes* in society and culture where mediatization processes are involved. The last part addresses *consequences* of mediatization in different arenas and aspects of social life. There are no simple causal relationships here. The processes that are here treated as 'consequences' are, of course, changes within the said social fields. The chapters dealing with 'changes,' in a similar way, discuss consequences of the interplay between mediatization and some other major transformations on various levels.

Friedrich Krotz argues that 'mediatization' is a concept with which to grasp media and social change. Andrea Schrott follows with tools to specify dimensions and levels of mediatization. Norm Friesen and Theo Hug work from related concepts within 'the mediatic turn' with emphasis on how they could be applied in media pedagogy. Lynn Schofield Clark relates mediatization theory to media ecology approaches. Knut Lundby concludes the concept section with a critical discussion of the term 'media logic,' which is made central in many presentations of mediatization.

The 'changes' under this second section are on different levels and with different time perspectives. With the outset in a historical view on the transformations, Stewart M. Hoover deals with contemporary complexities of mediatization. The changing religious cultures is his case, pointing specifically to transformations of authority. Andreas Hepp analyses three other macro processes that create differentiation in the relationship between mediatization and cultural change. These are individualization as a social dimension, deterritorialization as a spatial dimension, and the coming of intermediacy as a temporal dimension. Stig Hjarvard follows up on aspects of individualization, namely, how social character has been influenced by mediatization. This chapter revisits David Riesman's classic, *The Lonely Crowd* (1950). Synne Skjulstad brings the analysis of change into digital texts on the Web. She is concerned with textual shaping of symbolic and cultural expressions online via a variety of semiotic modes. Fashion online provides the cases for this chapter.

In the section on 'consequences,' Jesper Strömbäck and Frank Esser observe and analyse how mediatization shapes politics. Maren Hartmann relates studies of domestication to research on mediatization and brings this into the arenas of the everyday. André Jansson explores textures and stratification in mediatization processes when people are mobile but still develop patterns of social belonging. Tanja Thomas looks into the social inequalities that are produced and reproduced through mediatized individualism. Finally, Eric Rothenbuhler rounds it off with an essay on continuities. He considers the centrality of communicative form as well as the constraints of institutionalization. His communication approach to mediatization brings some fresh observations for further scholarly explorations.

Of course, these authors do not keep one strict definition of mediatization. The whole idea of this book is to offer a prism of perspectives on the mediatization processes.

REFERENCES

Altheide, D. L., and Snow, R. P. (1979). *Media Logic*. Beverly Hills: Sage.

Altheide, D. L., and Snow, R. P. (1991). *Media Worlds in the Postjournalism Era*. New York: Aldine de Gruyter.

Asp, K. (1990). Medialization, media logic and mediarchy. *Nordicom Review*, 11(2), 47–50.

Auslander, P. (2008). *Liveness. Performance in a Mediatized Culture* (2nd ed.). London: Routledge.

Baudrillard, J. (1993). *Symbolic Exchange and Death*. London: Sage.

Baudrillard, J. (1994). *Simulacra and Simulation*. Ann Arbor: University of Michigan Press.

Bolter, J. D., and Grusin, R. (1998). *Remediation. Understanding New Media*. Cambridge, MA: The MIT Press.

Bourdieu, P. (1991). *Language and Symbolic Power*. Cambridge, UK: Polity.

Bratteteig, T. (2008). Does it matter that it is digital? In K. Lundby (Ed.), *Digital Storytelling, Mediatized Stories: Self-representations in New Media*. New York: Peter Lang.

Chouliaraki, L. (2006). *The Spectatorship of Suffering*. London: Sage.

Cottle, S. (2006a). *Mediatized Conflict*. Maidenhead: Open University Press.

Cottle, S. (2006b). Mediatized rituals: beyond manufacturing consent. *Media Culture Society*, 28(3), 411–432.

Couldry, N. (2000). *The Place of Media Power. Pilgrims and Witnesses of the Media Age*. London: Routledge.

Couldry, N. (2003). *Media Rituals. A Critical Approach*. London and New York: Routledge.

Couldry, N. (2008a). Digital storytelling, media research and democracy: Conceptual choices and alternative futures. In K. Lundby (Ed.), *Digital Storytelling, Mediatized Stories: Self-representations in New Media*. New York: Peter Lang.

Couldry, N. (2008b). Mediatization or mediation? Alternative understandings of the emergent space of digital storytelling. *New Media & Society*, 10(3), 373–391.

Dayan, D., and Katz, E. (1992). *Media Events. The Live Broadcasting of History*. Cambridge, MA: Harvard University Press.

Drotner, K. (2008). Boundaries and bridges: Digital storytelling in education studies and media studies. In K. Lundby (Ed.), *Digital Storytelling, Mediatized Stories: Self-representations in New Media*. New York: Peter Lang.

Eisenstein, E. L. (1979). *The Printing Press as an Agent of Change. Communication and Cultural Transformations in Early-Modern Europe* (Vol. I–II). Cambridge, UK: Cambridge University Press.

Entman, R. M. (1993). Framing: Toward clarification of a fractured paradigm. *Journal of Communication*, 43, 51–58.

Fornäs, J. (1995). *Cultural Theory and Late Modernity*. London: Sage.

Greenberger, M. (Ed.). (1971). *Computers, Communications and the Public Interest*. Baltimore: John Hopkins University Press.

Habermas, J. (1987). *The Theory of Communicative Action. Lifeworld and System: A Critique of Functionalist Reason* (T. McCarthy, Trans. Vol. 2). Cambridge, UK: Polity Press.

Heyer, P. (2003). *Harold Innis*. Lanham, MD: Rowman & Littlefield.

Hjarvard, S. (2004). From bricks to bytes: The mediatization of a global toy industry. In I. Bondebjerg and P. Golding (Eds.), *European Culture and the Media* (pp. 43–63). Bristol, UK: Intellect.

Hjarvard, S. (2007). Changing media—changing language. The mediatization of society and the spread of English and medialects. Paper presented at the International Communication Association 57th Annual Conference, San Francisco, May 24–28, 2007.

Hjarvard, S. (2008a). *En verden af medier. Medialiseringen af politik, sprog, religion og leg*. Fredriksberg: Samfundslitteratur.

Hjarvard, S. (2008b). The mediatization of society. A theory of the media as agents of social and cultural change. *Nordicom Review*, 29(2), 105–134.

Hjarvard, S. (2008c). The mediatization of religion. A theory of the media as agents of religious change. In S. Hjarvard (Ed.), *The Mediatization of Religion: Enchantment, Media and Popular Culture* (pp. 9–26). Northern Lights. Film & Media Studies Yearbook 6. Bristol, UK: Intellect.

Imhof, K. (2006). Mediengesellschaft unde medialisierung. *Medien & Kommunikationswissenschaft*, 54(2), 191–215.

Jameson, F. (1991). *Postmodernism, or, The Cultural Logic of Late Capitalism*. Durham, NC: Duke University Press.

Jansson, A. (2002a). Spatial phantasmagoria: The mediatization of tourism experience. *European Journal of Communication*, 17(4), 429–443.

Jansson, A. (2002b). The mediatization of consumption. Towards an analytical framework of image culture. *Journal of Consumer Culture*, 2(1), 5–31.

Kress, G. (2003). *Literacy in the New Media Age*. London: Routledge.

Kress, G., and van Leeuwen, T. (2001). *Multimodal Discourse: The Modes and Media of Contemporary Communication*. London, New York: Arnold.

Krotz, F. (2007). *Mediatisierung: Fallstudien zum wandel von kommunikation*. Wiesbaden: VS Verlag für Sozialwissenschaften.

Krotz, F. (2008). Media connectivity: Concepts, conditions and consequences. In A. Hepp, F. Krotz, S. Moores and C. Winter (Eds.), *Connectivity, Networks and Flows. Conceptualizing Contemporary Communications* (pp. 13–32). Cresskill, NJ: Hampton Press.

Lash, S. (2005). Intensive Media—Modernity and Algorithm. *Roundtable: Research Architecture*. London: Centre for Research Architecture, Goldsmith's College, University of London. Accessed 9 January 2009 from http://roundtable.kein.org/node/125

Livingstone, S. (2009). On the mediation of everything. *Journal of Communication*, 59(1), p. 1–18.

Ludes, P. (Ed.). (2008). *Convergence and Fragmentation. Media Technology and the Information Society*. Bristol, UK: Intellect.

Lundby, K. (2008). Introduction: Digital storytelling, mediatized stories. In K. Lundby (Ed.), *Digital Storytelling, Mediatized Stories: Self-representations in New Media*. New York: Peter Lang.

Martín-Barbero, J. (1993). *Communication, Culture and Hegemony: From the Media to Mediations*. London: Sage.

Mazzoleni, G. (2008a). Media logic. In W. Donsbach (Ed.), *The International Encyclopedia of Communication*, vol. VII (pp. 2930–2932). Malden, MA: Blackwell.

Mazzoleni, G. (2008b). Mediatization of politics. In W. Donsbach (Ed.), *The International Encyclopedia of Communication*, vol. VII (pp. 3047–3051). Malden, MA: Blackwell.

Mazzoleni, G. (2008c). Mediatization of society. In W. Donsbach (Ed.), *The International Encyclopedia of Communication*, vol. VII (pp. 3052–3055). Malden, MA: Blackwell.

Mazzoleni, G., and Schultz, W. (1999). 'Mediatization' of politics: A challenge for democracy? *Political Communication*, 16, 247–261.

McCombs, M. (2004). *Setting the Agenda. The Mass Media and Public Opinion*. Cambridge, UK: Polity Press.

McLuhan, M. (1962). *The Gutenberg Galaxy: The Making of Typographic Man*. Toronto: University of Toronto Press.

McLuhan, M. (1964). *Understanding Media: The Extensions of Man*. New York: McGraw-Hill.

McQuail, D. (2006). On the mediatization of war. *The International Communication Gazette*, 68(2), 107–118.

Meyrowitz, J. (1985). *No Sense of Place. The Impact of Electronic Media on Social Behavior*. New York: Oxford University Press.

Meyrowitz, J. (2008). Medium Theory. In W. Donsbach (Ed.), *The International Encyclopedia of Communication*, vol. VII (pp. 3055–3061). Malden, MA: Blackwell.

Moring, T., and Mykkänen, J. (2008). Mediatization of politics—a reality check. Paper presented at the IAMCR, Stockholm, 21–25 July 2008.

Newton, J. H. (2008). Media Ecology. In W. Donsbach (Ed.), *The International Encyclopedia of Communication*, vol. VII (pp. 2857–2860). Malden, MA: Blackwell.

Pan, Z. (2008). Framing of the news. In W. Donsbach (Ed.), *The International Encyclopedia of Communication*, vol. V (pp. 1869–1873). Malden, MA: Blackwell.

Schulz, W. (2004). Reconstructing mediatization as an analytical concept. *European Journal of Communication*, 19(1), 87–101.

Silverstone, R. (1999). *Why Study the Media?* London: Sage.

Silverstone, R. (2002). Complicity and collusion in the mediation of everyday life. *New Literary History*, 33, 745–764.

Silverstone, R. (2005). The sociology of mediation and communication. In C. Calhoun, C. Rojek and B. Turner (Eds.), *The Sage Handbook of Sociology* (pp. 188–207). London: Sage.

Silverstone, R. (2007). *Media and Morality. On the Rise of the Mediapolis.* Cambridge, UK: Polity Press.

Strömbäck, J., and Nord, L. W. (2008). Media and politics in Sweden. In J. Strömbäck, M. Ørsten and T. Aalberg (Eds.), *Communicating Politics. Political Communication in the Nordic Countries* (pp. 103–121). Gothenburg: Nordicom.

Thompson, J. B. (1995). *The Media and Modernity.* Cambridge, UK: Polity Press.

Thumim, N. (2008). 'It's good for them to know my story': Cultural mediation as tensions. In K. Lundby (Ed.), *Digital Storytelling, Mediatized Stories: Self-representations in New Media.* New York: Peter Lang.

Weber, M. (1978). *Economy and society. An outline of interpretive sociology* (Guenther Roth and Claus Wittich, Eds., Vol. I). Berkeley, Los Angeles, London: University of California Press.

CONCEPT

CHAPTER ONE

Mediatization: A Concept With Which TO Grasp Media AND Societal Change

FRIEDRICH KROTZ

INTRODUCTION: WHY DO WE NEED A CONCEPT LIKE MEDIATIZATION?

If today we read empirical studies or theoretical concepts about children grow-ing up that were written thirty years ago, we see that media already played a role in those texts, albeit a less important one than today. Three decades ago, there were no mobile phones to constantly accompany nearly all adolescents, whatever they were doing, with the phones being almost a part of their person-alities. The internet didn't exist as a mass medium. Computer games could not be played at home and were much simpler than today. Nevertheless, growing up already involved media: music and cinema played an important role in develop-ing identity and lifestyle, and parents and children fought about how much and which TV the children were allowed to watch. In general, academic researchers, educators, and teachers identified four distinct institutions relevant for growing up: family, peer group, school respectively work, and the media. Each had to be seen as a separate institution with its own influence on the socialization of chil-dren and young people.

Today, this is no longer true. Of course, family, peer group, school, and the media are still the institutions of main importance for socialization processes.

But evidently, the media have changed their role, as today none of the other institutions can be understood without taking the media into account. No one nowadays would describe peer group relations, peer group structure, and peer group communication without referring to the media as a topic and as a means of communication. The same is true with the family, which today cannot be seen as independent of media. Instead, at least in the Western world and increasingly in Asian and other societies, the media play a crucial role in how a family works, in how relations are maintained and developed, and in how everyday life is organized. In addition, school was developed to teach the use and production of print media and thus always was a media-related institution. Today, in the age of so-called 'digital divides,' even schools, which traditionally focused on print media, cannot afford to neglect electronic media. This is because it is important for children to be familiar with all forms of media if they want to improve their life chances within society as a whole and the economy in particular. In addition, schools increasingly insist that children and young people have access to and are able to use electronic media in their schoolwork. Finally, media themselves refer much more to other media than they did three decades ago, as they all compete on the internet and as they all converge.

To sum up, families, peer groups, and schools as institutions are still the most important actors for the socialization of children and young people today. Nevertheless, none of them can be understood without taking into account the role that the media plays. In other words, we should speak of new mediatized forms of socialization and of growing up in or into a mediatized society. We should speak of the mediatized institutions 'family' and 'school,' mediatized social relations, mediatized peer groups, and even mediatized media.

Now what, then, is meant exactly by 'mediatized' and by 'mediatization'? It is the aim of this chapter to define and explain these concepts and to show how they are helpful in grasping social and cultural changes with reference to media and communication. To do so, in the next section we discuss the concept and some of its underlying assumptions. In the third section, we will go into details by defining an adequate understanding of communication and media using some of George Herbert Mead's ideas. This will help to make clear how the concept of 'mediatization' may be helpful when collecting and classifying empirical research about media and communication change. This we present in the fourth section. The fifth section relates the concept of 'mediatization' to the theoretical approaches of Juergen Habermas, Pierre Bourdieu, and Norbert Elias so as to show how fruitful it may be. Finally, we give some further hints about possible theoretical connections.

THE CONCEPT AND SOME UNDERLYING ASSUMPTIONS

If one, similar to Thompson (1995), aims to develop a social and cultural theory of the media, the starting point must be communication or communicative action. This is because the complex forms of human communication must be seen as a specific ability and a specific necessity for human beings. Communication is even their core activity, and no human practices can be considered without taking into account the complex forms of communication that humans need in order to live together, to think, and to develop their individuality. Human beings even can be defined as those beings who have complex forms of communication—this, for example, is the basis of the idea of Juergen Habermas (1987) to develop a critical sociology that is rooted first and foremost in the theory of communicative action.

Although we will deal later with the question of how to understand communication, we first concentrate on media and mediatization. If we start with communication, *media*[1] in a general sense is something that modifies communication.[2] If we confine ourselves to what is usually understood to be a medium (e.g., radio, television, print media, and the internet), we can say it in a more precise way: *media work at the same time on four different levels: as a technology, as a societal institution, as an organizational machine and a way of setting content in a scene, and as a space of experience of a recipient.*

Now, in the long history since the invention of communication and media, more and more media have been invented, and more and more media have been used by people to make communication more convenient, to make communication independent of the actual face-to-face situation, to store information, and so on. Harold Innis (1950, 1951) was one of the first academics who described the above and analyzed under which conditions media spread in societies with specific needs, what effects that spread has had, and so on. Here, of course, many questions are still open.

In consequence, it makes sense to speak, on the one hand, of face-to-face communication and, on the other, of mediated communication. *Being mediated* thus is an attribute that may refer to communication. Of course, mediated communication already comes into existence with the human ability to communicate. This is because communication happens by the use of signs and symbols, and people can use material things to express signs and symbols. The use of these materialized signs and symbols then is a form of mediated communication. People do so in order to produce messages that last longer than just a gesture or a sound. But then media do not serve only to mediate communication; they can also be used to control communication, to construct social relations, to earn money, and so on. In other words, here we find the social and cultural dimensions of media and media use—and they exist not by media but because of communication as an active process of the people using media.

Now, human beings construct their social and cultural reality by communicative action, as has been described by George Herbert Mead (1967), Alfred Schuetz (1971), Peter Berger and Thomas Luckmann (1980), Juergen Habermas (1987a), and others. But then, insofar as media are used for that purpose, this occurs by mediated communication. Thus we can assume that, throughout the history of humankind, media have become increasingly relevant for the social construction of reality as people in their communicative actions refer more and more to the media and use them. We, in consequence, should understand the social and cultural reality, and thus each individual social and cultural phenomenon, as also depending on the media. This is what we refer to as *mediatized*. We do not call it mediated, as this is quite different from what happens with communication as it becomes mediated. This is because it may be much more complicated to find out what a mediatized social phenomenon or field is than just to state that it is in relation with media. *Mediatization* thus should be defined[3] as a historical, ongoing, long-term process in which more and more media emerge and are institutionalized. *Mediatization* describes the process whereby communication refers to media and uses media so that media in the long run increasingly become relevant for the social construction of everyday life, society, and culture as a whole. This is shown in Figure 1.

More exactly, we speak of the *meta-process of mediatization* (Krotz 2003). By this we mean the following: first, that mediatization must be understood as a long-term process that has, in each historical phase, a specific realization in each single culture and society. Mediatization thus has specific stages of development

Mediatized forms of social and cultural life: The relevance of media for everyday life, work and leisure, for social relations, groups and identity, enterprises and institutions, politics and economy, socialization, culture and society
Mediated communication: Three main forms, classified according to whom a person communicates: mediated interpersonal communication, interactive communication, communication as production/reception of standardized content (mass communication)
Communication as the basic human practice: Face-to-face, gestures and language

Figure 1: Face-to-face-communication, mediated communication, and the mediatized conditions and forms of life.

that may be different at the same time. Second, mediatization as a *meta-process* should be understood as a concept similar to globalization, individualization, and commercialization. Each of these meta-processes is an ordering principle, which helps us to think of specific events and developments as belonging together, as each one takes place in specific fields of culture and society and then affects many other fields. Each of these concepts in this sense is a model, and the question is not whether such a model is true but whether it makes sense, and whether it is helpful to put individual phenomena into a common relation and order and under a common concept, even if they happen in different cultures and societies and in different times.

Of course, this definition is based on some *underlying assumptions* that give it a place in communication and cultural studies. The concept of mediatization also has relations to other theories and concepts commonly used by sociology, politics, psychology and other disciplines. Some of these assumptions and relations will now be outlined.

1. We defined *mediatization* as a meta-process that is grounded in the modification of *communication as the basic practice* of how people construct the social and cultural world. They do so by changing communication practices that use media and refer to media. Hence, mediatization is *not* a technologically driven concept, since it is not the media as a technology that are causal, but the changes in how people communicate when constructing their inner and exterior realities by referring to media.

2. Nevertheless, the technological evolution is also relevant for mediatization, especially as technologies are not merely a neutral means but are produced, modified, and developed by industry for capitalist purposes. Hence, *domestication theory*, which may be seen as an interesting approach to understanding how technologies are introduced into households (Silverstone and Haddon 1996; Roeser 2008; Hartmann 2008), fits rather well to the mediatization approach. Of course, there are further approaches that are rooted more in the sociology of technology, for example, van Loon (2008).

3. It is common knowledge that there are some discussions about whether 'mediation' or even 'medialization' would be better names than 'mediatization' (for an overview on terminology, see Livingstone 2008) as well as whether a mediation concept is more general or more specialized than a mediatization concept (cf. Couldry 2008; Hjarvard 2008; Livingstone 2008; Lundby 2008; Mazzoleni and Schulz 1999). Some of these researchers argue with the concept of *media logic* that was introduced by Altheide and Snow (1979).

We should not overemphasize these problems but find a common language for the analysis of an important development. The terminological question should be solved pragmatically: mediatization is more easily understood than medialization. 'Mediation' as introduced in this text should be dealt with as something different from 'mediatization'—only to differentiate face-to-face communication from mediated communication. The reason is that it is a conceptual and an empirical problem to find out how mediated communication is relevant for mediatized social and cultural phenomena. More exactly, a mediatized social structure cannot be analyzed by calling it *mediated*. Instead, it is produced by the people by rather complicated processes under specific conditions with specific consequences, which must be analyzed in detail, and thus one should not call this simply 'mediated.' Also, the 'media logic' concept may be misleading, as there is no (technically based) media logic, even if one adopts Altheide and Snow's definition of media logic as a mass-communication-based form of social actions according to Simmel (cf. Lundby's chapter in this book). The 'media logic' of TV today is not the same as of a decade ago, and the 'media logic' of a mobile phone is quite different for a 14-year-old girl as compared to a 55-year-old banker. Thus, there is no media logic independent of cultural and societal contexts and independent of history.

In summary, what we need is a social theory of media and media changes, and the label *mediatization* can make it clear that we are concerned with a development of culture and society that by importance, impact, and meaning for culture and society should be treated in a similar way as globalization, individualization, and similar meta-processes.

4. An underlying assumption of a theory of mediatization is the hypothesis that the development of media is a *nonsubstitutional* one. This has been well known in academic studies in Germany, for example, since Riepl's book (1972, first 1913). In more detail, this means that existing media have specific functions for their users, and media development is an evolution that must be characterized as a process of differentiation, as more and more needs and intentions refer to media and people use media for more and more specific purposes—and vice versa, media offer and fulfill more functions.

During the present phase of mediatization, we can observe many such developments. For example, in the age of e-mail and the mobile phone, which was preceded by the fax phase, the telegram still exists. In Germany, for example, you can still send a telegram to congratulate a person on her or his birthday, and this is delivered to this person by a specific carrier. Thus, we observe here that the old medium 'telegram' has lost its original function, which was to inform people rapidly about something. Historically, because telegrams were expensive, mainly 'important people' received telegrams. To receive a telegram thus may indicate that a person is important. Hence, this formerly secondary function of the telegram has now become its primary function, namely, to send a telegram to pay respects to someone. (Maybe this is even a good example indicating that there is no overall media logic for 'telegram.')

5. By *media environment*, we mean the set of media and media functions that a person can access and use. How this happens depends on the world this person inhabits, on the way she or he acts in everyday life, and on further contexts in which the person acts. For example, if we look at the more stable relations a person has and maintains, this person usually knows whether it is better to contact others by e-mail or by phone. This may depend on the time of a day or the day of a week, on what we actually know about the other person, or on the topic. People thus, driven by the forces of everyday life, culture and society, and their intentions and creativity, use the media for communication in an experienced and connected way, and thus their media environment is contextualized by a whole complex of practices, assumptions, habits, competencies, and so on.[4]

6. Above, we defined *mediatization* as an ongoing historical process that, in each specific epoch, has a specific form. This concept should not be confused with the *process of diffusion of innovations*, as described by Everett Rogers (1995). The main difference of his concept compared with the meta-process discussed here lies in the societal and cultural understanding of such a process. 'Diffusion of innovation' refers to the distribution of a fixed innovation in a population with a clear advantage for its users. But the computer or the internet are not innovations in this sense, as they do not have a fixed and unchangeable form of use. The internet of today is in a relevant way different from the internet we used a decade ago; the same is true for computers. Thus, the concept of a fixed given innovation does not work in this case (for a detailed critique, see Krotz 2006).

Compared with this, mediatization theory is not so much interested in the single media technology but in the *communicational practices associated with the media*. And, as this depends on how people understand a medium on the basis of their own position in their culture and society, mediatization is not a modernization theory but part of an approach to a social theory of media and communication.

7. We, of course, must understand mediatization as a process that takes place under the condition that there are further meta-processes such as globalization (Giddens 2001; Hepp 2004), individualization (Beck 1986, 1996; Krotz 1998), and commercialization (Schiller 1989; McAllister 1996). It is worth studying the relations between changes to culture and society resulting from mediatization and other long-term developments if we want to develop a social theory of the media. For example, as Castells describes it, media are a presupposition for globalization (Castells 1996; Castells and Cardoso 2006), and globalization is a reason why people use more and more media. Similar relations can be found for other meta-processes. Of course, the consequences of such relations do not necessarily have to fit together. For example, to act under the conditions of globalization, it would

be helpful to be able to refer to credible media. But in a commercialized media system, credibility may be problematic or at least extremely expensive. Thus, the different meta-processes must be analyzed simultaneously.

8. Finally, we would like to mention the connection between the mediatization approach and *medium theory*, especially as it was defined by Joshua Meyrowitz (1985, 1995) (cf. also Innis 1950, 1951; McLuhan 1967; Ong 1995; Goody et al. 1986; and Clark's chapter in this book). Obviously, both approaches refer to the basic idea that the content transported by media is not relevant for ongoing changes of culture and society, but rather the changing communication practices of the people who refer to media.

Nevertheless, the main difference lies in the fact that medium theory tries to describe fixed social and cultural states as a consequence of technologically given media logics, while mediatization is a social and cultural approach that is more interested in understanding developments made by human beings and not as a consequence of a technology. It also is not media centred. Thus, the concepts are close together and in the long run may find a common language.

UNDERSTANDING COMMUNICATION

We defined *media* pragmatically as a modifier of communication, and mediatization then is the concept used to grasp the social and cultural consequences of the changing conditions for communication as offered by the media's development. It is now obvious that the meaning and importance of the concept of mediatization then depends on how communication as a concept is understood.

To make this clear, we will differentiate heuristically between two approaches to understanding communication; a behaviouristic or functional approach, and a societally or culturally related perspective. This contrast is similar to the possible understandings of culture: Talcott Parsons, as is well known, understood *culture* as the set of values and norms of a given society (cf. Parsons and Shils 1962), whereas Raymond Williams conceptualized culture as the 'whole way of life' (Williams 1958, 1981; cf. also Geertz 1991) of people and, on the basis of this James Carey (1989), said that culture and communication are just different views of the same thing. The meaning of *culture* in both perspectives, is evidently rather different. On the basis of these contrasting understandings of what mediatization is, it is possible to outline the role that the concept mediatization may play.

First, from a *behaviouristic or functional perspective*, communication is the human answer to functional problems of human life. The problem is: how can cooperation be possible and take place? This problem is solved by the transport of information, which from this perspective is in itself an adequate definition of communication. As a consequence of this view, communication is seen to be a specific type of behaviour, and media appear to be technologies that may support communication under specific conditions. For instance, a message can be stored or more easily transported using media. For example, such a functionalistic perspective, which separates communication from culture and society, is behind the mediatization approach of Mazzoleni and Schulz (1999).

Second, from a *cultural or societal perspective*, communication in its complex human forms is an important element of the set of practices by which human beings construct their environment and themselves; their social relations and their everyday lives; their identities; and the social phenomena, sense, and meaning. Culture and society as a whole are then the results of this communicative production of reality. This perspective is behind Williams' idea of culture and the work of Carey, who understood culture and communication as both sides of the same coin (Carey 1989); it is behind the work of Juergen Habermas, who conceptualized systematically a whole sociology by starting with the problem of communicative action (1987a); it is behind the well-known work of Berger and Luckmann about the social construction of reality and society (1980); and behind the phenomenological sociology of Alfred Schuetz (1971) (cf. also Burkitt, 1991). In addition, the communication model of George Herbert Mead is based on these ideas, as argued below.

From such a point of view, and as was asserted by the Sapir-Whorf hypothesis, communication in its complex forms today is not only the characteristic feature of humankind, it is also the basis of all our thinking and experiences (cf. Whorf 1963). In these complex forms the mechanisms are also inscribed by which people maintain or overcome power and hegemony and by which they construct sense and meaning. And, most importantly, communication has its own history, as today it is not the same as communication was 100 years ago or will be in the even more mediatized societies of the future. Of course, mediatization as the consequence of the ongoing intertwining of communication and media is thus much more relevant for such a cultural perspective, since it is much more than an intervening variable.

Obviously, such a social and cultural based perspective is compatible with a semiotic understanding of communication, for example, with the encoding/decoding model of Stuart Hall (1980). Here, communication happens if people interpret something observable as an intended sign, produced by somebody who was attempting to express something. In addition, from a semiotic and a symbolic interactionist view, parallel non-observable, 'inner' processes within the participating people must be assumed. They happen on the side of the communicator, who usually tries to refer with his communication to an imagined other and some given situational conditions. And this inner process happens on the side of the listener and includes the production of meaning, the interpretation of the signs, plus the construction of an idea about the intentions of the other and of one's own as a basis for producing an answer.

Both processes, the inner and the exterior, are necessary for communication to be successful, and this shows the importance of what the concept mediatization intends to grasp: if the participants use media and refer to media in such a way that we speak of mediated communication, we find basic differences compared with face-to-face-communication. Other forms of expression and representation and other senses must be used, other habits and social norms come into existence, other content will be produced, and interpretations change. All in all, other conditions must be fulfilled, and third parties such as providers or producers and distributors or regulating institutions, which have their own interests, are participating. Thus, communication, which of course is historically and culturally contextualized as a social phenomenon and a human activity, today differs greatly from that of earlier generations, as it is dependent on society, politics, and the economy. We can assume that the individuals of today communicate in a very different way from people of other cultures and other times (cf., e.g., Goody et al. 1986; Ong 1995; Assmann 1990), that mediated communication is different to non-mediated communication, and that the process of mediatization defined here is of huge importance for any description of societal and cultural change.

To make this even clearer, let us emphasize the still underestimated position of George Herbert Mead (1969, 1973). He not only constructed a model of communication that explains how one person can understand another, he even is the only thinker who has tried to show how human beings in their structure are produced by communication, since such features as self-consciousness and self-awareness or learning from communicational experiences emerge into existence through the conditions of communication and thus as the result of the necessity of social cooperation.

In a soccer game (this is Mead's example), the players must anticipate what the others will do. This is possible because, in principle, each player knows what it is to be part of a soccer team and how to act in such a situation. Thus, by means of empathy or, more precisely, by imaginatively adopting the roles and perspectives of the others and by creating an idea about what one would do in the others' situation, each player develops an idea of what will happen. This enables a player to support what happens (if the other player is in the same team) or to operate against it (if the other player is in the other team). Just the same happens in every form of cooperation and in every communication. Obviously, this idea includes Erving Goffman's microsociological descriptions of how people present themselves and answer others.

Of course, this model is described here only very roughly (cf. Krotz 2007). Nevertheless, it makes clear what the change from face-to-face communication to mediated communication, and the change from one form of mediated communication to another, may mean and which consequences mediatization thus may have for various forms of living together, societal meaning, social relations, and cultural phenomena. It also illuminates which questions have to be answered as the consequence of the developments we are part of today. Some of these questions will be discussed in the remaining parts of this chapter.

MEDIATIZATION AS A FRAMEWORK FOR EMPIRICAL WORK

The following text aims to show why mediatization is a helpful concept. Here, the starting point is the rather general definition of mediatization as a meta-process that is similar to such concepts as globalization, individualization, and commercialization. All of these concepts help to unite a specific type of empirical phenomenon under a common label. This is an important advantage of a mediatization approach, as we argue in the following.

Today we live in an age that is characterized by the rapid evolution of media. From a technical perspective, our media environment is becoming more and more complex, as the variety of devices that can take over communicative functions for people increases. This creates uneasiness in the public as, for example, the growing use of computer games may have problematic consequences for the way we live together. In addition, the internet has been analyzed again and again as to whether it is disturbing existing social relations (Wellman and Haythorntwaite 2002). We know that complex processes take place if an important medium is introduced into households and enterprises (Silverstone and Haddon 1996). We also know that politics may change if people acquire new ways of informing themselves or discussing political topics, and the consequences, for example, can be the media-driven creation of manifestations or even revolutions (cf. Nyíri 2005). In the meantime, a huge amount of empirical research on questions such as these has been done, and there is also a growing amount of research into digitalization, the computer and its use for communication, and so on. Nevertheless, still missing are broader theoretical approaches and helpful principles to systematize all this knowledge and to put it into a useful order. This is especially necessary, because all of this knowledge is being collected within different disciplines.

The above-defined concept of mediatization now may be helpful in doing so, as described below.

1. The mediatization concept defines communication as the core activity of human beings; thus, a starting point for classifying knowledge should be the *different forms of mediated communication,* not the single medium.

Systematically, we can differentiate with whom communication is done. There is mediated interpersonal communication in its different forms; communication that is the production or reception of given standardized and generally addressed messages as found on TV, radio, internet websites, or in books; and as a new form of communication interactive communication. This may be helpful to systematize and categorize the existing empirical results, to emphasize missing links, and to create theory. A special advantage is that here the communicational practices are the starting point, not the single media, as is necessary if one wants to construct a social theory of the media and their change (Thompson 1995; Krotz 2001, 2007).

2. Mediatization theory mainly is interested in changes to the different fields of everyday life, culture, and society. Empirical questions and results thus can be classified according to whether these changes take place on a *micro*, *mezzo*, or *macro level*. For example, on the micro level, the use of mobile communication devices such as the cellular phone or the notebook are relevant to the actual situation in which a person acts. These devices make the situation more complex, as the owner becomes dependent on external influences, or he or she can change the situation by using that medium. In particular, an everyday life approach here would make sense, as that is the place where new developments must begin (cf. Thomas 2008). Furthermore, the digital media have a great impact on political parties, the way enterprises earn money, how universities teach, and on how institutions such as the police do their jobs—effects on the mezzo level. There are also effects on the macro level, such as the imagination of what is specific and unique to be a human being (Turkle 1996) and how socialization may change (Livingstone 2008).

3. Furthermore, we can order existing knowledge and unanswered questions by studying the mediatization of different fields, such as political communication and democracy, the communication of economic relevance, the effects on the social relations, effects on entertainment, and so on. Of course, this can also be structured more systematically. If we want to understand how life will be in the mediatized societies of the future, we must classify this knowledge. Finally, we do not need only a description and structured theories of what happens, but also a critical theory of mediatization that refers to Bourdieu, Foucault, and others (see below and other chapters in this book).

Thus, in its present state, mediatization may be a helpful way of asking relevant questions, making them empirically accessible, and collecting and classifying what we know already.

THEORETICAL RELATIONS AND ENLARGEMENTS:
HABERMAS, BOURDIEU, ELIAS, AND OTHERS

As it was argued above, we can study mediatization as a process that is rooted in the mediation of communication and takes place in society, culture, and the everyday life of the individual. As we understand communication as a simultaneous inner and exterior process, we obviously refer to an understanding of human action as meaningful, where this meaning is constructed by the acting individual in personal societal and cultural contexts. On that basis, the mediatization approach can be linked to other theories; here we will describe just a few.

Juergen Habermas uses the word mediatization in his book on communicative action and the corresponding German word, 'Mediatisierung,' in the original version (Habermas 1987a, vol. 2, p. 452). But he does not define it explicitly, as far as I know. The core difference between Habermas' use of *mediatization* and the concept as it is used here is what is understood as *media*. Here, mediatization refers to what may be called communicational media—books, newspapers, TV, radio, the internet, and so on. However, Habermas does not specify the media to which he refers. Instead, he writes about the dependency of people 'resulting from the *mediatization* of the lifeworld by system imperatives...' (Habermas 1987b, vol. 2, p. 305, emphasis in the original).

As a result, Habermas' concept is closer to the historical concept of mediatization, which is mainly used to describe how former immediate institutions of the historical Deutsches Reich became mediated with reference to a modern understanding of state (cf. Livingstone 2009). Nevertheless, in his view, mediated communication is a process that integrates a person more and more into the systemically structured world of society and economy, and this fits the perspective used here.

The approach of *Pierre Bourdieu* is in at least two ways highly important for a medatization approach—in his concepts of capital and habitus and in his concept of symbolic power. This is because research does not only consist of a description and discussion of what happens, it also must set its results in relation to society as a whole. Academic research is responsible not only for results but also for the interests that are behind it. Bourdieu's work then is helpful for evaluating research results and for giving them a meaning in society.

The concepts of cultural, social, and symbolic capital (Bourdieu 1993) are generalizations of Marx's idea of economic capital. He defined them so as to be able to analyze the life chances of persons in a given culture and society in a broad way. Cultural capital consists, for instance, of collected experiences, the ownership of cultural goods, and institutional titles. This capital may be incorporated, objectively present, or institutional. Social capital includes, among other things, the knowing of the right persons with reference to specific questions if one needs a job or some information. And symbolic capital is the concept that describes every influence or advantage a person gains through honour or credibility.

These three concepts now can be seen as generalizations of the economic capital concept, since all forms of capital

- have a value defined by society and culture
- are important for power and life chances
- can be accumulated, and
- can be exchanged against any other capital

Thus, Bourdieu's generalization can be used to describe how society functions in dependence of the resources of actors, and these four forms of capital relate all social phenomena to the categories of power and hegemony. The different types of capital thus provide a better description of inequality than the digital divide approach (cf. Krotz 2006).

In relation to mediatization, Bourdieu's capital concept may serve to describe changes in the life chances of people caused by media and communication development. Cultural capital may be devaluated by software such that specific skills are no longer necessary: the knowledge to write and to spell a word in a correct way, today is of less importance for a person, as one may be supported to write correctly by an adequate software programme. It is also possible by social changes that new forms of literacy may contribute to one's cultural capital. The same can happen with other types of capital. For example, in the process of mediatization, new elites may become influential in enterprises or institutions, or traditionally oriented experiences and images lose their binding force. Such processes, of course, must be analyzed not only in terms of what is won or lost by a person, but from a political perspective with reference to groups and classes.

A further concept of Bourdieu that is relevant with reference to mediatization is that of symbolic violence, which '... is the imposition of systems of symbolism and meaning (i.e., culture) upon groups or classes in such a way that they are experienced as legitimate' (Jenkins 1992, p. 104). Symbolic violence works by addressing people in their habitus such as their dispositions, used categories, and generative schemes, so that their social practises, individual experiences, and views and expectations of culture and society are included.

Bourdieu developed this concept in his studies about education in France. When we grow up, we do not only learn this and that—learning means to inscribe the rules of society into our bodies, our thinking, our emotions, and intentions. We in some sense *consist of these rules* that give us a structure, which we learn through interaction with our parents, in school, and nowadays with the media. With reference to Bourdieu, we can even assume that media in mediatized societies are a mighty instrument for influencing body and habitus and for transporting norms and rules to people—of course, this assumption needs empirical analysis to find out how this happens and in which fields.

Finally, let us have a look at the *Theory of Civilization* of Norbert Elias (1972, 1993, 1994, cf. also Burkitt 1993). Elias aims to show society and culture as an ongoing and everlasting process, which he called the process of *civilization*. His conceptual idea was to overcome the dualism of individual and society, which—since Descartes—is fundamentally inscribed into Western-based thinking and understanding of the world, and thus also into academic social and cultural science. Hence, for empirical work, he referred to two core concepts:

- First, the concept of *figurations*, in which people experience and act on the basis of interdependencies. Such figurations are, for example, the family or the society as a whole, but also a group of passengers on a ship. Such a figuration may last for some time or may exist more briefly; in each case, a figuration depends on its contexts (if the ship sinks, this will influence the figuration of the passengers in a relevant dimension).
- And second, the concept of *personality formation* or *habitus*, which describes the individual as a member of a figuration that demands and produces a specific behaviour and the fulfilling of specific norms by its members. His favourite example here is an understanding of society as a dance, which shows very well how the figuration exists only through the activity of its members but has its own rules and reality, and that it comprises of its members as dancers.

Now, Elias' two core concepts, figuration and habitus, in some sense are the two sides of the same coin as the habitus is generated by membership in figurations, and figurations just work because people interact and behave in an adequate way. Elias, using this as a basis, showed empirically that the historical development in Europe in the last 1000 years can be understood as a socio- and psychogenesis happening in association with one another. Of course, these two intertwined developments were rather sophisticated and complex but led to fitting results: the sociogenesis consisted of the development of hierarchy, economy, politics, and society so that the relations between the people become more and more complex, and every single activity has consequences for more and more other persons. This is especially true in the case of the economy. Of course, these developments must be understood in relation to power and power balances in the different figurations. On the other hand, the closely corresponding process of psychogenesis describes how people increasingly learn to incorporate norms and rules into their personalities so that their superegos evolved, and they became able to control their emotions. This guaranteed the behavior that was necessary to live under more and more complex conditions within economy, politics, and society. Of course, these ongoing developments were not planned; they just happened in the collective people lived in.

Empirically, Elias analyzed the evolution of norms, rules, and manners; laws and habits; and also, if possible, their real behaviour. For example, learning to eat from one's own plate using a knife and fork instead of eating by hand from a common plate, how to sneeze and not to spit on the table—learning manners like these are expressions of these general developments. Not only have laws been relevant for success, but all forms of self-socialization, whereby people learned what is normal and that being not normal may be disgusting, and so on. Most or all of these norms were first developed at the royal court of a country and then spread out to the 'ordinary' people. Thus, one could say that the adoption of these rules intermingled power and violence with the wish to gain a higher status in society by improving behaviour.

In detail, Elias mainly analysed media. This work includes his view that people use these media to understand other ideas and in doing so may change themselves—an active process of socialization for a more fitting life under changing conditions. Of course, other processes were also relevant for this development: values and norms changed by religion or other institutions; laws and rules that emerged in growing cities that had their own conditions of life; different classes that compared each other's manners; and face-to-face communication with neighbours, friends, or other persons.

Nevertheless, this is the point at which we can refer to mediatization. Communication obviously is the hinge or joint at which personality formation becomes typical and changes in accordance with the necessities of a society. These necessities of society are realized in the interdependent figurations that we are forced to be part of in order to organize our lives for producing goods, for guaranteeing shelter from violence and so on, economically, politically, culturally, and socially. As stated above, today no single figuration can, in the age of mediatized cultures and societies, be understood without taking into account the communication practices that refer to media. Media thus are the hinge and joint between the figurations and the habitus of a person of today: TV and the media of standardized messages, such as radio and books, explain to us how the world works. (Reality) TV and similar entertainment forms today, for example, show us how people 'really' are and what they are doing and in which ways. As already mentioned, mobile phones make their owner accessible everywhere and at all times. They also make it possible for the cell phone owner to leave at any moment, no matter where he or she is. It also makes it possible for the owner to share each single experience immediately with selected others whom he or she can call. All this then guarantees that, even in the rapidly changing world of today, social coherence may exist, at least inside specific groups and possibly in new short-term forms. Interactive media then show development in a different but fitting direction: interactive communication takes place between a person and a complex computer hardware/software system, including artificial intelligence products. Thus, we will increasingly live in a world where all objects react 'intelligently.' It then may become more and more complicated to differentiate between an inner dialog and a dialog with such 'living' objects. This sounds paradoxical, but it is not. For example, a verbal dialog between an owner with a dog cannot be seen only as a dialog with an animal but must be viewed as an inner dialog of the owner of the dog, which constitutes the dog as a simulated opposite—and this also happens with 'intelligent' objects with which we communicate (Krotz 2007).

In conclusion, we can derive very interesting relations from the theory of civilization and the way it works by applying the mediatization approach.

FINAL REMARKS

Of course, much further empirical research and further theoretical approaches could be taken into account to make a mediatization approach fruitful and to gain an empirically based, theoretically helpful understanding of what is taking place today. To these belong Shibutani's ideas of the difference between membership and reference groups, which was discussed in the 1950s within sociology; the social world concept of Anselm Strauss and Tamotsu Shibutani (cf. Shibutani 1955; Charon 1979), which could be used to describe online communities, the concept of different realities in contrast to everyday life reality, as was developed by Alfred Schuetz (1971a), and so on. We also explicitly refer to other chapters in this book.

What we need is much more empirical research on that and in larger academic 'figurations.' But all empirical research makes sense only if we are able to develop adequate theoretical approaches and bind them together with the existing theories into a close network of academic knowledge. This is what mediatization could be helpful for.

NOTES

1. Some researchers in a media-centered view understand communication always as being mediated— for instance, mediated by air or something like this. This is not the position presented here.

Of course, there are some conditions that must be fulfilled if we speak of communication, but the important thing to construct a theory about being human is communication, not the physical conditions for that.

2. We would even suggest that the other way round also works: what modifies communication should be understood as media. But of course, we here confine ourselves to what usually is understood as media in communication studies—letters and TV, the internet and print, and so on.

3. Similar or compatible definitions are given by Hjarvard (2008), van Loon (2008), and others, and different definitions are given, for example, by Mazzoleni/Schulz (1999).

4. The media environment of institutions can be defined similarly, of course, with reference to the goals and interests of that institution.

REFERENCES

Altheide, D. L., and Snow, R. P. (1979). *Media Logic*. Beverly Hills, CA: Sage.

Assmann, J. (1999). *Das kulturelle Gedächtnis. Schrift, Erinnerung und politische Identität in frühen Hochkulturen*. München: Beck.

Beck, U. (1986). *Risikogesellschaft*. Frankfurt am Main: Suhrkamp.

Beck, U. (1994). The Debate on the 'Individualization Theory' in Today's Sociology in Germany, *Soziologie*, Special ed. 3 (1994), pp. 191–200 (Journal of the Deutsche Gesellschaft für Soziologie).

Berger, P. L., and Luckmann, T. (1980). *Die gesellschaftliche Konstruktion der Wirklichkeit*. Frankfurt am Main: Fischer.

Bourdieu, P. (1993). *Die verborgenen Mechanismen der Macht*. Hamburg: VSA.

Burkitt, I. (1991). *Social Selves*. London: Sage.

Carey, J. W. (1989). *Communication as Culture. Essays on Media and Society*. Boston: Unwin Hyman.

Castells, M. (1996). *The Rise of Network Society. The Information Age*. Vol. 1, Oxford, UK: Blackwell.

Castells, M., and Cardoso, G. (Eds.) (2006). *The Network Society*. Washington, DC: Center for Transatlantic Relations.

Charon, J. M. (1979). *Symbolic Interactionism*. Englewood Cliffs, NJ: Prentice Hall.

Couldry, N. (2008). Mediatization or mediation? Alternative understandings of the emergent space of digital storytelling. *New Media and Society*, 10(3), 373–391.

Elias, N. (1972). *Über den Prozeß der Zivilisation*, 2 Bände, 2. Auflage, Frankfurt am Main. Suhrkamp.

Elias, N. (1993). *Was ist Soziologie?* 7. Auflage, Weinheim, and München: Juventus.

Elias, N. (1994). *Die Gesellschaft der Individuen*, 2. Auflage, Frankfurt am Main: Suhrkamp.

Geertz, C. (1991). *Dichte Beschreibung*, 2. Auflage, Frankfurt am Main: Suhrkamp.

Giddens, A. (2001). *Entfesselte Welt. Wie die Globalisierung unser Leben verändert*. Frankfurt am Main: Suhrkamp.

Goody, J., Watt, I., and Gough, K. (1986). *Entstehung und Folgen der Schriftkultur*. Frankfurt am Main: Suhrkamp.

Habermas, J. (1987a). *Theorie kommunikativen Handelns*, 2 vol., 4. ed., Frankfurt am Main: Suhrkamp.

Habermas, J. (1987b). *The Theory of communicative Action*. 2 vol. Cambridge, UK: Polity Press.

Hall, S. (1980). Encoding/Decoding, Hall, Stuart, Hobson, D., et al. (Eds.). *Culture, Media, Language*, London: University of Birmingham Press, pp. 128–138.

Hartmann, M. (2008). Domestizierung 2.0: Grenzen und Chancen eines Medienanegnungskonzepts. Winter, C., Hepp, A., and Krotz, F. (Eds.) (2008). *Theorien der Kommunikations- und Medienwissenschaft*. Wiesbaden: VS, 401–416.

Hepp, A. (2004). *Netzwerke der Medien. Medienkulturen und Globalisierung*. Wiesbaden: VS.

Hjarvard, S. (2008). The mediatization of society. A theory of the media as agents of social and cultural change. *Nordicom Review*, 29(2), 105–134.

Innis, H. A. (1950). *Empire and Communications*. Oxford, UK: Clarendon Press.

Innis, H. A. (1951). *The Bias of Communication*. Toronto: University of Toronto Press.

Jenkins, R. (1994). *Pierre Bourdieu*. London: Routledge.

Krotz, F. (1998). Media, Individualization, and the Social Construction of Reality. In Giessen, H. W. (Ed.). *Long-Term Consequences on Social Structures through Mass Media Impact* (pp. 67–82). Saarbrücken: Vistas (Reihe der LAR).

Krotz, F. (1999). Individualisierung und das Internet. In Latzer, M., Siegert, G., and Steinmaurer, T. (Hrsg.). *Die Zukunft der Kommunikation. Phänomene und Trends in der Informationsgesellschaft* (pp. 347–365). Innsbruck and Wien: Studienverlag.

Krotz, F. (2001). *Die Mediatisierung kommunikativen Handelns. Wie sich Alltag und soziale Beziehungen, Kultur und Gesellschaft durch die Medien wandeln*. Wiesbaden: Westdeutscher Verlag.

Krotz, F. (2003). Metaprozesse sozialen und kulturellen Wandels und die Medien. *Medien Journal*. 27, 7–19.

Krotz, F. (2006). Rethinking the Digital Divide-Approach: From a technically based understanding to a concept referring to Bourdieu's social Capital. Carpentier, N. et al. (Eds.). *Researching Media, Democracy and Participation* (pp. 177–189). Tartu University Press (available also at www.ecrea.com/summer).

Krotz, F. (2007). *Mediatisierung: Fallstudien zum Wandel von Kommunikation*. Wiesbaden: VS.

Livingstone, S. (2009). On the mediation of everything. *Journal of Communication*, 59(1), p. 1–18.

Lundby, K. (2008). Editorial: mediatized stories: mediation perspectives on digital storytelling. *New Media and Society*, 10(3), 363–371.

Mazzoleni, G., and Schulz, W. (1999). 'Mediatization' of Politics: A Challenge for Democracy? *Political Communication*, 16(3), 247–261.

McAllister, M. P. (1996). *The Commercialization of American Culture. New Advertising, Control and Democracy*. Thousand Oaks, CA: Sage.

McLuhan, M. (1967). *Understanding Media: The Extension of Man*. London: Sphere Books.

Mead, G. H. (1967). *Mind, Self and Society*. Chicago: University of Chicago Press.

Mead, G. H. (1969). *Philosophie der Sozialität*, Frankfurt am Main: Suhrkamp.

Meyrowitz, J. (1985). *No Sense of Place*. Oxford, UK: Oxford University Press.

Meyrowitz, J. (1995). *Medium Theory*. In Crowley, D. J., and Mitchell, D. (Eds.). *Communication Theory Today* (pp. 50–77). Cambridge, UK: Polity Press.

Nyíri, K. (Ed.) (2005). *A Sense of Place. The Global and the Local in Mobile Communication*. Wien: Passagen Verlag.

Ong, W. J. (1995). *Orality and Literacy. The Technologizing of the World*, London, New York: Routledge.

Parsons, T., and Shils, E. (Eds.) (1962). *Toward a General Theory of Action*. New York: Harper & Row.

Riepl, W. (1972). *Das Nachrichtenwesen des Altertums*. Reprint of 1913. Hildesheim: Olms.

Roeser, J. (Ed.) (2007). *MedienAlltag*. Wiesbaden: VS.

Rogers, E. M. (1995). *Diffusion of Innovations*. 4th ed. New York: The Free Press.

Schiller, H. I. (1989). *Culture, Inc.: The Corporate Takeover of Public Expression*. New York: Oxford University Press.

Schuetz, A. (1971). *Gesammelte Aufsätze*, 2 vol., Den Haag: Nijhoff.

Schuetz, A. (1971a). Über die Mannigfaltigen Wirklichkeiten. Schütz, A.: *Gesammelte Aufsätze, Bd 1: Das Problem der sozialen Wirklichkeit* (pp. 237–298). Den Haag: Martinus Nijhoff.

Shibutani, T. (1955). Reference Groups as Perspectives. *American Journal of Sociology LX*, 562–569.

Silverstone, R., and Haddon, L. (1996). Design and the Domestication of Information and Communication Technologies: Technical Change and Everyday Life. Mansell, R., and Silverstone, R. (Eds.). *Communication by Design. The Politics of Information and Communication Technologies* (pp. 44–74). Oxford, UK: Oxford University Press.

Thomas, T. (Eds.) (2008). *Medienkultur und soziales Handeln*. Wiesbaden: VS.

Thompson, J. (1995). *The Media and Modernity*. Cambridge, UK: Polity Press.

Turkle, S. (1998). *Leben im Netz. Identitaet in Zeiten des Internet*, Reinbek b. Hamburg: Rowohlt.

Wellmann, B., and Haythornthwaite, C. (2002). *The Internet in Everyday Life*. Malden, MA: Blackwell.

Whorf, B. L. (1963). *Sprache, Denken, Wirklichkeit*. Reinbek bei Hamburg: Rowohlt.

Williams, R. (1958). *Culture and Society*. New York: Chatto and Windus.

Williams, R. (1981). *The Sociology of Culture*. London: Fontana.

CHAPTER TWO

Dimensions: Catch-All Label OR Technical Term

ANDREA SCHROTT

There is a decided lack of a consistent and commonly shared concept of mediatization, a shortfall that leads to a limited transferability of the latest research contributions to the field. The aim of this chapter is to develop an analytical concept of mediatization that can be adopted within a wide thematic range of communication studies.

The core of the discussion on "mediatization" is about societal media effects that are a result of the modernization of mass media and the media organizations. There is a proximity to established concepts in the research field of media effects such as the *spiral of silence* (Noelle-Neumann 1993). But whereas the spiral of silence focuses on the connection between the climate of opinion and political opinion-making, mediatization focuses on societal change that is activated by the alteration of the media system, or at least is aided by this alteration. The main question then is not, "What does this mean for the processes of political opinion-making before, say, elections?" Rather, it is, "What does this mean for the society as a whole or, in particular, for the political system?" Despite the intensity of the discussion on the theoretical level, there is a striking lack of concrete research on mediatization and its effects, and the research community has not come up with a commonly shared concept of what mediatization is and does.

The focus of this chapter is on societal structures, in particular on institutions as the central elements of organization in modern societies. It doubtlessly makes a difference for the existence and continuity of societal structures whether societies have modern and therefore differentiated media systems at their disposal. The central question revolving around the term "mediatization" is, therefore, "How and under what circumstances do modern mass media affect and even change a society's structures?" It is almost impossible to answer this question conclusively. However, what can be achieved is the inception of an urgently needed discussion about the possibility of how to answer this question.

Processes of mediatization involve media effects of a special type, namely supra-individual media effects that cannot be traced back to individual media content but are caused by the existence and the meaning of the media.[1] This chapter first gives some thought to the need of such a term, shows its theoretical classification, and offers a short compilation of the current knowledge in the field. It then discusses the main causes for the lack of a commonly shared concept of mediatization and constructs an analytical model designed to capture mediatization for empirical research.

RELEVANCE

The core of mediatization consists in the mechanism of the institutionalization of media logic in other societal subsystems. In these subsystems, media logic competes with established guidelines and influences on the actions of individuals.[2]

What, then, is the point of such efforts of discussion and definition? *First*, the term "mediatization" bears great potential for explaining many phenomena linked with the growing social impact of modern mass media regarding media content, media organization, media effects, and the individual and social relevance of media consumption. Thus, it becomes possible to construct a wide-ranging theory of the social impact of mass media based on the term "mediatization."[3] *Second*, a specific advantage in describing mediatization as an ongoing process with a multidimension model consists in its vague and, at the same time, dynamic character. A *third* advantage of describing mediatization as an ongoing process lies in its possibility to create indicators that measure the direction and force of media influence. This facilitates the construction of a system of assumptions concerning social structures that influence the magnitude and direction of this process.

STATE OF THE ART OF KNOWLEDGE ON MEDIATIZATION

Although the topic has been on the research agenda for some decades, the research on media society, or media democracy as a result of mediatization, has only recently become a favorite topic of analyses in mass communication research. It must be noted, though, that the research based in English-speaking countries and the studies performed by the German-speaking scientific community vary in their approaches and thus arrive at different conclusions about the impact of mass media on modern society and democracy. Research that broaches the issue of mediatization and mediatization phenomena have been experiencing a continuous boom in Western European mass communication sciences (e.g., Hjarvard 2008; Kaase 1998; Kepplinger 2002; Krotz 2007; Marcinkowski 2005; Saxer 2004; Schulz 2004)— particularly the German-language communication sciences.

In the German literature, the term "mediatization" has established itself and has been implemented in English publications in Europe, especially in the *European Journal of Communication* (Bentivegna 2006; Fairclough 2000; Jansson 2002; McQuail 2005; Schulz 2004; Schulz, Zeh, and Quiring 2005). In publications outside of Europe, the term is used seldom and, if used, is usually the translation of the German term. But, just because the term is used more frequently in German publications, this does not mean that the community sees eye to eye on the correct definition. Therefore, definitions of mediatization are manifold. Steinmaurer speaks of mediatization as the contamination of society with media content (Steinmaurer 2003); Saxer characterizes it as a social phenomenon with the characteristic of totality (*Totalphänomen*) that develops a ubiquitous impact on all dimensions of social existence (Saxer 2004, p. 151). Especially in political communication research, the term "mediatization" refers to negative impacts on modern democracy:

> The term mediatization denotes problematic concomitants or consequences of the development of modern mass media. It is distinguished from mediation, which refers in a neutral sense to any acts of intervening, conveying, or reconciling between different actors, collectives, or institutions." (Mazzoleni and Schulz 1999, p. 249)

Two anthologies summarize recent empirical findings and ongoing research (Imhof et al. 2004; Rössler 2005). This could be seen as an indicator for the current prominence of the debate, even though it seems that the scientific hype around media society has been declining. In this context, mediatization was predominantly defined as a process of social change that results in a media society, albeit some authors use the term for the fact that mass media increasingly obtain influence on the formation of social reality perceptions.

Nevertheless, there is one small common denominator: the term "mediatization" generally refers to the penetration of mass media, and of the functional and operational logic of all social systems, as well as to the challenge it poses to established patterns among and within social actors and institutions. In the area of political communication, the term "mediatization of politics" stands for the rising importance and the mass medial penetration of the political system and for the displacement of political logic through media logic.[4]

In the original English publications, a variety of terms are used that can only partially, and only with reference to the source, be used as synonyms. Mazzoleni and Schulz (1999) use the term "mediatization," Louw (2005) uses "media-ization," and Altheide and Snow (1979) "mediation." Brian McNair (2000), Bennett and Entman (2001), and Nimmo and Combs (1990) concentrate on the political system and the influence of modern mass media on the political process and therefore talk about "mediated politics" and "mass mediated political realities."

Having so many descriptions of the term used can lead to the impression that everyone is talking about the same or at least very similar processes and aspects. On the other hand, it makes it very complicated to connect the different research results.

This field lacks comparative studies because of their different understanding and therefore varying operationalization of mediatization. Winfried Schulz's work on "Reconstructing Mediatization as an Analytical Concept" (Schulz 2004) forms an important contribution to the general research on mediatization and its effects. Schulz defines mediatization as a process of social change that could be understood as partial processes of "extension," "substitution," "amalgamation," and "accommodation" (Schulz 2004, p. 88ff). It nevertheless remains unclear whether these partial processes are results of mediatization itself or of social change in general, assuming they are parts of mediatization, its effects, or its basic causes.

Another important contribution in this context is the conceptualization of mediatization by Frank Marcinkowski (2005). He defines mediatization as a social process in which various procedures or action patterns come up against mass media logic. The consequences of this encounter fundamentally depend on preconditions of a different order. First, there are preconditions in society in general, such as structures of governance, structures of the media system, levels of regulation, the technological development status, etc. Second, there is the specific media system itself (cf. Hallin and Mancini 2004), which can be characterized by many questions: "To what extent are media reconstructing a reality of their own quality?" "Have they developed their own criteria for selecting and interpreting social reality?" "To what extent do their reconstructions have a social-binding character?" Third, there are also preconditions with respect to the object of investigation. A social actor is assumed to depend on public communication in order to fulfill his or her social functions. The probability that such a dependency exists, as well as its extent, are predicated to be affected by media logic (Marcinkowski 2005). There are doubts about the idea that, for example, political institutions or institutions of other social systems are completely determined by media logic. The suggestion that there is coexistence of various logics that might function as an orientation system for politics appears more convincing (Marcinkowski 2005, p. 346). Whether additional media logic causes mediatization effects in political institutions mainly depends on two aspects. They are (1) the type of political institution, and (2) the correlation of their logic and media logic (Marcinkowski 2005, p. 346ff). Thus, mediatization effects may vary from one political institution to another.

In all of the conceptualizations of mediatization presented, the basic assumptions of modern effects research is mirrored, regardless of labels and approaches used: (1) The media construct their own reality; they pick and choose news that is newsworthy and then present it in a specific way. Their media logic defines the selection and presentation rules. (2) The power of the effectiveness of the media depends on a handful of social variables that, on the one hand, affect society and the subsystem society and, on the other hand, can just be applied for the object/actor that is being analyzed. The potential influence of the media can vary and depend on the actual (also the historical) situation and the actual object that is being analyzed. (3) The existence and the functional logic of modern mass media yield indirect and direct effects that have considerable consequences for social communities.

Despite the fact that empirical verifications are rare and scattered in the field, there are interesting recent theoretical and empirical findings. Existing empirical studies of mediatization broadly deal with phenomena in the field of political communication, mainly election campaigns (Holtz-Bacha 2003; Sarcinelli and Schatz 2002; Strömbäck 2008; Swanson and Mancini 1996b) and especially focus on the contents of election communication (e.g., Hallin 1992; Patterson 1993). Examples of studies that focus on media-induced change on the organizational level are the panel surveys conducted by Jay G. Blumler and Michael Gurevitch. They have been doing newsroom observations during election periods since 1966 (Blumler and Gurevitch 2001; Gurevitch and Blumler 1993). Almost as rare as studies on organizational consequences are studies that focus on the effects of the mediatization of the political system for individuals in the role of voters, citizens, or individuals involved in policy making. The electorate perspective of the intertwining of political processes with mass medial communication is presented in publications by Schulz, Zeh, and Quiring (2005). The authors attribute the following characteristics to mediatization: "(1) an enormous expansion of supply of new types of media and content genres, (2) the growing importance of television in political communication, and (3) the transformation of election campaigning" (Schulz et al. 2005, p. 55). The authors then try to find whether this process of change has any influences on voting behavior, especially on the mobilization of the electorate; on the meaning of the television in comparison to other media types (dependency theory of mass communication); and on tendencies toward more personalization, meaning candidate-centered voting decisions. Apolitical individuals in particular inform themselves (or are informed) about politics and policies through television, whereas the most relevant medium for information about politics and political factual issues for individuals who do not belong to a party is still the print news. This only partially supports the mediatization thesis.

As can be seen, research on mediatization so far only deals with selected aspects of public communication in specific cases, even though existing studies provide interesting findings of fundamental changes caused by mediatization effects. The biggest challenge in researching mediatization is that the postulated changes, or the alterations that are to be analyzed, can be monitored only through longitudinal studies and can be verified only through comparative research designs. This makes research even more difficult. Esser and Pfetsch's (2004b) anthology, comparing theories of political communication, shows that, on both sides of the Atlantic, similar questions are asked regarding the meshwork of mass media and politics and that research in this area of international comparative research is desperately needed. Mediatization, especially "mediatization of politics," is one of the expressed research desiderata:

> ...we still lack precise information as to its varying intensity and consequences in different political systems. Mediatization is caused by processes rooted in the media system...It can be tracked back to the media's primary function: the creation of publicity by selecting, processing, and conveying information according to media-specific criteria, formats, and presentational styles. (Esser and Pfetsch 2004a, p. 387)

AN ALTERNATIVE DEFINITION OF MEDIATIZATION

Mass media are the nervous system of modern societies that carries information, emotions, stimuli, expectations, valuations, and valuation standards farther than just into a directly accessible environment. This is why the mass media gain more and more power of information, definition, and interpretation in almost all social areas and for almost all actors that depend on the media's output. These social areas and actors are being "mediatized." How can we describe this mediatization, and how do we measure it? This chapter is based on one main assumption, which sounds trivial at first: mediatization exists as soon as the media become influential and formative, beyond their merely neutral role as mediator and channel of information. Therefore, the media affect macro structures. If it is possible to find evidence for a formative influence of the media and their way of depicting "reality" on the state of (parts of) society, we can assume that society, or parts of it, are mediatized. In order to do so, an exact description of the mediatization process has to be developed. On this basis, it is then possible to design an analytical framework that allows empirical implementations.

What turns modern mass media into modern mass media is the "media logic." This media logic is based on the type of media, on the processing routines of journalistic work, on the technological possibilities and capacities, and finally on the economic organization of the media system. An "emission" of this logic and its establishment in other social fields (alongside their usual logic of functioning) would be a sufficient indicator for the social impact of the media that exceeds their original mediating function. Therefore, this chapter defines *mediatization as a social process of media-induced social change that functions by a specific mechanism. This mechanism is the institutionalization of media logic in social spheres* that were previously considered to be separate from the mass media. Thus, "mediatization" refers to whether social change is caused by the mass media. The question to be answered is: Does the above-mentioned process, with its specific way of functioning, exist or not? In looking at the institutionalization of the media logic, we also try to find out in what way, and according to which rules, the mediatization process works: what are the rules and contexts that form the grounds of the "mechanism" of the mediatization process?

When doing empirical research on mediatization and its possible features, it is therefore important to first find out if media-induced change has taken place: Have new regulations for the exposure to the public sphere been implemented within an organization? Has a new corporate design been created? etc. Secondly, it is essential to explain this phenomenon by means of searching for the mechanism of institutionalization of the media logic. This mechanism can be identified and described in terms of five characterizing features, which shall be specified later in the chapter.

If indicators of mediatization can be identified, we need to consider the consequences for specifically affected social subsystems and for society as a whole. We can then speak of mediatization effects as effects perceivable on a macro level. Moreover, we need to differentiate between mediatization effects and "traditional" media effects, which take place between media and the public on an individual level, and for which media coverage becomes the triggering stimulus. In contrast to this classic meaning of media effects, mediatization effects focus on social impacts of mass media. Therefore, if mediatization effects occur, we encounter them as second-order media effects, or as indirect, long-time media effects on the macro level. Thus, diverging from the classical perception of media effects, mediatization impacts actors not only through the content of media coverage but rather through its very existence. Actors are under pressure to conform to media logic, because they causally attribute power to the mass media to define and interpret socially binding reality. This attribution can be rooted in the organizational power of media organizations as autonomous actors, in the presentation power of media as mediators of information and meaning, as well as in the interpretation power of media as mediators of orientation.

The main point is that mediatization effects are predominantly latent. We are scarcely aware of the orientation frame "media logic" with which we align our activities. Just as rare are explicit indicators of an actor following media logic. Media logic, understood as an orientation frame, first of all defines a hidden arrangement of action patterns and sets a space of possible rational actions in the context of public or partial public communication. We are confronted with media logic patterns in nearly every public or semipublic situation—even at presentations in university courses. Presentation techniques conforming to media logic increasingly compete with the presented content, so that presentation skills become a core competence for nearly every field in professional and in private life. Nevertheless, the rising importance of presentation, and therefore entertainment, need not stand for a loss in the dimension of content, although it poses a great risk for political or scientific communication. So it is not surprising that findings in political communication research suggest that modern presentation necessities have an impact on political decisions.

THE MECHANISM OF MEDIATIZATION:
INSTITUTIONALIZATION OF MEDIA LOGIC

The term "institutionalization" means both *condition* and *process*. As a process, institutionalization refers to a *transaction* of social relations and actions to indisputable parts of situations that are commonly seen as objective. The case at hand refers to routines of selection and depiction of the mass media that are summarized with the term 'media logic.' Thus, institutionalization as a process means that the rules of production for mass media content become independent for the content of merely every kind of communication in almost every social area. Institutionalization as a condition refers to social or cultural shared opinions of what is "reality," what is relevant, and which actions are accepted and feasible (Walgenbach 2002). Institutions as contextual factors do have the character of regulations, but they are more than just norms and values. They gain their commitment also by "taken-for-granted scripts, rules, and classifications." Therefore institutions are "macrolevel abstractions" (DiMaggio and Powell 1991, p. 15).

In this sense, "mediatization" functions by the implementation of a new socially shared interpretation system that is seen as objective and true, and is therefore not questioned. Thus, media logic is established in different functional systems as a pattern of orientation and interpretation for public communication, and which thereby changes the functional spheres themselves. These patterns of orientation become implicit regulation systems, which overlay or even complement political or economic or scientific regulation systems. This means that not only what we consider as newsworthy (selection), but also the chosen form of depiction (presentation) and interpretation of the reported information in relation to "reality" (mediation), is deeply connected to the form and content of modern mass communication.

The process of institutionalization bears contextual effects on the actors of social systems (individuals, organizations and institutions). It indirectly affects the social system itself and all of society, because it puts pressure on every type of actor and institution to conform to media logic.

INDIVIDUAL BEHAVIOR AND EFFECTS ON THE MACRO LEVEL

As the preceding sections suggest, the definition of mediatization in use here indicates the decision for a clear methodological perspective, namely the perspective of the methodological individualism. This discussion refers to James Coleman's (1990) thesis, according to which, effects on a macro level of society can never be direct effects. The behavior of individuals in a specific situation is always crucial. These single actions aggregate to an effect phenomenon on the macro level. However, social phenomena, "corpi delicti," form the basis for individual behavior and prestructure the concrete situation in which the individual acts. In doing so, the individual always has different options of actions to choose from; this choice is determined by individual criteria of rationality. It is of essential importance, along with which goals and acting principles these rational criteria orient themselves. From this point of view, the individual sees himself confronted with conflicts of goals in concrete situations of action: following the tradition of the *rational choice theory*, Coleman assumes the determinative action principle of maximization of benefit. The individual maximizes his personal benefits by means of his actions. There are a few principles that compete with the latter, which can be summarized in the superordinate concept of "social conformity." Elisabeth Noelle-Neumann (1993) identifies the pursuit of social conformity as a central criterion for the accomplishment and effects of public opinion. The social nature of man causes him to seek accordance and consent; social control and individual fear of isolation are the mechanisms that trigger socially conformable behavior.

From this standpoint, people act rationally when they act according to the rationality criteria that fit the pursued principle of action. An example of this is: A company wins an award for an innovative project and now has to find someone to do the acceptance speech at the public award show. The manager of the company sees this as a chance to promote himself for possible future employers.

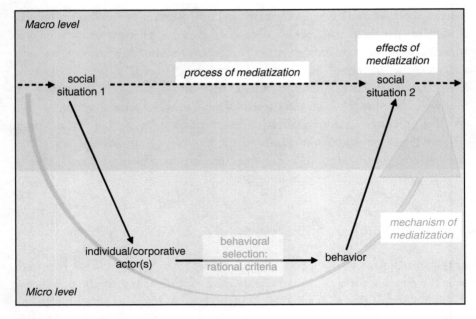

Figure 1: Mediatization on macro and micro level (following Coleman 1990).

The project team and its team leader interpret the whole trip, the show, and the speech as a successful conclusion of their work and would also like to seize this opportunity. Both manager and project team act rationally, but they do so on the basis of different principles of action.

The rationality criteria are decision rules, which give individuals the chance to choose from possible options of action. Individual rational actions then trigger collective effects on the macro level, which do not necessarily have to be intended by the individual actors (see Figure 1). The collective phenomenon is caused by single decisions for specific rationality criteria, even though it is not determined by them. Therefore, effects of mediatization are the result of individual or corporate actors' behavior. These actors deliberately or unconsciously make their decisions according to rationality criteria, which, again, result from the maxim of "positive public attention."

FIVE DIMENSIONS OF MEDIATIZATION

Mediatization inherently implies the assumption that modern mass media influence society in a formative manner, that they change its form and social mutual expectations of specific actions. This hypothesis still requires verification.

Specifically applied to political communication, mediatization denotes the process of change, which is initiated by the "emergence of the mass media as the essential conduit between the public and political actors and as an autonomous power centre in the political process" (Swanson and Mancini 1996a, p. 254). If parts of the political system are mediatized, we should be able to find indicators of media logic as a concurrent orientation frame for political actors. Five specific dimensions of the mechanism of mediatization describe the circumstances under which this mechanism works. These five dimensions also define the orientation frame "media logic" and allow the explanation of mediatization phenomena. Lepsius' model of the characteristic space of institutions (1994, 1997) helps to identify these "five dimensions of mediatization," which help to predict the probability of individual or organizational actors feeling the pressure to conform due to mediatization.

Since the 1980s, the so-called *neo-institutionalism* has drawn much attention in sociology, economics, and political science. "Institutions" develop a formerly unknown level of attractiveness. Despite a very small number of publications on this topic, a theory of Rainer Lepsius has a crucial influence, in particular on analyzes in the German-speaking field of social science. His most important pieces of work do not exist in English, which is why his central assumptions need to be described in more detail here. Lepsius' starting point concerning the analysis of institutions is a very pragmatic one: "An analytical content of the term 'institution' results only from a concrete problem. Not the question: What are institutions? but rather the question: Which problem should be dealt with? gives access to an analysis of institutions" (Lepsius 1994, p. 393). So he suggests a model that allows analyzing institutionalizations rather than institutions.

The *first dimension* is the dimension of *causes* and *rational criteria* and defines the structuring and classifying idea of the institutionalization process.[5] It constitutes the context of argumentation and justification, which puts pressure to conform on the object of mediatization: "The cause of institutional pressures refers to the rational set of expectation, or intended objectives that underlie external pressures for conformity" (Oliver 1991, p. 161). While the cause of mediatization is positive public attention, the way to achieve it is defined by the rational criteria of mediatization that are thought rational only in certain situations, and in a specific context. This dimension is about concrete action principles, which, on the one hand, allow the interpretation of the situation the actor is in. But, on the other hand, they determine the range of possible actions. Criteria of interpretation and selection correspond with the so-called rationality criteria, which specify the general action principle for the specific situation. That is why the specific rational criteria are different in every situation, even if they always apply to the same actor. From this perspective, it also depends on which public sphere attention should be attracted. Before analyzing a phenomenon for mediatization criteria, we must ask ourselves whether the phenomenon is a consequence of acting on the maxim "positive public attention."

The *second dimension*, the dimension of *context*, limits the impact of media logic on the sphere of public communication. Whenever actors communicate in public, the probability that they follow media logic is particularly high if they are under the pressure to conform due of mediatization. This orientation is important in that it increases the chances to be understood by an audience—relatively independently from its size. Therefore, a huge audience is not a necessary condition, but it is necessary that an audience exist. So, there have to be people who watch and listen, whereas the different roles of actors and observers could change. With every kind of public information, we associate a particular idea about how it should be presented. Here, we have to ask: How publicly accessible, observable, or changeable is the context in which the phenomenon is being observed?

The *third dimension* refers to the power to exert sanctions (*control*) inherent in mediatization. The power of sanctioning is important for the widened behavioral space but also narrowed by the process of institutionalization and its criteria. Such power is substantially rooted in its context: Public communication aims at publicity. The fact that any mobilization against actors or organizations or even institutions will be publicly visible constitutes the most severe sanctioning that mediatization can impose, besides absolute non-observance. The potential of threat grows with the rate of how independent, organized, and concentrated media corporations are, so that in societies, in which media organizations show a low level of independence, organization, and concentration, the power to exert sanctions through mediatization is also low. In consequence, it can be assumed that a highly independent and organized media system fosters mediatization effects in other social systems under its observance. The greatest sanctioning potential of the mediatization mechanism lies outside the media system. The best control over the individual compliance with rational criteria lies in the fear of not being heard or, even worse, of being rejected. Every public action brings the potential danger of making an exhibition of oneself in front of one's audience. Rationality criteria of the media logic serve as a frame of orientation to escape such a situation. This sanctioning potential does not work, though, if the audience consists of listeners who make sense of the situation according to different criteria. Considering an existing phenomenon, the question to ask should be: When acting differently, would the actor have been in danger of social exclusion or non-observance?

The *fourth dimension* is the dimension of externalization of *contingencies*. The other dimensions define a spectrum of problems solvable through media logic and predict that media will deal only with those problems that can be solved by media logic. Other problem solutions are suppressed. Problems or contingencies that emerge from such limitation of possible solutions will be rejected and solutions applied in other contexts. What happens with problems that arise from focusing on media logic by public actors? What happens if, for example, journalists disregard established rules for a more sensational coverage? The existence of patterns of arrangements for the externalization of unsolvable problems is an indicator for the consolidation of institutionalization processes. Considering this dimension, the research question is: In which way are unintended consequences of mediatized actions processed?

The *fifth dimension* is the dimension of competing institutions. Social life is fundamentally affected by the competition of different regulatory models. The higher the social order, and the more consolidated the processes of institutionalization are, the more probable it becomes that an intermediate structure will be constructed to balance the institutional equilibrium. Evidence for established intermediate structures between media and other functional spheres can serve as an indicator of mediatization effects, particularly if their establishment is recent. Considering this phenomenon, we need to ask: What other institutions are in conflict with the actor's behavior?

The above-mentioned aspects are summarized in the following table (Table 1). Every analyzed phenomenon that needs to be checked as to whether it is a mediatization effect has to be analyzed for each of the depicted dimensions. We can

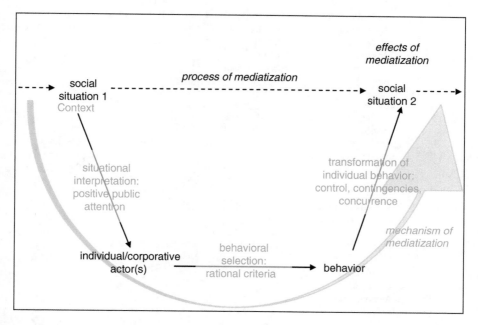

Figure 2: Dimensions of the mechanism of mediatization.

Table 1: "The characteristic space" of the mechanism of mediatization.

	General question for institutionalization	Concrete question for the mechanism of mediatization	Process of mediatization	Examples
Causes and criteria	Why is an actor being pressured to conform to institutional rules or expectations?	– Is the phenomenon a cause of action that resulted out of the maxim 'positive public attention'? – Are the actions of the actors oriented by criteria of media logic?	Positive publicity and media logic	Expectations, decisions have to be announced in public as a source of legitimacy of decision makers
Context	In which context can the dimensions "causes" and "rational criteria" evolve into orientation frames for actors?	How publicly accessible, observable, and/or changeable is the context in which the phenomenon is being observed?	Public communication	Following patterns of media presentation in situations without media attention
Control	What forms of sanctioning are used to enforce conformist behavior?	When acting differently, would the actor have been in danger of social exclusion or non-observance?	– Disobedience/ nonobservance – Social disregard	Moral panics triggered by media coverage
Contingencies	Which regulation mechanisms for contingencies were formed?	In which way are unintended consequences of mediatized actions processed?	– Regimes of governmental regulation – Regimes of self-regulation	Swiss Press Council Foundation (*Schweizer Presserat*) as a regime for the self-regulation of Swiss press
Concurrence	Which concurring regulation patterns can be seen in one context? Which responses are established for the reduction of frictions?	What other institutions are in conflict with the actor's behavior?	– Politics – Economics – Law – Religion/moral	– Media law – Labor law

assume that the analyzed case is a mediatization effect if the phenomenon can be traced back to every single dimension of the mediatization mechanism.

If these assumptions were confirmed through empirical research, they would provide strong evidence for the relevance of mediatization as a process of social change. It would also be possible to estimate how far this process has already been established. The suggested steps of analysis and their interpretations are designed in a rather careful manner so as to avoid the dangers of misinterpreting macro phenomena as effects of a macro process. In effect, even if every single dimension has been analyzed, it is still possible that the phenomenon results from numerous social processes or a completely different process, which we have not seen simply because we have not looked for it. This possibility should not discourage us but rather lead to even better instruments of analysis. The research done in the field of media and communication studies is valuable and will be even more so if we are able to make more precise statements about communication, its meaning, and its value for society.

Testing the Instrument and Discussion

Eric Louw says that "different parts of the political process have been substantively media-ized" (Louw 2005, p. 141). To demonstrate this statement, he gives some examples, which shall be used here to investigate usability and significance of the instrument introduced. The example chosen is "selling politicians and creating celebrity" (p. 172), because it uses a similar understanding of mediatization and gives concrete examples of mediatization effects—and therefore of analyzable phenomena. Louw says "that politicians have had to become experts in creating 'faces' (or 'masks') by *performing* scripts written by spin-doctors for television audiences" (Louw 2005, p. 172). Politicians are thus a "key product" of successful political PR machinery, which has developed due to the increasing social importance of media reality and its construction rules. The key term here is "impression management," which offers an image for the mass audience that promises to give the most positive overall impression. Hence, Eric Louw provides us with two analyzable phenomena: (a) the emergence of a particular industry of political PR: spin doctoring; and (b) the construction of prominent personalities, relatively independent from "real" competence and achievements. For the two phenomena, we assume the following preconditions: (1) The phenomena are relatively young, meaning that they did not exist before the technological possibilities of modern mass communication; (2) the developments can be generalized and do not only apply to a small number of isolated cases; and (3) it is feasible to differentiate between the public appearance of a politician and his or her actions, meaning that there is a clear difference between the production and the depiction of politics. The following table (Table 2) examines whether the phenomena show the different dimensions of the mechanism of mediatization.

Table 2: "The characteristic space" of the mechanism of mediatization with examples.

	Dimension		Examples	
	Process of mediatization	Concrete question for the mechanism of mediatization	Spin-doctoring	Constructed celebrity of a politician
Cause criteria	Positive public attention media logic	– Is the phenomenon a cause of action that resulted out of the maxim, positive, public attention'? – Is the actor's guideline the criteria of media logic?	– Yes; a different maxim of action is not an option in this case. – Yes; the guideline is classic news factors and it offers tailored content.	– Yes: as a foundation for a possible election success or the acceptance of the citizens. – Yes; the guideline is a central news factor: prominence that is self-constructed.
Context	Public communication	How publicly accessible, observable, and/or changeable is the context in which the phenomenon is being observed?	This is about public communication in front of an audience that is as large as possible, the concrete action itself is also undertaken secretly.	The core is about public communication in front of a audience that is as large as possible.
Control	– Disobedience/ nonobservance – Social disregard	When acting differently, would the actor have been in danger of social exclusion or non-observance?	The spectrum of action is within the frame of action corresponding with media logic; changing action in itself also refers to media logic (e.g., a deliberately factual-based presentation) as a difference to the 'usual' approach.	No, not necessarily. There are examples for prominent politicians that do not need impression management. Sometime it can be disadvantageous for a politician to depend on the criteria of media logic to strongly.
Contingencies	– Regimes of governmental regulation – Regimes of self-regulation	In which way are unintended consequences of mediatized actions processed?	e.g., – Cancellation of a job – Discrediting – Judicial action	e.g., – Non-vote – Exclusion from party
Concurrence	– Politics: political competition – Law – Religion/moral	What other institutions are in conflict with the actor's behavior?	Coded implementation of democracy (conflict between constitutional text and constitutional reality)	Coded implementation of democracy (conflict between constitutional text and constitutional reality)

By analyzing the two examples (which are still in need of further, more detailed analysis), we can see that they cannot automatically be considered as mediatization effects. The best indication for an increasing mediatization of political fields would probably be the spin-doctoring. The constructed prominence of politicians, though, still needs to be checked more critically. The question to be asked here is: Is it possible to construct prominence without recourse to competence and achievements (real or made up), and does it seem credible in the eyes of the voters? Therefore, it is crucial to search for the sources of the prominence of a certain politician: Is he prominent because his appearance, his look, and his utterances fit our imagination of a prominent person? Or is he prominent because he would look and act in the exact same way without the possibility of being watched by a mass audience? It is not really plausible to generally assume a mediatization effect in this case. A number of single cases would have to be analyzed to find out in which way they could be generalized.

Concerning the instrument itself, we can see that it allows the partial explanation and agreement with, or the rejection of, an analyzed phenomenon as a mediatization effect. In any case, it allows a more differentiated judgment and a more detailed analysis than previous—usually very global—attributions of mediatization. However, the instrument needs to be refined and improved so as to make it more precisely applicable to specific problems. In addition, the question of how this instrument could be applied to other cultures needs to be discussed. Until now, only Western democracies and media systems are possible points of reference. Let me also refer to the history of the mediatization process. As mentioned above, the key to the explanation of the mediatization process can be found in the emergence of new techniques of mass communication. Technological jumps of journalistic communication channels have repeatedly occurred in the last centuries. If we want to expand this concept and apply it to the explanation of historical social change influenced by the development of the mass media, we need to specify the proposed analytical scheme even more (e.g., concerning the definition of the "actor"). This demonstrates that we are still at the very beginning of understanding and analyzing media-induced social change. Let us hope that this does not serve as a deterrent, but rather as a challenge, to do more intensive research.

CONCLUSIONS

What can be said to conclude these efforts? First of all, we have to admit that there is a wide area of controversy, which complicates the settlement of the different definitions of mediatization. In the end, we have to concede to Doris

Graber (2005) being correct in saying: The important thing for modern mass communication research is "to collectively create a road map for more systematic research development, rather than leaving the outcome to chance" (Graber 2005, p. 498). Added to that, it is important to recollect and rearrange existing research approaches in a sustainable framework of mass media theories.

Finally, how do we judge the described process of mediatization? Mediatization is a process that is impossible to either condemn or support. It exists as a social fact, and its extent differs from social area to social area. It is a normal process of social change that features sources of social self-assurance and social acceptance. And social acceptance, combined with the fear of social exclusion, is the central impetus for human existence (cf. Noelle-Neumann 1993). In the past, what we have learned in school and in specific social situations—rules of social acceptance by means of comparison with classmates, the teacher as a role model, the lessons learned every Sunday in church or by practicing with parents—is now what also we learn through TV and the media. They provide us with pictures that teach us social behavior, social standards, and finally the value of social acceptance. The media have become one of society's central institutions of socialization. Media reality therefore becomes a social fact that we have to cope with. This media reality defines social standards that decide what is socially acceptable and what is not. The question now is how stable these standards are—for example, youth as criterion of social acceptance in opposition to former "modesty" or respectability. But at least spoken in medium-term timelines, they are of crucial importance for the constitution of community. And it is probable that new criteria of social acceptance are to be spread through and influenced by the media.

NOTES

1. With this definition, the term *mediatization* identifies with the definitions provided by McLuhan and Meyrowitz. This conceptional closeness shows the preeminent importance of television in this model as an intermediary of meaning and orientation.
2. "Mediatization" exceeds the idea that the media have potential power by distributing knowledge and includes the *way* in which knowledge—and also entertainment—is communicated. This view of the media system, therefore, does not limit the system to the form of its organization but expands it by seeing the media as a cultural institution.
3. It would exceed the scope of this chapter to discuss the problem that this effect might be an aggregated individual effect on the macro level. I favor the macro-micro-macro approach in the way that James E. Coleman (1990) and his followers have designed and modified it.
4. Media logic in its most basic form posits that the message being communicated must pass through two filters: the first filter is the filter of selection; the second is the filter of presentation. Both filters are specifically constricted to fit the communication channel that is publishing the message. However, all media and media types share a common set of general rules for filtering (e.g.,

novelty, immediacy, conflict, dramatization…). These rules are altered to fit the characteristics and constraints of the media. The constraints create a picture of the world that is particular to the media: Media logic defines "how material is organized, the style in which it is presented, the focus or emphasis of particular characteristics of behaviour, and the grammar of media communication […] a perspective that is used to present as well as interpret phenomena." (Altheide and Snow 1979, p. 10).

5. Social situations are characterized by its multi-causality. But for the individual interpretation of a social situation mostly one action principle dominates though other action principles could be also important.

REFERENCES

Altheide, D. L., and Snow, R. P. (1979). *Media Logic*. Beverly Hills, CA: Sage.

Bennett, W. L., and Entman, R. L. (Eds.) (2001). *Mediated Politics: Communication in the Future of Democracy*. Cambridge, UK: Cambridge University Press.

Bentivegna, S. (2006). Rethinking politics in the world of ICTS. *European Journal of Communication*, 21(3), 331–343.

Blumler, J. G., and Gurevitch, M. (2001). "Americanization" reconsidered: UK-US campaign communication comparisons across time. In W. L. Bennett and R. L. Entman (Eds.), *Mediated Politics: Communication in the Future of Democracy* (pp. 215–235). Cambrdige, UK: Cambridge University Press.

Coleman, J. S. (1990). *Foundations of Social Theory*. Cambridge, MA: Belknap Press.

DiMaggio, P. J., and Powell, W. W. (1991). Introduction. In P. J. DiMaggio and W. W. Powell (Eds.), *The New Institutionalism in Organizational Analysis*. (pp. 1–40). Chicago: University of Chicago Press.

Esser, F., and Pfetsch, B. (2004a). Meeting the challenges of global communication and political integration. The Significance of comparative research in a changing world. In F. Esser and B. Pfetsch (Eds.), *Comparing Political Communication: Theories, Cases, and Challenges* (pp. 384–410). Cambridge, UK: Cambridge University Press.

Esser, F., and Pfetsch, B. (Eds.) (2004b). *Comparing Political Communication. Theories, Cases, and Challenges*. Cambridge, UK: Cambridge University Press.

Fairclough, N. (2000). *New Labour, New Language?* London: Routledge.

Graber, D. (2005). Political communication faces the 21st century. *Journal of Communication*, Sept. 2005, 479–507.

Gurevitch, M., and Blumler, J. G. (1993). Longitudinal analysis of an election communication system: Newsroom observation at the BBC 1996–1992. *Österreichische Zeitschrift für Politikwissenschaft*, 22, 427–444.

Hallin, D. C. (1992). Sound bite news: Television coverage of elections 1968–88. *Journal of Communication*, 42(2), 5–24.

Hallin, D. C., and Mancini, P. (2004). *Comparing Media Systems: Three Models of Media and Politics*. Cambridge, UK: Cambridge University Press.

Hjarvard, S. (2008). The mediatization of society. A theory of the media as agents of social and cultural change. *Nordicom Review*, 29, 101–130.

Holtz-Bacha, C. (Ed.). (2003). *Die Massenmedien im Wahlkampf. Die Bundestagswahl 2002 (Mass Media in election campaign. The Election of the German Bundestag in 2002)*. Wiesbaden: Westdeutscher Verlag.

Imhof, K., Blum, R., Bonfadelli, H., and Jarren, O. (Eds.). (2004). *Mediengesellschaft. Strukturen, Merkmale, Entwicklungsdynamiken (Media Society. Structures, Characteristics, Dynamics)*. Wiesbaden: VS Verlag für Sozialwissenschaften.

Jansson, A. (2002). Spatial phantasmagoria: The mediatization of tourism experience. *European Journal of Communication*, 17(4), 429–443.

Kaase, M. (1998). Demokratisches System und die Mediatisierung der Politik (Democratic system and mediatization of politics). In U. Sarcinelli (Ed.), *Politikvermittlung und Demokratie in der Mediengesellschaft* (pp. 24–51). Opladen; Wiesbaden: Westdeutscher Verlag.

Kepplinger, H. M. (2002). Mediatization of politics: Theory and data. *Journal of Communication* 52(4), 972–986.

Krotz, F. (2007). *Mediatisierung: Fallstudien zum Wandel von Kommunikation*. Wiesbaden: VS Verlag für Sozialwissenschaften.

Lepsius, M. R. (1994). Institutionenanalyse und Institutionenpolitik (Institutional analysis and institutional politics). In B. Nedelmann (Ed.), *Politische Institutionen im Wandel (Political institutions in change)* (pp. 392–403). Wiesbaden: Westdeutscher Verlag.

Lepsius, M. R. (1997). Institutionalisierung und Deinstitutionalisierung von Rationalitätskriterien (Institutionalization and de-institutionalization of rational criteria). in G. Göhler (Ed.), *Institutionenwandel (Institutional Change)* (pp. 57–69). Opladen: Westdeutscher Verlag.

Louw, E. (2005). *The Media and Political Process*. London; Thousand Oaks, CA; New Delhi: Sage.

Marcinkowski, F. (2005). Die 'Medialisierbarkeit' politischer Institutionen (The ability of becoming mediatized in case of political institutions). In P. Rössler and F. Krotz (Eds.), *Mythen der Mediengesellschaft—The Media Society and its Myths* (pp. 341–370). Konstanz: UVK.

Mazzoleni, G., and Schulz, W. (1999). 'Mediatization' of politics: A challenge for democracy? *Political Communication*, 16(3), 247–261.

McNair, B. (2000). *Journalism and Democracy: An Evaluation of the Political Public Sphere*. London: Routledge.

McQuail, D. (2005). *Mass Communication Theory* (5th ed.). London: Sage.

Nimmo, D., and Combs, J. E. (1990). *Mediated Political Realities*. New York: Longman.

Noelle-Neumann, E. (1993). *The Spiral of Silence: Public Opinion—Our Social Skin* (2nd ed.). Chicago: University of Chicago Press.

Oliver, C. (1991). Strategic responses to institutional processes. *Academy of Management Review*, 16(1), 145–179.

Patterson, T. E. (1993). *Out of Order*. New York: Alfred A. Knopf.

Rössler, P. (Ed.). (2005). *Mythen der Mediengesellschaft. The Media Society and Its Myths*. (vol. 32). Konstanz UVK Verlagsgesellschaft.

Sarcinelli, U., and Schatz, H. (Eds.). (2002). *Mediendemokratie im Medienland? Inszenierungen und Themensetzungsstrategien im Spannungsfeld von Medien und Parteieliten am Beispiel der Nordrhein-Westfälischen Landtagswahl im Jahr 2000 (Media democracy in media country?)*. Opladen: Westdeutscher Verlag.

Saxer, U. (1998). Mediengesellschaft: Verständnisse und Missverständnisse (Media society: Understandings and misunderstandings). In U. Sarcinelli (Ed.), *Politikvermittlung und Demokratie in der Mediengesellschaft* (pp. 52–73). Bonn: Bundeszentrale für politische Bildung.

Saxer, U. (2004). Mediengesellschaft: auf dem Weg zu einem Konzept (media society: on the way to a concept). In K. B. Imhof, Roger; Bonfadelli, Heinz; Jarren, Otfried (Eds.), *Mediengesellschaft. Strukturen, Merkmale, Entwicklungsdynamiken (Media Society: Structures, Characteristics, Dynamics)* (pp. 139–155). Wiesbaden: VS Verlag für Sozialwissenschaften.

Schulz, W. (2004). Reconstructing mediatization as an analytical concept. *European Journal of Communication*, 19(1), 87–101.

Schulz, W., Zeh, R., and Quiring, O. (2005). Voters in a changing media environment. A data-based retrospective on consequences of media change in Germany. *European Journal of Communication*, 20(1), 55–88.

Steinmaurer, T. (2003). Medialer und gesellschaftlicher Wandel. Skizzen zu einem Modell (Medial and social change. Outlines for a model). In M. Behmer, F. Krotz and R. Stöber (Eds.), *Medienentwicklung und gesellschaftlicher Wandel. Beiträge zu einer theoretischen und empirischen Herausforderung (Media Development and Social Change)* (pp. 103–119). Wiesbaden: Westdeutscher Verlag.

Strömbäck, J. (2008). Four phases of mediatization: An analysis of the mediatization of politics. *The International Journal of Press/Politics*, 13(3), 228–246.

Swanson, D. L., and Mancini, P. (1996a). Patterns of modern electoral campaigning and their consequences. In D. L. Swanson and P. Mancini (Eds.), *Politics, Media, and Modern Democracy* (pp. 247–276). Westport, CT: Praeger.

Swanson, D. L., and Mancini, P. (Eds.). (1996b). *Politics, Media, and Modern Democracy. An International Study of Innovations in Electoral Campaigning and Their Consequences*. Westport, CT: Praeger.

Walgenbach, P. (2002). Institutionalistische Ansätze in der Organisationstheorie (Institutional approaches in organizational theory). In A. Kieser (Ed.), *Organisationstheorien (Organizational Theories)* (pp. 319–353). Stuttgart: Kohlhammer.

CHAPTER THREE

The Mediatic Turn: Exploring Concepts FOR Media Pedagogy

NORM FRIESEN AND THEO HUG

I don't know who discovered water but it certainly wasn't a fish.

—MARSHALL MCLUHAN[1]

INTRODUCTION

The roots of terms such as 'mediatization,' 'medialization,' and 'mediality' can be traced back through much of the history of Western thought. This goes as far back as Aristotle's consideration of various media of expression in the context of his *Poetics*; the question appears again (among other places) in Augustine's discussion of the medial characteristics of the biblical "Word" in Book 11 of his *Confessions*. The question of media and the mediatic reemerges more recently in Peirce's proto-semiotic theory, and again in Cassirer's consideration of the fundamental mediality of culture and human knowing in *Philosophy of Symbolic Forms* (1953). However, it is with Marshall McLuhan's more recent and famous claim that "the medium is the message" that the contemporary significance of media—and with it, of 'mediatization,' 'medialization,' and 'mediality'—begins to take shape. Indeed, it is relatively uncontroversial in German-language media studies that with this declaration (and its exposition in *The Gutenberg Galaxy* and

Understanding Media), McLuhan's place was secured as "the founder and figure-head of modern media theory" (Margreiter 2007, p. 135):

> With the thesis that media themselves are the message, and the implied transition of research interests to mediatic forms, McLuhan himself actually created the terrain for an independent science of the media (*Medienwissenschaft*). (Leschke 2003, p. 245)

The "transition of research to mediatic forms" invoked here by Leschke has been surprisingly interdisciplinary and widespread in German-language scholarship. Conspicuous attention to mediatic forms began in German literary theory (e.g., Kittler's 1985 *Aufschreibesysteme 1800/1900*). It subsequently extended to philoso-phy (e.g., Hartmann's 2000 *Medienphilosophie*), and it has recently been evident in cultural and historical studies as well (e.g., Giesecke 2002, 2007).

It is our contention that these texts and others like them, and more impor-tantly, the theoretical and empirical developments they present, are not exhausted by the ideas such as mediality and mediatization. Instead, they are all illustrative of what can be called a *mediatic turn*. The phrase refers not simply to a recent trend in research and thinking, but something that can be articulated in the more foundational terms of a cultural or, indeed, an epistemological and existential condition or exigency. This chapter focuses on the *mediatic turn* as an empirical, sociocultural "event," and also as a related development in theory and philosophy. The idea of such a "turn" serves as a way of developing an integrated perspective on concepts such as 'mediation,' 'mediatization,' 'medialization,' and 'mediality.' Giving special emphasis to theoretical developments in German-language dis-courses, this chapter then explores a number of consequences of these empirical and theoretical developments in the area of media literacy and education.

THE SOCIOLOGY OF THE MEDIATIC TURN

It hardly bears repeating that in today's world, media, in their different forms, have thoroughly interpenetrated everyday life and knowledge, making even the most banal tasks all but unimaginable without these forms and technologies. We listen to or look up the weather forecasts rather than checking the color of the sky at night. E-mail, texting, voicemail, and Facebook increasingly connect us interpersonally. And the internet and the Web have opened up multiple chan-nels for instant access to specialized knowledge that previously would have been available only in print or face to face. Media and the messages they broadcast can consequently be said to penetrate more deeply into everyday consciousness. And newer interactive or participatory media (e.g., mobile phones, texting, blog-ging, etc.) increasingly *inter*penetrate everyday practical activity. Media in this sense profoundly influence the realm of everyday, unstructured understandings and activities (or what German philosophers and sociologists have termed the *Lebenswelt* or lifeworld). As Sybille Krämer puts it, "Everything we can say, find out and know about the world is being said, found out and known with the help of media" (Krämer 1998, p. 73).

There are many different ways in which this "mediatic turn" as an empirical, sociological development has been understood in German-language scholarship. Gebhard Rusch, for example, describes such a turn in terms of a *"historically unique degree"* of integration of the technological and the sociocultural. Referring to information and communication technologies (ICTs) generally, Rusch identifies the processes and effects specifically of digitization as being decisive in this sociotechnical integration:

> Actually, from a technological perspective this integration appears as a deepening penetration of public and private spheres by ICT-infrastructures. From a sociological point of view this means an immensely increased accessibility of different kinds of information, people and services together with a corresponding multi-optionality. From a sociotechnical perspective, finally, this integration sets up a restructuration of media and communication following the infrastructural connectivity and processablity...And this is because the "ICT-sation" of our lifeworlds also includes the digital conversion of communication and media. (Rusch 2008, p. 33)

The mediatic turn is manifest here in terms of increased access and flexibility, in which the widespread digitization of mediatic forms and contents plays a decisive role.

Others, referring to Habermas' familiar system-lifeworld distinction, give expression to the mediatic turn in terms that are less sanguine. For example, Göran Sonesson, a Swedish semiotician explains that Habermas describes the lifeworld principally "in opposition to organized society, the so-called 'system world.'" One of Habermas' points, of course, is that lived, informal, and culturally grounded understandings and activities are gradually being permeated or "colonized" by instrumental-scientific and technical structures and controls. "Now we are suggesting," Sonesson ventures, that media could be "playing a similar role to this instrumental system." Media, in other words, are seen as gradually systematizing and organizing the relatively unstructured realm of the everyday. A lifeworld free from this systematizing influence, Sonesson explains,

> ...would be *immediate* (or as little mediated as possible) and *taken for granted—but* more than science and social institutions, media may well be able to transform secondary interpretations into significations taken for granted. Media, rather than the system world, may already be "colonizing" the Lifeworld. (Sonesson 1997, p. 67)

Sonesson sees the mediatic turn, in other words, not in terms of increased flexibility and accessibility, but in terms of a process with unambiguously baleful consequences. Media, mediatization, or mediality are increasingly structuring and controlling the realm of subjectivity and freedom of the lifeworld, and they are doing so in a way that is not readily evident, or at least "taken for granted."

Knuth Hickethier (2003) takes this further by contending that these kinds of processes have resulted in identifiable effects on consciousness. "If people as cultural beings are modeled through media (and these media are not isolated cultural instances), then [it should be possible to] create a open and changeable catalogue of associated *medial effects*" (emphasis in original; p. 230). He includes in this catalog of effects the construction and standardization of temporality; the shaping of attention and emotions; and an emphasis on the semiotic nature of individuals' relationships to the world around them, among others (Hickethier 2003, pp. 230–242; see also Schmidt 2008, p. 96). Media, in this sense, can be said to constitute a kind of a priori condition, in the sense similar to Kant's transcendental a priori. Just as water constitutes an a priori condition for the fish, so do media for humans. Like Kant's understanding of the "always-already" existing categories of time and space that are constitutive of experience, media today can be said to structure our awareness of time, shape our attentions and emotions, and provide us with the means for forming and expressing thought itself. Media, in slightly different terms, become epistemology: the grounds for knowledge and knowing itself.

THE PHILOSOPHY OF THE MEDIATIC TURN

With the notions like the mediatic a priori and media as epistemology, we move from the study of the social and empirical of realm of philosophy. Just as knowledge is seen as being increasingly contingent on media in empirical, quotidian terms, a similar mediatic contingency has been articulated in terms of the philosophy of language, culture, and knowledge (or epistemology). Referring to the work of Mead, Cassirer, Whitehead, and others, Reinhard Margreiter (2007), explains that thought itself has gradually come to be seen as mediatically contingent:

> ...the sign- and symbol-systems that determine thought stand in close relationship to media, or can even be said to be identical with media. Media can be defined in terms similar or identical to those of sign or symbol-systems. This further reflexive move must then be formulated as follows: *Thought [itself] takes place symbolically-medially.* And this can then be characterized as the "mediatic turn." (p. 32)

Media not only present a necessary precondition for knowledge in everyday practice, understood as semiotic systems, media also shape what it is possible to know and also to think. In their 1999 preface to Kittler's *Gramophone, Film, Typewriter*, Winthrop-Young and Wutz come to a similar conclusion. They arrive at it not by following Mead, Cassirer, and Whitehead, but by tracing continuities in the thought of Saussure, Derrida, and Foucault, and presenting these in terms of a genealogy of discrete phases or steps:

> Step 1: We recognize that we are spoken by language. Step 2: We understand that language is not some nebulous entity but appears in the shape of historically limited discursive practices. Step 3: We finally perceive that these practices depend on media. (p. xx)

In other words: We are not masters of language, but language—as a highly structured system of signs and meanings—instead "masters" us and our thoughts and our efforts to communicate. Foucault's understanding of discourse-as-power extends this ontological "ventriloquism" to the dimensions of the political and historical, making the case that official and historically contingent vocabularies and means of expression enable some meanings while limiting or excluding the expression of others. McLuhan and his (largely German) successors remind us, finally, that this also extends to *technologies* through which language and discourse become manifest:

> All our cognitive and communicative processes are suppositions which rely on presuppositions. The most important presuppositions in this respect are language and media, modeled in terms of frameworks of interactive dependencies which interrelate materialities and possible semantic contents in a systematic way, followed by collective cultural knowledge as the basis and outcome of socialization...Discourses function via the co-presence of materiality and meaning construction processes. This contemporarity defines the mediality of our relation to the world. Language is inseparably bound to materialities; media are necessarily bound to technicality. (Schmidt 2008, p. 101)

The linguistic turn, in other words, led to the discursive turn, and this led, finally, to a mediatic turn. "In short, structuralism begot discourse analysis, and discourse analysis begot media theory. Media," as Winthrop-Young and Wutz conclude, "are [at] the end of theory because in practice they were already there to begin with" (1999, p. xx). The practical and material characteristics of media systems and technologies shape what can be thought and expressed. Print, as McLuhan and others remind us, is relentlessly linear and centralizing: Information that is mass produced in the form of lines of standardized type on a page only radiates from places where print-based "information technologies" have attained critical mass. Broadcast media follow a similar centralizing logic, relying as they do on expensive and advanced means for gathering, assembling, and distributing information.

But unlike book culture, what radiates from the centralized broadcast media is not rigidly fixed and linear like print, demanding the quiet, reflective repose of its audience. It instead takes the form of an audiovisual flow, demanding of its audience more emotionally involved or visceral reception. The conditions of what is possible and impossible in human communication, expression, and social organization are in this sense shaped and conditioned by mediatic forms. Through the mediatic turn, the material and logical characteristics of media present the conditions for the possibility of forms of, and of collective and personal, knowledge and also social organization.

The mediatic turn designates a point in theory and practice in which media are no longer seen as constituting a special case or merely one element among many. In this sense, media contain these other social and epistemological elements rather than being contained by them. Just as we are spoken by language, rather than being its speakers, media express themselves through us rather than serving as neutral tools ready to do our own expressive bidding.

It goes without saying that invoking the mediatic turn, like earlier invocations of the semiotic and discursive turns before it, represents a theoretical move of some audacity. In its more extreme articulations, the mediatic turn can be understood as tantamount to making the assertion attributed to Derrida, that "there is nothing outside of the text." Elevating media technologies to a position of this importance—casting them, in effect, as that which contains, causes or explains all else—is to open oneself to the charge of determinism (or worse). Determinism, of course, refers the idea that every event is ultimately determined by particular kind of event or cause—in this case, a particular medium or set of media. Such a view would ascribe to media a power so total that they would ultimately be seen as capable of "creating what they transport" rather than "merely setting and shaping limits to what they transport. Such an understanding is termed "fundamentalist" by media theorist Sybille Krämer. Like her, the authors of this chapter wish distance themselves from such a totalizing take on the mediatic turn. Like Krämer, we wish to articulate

> an approach to media that is nondeterministic, [in which] the phenomena that become interesting are related to the heteronomy or the other-determined character of the [medium or] messenger. For media simply do not present themselves as autonomous "givens." We understand therefore the medium less as a conduit than as "middle" or as "mediator." There is always something outside of the medium. (p. 16)

Similarly, we seek to articulate an understanding of media that sees it a related to heteronymous factors, that recognizes it as manifest in terms of cultures and practices that are not entirely reducible to media's materiality or logical form.

MEDIALITY, MEDIATIZATION, AND MEDIALIZATION

Keeping this discussion of the mediatic turn and the mediatic a priori in mind, the meaning of the terms mediality, mediatization, and medialization can be readily defined. In experience that is significantly contingent on mediation, *mediality*, first, refers to the changing constellations of interrelated media that at any point in history constitute the condition of the mediatic a priori (Margreiter 1999, p. 17). Margreiter understands mediality as central characteristic of human thought and as adequate redefinition of transcendental philosophy. But in contrast to the Kantian concept of the a priori, Margreiter sees the constructive character of the mediatic a priori condition as historically relative. It should not be confused with a putatively timeless and unchanging cognitive structure. It is instead a relational, alterable structure that can be described empirically to some extent. In other words, similar to implicit knowledge as described by Polanyi (1966) and others, these historically relative conditions cannot be expatiated fully, but only partially. Theories of media dynamics as developed by Rusch (2007) and previously by McLuhan (1964) and Postman (1986) provide good examples of how historic media conditions can be tracked.

The term "mediality" can be understood, in other words, as designating the interaction of technology, society, and cultural factors through which institutionalized media of communication such as the press, television, or the World Wide Web produce, transform, and circulate symbols in everyday life. It is this total media system, and not specific instances of communication, that are of principal importance. Mediality in this sense can be said to develop out of or to supersede communication activity or communicativity:

> The evolution of the total media system of modern media-culture societies from writing to the internet has fundamentally changed our relation to the world and our modes of communication. This change can be described as [the] transition from communicativity to mediality. (Schmidt 2008, p. 95)

Mediality in this sense is conspicuously resonant with what in North America is referred to as *media ecology*. Again, if it is the water in which the fish swims that is of interest, then this ambient condition is best studied as an environment or ecology. Neil Postman describes this approach to media as follows:

> Media ecology is the study of media as environments... In the case of media environments (e.g., books, radio, film, television, etc.), the specifications are more often implicit and informal, half concealed by our assumption that what we are dealing with is not an environment but merely a machine. Media ecology tries to make these specifications explicit. (Postman 1970, p. 161; see also Fuller 2005; Tabbi and Wutz 1997)

Media ecology, in other words, is about the "total media system" as it is constituted by a gradually changing constellation of mediatic forms, from books and radio through television and the internet.

By way of contrast, the term *mediatization* refers not to a continuous process evolving over history, but to developments that are emphatically contemporary. Broadly speaking, it refers to the processes of the (inter)penetration, integration, saturation, or "colonization" of the sociocultural lifeworld by media of various sorts. Krotz (2007), for example, describes mediatization as one of a number of "meta-processes," which he defines as closely interrelated, overarching "constructs which describe and explain theoretically specific economic, social, and cultural dimensions and levels of actual change" (p. 257). These include general transformative processes such as globalization, individualization, and commercialization; but among these, Krotz says, the one that is likely most important

> ...is that of *mediatization*. By this we mean the historical developments that took and take place as a change of (communication) media and its consequences, not only with the rise of new forms of media but also with changes in the meaning of media in general. (emphasis in original; p. 258)

Although they have been manifest in the past, processes like mediatization (or globalization, commercialization, etc.) are prominent in the present as elements of relentless change. Medialization, finally, can be explained as a derivative designation for this transformative meta-process. The preferred designation for this development would translate in German most directly as "medialization," hence the occasional appearance of this term in English as well.

(MEDIA) EDUCATION AND THE MEDIATIC TURN

Given its general significance in philosophical theory and in everyday life, it is not surprising that the *mediatic turn* has implications for pedagogy that are both broad and urgent. This section explores these implications but will begin first by considering the current significance of media in both English- and German-language educational research and practice. Discourse in both linguistically defined traditions has generally approached the question of media in two particular ways: first and primarily, media is studied and addressed in education in terms of popular, youth, and mass media as they are encountered every day. In English-language contexts, this educational approach to media is associated with the term "media literacy," which has been defined as

> The process of understanding and using the mass media in an assertive and nonpassive way. This includes an informed and critical understanding of the nature of the media, the techniques used by them and the impact of these techniques. (Boles 2008)

Needless to say, the implication is that the mass media are principally deleterious in their effects on students, adult learners, and educational efforts generally. As the above definition makes clear, the typical response of educational research and practice is to aim at equipping students with skills and abilities for resisting the otherwise prevailing influence of media. This response, furthermore, sometimes extends to include the political and pedagogical implications of "media socialization," the notion that the effects of media extend to the way that entire generations are brought up to think and act.

Secondarily, media are also defined in education specifically in terms of instructional media, instructional *multimedia* (and also as "multimedia learning," "instructional materials," or "message design," all of which are generally classified as subdomains of instructional design and development). These terms refer to the intentional and systematic use of computer, broadcast, and other technologies for instructional purposes, and generally in instructional settings. "Multimedia learning," for example, is described as

> ...focus[ing]...on how people learn from words and pictures in computer-based environments. [These] environments include online instructional presentations, interactive lessons, e-courses, simulation games, virtual reality and computer-supported in-class presentations. (Mayer 2005, p. ix)

The issue driving research and practice in this subdiscipline is the efficient use of media for instructional ends. Efficiency, moreover, tends to be defined in terms of fixed, physical and logical characteristics of media and their correlation with curricular content and individualized cognitive functions (e.g., Mayer 2005).

In educational discourse, media are also thus subsumed firstly as a cultural element *outside* of the institution, and secondly as a technical element instrumentalized *within* educational contexts. The twofold significance of media in educational discourses and systems is indicated in Figure 1, a diagram of the "student academic learning model" by Michael Molenda.

The term "media" appears twice in this schematization. First, it appears in the form of mass media, directly connected with culture, and located as an element outside of the sphere of influence of the school and classroom environments. Second, "media" appears closer to the center of the diagram, unambiguously within the institutional environments of the school and classroom, contiguous with instructional methods, directly connected with the teacher characteristics, and feeding directly into student instruction and motivation (or "effort").

This duality is defined in surprisingly similar terms in both English- and German-language discourses. The one difference separating these discourses in this regard, though, is that both conceptions of media are subsumed in German under the term *Medienpädagogik* (media pedagogy), whereas they appear separately

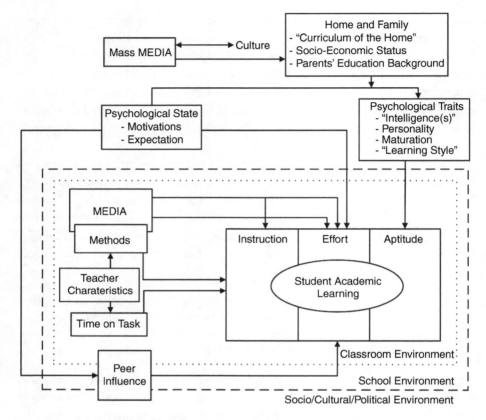

Figure 1: Student academic learning model. © M. Molenda. Used with permission.

in English. Media pedagogy is defined in the most inclusive terms, for example as "the treatment of pedagogical questions of a theoretical and practical nature, raised in connection with media" (Merkert, 1997, p. 1057). As a field of this breadth, it is not surprising that *Medienpädagogik* encompasses a range of wide emphases for both research and teaching, including:

- a focus for both research and teaching on the academic, ideological, and theoretical implications of the production, distribution, and transmission of knowledge in society;
- the treatment of media and media related questions specifically as subjects in school curricula; and
- a practical field of media pedagogical activity or praxis for and in kindergartens, schools, parent-teacher associations and various areas of youth work, and adult and continuing education.

Thus designating research, teaching, and social action related to media in the broadest sense, *Medienpädagogik* also encompasses a number of subdisciplines or subspecializations. These include media didactics (*Mediendidaktik*), media education (*Medienerziehung*), ICT competency (*informationtechnische Bildung*), as well as the tellingly named tradition of the pedagogy of protection (*Bewahrpädagogik*). This protective pedagogy, together with "media education" and corresponding ICT competencies, can be said to correspond broadly to English-language "media literacy" as defined above. Media didactics, for its part, provides a counterpart to the English-language subdomain of "instructional media." Media didactics has been defined as focusing on "the functions, effects, and implementation of media in teaching and learning contexts," specifically for the purpose of "the optimization of teaching and learning processes" (Hug 2002, p. 195).

As indicated in the diagram above, in both ways of defining media in education—in terms of media literacy or education, and in terms of instructional media or media didactics—mediatic technologies and forms are relegated to two relatively minor subcomponents or subsystems in a much larger system of learning or education. These components are firmly contained and suspended within the encompassing environment of the classroom, school and social, cultural, and political systems. In other words, media are generally *not* seen in educational theory in such a way that they would constitute the "water" in which teachers and students would figuratively "swim."

Needless to say, in the light of the mediatic turn, this bifurcated and limited educational definition of media appears inadequate. To understand media as a "mass" phenomenon external to educational purposes (on the one hand) and as an instrument entirely defined by these purposes (on the other) is problematic for education on both empirical and theoretical grounds. Empirically speaking, these ways of conceptualizing media are rendered insufficient by the increased penetration of media generally, and also by the increasing importance of more personal or participatory (rather than "mass") media. Theoretically speaking, these traditional roles of media in education are put into question in terms of the mediatic a priori: the contention that media play an important role in defining the epistemological preconditions or characteristics of cognition, such as the perception of time, space, and the shaping of attention and communication. Understood in this way means that media themselves can be aligned with educational purposes in a number of ways rather than simply being regarded as a problem for education or as a mere conduit for instructional content.

What changes to the traditional bipartite educational definition of media would be adequate to the mediatic turn? Some would answer this question in quite ambitious terms, envisioning the emergence of a vast "media research program" for a range of disciplines:

> As soon as we realize that there are no contents outside the media, we have to accept that research in media has to invest deliberately in all possibilities of observation and description offered by all media. In the times to come, new concepts of science and aesthetics, of rationality and creativity should and will...be developed in order to serve the needs of a media research programme we can only imagine today. (Schmidt 2008, p. 103)

Certainly, some of these new disciplinary concepts would relate to matters educational as well as scientific and aesthetic; but at the same time, such grandiose visions for the future shed little light on present or short-term possibilities. Speaking perhaps more practically, and focusing again on Figure 1, recognition of the mediatic turn would first mean that media would be freed from their schematic containment, as either mass phenomena or instructional tools. Whether one is thinking along the lines of the recent proliferation of internet-based communication media (e.g., chats, blogs, wikis, and social software generally) or of the possibility of mediatically conditioned cognitive characteristics, "media" as a term would be more accurately depicted as interpenetrating all elements in the "learning model." Media, in other words, would need to be redefined diagrammatically as being ubiquitous, as encompassing the school and classroom environments, as having a scope that is contiguous with the socio/cultural/political environment as a whole.

This further implies that the practices and institutions of education need to be understood in a frame of reference that is *mediatic*: in terms of what has been referred to above as mediality, as a part of a media-ecological configuration of technologies specific to a particular age or era. Of course, in this context as well, institutional education cannot be defined through a series of boxes and arrows, in which media is are given discrete and tightly circumscribed roles. Education as a whole instead appears as deeply interconnected with the gradually changing configuration of mediatic forms that surround and saturate it. As has been widely noted in North American writing in media ecology, this configuration is one in which *print* has been dominant. McLuhan, for example, has described the role of the school specifically as the "custodian of print culture" (1962, p. 215). It provides, he says, a socially sanctioned "civil defense against media fallout" (1964, p. 305)—against threatening changes in the mediatic environs. Neil Postman expresses this in slightly less figurative terms, saying that "school was an invention of the printing press and must stand or fall on the issue of how much importance the printed word will have in the future" (1982, p. 42). Postman further describes this typographically centered mediatic constellation as being one that crystallized during the seventeenth century.

He points out that it was during this century of enlightenment that particular meanings of school and childhood developed that remain familiar today:

> Since the school curriculum was entirely designed to accommodate the demands of literacy, it is astonishing that educationists have not widely commented on the relationship between the "nature of childhood" and the biases of print. For example, a child evolves towards adulthood by acquiring the sort of intellect we expect of a good reader: a vigorous sense of individuality, the capacity to think logically and sequentially... [as well as] the capacity to manipulate high orders of abstraction...Infancy ended at the point at which a command of speech was achieved. Childhood began with the task of learning how to read... *childhood became a description of a level of symbolic achievement.* (1982, pp. 42, 46)

Childhood can be thus defined in terms of mediatic competency, as a transitional state that begins with mastery of spoken communication and ends with much more laborious accomplishments in written communication. These characteristics of literacy listed by Postman have become so familiar that they are generally understood as part of the natural processes of human development—registered in Piaget's concrete and operational stages, for example. Schooling and education, by extension, appear as the formal setting that is the necessary institutional correlative to this conception of development. As the "custodian of print culture," it is the task of education to provide students with a structured, controlled environment that is conducive to the quiet repose that print media demand of their audiences. This further positions the school as a kind of separate, reflective, critical pedagogical "space," isolated from the multiple sources of informational "noise" in an otherwise media-saturated lifeworld.

Sustained discussions of the effect of mediality and the design and evolution of educational forms seem to be as rare in German-language discourse as they are in Anglo-American scholarship. A conspicuous if unusual exception appears in pedagogical literature in German-speaking Europe in the work of Klaus Mollenhauer, who observes in his book, *Forgotten Connections* (1983), that in the seventeenth century

> ...the ground rules through which reality is constructed for children [were] not simply transformed; but a whole new system of rules emerge[d]. The culture [was] no longer presented to the child in its entirety, but only in part: namely, via [a kind of] pedagogical rehearsal or practice, as it would be for someone from a foreign land. This makes certain institutions necessary [such as] schools...orphanages...[and] kindergartens... (p. 50)

Instead of only and simply learning directly from what adults around them said and did, an emphasis on print literacy meant that children learned of the world indirectly, through books—almost as someone would read about a far-away place. And such learning by proxy requires the forms and functions of the school. Intervening changes in media and their interrelationships have, of course, challenged the centrality of this print-based "pedagogical rehearsal or practice" that Mollenhauer describes. These changes, occurring through the introduction first of radio, then of television, and finally of newer media technologies, have been described by Postman and others as constructing a reality for children that in many ways undermines the one arising via print and literacy. In this way, mediatic changes have challenged the raison d'etre of the school, making its disposition or posture increasingly "custodial" or defensive. McLuhan describes this from the perspective of the student, socialized to audiovisual media, who is suddenly confronted with "baffling" customs and values shaped by rather different mediatic circumstances:

> The youngster today, stepping out of his...TV environment, goes to school and enters a world where the information is scarce but is ordered and structured by fragmented, classified patterns, subjects, schedules. He is utterly bewildered because he comes out of this intricate and complex integral world of electric information and goes into this nineteenth-century world of classified information that still characterizes the educational establishment...The young today are baffled because of this extraordinary gap between the two worlds. (McLuhan 1995, p. 222)

These media, in McLuhan's view, would ultimately lead to students' liberation from schooling and thus to the end of the school as an institution (Lynch 2002). Following in McLuhan's footsteps, Neil Postman interprets the end result of this clash of media cultures in more baleful terms:

> In the long run, television may bring an end to the careers of school teachers, since school was an invention of the printing press...There is no chance, of course, that television will go away, but schoolteachers who are enthusiastic about its presence always call to my mind an image of some turn-of-the-century blacksmith who not only is singing the praises of the automobile but who also believes that his business will be enhanced by it. (Postman 1997)

In the light of the mediatic turn, the defensive position of the school in the era of proliferating electronic media is evident in the way it has responded to media as form and culture, summed up in the term "media literacy": the terminology and the critical arsenal of a previous era of mediality ("literacy") is directed against what is interpreted as a forces in need of active and vigorous critique and deconstruction ("media"). Given the position of the school in the current configuration of mediality, it is no surprise that they are at the center of the school's efforts to work against subsequent changes in the medial constellation. It is therefore not surprising that both *Medienpädagogik* and media literacy have in common a central affirmation of the school as a place of quiet reflection, insulated from the sounds and images of the external mediatic environment.

But at the same time, and as has been indicated earlier, McLuhan, and Postman's descriptions of the mediatic environment as an "electronic," televisual environment sounds dated. Postman's claim that "there is no chance, of course, that television will go away," for example, carries and inappropriately finality in an age in which viewership (especially among the young) is declining. The intervening mutation and combination of mediatic forms, including text, image, video, and audio present a significant challenge McLuhan's and Postman's divergent prognoses. Any simple binary opposition between logical, hierarchical print culture on the one hand, and the visceral visual and audio flows on the other, has seriously undermined by the eclectic mix of media available via the internet, Web, and mobile communications. This is illustrated with special clarity in the case of textual forms of communication that have been collectively labeled "Web 2.0" or "the read-write Web." These include chat and texting, Wikis and Wikipedia, blogging (including audio podcasting and video blogging), and "social software" generally. Especially in the case of chat, texting, blogging, and social software like Facebook, these forms have brought with them new kinds of writing and written expression: The abbreviated, telegraphic textuality of synchronous chat and texting has attracted the attention of linguists and communications scholars, and the varied combinations of text and other visual media common on blogs and other social software have been widely studied in terms of identity construction and self-expression.

In upsetting the binary opposition between textual and audio/visual cultures posited by McLuhan, Postman, and others, these new forms and combinations present radically new opportunities for media pedagogies in particular and education in general. Simply put, these new additions to the mediatic environment relieve education of its unambiguously defensive role as "the custodian of print culture" against an audio/visual mediatic onslaught. Education, fighting on the side of literacy, no longer needs to fend off the attacks of "mass media" on the one hand while wielding instructional media from its curricular arsenal on the other. Instead of working against media and insulating its use of media against the mass mediatic environment, education now has the opportunity of working *with* media, in greater consonance with the larger mediatic ecology.

(MEDIA) EDUCATION AFTER THE MEDIATIC TURN

The question then becomes, "How can pedagogy work *with* media, in concord with the mediatic environment, in the wake of the mediatic turn?" Answering this question requires a flexible understanding of pedagogy, its forms and functions, and, of course, of its relationship medial environment in which it is immersed. This concluding section of the chapter explores a number of possible pedagogical responses and considers possibilities developed in recent scholarship as well as those implied by the preceding discussions of mediality and mediatization.

One prominent response has been presented by Henry Jenkins under the rubric of "participatory technologies" and "cultures." In a report entitled *Confronting the Challenges of the Participatory Culture: Media Education for the 21st Century*, Jenkins and a number of coauthors describe a number of applications characteristic of Web 2.0 in terms that can also be seen as reflective of the mediatic turn:

> Rather than dealing with each technology in isolation, we would do better to take an ecological approach, thinking about the interrelationship among all of these different communication technologies, the cultural communities that grow up around them, and the activities they support. Media systems consist of communication technologies and the social, cultural, legal, political, and economic institutions, practices, and protocols that shape and surround them. (Jenkins et al. 2006, p. 8)

In keeping with the nondeterministic emphasis discussed earlier in this chapter, Jenkins and his coauthors see media as related to a variety of different factors outside of themselves, including institutions, cultures, and practices that appear quite heteronymous in nature. In this context, it is not simply a question of the material and functional character of the technologies that is important (or their correlation to curricular or cognitive characteristics). Instead, Jenkins and his collaborators emphasize a much wider set of elements, which they see as all having contributing to a new "participatory culture." They define such a culture as one

> ...with relatively low barriers to artistic expression and civic engagement, strong support for creating and sharing one's creations, and some type of informal mentorship whereby what is known by the most experienced is passed along to novices...Participatory culture is emerging as the culture absorbs and responds to the explosion of new media technologies that make it possible for average consumers to archive, annotate, appropriate, and recirculate media content in powerful new ways. (pp. 3, 8)

The specific skills that Jenkins and his coauthors describe as arising through involvement of "average consumers" in this "participatory culture" include ludic forms of problem solving, identity construction, multitasking, "distributed cognition," and "transmedial navigation" (p. 8). Specific sites and programs that Jenkins and his coauthors see as illustrative of such a culture include popular commercial offerings such as "Neopets," "The Sims Online," and "My Pop Studio."

However, it is precisely this emphasis on commercial media and "average *consumers*"—and the concomitant centrality of leisure and entertainment—that have given rise to misgivings concerning Jenkins' and his coauthors' vision of the educational potential of participatory media cultures. The emphatically commercial nature of some of the sites and communities mentioned as examples by Jenkins and his coauthors compound the problem. In opposition to this emphasis on consumption and commercial culture, schooling and education not only present a critical print-cultural bias, they also retain a clear (albeit contested) noncommercial character. The space that education provides for critical reflective practices must remain in some significant ways distinctive from the commercially culture and methods of advertising and consumption. The point is not that there is nothing to be learned from practices for maximizing profit; the point is that the circumscribed cultural and technical parameters of the communities and activities—ultimately designed to mobilize profit and circulate consumer and advertising data—must not simultaneously circumscribe learning and education.

In urging education to work *with* rather than *against* the positive potential of the surrounding mediatic environment, we have a somewhat different set of possibilities in mind. These combine the reflective, critical reflexivity or self-awareness characteristic of literacy with a number of new mediatic forms and implications. The first of these possibilities is to develop critical and self-aware participation in commercial and especially *non*commercial Web 2.0 technologies; the second is to develop a similarly reflexive appreciation of the role of media in pedagogical research; the third and most important is to develop a particular emphasis on *framing*, to cultivate an awareness of the role of the mediatic a priori, epistemological character of media.

The increasing expansion and penetration of mediatic forms and technologies (as a part of meta-process of mediatization) is generally accompanied by increased commercialization (as a parallel meta-process). In this context, a significant function of schooling and education is to foster noncommercial or even countercommercial mediatic forms and engagement. Of necessity, these forms will involve different tools and different types of use from what "average consumers" would be typically be accustomed to. For example, Wikis and blogs (even if these may be hosted on commercial sites) can be adapted for critical, reflective writing—rather than, say, passive browsing. Instead of remixing existing clips from television or top-forty radio, as another example, children should be encouraged to generate and recombine audio and/or video elements from their own contexts and situations. In this way, participation can be encouraged to break through patterns of inscribed by the circulation of data, commodities, and monetary value that can otherwise limit the use of these media.

In terms of pedagogical research, the mediatic turn calls for a reconsideration of the value and position of media in the way in which educational theories and practice are developed and researched. In research work, just as in the activities of learners described above, a self-aware engagement with mediatic representation in both creation and dissemination of data needs to be exercised. This includes investigative processes such as in software-supported methods of data analysis and also extends to the ways in which objects of investigation are defined through mediatic representation (e.g., in the case of the emergence and passing of internet subcultures). These questions need to be seen as relevant not only to empirically oriented approaches of educational research but also to educational philosophy and its discursive and representational modalities.

Finally, understanding media as presenting the a priori or the epistemological preconditions for both specialized and everyday knowledge can be seen to entail an emphasis on epistemological orientation or *framing*. This arises as follows: If the acquisition, refinement and circulation of knowledge all occur as mediated processes, it only makes sense that an awareness of the current and potential role of media in forming knowledge should follow. Student and teacher competencies need to be reconsidered along the lines of this awareness, with the capability to effectively select, utilize and thus *frame* media and mediatic contents being the most important. In understanding this kind of "framing," Hans Blumenberg's notion of the fundamental "readability of the world" (*Lesbarkeit der Welt*) can be helpful: It refers to the foundationally *hermeneutic* nature of the human condition, the fact that our orientation in the world around us—whether it is presented to us as text, image, sound, or a multimedial mixture—carries meanings that call out to be actively interpreted (Blumenberg 1981). In responding to this often-mediated call to interpretation, familiarity with the way these meanings are shaped, distorted, or even sometimes erased through this mediation is indispensible. Of course, the curriculum requisite to such "framing competencies"—like the new rationalities and aesthetics invoked by Schmidt—is something that "we can only" begin to "imagine today."

CONCLUSION

Of course, education does not become obsolete simply because rapid and multiple developments in media and its cultures and technologies have increased uncertainty about the creation, acquisition, and circulation of knowledge. Instead, the need for education becomes more urgent: the importance of differentiated understandings of media-induced forms of knowledge and accounts of underlying mediatic structures is instead heighted. As certainties become fewer, the importance of education becomes greater:

> When only particular—and only dimly perceivable—structures come to visibility, then humans need more than qualifications and certification, more than even learning that is lifelong. People must be given the ability to deal with significantly weaker forms of knowledge and consciousness; for that purpose, people need technological skills, capacities for self-construction in front of screens. They still need some small degree of metaphysical comfort. They must be capable of enduring an existence in flickering and distributed networks and competencies for cooperation with emotional beings under the conditions of unleashed communication. Education after the mediatic turn is nothing less than this. (Schönherr-Mann 2008, pp. 206–207)

The precise ways in which digital media might eventually contribute to the "readability of the world"—and not only to the processes of commercialization, globalization, and trivialization of life—have yet to be fathomed.

NOTE

1. Although this quote is frequently attributed to McLuhan (e.g., see McLuhan in Wikiquotes, 2008), it is clear that its ultimate origins lie elsewhere. The question, "What does a fish know about the water in which it swims all its life?" has been attributed to Albert Einstein (see http://www.knowprose.com/node/11678). And a similar fish–water analogy is clearly evident in an undated Zen Koan; see http://www.zenki.com/GenjoKoan.htm.

REFERENCES

Bakardjieva, M. (2008). The (Wo)man on the Net: Exploring the New Social Distribution of Knowledge. In T. Hug (Ed.), *Media, Knowledge & Education— Exploring New Spaces, Relations and Dynamics in Digital Media Ecologies* (pp. 151–169). Innsbruck: Innsbruck University Press.

Blumenberg, H. (1987). *Die Lesbarkeit der Welt*. Frankfurt a. M.: Suhrkamp.

Boles, D. (2008). The Language of Media Literacy: A Glossary of Terms. *Media Awareness Network*. Accessed October 29, 2008 from: http://www.media-awareness.ca/english/resources/educational/teaching_backgrounders/media_literacy/glossary_media_literacy.cfm.

Cassirer, E. (1956). *Philosophy of Symbolic Forms* (three vols.). New Haven, CT: Yale University Press.

Fuller, M. (2005). *Media Ecologies: Materialist Energies in Art and Technoculture*. Cambridge, MA: MIT Press.

Giesecke, M. (2002). *Von den Mythen der Buchkultur zu den Visionen der Informationsgesellschaft: Trendforschung zur aktuellen Medienökologie*. Frankfurt a. M.: Suhrkamp.

Giesecke, M. (2007). *Die Entdeckung der kommunikativen welt. Studien zur kulturvergleichenden mediengeschichte*. Frankfurt a. M.: Suhrkamp.

Hartmann, F. (2000). *Medienphilosophie.* Vienna: WUV-Universitätsverlag (UTB).

Hickethier, K. (2003). *Einführung in die Medienwissenschaft.* Stuttgart, Weimar: Metzlar.

Hug, T. (2002). Medienpädagogik—Begriffe, Konzeptionen, Perspektiven. In G. Rusch (Ed.), *Einführung in die Medienwissenschaften* (pp. 189–207). Opladen: Westdeutscher Verlag.

Kittler, F. A. (1985). *Aufschreibesysteme 1800/1900.* München: Fink.

Krämer, S. (1998). Das Medium als Spur und als Apparat. In Krämer, S. (Ed.). *Medien, Computer, Realität. Wirklichkeitsvorstellungen und Neue Medien* (pp. 73–94). Frankfurt a. M.: Suhrkamp.

Krämer, S. (2005). Boten, Engel, Geld, Computerviren. Medien als Überträger. *Paragrana: Internationale Zeitschrift für Historische Anthropologie, Themenheft: Körpermaschine Maschinenkörper. Mediale Transformationen,* 14(2), 15–24.

Krotz, F. (2007). *Mediatisierung: Fallstudien zum Wandel von Kommunikation.* Wiesbaden: Verlag für Sozialwissenschaften.

Jenkins, H., Purushotoma, R., Clinton, K.A., Weigel, M., and Robison, A. J. (2006). *Confronting the Challenges of Participatory Culture: Media Education for the 21st Century.* White paper co-written for the MacArthur Foundation. Accessed July 14, 2008 from: http://www.projectnml.org/files/working/NMLWhitePaper.pdf.

Leschke, R. (2003). *Einführung in die Medientheorie.* München: Fink.

Lynch, J. (2002). What can we learn from McLuhan? Electronic communication technologies and the future of schooling. In P. Jeffrey (Ed.), *Problematic Futures: Educational Research in an Era of Uncertainty—AARE 2002 Conference Papers,* pp. 1–16, AARE, Melbourne.

Margreiter, R. (1999). Realität und Medialität: Zur Philosophie des 'Medial Turn.' *Medien Journal,* 23(1), 9–18.

Margreiter, R. (2007). *Medienphilosophie: Eine Einführung.* Berlin: Parerga.

Mayer, R. E. (2005). *The Cambridge Handbook of Multimedia Learning.* Cambridge, UK: Cambridge University Press.

McLuhan, M. (1962). *The Gutenberg Galaxy: The Making of Typographic Man.* Toronto: University of Toronto Press.

McLuhan, M. (1964). *Understanding Media: The Extensions of Man.* New York: McGraw-Hill.

McLuhan, M. (1995). Address at Vision 65. In F. Zingrone and E. McLuhan (Eds.), *The Essential McLuhan.* New York: Basic Books.

Merkert, P. R. (1997). Medienpädagogik. In H. Hierdeis & T. Hug (Eds.), *Taschenbuch der Pädagogik,* Vol. 3 (pp. 1057-1066). Baltmannsweiler: Schneider-Verlag-Hohengehren.

Molenda, M., and Pershing, J. A. (2008). Improving Performance. In A. Januszewski and M. Molenda (Eds.), *Educational Technology: A Definition with Commentary.* New Jersey: Lawrence Erlbaum Associates.

Mollenhauer, K. (1983). *Vergessene Zusammenhänge. Über Kultur und Erziehung.* Munich: Juventa.

Polanyi, M. (1966). *The Tacit Dimension.* Garden City, NY: Doubleday.

Postman, N. (1970). "The Reformed English Curriculum." In A. C. Eurich (Ed.), *High School 1980: The Shape of the Future in American Secondary Education* (pp. 160–168). New York: Pitman.

Postman, N. (1982). *The Disappearance of Childhood.* New York: Random House.

Postman, N. (1997). Five Things We Need to Know About Technological Change. Accessed October 27, 2008 from: http://itrs.scu.edu/tshanks/pages/Comm12/12Postman.htm.

Rusch, G. (2007). Mediendynamik. Explorationen zur Theorie des Medienwandels. *Navigationen. Zeitschrift für Medien- und Kulturwissenschaften,* 7(1), 13–93.

Rusch, G. (2008). The Many Mediatic Turns…and a Significant Difference. In T. Hug (Ed.), *Mediale Wende—Ansprüche, Konzepte und Diskurse,* 25(1), 23–34.

Schmidt, S. J. (2008). Media Philosophy—A Reasonable Programme? In H. Hrachovec and A. Pichler (Eds.), Philosophy of the Information Society. *Proceedings of the 30th International Ludwig Wittgenstein Symposium*, Kirchberg am Wechsel, Austria 2007, Vol. 2 (pp. 89–105). Frankfurt u. a.: Ontos.

Schönherr-Mann, H-M. (2008). Bildung im Zeitalter des weltbildenden Bildschirms— Ein Essay. In T. Hug (Ed.), *Media, Knowledge & Education—Exploring New Spaces, Relations and Dynamics in Digital Media Ecologies* (pp. 195–207). Innsbruck: Innsbruck University Press.

Sonesson, G. (1997). The multimediation of the lifeworld. In N. Winfried (Ed.), *Semiotics of the Media. State of the Art, Projects, and Perspectives. Proceedings of an international congress, Kassel, March 1995*, p. 61–78. Berlin, New York: Mouton de Gruyter. Accessed October 9, 2008 from: http://filserver.arthist.lu.se/kultsem/sonesson/media_2.html.

Tabbi, J., and Wutz, M. (1997). *Reading Matters: Narrative in the New Media Ecology*. Ithaca, NY: Cornell University Press.

Wikiquote. (2008). Marshall McLuhan. Accessed October 30, 2008 from: http://en.wikiquotes.org/wiki/Marshall_McLuhan.

Winthrop-Young, G., and Wutz, M. (1999). Translators' introduction: Friedrich Kittler and media discourse analysis. In *Gramophone, Film, Typewriter*. Stanford, CA: Stanford University Press.

Zuboff, S. (1988). *In the Age of the Smart Machine: The Future of Work and Power*. New York: Basic Books.

CHAPTER FOUR

Theories: Mediatization AND Media Ecology

LYNN SCHOFIELD CLARK

In the film *Annie Hall* (1977), Alvy (Woody Allen) and Annie (Diane Keaton) are standing in a movie line, with a very loud professor type talking behind them, pretentiously offering opinions to his girlfriend on Fellini films, Samuel Beckett, and Weltanschauung. Finally he works his way around to television. The professor says:

> "You know what it is? It's the influence of television! Marshall McLuhan deals with it in terms of it being a high intensity, you understand? A hot medium, as opposed to the cool medium of print."
>
> Woody Allen (agitated, turns to speak directly to the camera): "What do you do when you get stuck in a movie line with a guy like this behind you?"
>
> Professor (joins Allen in speaking to the camera): "Wait a minute, why can't I give my opinion? It's a free country!"
>
> Woody Allen: "He can—you can give it—but do you have to give it so loud?! I mean aren't you ashamed to be pontificating like that? And the funny thing is, Marshall McLuhan, I mean, you don't know anything about Marshall McLuhan's work!"
>
> Professor: "Really? Really? I happen to teach a class at Columbia on TV, media, and culture. So I think that my insights into McLuhan have a great deal of validity."
>
> Woody Allen: "Oh, do you? Well, I happen to have Mr. McLuhan right here." (Walks over to a cardboard display and reaches behind it to pull Marshall McLuhan into the frame.)

McLuhan (speaking to the professor): "I heard what you were saying. You mean my
    whole fallacy is wrong. You know nothing of my work. How you ever
    got to teach a course in anything is totally amazing!"
Allen (speaking to the camera): "Boy, if life were only like this."

This is a funny excerpt for many reasons: the ridiculous professor who gets
one-upped by Allen's Alvy; the unexpected breaking of realism when Allen and
the professor speak to the camera and when McLuhan appears incongruously
to champion Allen's point; and Annie's comments about sexuality and therapy
that occur before this interchange and that make Alvy uncomfortable enough to
drive him to confront the professor in the first place. Also funny is the seemingly
incomprehensible line from McLuhan: "You mean my whole fallacy is wrong."
Some have seen this as a particularly brilliant line (Mitchell 2006). All fallacies
are wrong, of course, but having McLuhan say this parodied the way his own
work tended to be viewed by others as inscrutable and circular. And the fact that
McLuhan himself is saying it allows us as audience members to relish both Allen's
and McLuhan's love of irony.

By 1977, when *Annie Hall* received its Best Picture Oscar, the film rein-
forced what many media scholars at the time seemed to think: that while some
of McLuhan's thoughts were quite compelling (the role of media in the rise of
the "global village," for instance), his ideas and the style in which he wrote about
them had largely fallen out of favor. He could, then, become a parody of himself.
Although still a celebrity, McLuhan's reception in university life had chilled, particularly in the then-growing field of media studies. There, his writings were dismissed for their "fallacies" and his grand theories fit uneasily with a field that was
divided into those enchanted with positivism and those compelled to bring media
studies into a broader conversation with neo-Marxism, feminism, and critical race
theory. Both approaches worked against what seemed to be the "metatheorizing"
work of Marshall McLuhan.

So why resurrect media ecology in the context of a new and seemingly
vibrant conversation about mediatization theory? There are several reasons for
this, but it is not the aim of this chapter to argue that McLuhan was right and
that therefore all of the contributions of media studies over the past twenty
years have been wrong or at least misguided (see Morley 2006, on the overlook-
ing of media studies research in Lash 2002 and Kittler 1999). Rather, I wish
here to adopt an approach once attributed to Stuart Hall: that of a "productive eclecticism in intellectual life . . . a selective, syncretic inclusiveness in which
one attempts to take what is best from various intellectual traditions and work
with those elements towards new synthesis" (Morley 1997, p. 303). Therefore,
I aim to put some of the issues facing mediatization theory in conversation

with research within media ecology that seems consistent with mediatization's impulses.

Mediatization has become an interesting way to theorize the transformative role of the media within social life in the contemporary period (Hepp 2007, Hjarvard 2008, Mandaville 2007). Schulz (2004) has proposed four different aspects of mediatization: (1) Media extend the natural limits of human communication capacities, (2) the media provide a substitute for social activities and social institutions, (3) media amalgamate with various non-media activities in social life; and (4) actors and organizations of all sectors of society accommodate to the media logic. Mediatization, therefore, refers to both the processes by which social organizations, structures, or industries take on the form of the media, and the processes by which genres of popular culture become central to the narratives of social phenomena.

The first reason for looking to media ecology, then, is that mediatization and media ecology do share many of the same impulses. At root, both are concerned with how we might discuss the role that technologies of communication have played in shaping culture, and conversely, the ways in which we might take account of how cultural practices shape communication technologies. But a second reason for a reexamination of media ecology is that McLuhan's popularity and influence were at their peak just as the tradition of cultural studies was on the rise in North and South America and in the South Pacific. Some in cultural studies therefore shared with McLuhan followers a tradition in literary criticism, while others were writing their own thoughts in response to those of media ecology; Raymond Williams both shares some of McLuhan's scholarly traditions and explicitly critiqued his work, as will be discussed below. A third and final reason for exploring media ecology in relation to mediatization is that, whereas Marshall McLuhan's own popularity may have faded, his legacy has continued to inform a field that has grappled with some of the same challenges that mediatization now faces: charges of technological determinism, a desire to put forth an ecological or environmental understanding of media, a concern with the relationship between humans and the technologies they create, and a wish to explore the way in which cultures evolve. It is worth exploring how scholars in media ecology have addressed themselves to these various challenges as we contemplate the development of mediatization theory and its similar concerns.

WHAT IS MEDIA ECOLOGY?

Neil Postman first introduced a definition of media ecology in 1968 and developed it further in his keynote address at the inaugural meeting of the Media

Ecology Association. In that lecture, he told the gathered alumni, graduate students, and associates:

> Our first thinking about the subject was guided by a biological metaphor. You will remember from the time when you first became acquainted with a Petri dish, that a medium was defined as a substance within which a culture grows. If you replace the word "substance" with the word "technology," the definition would stand as a fundamental principle of media ecology: A medium is a technology within which a culture grows; that is to say, it gives form to a culture's politics, social organization, and habitual ways of thinking. Beginning with that idea, we invoked still another biological metaphor, that of ecology...We were not simply interested in media, but in the ways in which the interaction between media and human beings gives a culture its character and, one might say, helps a culture to maintain symbolic balance. (Postman 2000, pp. 10–11, in Strate 2006, p. 15)

There are three things to note here. First, with its emphasis on an interest in "interaction between media and human beings" toward the end of his statement, Postman seemed interested in distinguishing the media ecological approach from technological determinism (the belief that a certain technology "causes" patterns in culture). He described culture as something that is constituted in the interaction between media and human beings. In fact, it's noteworthy that, in this part of his statement, Postman's interest in "interaction" has some limited resonance with Raymond Williams' (1977) definition of the patterns of culture as a "structure of feeling," the elements of which have "affective elements of consciousness and relationships" that exist as a kind of "practical consciousness of a present kind" (p. 132). Yet Postman adds a specifically ethical dimension to his description of culture by implying that there is some need for it to "maintain symbolic balance." In contrast, many in the tradition of media and cultural studies (including Williams) are more interested in the costs at which that balance in maintained, and how groups might productively upset the linkages between media and ideology that hold things in balance through hegemony (Hall 1982).

There is a second thing to note about Postman's definition of media ecology offered in this excerpt, and that is the style of his argument, which is presented in the form of a GRE-like analogy: Petri dish is to world as enzyme is to technology as resulting biological substance (or "culture") is to anthropological culture. Despite the stated emphasis on interaction, the analogical model set up here is one of cause and effect, for it is only after the technology enters the Petri dish that culture takes the particular shape that it does (e.g., the biological substance doesn't change or shape the nature of the enzyme, and thus the anthropological culture does not seem to change the shape or nature of the technological forms). Thus, although Postman claims that his model is interactive, the very use of a biological metaphor ("ecology") calls this into question and introduces a serious problem to its stated claims.

The third noteworthy aspect to Postman's words is that, according to those who have written intellectual histories of the tradition of media ecology, this is the first mention of media ecology as such. Indeed, it was Postman who first worked to draw together the scholarly traditions that now are defined within media ecology, as will be discussed below (Man Kong Lum 2006).

Postman's style of using metaphors and analogies follows directly from McLuhan, who had a great deal of influence on Postman when they were both in New York in the late 1960s (Man Kong Lum 2006). Indeed, as Strate has pointed out, in the title of his most respected work, *The Gutenberg Galaxy: The Making of Typographic Man* (1962), Marshall McLuhan uses the word galaxy as "a synonym for system, environment, or ecology" (Strate 2006, p. 22). But, of course, McLuhan's most famous metaphor is the one that defines both the field of media ecology and the media forms that it studies: "The medium is the message." McLuhan, Postman, Walter Ong, and Harold Innis are generally considered to be the main influences in media ecological thought (Strate 2006), and therefore it is worth reviewing some of their work here.

Although perhaps his most often cited and most frequently challenged work was *Understanding Media: The Extensions of Man* (1964), McLuhan's first major work appeared in 1951, with a similarly metaphor-informed title: *The Mechanical Bride: Folklore of Industrial Man*. Its study of advertisements was influenced by the literary critic Frank R. Leavis' work. Leavis similarly took the texts of fiction and the novel as the object for critical discussion (as opposed to studying the intentions and psychological dispositions of its creator, which was the popular mode of literary criticism at the time). Raymond Williams and Richard Hoggart, theorists associated with the tradition of cultural studies, were also influenced by Leavis' work, although they were critics of what they viewed as Leavis' elitism regarding English "high" popular culture. Rather than criticizing Leavis directly as Williams did (and indeed, Leavis did not interpret advertising as McLuhan did, but dismissed it as a symptom of cultural disease [Storey 1993]), McLuhan took Leavis' style of literary criticism into explorations of how human beings in a certain time period are constructed and how our core assumptions and needs are reflected in the advertisements of the time.

In addition to Leavis, McLuhan owed a debt of gratitude to Harold Innis (1951), the political economist and historian who was his colleague at the University of Toronto. In his study of empires, Innis was interested in how the media systems in differing societies lent themselves to how power can be exercised and subverted. He suggested that entire cultures had a "bias" toward either space or time, seeking either an enlarged empire (space) or a preservation of cultural tradition (time). Differing media similarly had a bias toward space or time, he argued; stone tablets, for instance, lasted a long time but were difficult to transport, whereas papyrus and paper made it possible for leaders to communicate their mandates across great distances (important in the maintenance of the Roman empire) but were also more easily subverted or changed. Innis suggested that when a particular culture's bias aligned with a particular development in communication, it was possible for that culture to succeed in its goals of expanding its empire through space or consolidating its cultural uniqueness and strength through time.

McLuhan also drew upon the work of Eric Havelock (1963), who was Innis' colleague at the University of Toronto before departing for Yale. Havelock, a classics scholar, argued that a significant shift occurred when the context of Greek philosophy changed from an oral to a literate form. Studying the development of the Greek language, he argued that the meaning of words changed once they were written down. They allowed for a self-reflective subject, or one who could see oneself as separate from what was articulated. The resulting change led to the end of an emphasis on the oral memorized tradition of Homer and the emergence of a style of argument that became central in knowledge and education, Havelock argued.

At the time of his writing, his colleagues in the Classics largely dismissed Havelock's work (Halverson 1992). It has remained controversial and is viewed as limited due to its reliance upon assumptions and conjectures in lieu of available evidence from the Homeric era. Yet Havelock's ideas were consistent with the interest in structuralism in literary criticism and anthropology popular throughout the 1960s, and therefore they became highly influential in media ecology, particularly in the work of Walter Ong.

Marshall McLuhan supervised Walter Ong's M.A. thesis, which was defended at St. Louis University in 1941. After completing a Ph.D. in English literature at Harvard University in 1954, Ong returned to St. Louis University, where he spent most of the remainder of his career. Ong wanted to map the ways in which technological developments provided a foundation for the changes that have occurred in Western civilization. He therefore divided history into epochs according to their relationship to communication: the preliterate society, the rise of the alphabet in Hebrew and Greek traditions, the rise of manuscript culture, the rise of the printing press, and, finally, developments in recorded sound. In his most acclaimed book, *Orality and Literacy: The Technologizing of the Word* (1982), Ong discussed the transition from an oral to a literate culture. He argued that writing moves communication from the realm of sound to the realm of sight. Yet despite his seeming focus on the importance of the medium of communication (speech, manuscript, printing press), Ong was perhaps the first to directly address the charge of technological determinism within media ecology:

> [My] works do not maintain that the evolution from primary orality through writing and print to an electronic culture, which produces secondary orality, causes or explains everything in human culture and consciousness. Rather, [my] thesis is relationist: major developments, and very likely even all major developments, in culture and consciousness are related, often in unexpected intimacy, to the evolution of the word from primary orality to its present state. But the relationships are varied and complex, with cause and effect often difficult to distinguish. (Ong 1977, pp. 9–10)

Indeed, like Harold Innis, Ong was interested not only in how certain media might account for social change, but in the contexts in which various media were able to gain a foothold in a culture. This becomes an interest in those who followed Innis and Ong into more focused cultural historical studies, as I discuss below.

Metaphorical allusions, poetic flourishes, and theories on a grand scale have remained some of the hallmarks of style within the field of media ecology itself and among the students of Postman, McLuhan, and Meyrowitz (1985) who have been associated, most recently, with the program at New York University that Postman directed for many years. Many of the criticisms of this body of work have centered on the grandness of media ecological theories and their tendency to disavow yet also reinscribe a "hard" or technological determinism (see Smith and Marx 1996). Yet, whereas an analogical writing style and the method of attempting to relate social practices to differing epochs was found to be problematic by many scholars not least for its scale, critiques of the claims of McLuhan and of others associated with media ecology have led to productive and highly influential scholarship in the field of media cultural history.

THE PROBLEM OF TECHNOLOGICAL DETERMINISM

The role of media in social change is a primary concern in media ecology, as demonstrated in Postman's (1970) discussion of his main concern:

> ...how media of communication affect human perception, understanding, feeling, and value; and how our interaction with media facilitates or impedes our chances of survival. The word *ecology* implies the study of environments: their structure, content, and impact on people. (p. 161)

Postman's interest in how media affect environments is evident here. Also worth noting is Postman's concern with human cognition, or how technology might make possible certain modes and patterns of human thought while closing off others. This moves beyond the interests in social change and focuses on how media might affect individuals. As such, Postman's work shared a common concern with the television effects tradition that was receiving quite a bit of U.S. federal funding and attention at the time (Bandura 1977; Comstock and Rubenstein 1972). Moreover, Postman's approach to media from the position of social critic garnered for Postman a wide range of opportunities for speaking, particularly among educators concerned with how media provided unique challenges for the classroom (e.g., Postman 1995). It also contributed to critiques made of his work and its social position (Jensen 1990).

Postman was not the first to hear the charge of technological determinism. In 1974, when Raymond Williams wrote of the need for "a very different model of cause and effect," he was surely meaning to provide a contrast to what he viewed as McLuhan's notion of causality. Williams wrote:

> If the medium—whether print or television—is the cause, all other causes, all that men ordinarily see as history, are at once reduced to effects. Similarly, what are elsewhere seen as effects, and as such subject to social, cultural, psychological and moral questioning, are excluded as irrelevant by comparison with the direct physiological and therefore 'psychic' effects of the media as such. (Williams 1974, p. 127)

The contrasting viewpoint to his own, Williams noted, is that "A technology, when it has been achieved, can be seen as a general human property, an extension of a general human capacity" (p. 129). As Lister and his colleagues (2003) have pointed out, Williams was concerned that we not dismiss the question of how a technology is achieved. He argued that technologies can become meaningful and useful only when social practices exist before them; the specific context in which the technologies can meet a preexisting desire or interest is important to consider. Whereas McLuhan was interested in how a particular medium changes the "pace and scale" of human affairs, Williams was instead interested in the power that certain social groups have to determine the "pace and scale" of technological development. McLuhan saw broad effects emerging as a result of a single technology; Williams pointed out that there are many possible outcomes, and thus there is nothing in a particular technology that leads to a certain set of uses or social effects (Lister et al. 2003).

Williams (1977) also objected to the way in which McLuhan collapsed the concepts of "medium" and "technologies." Using "medium" in McLuhan's sense leads to a reification of a social process, he argued. In Williams' view, technologies were not merely artifacts but were also embodiments of knowledge and skillful practices that are required for the use of any tools or machines. This insight is key to the emergence of the social construction of technology school of thought

(MacKenzie and Wajcman 1999). It is also important in how those in cultural studies think about the process of mediation as constitutive of reality, as noted in Sonia Livingstone's foreword to this volume.

McLuhan fell out of favor among those in British cultural studies and those in the tradition of communication history that followed from Raymond Williams' line of thought and his careful analysis of communication technologies as socially and materially achieved. Indeed, as one example in the United States, renowned communications scholar James Carey (1988) similarly expressed discomfort with the technological determinism he associated with Marshall McLuhan's work. Following Innis yet focusing on a particular epoch rather than comparing several, Carey's work explored the nineteenth century introduction of "new media," including the telegraph. Carey argued that this technology facilitated the rise of a national identity as it enabled messages to travel across space and allowed for (even necessitated) the standardization of time represented in the establishment of time zones. Carolyn Marvin (1988), a onetime student of Carey's, then extended this approach further, exploring how the introduction of electricity and the telephone built upon existing social practices while challenging existing social systems of hierarchy and authority. These scholars differentiate themselves from the media ecology school due to their differences with McLuhan's sweeping claims and Postman's ethical impulses and analogical method of analysis. They also pointed the way toward how we might explore the unfolding of communication technologies within particular contexts, thereby continuing in Williams' line of thought.

CULTURAL STUDIES' OBJECTIONS TO MEDIA ECOLOGY: A RECONSIDERATION THROUGH ACTOR-NETWORK AND CYBERNETICS THEORIES

Certainly, McLuhan's theories have served as an important set of questions to think with for those in media studies. Yet perhaps the body of work known as *media ecology* can also assist cultural studies, and in turn the theories of mediatization that have largely grown from that tradition, in considering the importance of the physicality of communications technologies. Communications technologies, after all, are real and material, both in their physicality and in their ability to change particular social practices, as Lister and his colleagues (2003) have argued:

> New technologies do produce highly tangible changes in the way everyday life is conducted: they affect the way in which labour power is deployed, how money is invested and circulates, how business is done, how and where identities are formed, and so

> on. In such ways, technology, both in its forms and its capacities, profoundly affects human culture...A consequence of sidelining questions of technology within media studies, except to roll back undisciplined euphoria and ideological overstatement by techno-enthusiasts, means that the field of media studies has largely failed to develop a means of addressing technology as a real and material phenomenon. (pp. 289, 290)

Indeed, as Bruno Latour (1993) argued, studies in the humanities have become so concerned with questions of discursive construction that we do not explore the material world itself, attributing agency only to "a small number of powers—human powers" (p. 138). Yet things like diseases have effects and must therefore be accounted for through medical sciences as well as systems of communication, transportation, and technologies. It is not the thing (the disease), the technology (the medical treatment), or the human that has agency; it is the network as a whole that acts, effects, and determines what is possible. Humans are involved in "local interactions," but they are not the agents that create the networks and are therefore not solely responsible for what is possible. When Latour therefore argued that social action results from humans and nonhumans, he allowed space for purposive social action that is not located in individual agency or in technological determinism. Our division of intellectual tradition into disciplines is what hampers our ability to consider the many intersections of technology and culture that make things as they are, Latour suggested.

We are more hybrid now than human, as Donna Haraway (1991) famously argued in her essay titled, "The Cyborg Manifesto," and as such we must refuse to demonize or ignore technology on its own terms, thereby taking responsibility for the way in which the human/technology interface is "reconstructing the boundaries of everyday life." This is the point at which the social construction of technology school meets media ecology and cultural studies. Indeed, some, such as Olivia Harvey (2006), have argued that McLuhan's view of the human is that of a subject co-constructed with technology and that, conversely, "the reproduction of the human subject is an inherently technological process" (p. 342). This puts McLuhan in dialogue with conversations of the cyborg (part machine, part human hybrid) as well as with the posthuman (the entity that confronts such a plurality of choices regarding human relationships, families, and bodies that there are no longer any definitions of these things can be thought of as universal [Hayles 1999]). This, then, also provides a way for those interested in mediatization theories to grapple with feminist rethinking of the human subject in light of cybernetics.

Lister and his colleagues (2003) have argued that those of us in media cultural studies have not sufficiently explored communications technology through this hybridized sense of the cyborg or through Latour's actor-network theory due to our commitment to Williams' interest in replacing the concept of causality with the concept of agency. This has led to the long line of interesting research into the social construction of technology, as noted earlier. Yet as Lister and colleagues (2003) have also argued, Williams has "bequeathed media studies a problematic humanism" (p. 298): one that is so interested in exploring human agency that it has been incapable of considering the agency of things, in Latour's and Haraway's models. Williams, Lister and colleagues argued, operated from a linear and mechanical conception of causality: there is a cause and an effect. Yet McLuhan, they pointed out, is working like Latour and Haraway, with a nonlinear causality based not in mechanics but in cybernetics.

Cybernetics is a field of science, mathematics, and engineering that is interested in prediction and control of possible outcomes. It is based on a system of negative and positive feedback. Negative feedback can be understood in relation to the example of an automatic thermostat that, to avoid overheating, turns heat off when a certain temperature is reached. Positive feedback is akin to the feedback that occurs when a microphone is too close to a speaker in an audio system: it keeps building pressure until the system (in this case the speaker) is destroyed. Cybernetics argues that all change is the product of positive feedback, and thus the goal of controlling a system lies in ensuring its predictability by maximizing negative feedback. Alternatives need to be eliminated, which means they exist in some sense as potential outcomes. As Lister and colleagues (2003) explain, "Cybernetic control works by eliminating possible actions rather than prompting particular ones" (p. 371; see also pp. 353ff.). This introduces what Lister and colleagues, borrowing from Deleuze (1986, 1989), term the "cybernetic circuit," which is meant to point to the lack of a beginning and end point in a system that is explained not only by interactions between humans and technologies, but rather in addition by a continuous, co-creating exchange. To put this in the terms of media cultural studies, we might say that humans and technologies are both simultaneously actors and acted upon, even if often temporarily, occasionally with unpredictable results, and in a relationship that is not so much collaborative (e.g., in equal measures of power) as constructionist (e.g., that the role of power within the interaction is not always able to be disaggregated and understood). This, as Lister and colleagues point out, is consistent, at least in part, with Marshall McLuhan's (1967) theory of communication technologies as "extensions" of humanity. In many ways, the theory of extension is also consistent with Marx's theory of alienation. As Lister and colleagues (2003) argue with respect to Marx's discussion of how the factory has transformed the human experience, "by extending the body (through the automated machine that does the human's work), the body becomes transformed by its own extensions" (p. 86). Marx, like Williams after him, was more concerned with the costs associated with this transformational process and the distribution of power it enabled than with the properties of the technology (in this case, the factory) that enabled the transformation itself. This is the basis of the charge on the part of numerous critical scholars that McLuhan's perspective is deeply apolitical (Man Kong Lum 2006). While this is clearly a problem in McLuhan and some subsequent McLuhanesque theorizing, there is no doubt that McLuhan points to an important dimension of social experience that is not in contradiction to that of Marx's and, later, Williams' understanding of the potentially transformative role of technology.

Moreover, McLuhan disavows the sequential, linear approach to the relationship of technology and humanity in a way that also is consistent with cybernetics and differs from the charge Williams leveled against him. McLuhan (1967) noted:

> [A]s David Hume showed in the eighteenth century, there is no principle of causality in mere sequence. That one thing follows from another accounts for nothing... So the greatest of all reversals occurred with electricity, that ended sequence by making things instant. With instant speed the causes of things began to emerge to awareness again... Instead of asking which came first, the chicken or the egg, it suddenly seemed that a chicken was an egg's idea for getting more eggs. (p. 20, quoted in Lister et al., p. 306)

This suggests a process that is nonlinear, one in which the physical nature of a technology might play a role in limiting its possible uses and outcomes, and the actual collective human uses of technologies in concert with the financial interests that shape their availability cohere to amplify certain uses over others, which in turn shapes a cultural environment that then lends itself to a new physically rendered technology. "Technique engenders technique," as Jacques Ellul (1954) put it (p. 87)—yet in this case, we might say that technology, human, and culture are all co-constructed, constituting and mediating each other in ways that open up new possibilities for thinking and acting.

McLuhan's extension thesis has been directly or indirectly influential in the thinking of a variety of scholars, from Baudrillard (1997) to Haraway (1991). Most recently, the idea of the externalization of the human nervous system appears in media historian Jeremy Stolow's (2008) analysis of how the religious movement of spiritualism (contact between the living and the dead) shared common ground with the telegraph and with emergent scientific understandings of the human nervous system in the nineteenth century. The nervous system, indeed, was the body's most vital communication network. And just as those in medical sciences borrowed discursive explanations of the connections between mind and body from the realm of the telegraph, the telegraph came to be viewed as a system of cables that linked distant senders and receivers within the public body. Moreover, spiritualism, as Stolow argues, "shared with the technoculture of its day a common set of performative goals to erase distance, freeze time, and to circumvent what seemed otherwise to be an inevitable route toward inertia and decay of bodies and things" (p. 5). Spiritualism, as John Durham Peters (1999) has argued, "was one of the chief sites at which the cultural and metaphysical implications of new forms of communication were worked out... It is also the source for much of our vocabulary today (medium, channel, and communication)... Dreams of bodiless contact were a crucial condition not only of popular discourse but of technical invention as well" (pp. 100, 104). The physicality of the technology of the telegraph, and its ability to enable communication of instantaneous presence at a distance, through its embeddedness in social practices made other imaginings possible. The telegraph, and the simultaneously available spiritualist discourse of disembodied communication, in turn shaped the future imaginings of the telephone and radio. This recursive approach to studying the interactions at the nexus of the actor-network seems a good model for the kind of scholarship that can take place in the study of mediatization as a process that explores media ecology's interest in communication technology and change and is "soft" rather than "hard" in its determinism.

A number of historians in North America similarly seem to write in response to both Williams and McLuhan. An interesting example is found in James Beniger (1989), who introduced his thesis in *The Control Revolution* by arguing against the idea, largely put forth in McLuhan's thesis, that we are currently living through an "information revolution." Instead, Beniger argued, what we are currently experiencing is the result of what he termed a "crisis of control" that had its seeds in the Industrial Revolution when production first outpaced human physical powers. In short, speed brings uncertainty, which leads to a need for greater control over information. Following Max Weber, Beniger noted that through standardization of procedures and responsibilities, bureaucracy enabled the exercising and decentralization of control, which in turn had many unintended consequences in other sectors of life. With the rise of information processing after World War II, Beniger argued, bureaucratic control was further embedded into information systems. Beniger's argument was therefore consistent in thrust with Raymond Williams': He wanted to point out that organizational systems contributed to the emergence of an infrastructure which drew upon, rather than was determined by, information technology. Yet the very interest in the role of technology in social change was sparked by McLuhan's assertions and lends a great deal to the overall exploration of how technologies can take on a nonhuman agency of their own in the further construction of a culture oriented to controlling through negative feedback.

CONCLUSION

Many problems with media ecology theories cannot be adequately dealt with here, from its adherents' interest in grand theories to its underlying and uncritically reiterated Judeo-Christian ethical framework to its penchant for sweeping conclusions and acolyte-like attention to its earlier scribes.

In the end, what is to be made of the impulses that media ecology shares with mediatization? As this chapter has demonstrated, whereas mediatization may not be identical to media ecology in its roots, in many ways it faces the same dilemmas. What I propose is that the strength of mediatization, like that of media ecology, lies in two directions that are to be found not within the theories of mediatization themselves but in the conversations that might be mobilized around these theories.

First, mediatization is a way to help bring media history scholarship to the attention of sociologists. Just as Walter Ong's historical focus came into dialogue with Neil Postman's social criticism in media ecology, so scholarship that brings together sociologists and historians can enliven the emergent explorations in mediatization. To the extent that mediatization continues to encourage sociologists to grapple with not only what historians study but the ways in which humanists approach their work, it is a theory that holds potential importance for encouraging scholars— perhaps especially new scholars and graduate students—into conversation.

Second, and as a related note, it may be true that the works of Marshall McLuhan, Neil Postman, and Walter Ong have fallen out of favor in the exciting multidisciplinary and internationally informed impulses that characterize media studies today. Yet McLuhan's theories of technologies as extensions of human capabilities suggest common ground with cybernetics, and particularly with the cyborg and the posthuman. As such, media ecology can point to fruitful avenues for further exploration that avoids linear and causal assumptions in favor of an approach that assumes change is recursive, continuous, and co-created as part of a cybernetic circuit.

Third, it remains true that, because media ecologists spoke in a language that resonated with the public (even if it also seemed to lend itself at times to pretentiousness), the key works of media ecology continue to bring intelligent and thoughtful students into a greater desire for understanding the role of media in society and in relation to ourselves. These students may begin with a "hard determinist" approach but can learn to explore the subtleties invoked at the intersections of media ecology, cybernetics, and mediatization. For this reason, even if its style is analogical rather than analytical, it is worth noting how well media ecology has succeeded in engaging members of the public and future students in the conversation. This, too, is something that mediatization theories should strive to maintain and build upon.

REFERENCES

Bandura, A. (1977). *Social learning theory.* Englewood Cliffs, NJ: Prentice Hall.

Baudrillard, J. (1997). *Simulacra and Simulations,* trans. Sheila Faria Glaser. Ann Arbor, MI: University of Michigan Press. Cited in Lister et al.

Beniger, J. (1989). *The Control Revolution: Technological and Economic Origins of the Information Society.* Cambridge, MA: Harvard University Press.

Carey, J. (1988). *Communication as Culture: Essays on Media and Society.* Routledge.

Comstock, G.A., and Rubinstein, E. A. (Eds.) (1972). *Television and Social Behavior: A Technical Report to the Surgeon General's Scientific Advisory Committee on Television and Social Behavior. Vol. 3. Television and Adolescent Aggressiveness* (DHEW Publication No. HSM 72–9058) (pp. 1–34). Washington, DC: U.S. Government Printing Office.

Deleuze, Gilles (1986). *Cinema I: The Movement Image,* trans. Hugh Tomlinson and Barbara Haberjam. London: Athlone.

Deleuze, G. (1989). *Cinema 2: The Time-Image.* London: Athlone.

Ellul, J. (1954 [1964]). *The Technological Society.* New York: Vintage.

Hall, S. (1982). The Rediscovery of 'Ideology:' The Return of the Oppressed in Media Studies (pp. 52–86), in M. Gurevitch, T. Bennett, J. Curran, and J. Woolacott (Eds.), *Culture, Society, and the Media.* London: Methuen & Co.

Halverson, J. (1992). Havelock on Greek orality and literacy, *Journal of the History of Ideas* 53(1): 148–163.

Haraway, D. (1991). A Cyborg manifesto: Science, technology, and socialist-feminism in the late twentieth century, in D. Haraway, *Simians, Cyborgs, and Women: The Reinvention of Nature.* New York: Routledge.

Harvey, O. (2006). Marshall McLuhan on technology, subjectivity, and 'the sex organs of the machine world," *Continuum: Journal of Media & Cultural Studies* 20(3), 331–344.

Havelock, E. (1963). *Preface to Plato.* Cambridge, MA: Harvard University Press.

Hayles, N. K. (1999). *How We Became Posthuman: Virtual Bodies in Cybernetics, Literature, and Informatics.* Chicago: University of Chicago Press.

Hepp, A. (2007*). Media Cultures and Religious Change: 'Mediatization' as 'Branding Religion'.* Paper presented at the annual meeting of the International Communication Association, San Francisco, CA, May 24–28, 2007.

Hjarvard, S. (2008). *The Mediatization of Society: A Theory of Media as Agents of Social and Cultural Change.* Nordicom Review 29(2): 105–134.

Innis, H. (1951). *The Bias of Communication.* Toronto: University of Toronto Press.

Jensen, J. (1990). *Redeeming Modernity: Contradictions in Media Criticism.* Newbury Park, CA: Sage.

Kittler, F. (1999). *Gramophone, Film, Typewriter.* Palo Alto, CA: Stanford University Press.

Lash, S. (2002). *Critique of Information.* London: Sage.

Latour, B. (1993). *We Have Never Been Modern.* Transl. Catherine Porter. Cambridge, MA: Harvard University Press.

Lister, M., Dovey, J., Giddings, S., Grant, I., and Kelly, K. (2003). *New Media: A Critical Introduction.* London: Routledge.

MacKenzie, D., and Wajcman, J. (1999). *The Social Shaping of Technology.* Buckingham and Philadelphia: Open University Press.

Mandaville, Pe. (2007). Globalization and the politics of religious knowledge: Pluralizing authority in the Muslim world. *Theory, Culture, and Society* 24(2), 101–115.

Man Kong Lum, C. (2006). *Perspectives on Culture, Technology, and Communication: The Media Ecology Tradition.* Cresskill, NJ: Hampton Press.

Marvin, C. (1988). *When Old Technologies Were New: Thinking about Electric Communication in the 19th Century.* New York: Oxford University Press.

McLuhan, M. (1962). *The Gutenberg Galaxy.* London: Routledge and Kegan Paul.

McLuhan, M. (1967). *Understanding Media: The Extensions of Man.* New York: McGraw-Hill, 1964; London: Sphere.

Meyrowitz, J. (1985). *No Sense of Place: The Impact of Electronic Media on Social Behavior.* New York: Oxford University Press.

Mitchell, W. J. T. (2006). *What Do Pictures Want? The Lives and Loves of Images.* Chicago: University of Chicago Press.

Morley, D. (1997). Theoretical orthodoxies, In M. Ferguson and P. Golding (Eds.), *Cultural Studies in Question.* London: Routledge.

Morley, D. (2006). Unanswered questions in audience research, *The Communication Review* 9, 101–121.

Ong, W. (2002). *Orality and Literacy: The Technologizing of the Word,* 2nd ed., London: Routledge.

Ong, W. (1977). *Interfaces of the Word.* Ithaca, NY: Cornell University Press.

Peters, J. D. (1999). *Speaking Into the Air: A History of the Idea of Communication.* Chicago: University of Chicago Press.

Postman, N. (1985). *Amusing Ourselves to Death: Public Discourse in the Age of Show Business.* New York: Penguin.

Postman, N. (1995). *The End of Education.* New York: Knopf.

Postman, N. (2006). The humanism of media ecology. *Proceedings of the Media Ecology Association* 1, 10–16, 2000. Excerpted in L. Strate, *Echoes and Reflections: On Media Ecology as a Field of Study.* Cresskill, NJ: Hampton Press, p. 15.

Schulz, W. (2004). Reconstructing mediatization as an analytical concept. *European Journal of Communication* 19(1), 87–101.

Smith, M. R., and Marx, L. (Eds.) (1996). *Does Technology Drive History?* Cambridge, MA: MIT Press.

Stolow, J. (2008). *The Spiritual Nervous System: Spiritualism, Technology, and the Electrical Mediation in the Nineteenth-Century Atlantic World,* paper presented at the annual conference of the American Academy of Religion, Chicago, IL, November.

Storey, J. (1993). *An Introduction to Cultural Theory and Popular Culture.* Athens, GA: The University of Georgia Press.

Strate, L. (2006). *Echoes and Reflections: On Media Ecology as a Field of Study.* Cresskill, NJ: Hampton Press.

Williams, R. (1974). *Television: Technology and Cultural Form.* London: Fontana.

Williams, R. (1977). *Marxism and Literature.* New York: Oxford University Press.

CHAPTER FIVE

Media Logic: Looking FOR Social Interaction

KNUT LUNDBY

Behind the concept of mediatization, there is frequently an idea of a specific 'media logic.' This media logic is considered inherent to the mediatization processes. The present chapter questions the validity and the usefulness of 'media logic' as a sweeping concept and the key to mediatization processes. Such big conceptual claims make the mediatization discourse vulnerable. This chapter looks into the sources to the idea of a media logic that are to be found in the writings of the German sociologist Georg Simmel (1858–1918). His focus on social forms leads to a preoccupation with social interaction in order to grasp the inner workings of mediatization.

'MEDIA LOGIC' IN THIS BOOK

In this book, thinking in terms of media logic is most prominent in the chapters by Andrea Schrott and Stig Hjarvard as well as in the contribution by Jesper Strömbäck and Frank Esser. In addition, Eric Rothenbuhler deals with media logic in an essayistic manner in his chapter. He points rather to communicative forms than to media logic as the key to mediatization. The focus on form will soon prove to be important in this chapter, opening the door to understanding mediatization through patterns of social interaction.

Schrott holds that the core of mediatization is to be found in the mechanisms where the logic of the media is institutionalized in societal subsystems other than the media themselves. In these other institutional settings, such as politics, media logic competes with established guidelines and influences on the actions of individuals. Media logic, then, is inherent to mediatization. Schrott defines mediatization as a social process of media-induced social change which functions by the institutionalization of media logic in various social spheres.

Hjarvard, in his chapter, maintains that 'mediatization is the process whereby society to an increasing degree is submitted to, or becomes dependent on, the media and their logic' (p. 160). Hjarvard understands the logic of the media as 'the institutional and technological modus operandi of the media. This includes the ways in which media distribute material and symbolic resources (e.g., according to ratings or reading figures) and operate with the help of formal and informal rules (e.g., news criteria)' (p. 160). Considering that institutions are characterized by their rules and allocations of resources (Giddens 1984, p. 86; Hjarvard 2008b), it is consequent when Schrott points to the institutionalization of media logic that takes place in media organizations and in other societal subsystems of society as the specific 'mechanism' of mediatization.

Media logic, for Schrott, becomes an 'orientation frame' for people and organizations that we are scarcely aware of. Media logic is established as a pattern of orientation and interpretation for public communication. These patterns become implicit regulation systems. Hjarvard follows suit when he concludes that 'one of the principal consequences of the mediatization of society is the constitution of a shared experiential world, a world that is regulated by media logic' (Hjarvard 2008b, p. 129). Media logic as an orientation frame, Schrott argues, may overlay, complement, or replace the patterns of orientation and interpretation in other institutions, as in politics.

Strömback and Esser relate media logic to political logic in Chapter 10. They admit that the concept of media logic is referred to more often than it is properly defined. However, they regard an understanding of media logic as a prerequisite if one wants to understand mediatization. Hence, they have to define 'media logic.' They understand it as 'a particular way of seeing, covering, and interpreting social, cultural, and political phenomena' (p. 212). Strömback and Esser, then, confirm Schrott's understanding of media logic as an orientation frame. Strömback and Esser pay attention to the extent that news media content and the behaviours of political actors and institutions are shaped by a media logic rather than a political logic. They see media logic as an engine of the mediatization of politics.

COINING THE TERM

Strömback and Esser, Schrott, and Hjarvard all refer back to David L. Altheide and Robert P. Snow for the term *media logic*. Altheide and Snow's book from 1979, titled *Media Logic,* has had a great impact on the research into mediatization processes in media studies on authors beyond those in the present book (e.g., Asp 1990; Mazzoleni and Schultz 1999; Mazzoleni 2008). Altheide and Snow's work has been cited without too much scrutiny. The scope of this chapter implies a critical re-reading of *Media Logic.*

Altheide and Snow themselves link media logic to mediatization, although they apply the term *mediation*. Moving 'Toward a Theory of Mediation,' they state, 'Mediation (some people prefer *mediatization*) refers to the impact of the logic and form of any medium involved in the communication process' (Altheide and Snow 1988, p. 195, emphasis in original).

Initially, Altheide and Snow observe media logic as 'a way of "seeing" and of interpreting social affairs' (1979, p. 9). Hence, Schrott is in line with their approach when she understands media logic as an orientation frame. Altheide and Snow add, 'As logic they also involve an implicit trust that we can communicate the events of our daily lives through the various formats of the media' (1979, p. 9). In general terms, they define media logic as 'a form of communication; the process through which media present and transmit information' (Altheide and Snow 1979, p. 10). Then they go on to list various elements of this form of communication, focusing the formats of the various media that are employed.

In a recent piece, Altheide summarizes the meaning of the concept: 'Media logic refers to the assumptions and processes for constructing messages within a particular medium.' (Altheide 2004, p. 294). The mediatization processes become visible in the institutional transformations: 'when media logic is employed to present and interpret institutional phenomena, the form and content of those institutions are altered' (ibid.).

A COHERENT MEDIA LOGIC?

Altheide and Snow (1979, 1988) apply 'media logic' in the singular, not logics in the plural. Although they point to various elements like 'how material is organized, the style in which it is presented, the focus or emphasis on particular characteristics of behavior, and the grammar of media communication' (1979, p. 10), these elements are media formats making up the 'form of communication' that is termed 'media logic.' So, although there may be many different expressions of this media logic when it comes to the formats and working procedures that are applied in different media, the idea seems to be a coherent logic behind them. This is a certain basic 'rationale, emphasis, and orientation promoted by media production, processes, and messages' that even 'tends to be evocative, encapsulated, highly thematic, familiar to audiences, and easy to use,' as Altheide formulates it in the recent article (2004, p. 294).

The authors who apply the concept of media logic in the present book seem to follow suit, although they may stress the complex mix of constraints and procedures behind the general media logic.

Strömbäck and Esser acknowledge the variety of media formats and 'frames' in the production processes and routines, with pressures to include conflict and good visuals in the media coverage. In a news organization, the operations of the media logic depend on the structural environment for the journalistic work, on cultural factors like journalistic attitudes, on degree of professionalization in the media organization, and on the kind of media system they operate within. But although the media logic is driven by a repertoire of 'media formats and grammar, professional norms and values, and commercial incentives and motives' (p. 219), Strömbäck and Esser subsume these mechanisms under one overall 'media logic.' As does Andrea Schrott.

She focuses the two 'filters' that are applied to communicated messages: the filter of selection and the filter of presentation. They are subsumed under 'a common set of general rules for filtering (e.g., novelty, immediacy, conflict, dramatization). These rules are altered to fit the characteristics and constraints of the media. The constraints create a picture of the world that is particular to the media' [NOTE 4, p. 58]. This, to Schrott, summarizes the term *media logic*. This 'logic,' then, is considered a coherent mechanism operating with the said conditions and processes, working as an orientation frame for those involved. However, this general media logic will appear in different contexts and have a variety of expressions as it 'is based on the type of media, on the processing routines of journalistic work, on the technological possibilities and capacities, and finally on the economic organization of the media system' (Schrott's chapter, p. 47).

Hjarvard takes a similar position. In a recent presentation, he emphasizes that the term *media logic* is 'a shorthand for the multiplicity of factors structuring media practices, not a singular, unified mechanism' (Hjarvard 2008c). Still, he uses the term in the singular. Although his definition of media logic encompasses 'institutional and technological modus operandi,' 'ways,' and 'rules' in the plural (Hjarvard 2008b, p. 105), it appears as a unified concept.

As long as the said contributors emphasize that there are a variety of factors operating behind the surface of the media logic, the use of this term may look like a question of presentation tactics. It may be convenient, but I will hold that the use of 'media logic' as an overall term weakens the scholarly argumentation about mediatization. Such a general concept hides the differentiation that people will know about. It is obvious that the conditions and practices vary and change. As Friedrich Krotz put it in his chapter in this book, 'The "media logic" of TV today is not the same as of a decade ago, and the "media logic" of a mobile phone is quite different for a 14-year-old girl as compared to a 55-year-old banker' (p. 26). It seems better to argue with the relevant specific constraints, formats, etc., that are at work in the mediatization processes. Andreas Hepp takes exactly this stand in his chapter, that 'we cannot suppose one single general logic of the media, but have to investigate the concrete interrelation between mediatization and cultural change for certain contexts and fields' (p. 154).

A LINEAR PROCESS?

The simple notion of a media logic may blur and simplify the complex mediatization processes at work and be easy to attack. Nick Couldry (2008) takes this opportunity. In an elaborate argumentation on the relative use of the concept of mediatization versus the concept of mediation (in this case to understand the emergent space of digital storytelling), Couldry considers the logic that underlies theories of mediatization to be of linear nature.

While Couldry (2008, p. 377) finds the concept of mediatization useful to describe 'the transformation of many disparate social and cultural processes into forms or formats suitable for media representation,' he relates it to a linear dynamic:

> The argument at its broadest is that, because they look for an essentially linear transformation from 'pre-media' (before the intervention of specific media) to 'mediatized' social states, theories of mediatization may be less useful. (Couldry 2008, p. 375)

Couldry raises his criticism with Winfried Schulz's article on 'Reconstructing Mediatization as an Analytical Concept' (2004). He also discusses the then-available works by Stig Hjarvard (2004, 2007) where Hjarvard defines 'media logic' as

> …the *'organizational, technological, and aesthetic* functioning, including the ways in which media *allocate material and symbolic resources* and work through *formal and informal rules.'* (Hjarvard 2007, p. 3, emphasis in original)

Hjarvard may, on a meta level, describe mediatization as somewhat linear historical transformations. However, it is difficult to see how the multifaceted understanding of the concrete mediatization processes in the citation above could be termed 'linear,' as Couldry does (Lundby 2008, p. 11). In any case, big claims on behalf of a general 'media logic' are seen to be vulnerable.

Couldry links the linearity to the concept of media logic as developed by Altheide and Snow (1979). Neither Schulz nor Hjarvard refer to Altheide and Snow's book on *Media Logic* (1979) in the pieces that Couldry criticizes. However, their concept of media logic is inspired by Altheide and Snow.

MEDIA LOGIC AS FORM—OR FORMAT

Altheide and Snow (1979, 1991) built their concept of media logic upon the concept of *form* proposed by Simmel. Media logic is regarded to constitute such a form. The German sociologist was introduced to English readers through the 'Chicago school' in the decades after Simmel's death (Levine 1971, pp. xlix–lxi).

Georg Simmel did not write much on communication specifically. An *Exkurs* on "Written Communication" is an exception, where he discusses the combined secrecy and public character of letters. This may be compared to today's e-mail practices. A few indirect influences over a long span of time may also be noted: Simmel came to contribute to media research when he inspired Robert Park, a founder of the 'Chicago school,' in his very early newspaper studies in the late 1920s (Levine 1971, p. xlix). The contemporary internet researcher Barry Wellman (2003) notes that Simmel has contributed to modern studies of social networks.

Simmel has inspired contemporary media studies beyond Altheide and Snow. Simon Cottle does not cite him, but Cottle's work *Mediatized Conflict* (2006) could be seen as a study of mediatization of conflict as a social form (cf. Simmel 1955 [1908]). In his chapter in this book and elsewhere (2003), Stig Hjarvard makes direct references to Simmel's understanding of the playful social form, 'sociability' (Simmel 1950 [1910]).

Altheide and Snow from the very beginning (1979) turned to Georg Simmel to understand media logic. Their approach, in order to understanding media as a social force in society, is to treat them 'as a form of communication that has a particular logic of its own' (1979, p. 9). Form is a key concept. 'In general terms, *media logic* consists of a form of communication' (Altheide and Snow 1979, p. 10, their emphasis). They work back and forth between the two concepts. They claim that 'the logic of the media provides the form for shared "normalized" social life' (1979, pp. 9, 12). In their 1988 theoretical outline on mediation (mediatization), 'logic' and 'form' are applied alongside each other (Altheide and Snow 1988, pp. 195, 218).

Simmel built much of his sociology upon the dialectics between content and form. Altheide and Snow pick up on his concept of form only and hence give priority to form over content (as also Simmel did). Altheide and Snow state,

> Simmel argued that form is a process through which reality is rendered intelligible. Form is not a structure per se, but a processual framework *through which* social action occurs. Media logic constitutes such a form. (Altheide and Snow 1979, p. 15, their emphasis)

However, in the 1979 book, this is their only reference to Simmel. He does not even appear in the index. Altheide and Snow on this occasion do no more than, as they say, 'consult' Simmel's works, listing only one book by this productive sociologist (Altheide and Snow 1979, p. 15). Altheide and Snow's reference to Simmel in *Media Logic* is vague and nearly nonexistent.

They claim 'form' as a key to media logic but apply rather more specific conceptual tools, especially 'format.' *Format* consists of how material is organized, the style of presentation, the focus or emphasis, and the 'grammar' of the mediated communication. A format has the more concrete 'subform elements' of a form (Altheide and Snow 1979, p. 10). The main aspects of format are the *selection, organization,* and *presentation* of experience and information they later summarized (Snow 1983; Altheide 1995, p. 11).

In their 1988 theoretical sketch, Altheide and Snow elaborate some on Simmel's concept of social forms, at least for almost one page. They regard Simmel's basic approach to sociology as essentially grounded in notions about communication processes and acknowledge the fundamental importance of social forms in this respect. 'For Simmel,' they state, 'people act through forms and use them to make sense of their empirical world...forms are procedural strategies used to guide behavior and to develop particular kinds of cultural content' (Altheide and Snow 1988, pp. 197–198).

In 1988, instead of pointing to media logic as a form, Altheide and Snow propose that 'Any medium on which we depend for imagery and information can be treated and analyzed as a social form' (Altheide and Snow 1988, p. 198). Again, they point toward *format:* The way media appear makes up their 'essential form.' They refer 'to the nature of this appearance as format, or the rules and logic that transform and mold information (content) into the recognizable shape and form of the specific medium' (Altheide and Snow 1988, pp. 198–199). The concept of media logic is being played down. The logic has become a characteristic of the format, not the overall form. However, the term 'media logic' survives.

In their 1991 book, Altheide and Snow have sharpened their focus on 'form,' giving stronger reference to Simmel, stating, 'Our theoretic concern is with the identification and description of social forms' (Altheide and Snow 1991, p. 7).

They build it into a larger concept of 'media worlds,' applying another key term from Simmel. 'Worlds' for Simmel are cultural formations, totalities of content, shaped within social forms (Levine 1971, p. xvii). However, Altheide and Snow stick to their initial media logic approach. Their basic postulate is still there, that media logic, in general terms, 'consists of a form of communication' (Altheide and Snow 1991, p. 9). Actually, Altheide and Snow in 1991 repeat, word for word, their opening reference to Simmel on form in *Media Logic* (1979, p. 15; 1991, p. 12), restating that media logic 'constitutes such a form' as Simmel had defined.

This form includes the various media that are applied and the formats used (Altheide and Snow 1991, p. 9). They deal with media logic as a general form by dealing with the subproperties of selected media—media formats. The assumptions and processes for constructing messages within a particular medium 'includes rhythm, grammar and format' (Altheide 2004, p. 294).

This chapter points out an alternative reading and application of Simmel's concept of *form* for the understanding of mediatization. I question whether the concept of 'media logic' could still make a conceptual core in nuanced or heterogeneous theorizing about the mediatization processes. Instead, the chapter advises a focus on the transformations as they appear in social interaction and through constraints on the mediated communication. The aim is to cultivate the concept of mediatization as a viable concept for scholarly analysis.

Either they hold that media logic constitutes a form, or that any medium can be regarded as a social form. I will argue that Altheide and Snow miss the core idea in Simmel's conceptualization of form. So what did Simmel mean by 'form'?

SIMMEL'S UNDERSTANDING OF FORM

For Simmel, form is *social* form. He worked to establish sociology as a new discipline. To him, society was not a fixed entity but continuously shaped through social interaction. This happens within a diversity of forms. Simmel, first, defines sociology as the study of the 'form of social interaction.' Later, he refined this by introducing the concept of 'sociation' (*Vergesellchaftung*) to denote the phenomenon that people engage with others in a variety of social processes (Frisby 2002, pp. xiv–xv). Sociation 'is the *form* around which the interests of human beings crystallize,' as Robert Park recalls from Simmel's lectures in Chicago (Frisby 1992, p. 12). Simmel thus redefines sociology as the study of the 'forms of sociation.' For him society is 'a constellation of *forms of sociation*, including emergent as well as permanent forms' (Frisby 2002, p. xv, italics in original).

Rooted in Kantian thinking, Simmel distinguishes form from content. His sociology focuses on forms as abstractions. A form gathers contents into a whole.

There are many kinds, levels, and degrees of form (Weingartner 1959, pp. 41–42). However, the diversity of contents is greater. The forms of sociation are less diverse than their content, since the same form of sociation can enter into the most varied material (Frisby 1994, p. 335). Simmel's image of sociation, however, is interaction with both form and content (Duncan 1959, p. 101). 'Any social phenomenon or process,' Simmel writes, 'is composed of two elements which in reality are inseparable: on the one hand, an interest, purpose, or a motive; on the other, a form or mode of interaction among individuals through which, or in the shape of which, that content attains social reality' (Simmel 1971 [1908]). Forms of interaction, then, may develop a certain objectified character.

This stress on social forms and social formations is part of the 'formal sociology' that Simmel proposed. This is an abstract approach compared to what he termed 'philosophical sociology,' dealing with epistemological questions, and 'general sociology,' engaging with historical and actual cases and developments (Wolff 1950, pp. xxxii–xxxiv). The formal, or 'pure' sociology of social forms, investigates the social forms themselves (Duncan 1959, p. 101); it 'abstracts the mere element of sociation...like grammar, which isolates the pure forms of language from their contents through which these forms, nevertheless, come to life' (Simmel 1950, pp. 21–22).

In the collection, *Georg Simmel on Individuality and Social Forms*, Donald Levine (1971) converts Simmel's often obscure explication of various social forms into a readable typology. As forms of social interaction described in Simmel's works, he presents a variety of these social forms: exchange, conflict, domination, prostitution, and sociability.

These forms of interaction are all types of relationships between people that may follow certain characteristic patterns. In *The Philosophy of Money* (1978 [1900]), Simmel analyses exchange as a basic form of sociation in the modern society. He regards conflict as part of the social dynamic (Simmel 1955 [1908]).

'Sociability' is the playful form of social interaction. This is the more spontaneous form of coming together, association related to art and play. This is the pure form of sociality, Simmel holds, 'the free-playing, interacting, interdependence of individuals' (Simmel 1950 [1910], p. 129).

Levine (1971, p. xv) sums up: forms, for Simmel, 'are the synthesizing principles which select elements from the raw stuff of experience and shape them into determinate units.'

The term 'form' is, in the media and communication literature, to be found specified as 'communicative form' or 'form of communication.' It could also be 'cultural form,' as in Raymond Williams' *Television: Technology and Cultural Form* (Williams 1975). According to Simmel, forms emerge to shape content, and sooner or later, 'the forms can be liberated from their connection with practical purposes and become objects of cultivation in their own right' (Levine 1971, p. xvi). Forms, then, may shape processes of mediatization. However, there is also a mediatization of forms, as Scott Lash points out in an article on 'Georg Simmel in the Information Age.' The mediatization of forms is also their technologization, he states. Mediatization is the collapse of form into technology (Lash 2005, pp. 16–17). This explains why Altheide and Snow slide from 'form' into 'format' and similar concepts largely dependent on the media technology.

SOCIAL INTERACTION AS THE KEY

Stig Hjarvard voices doubts on how key 'media logic' really is to Altheide and Snow's argument. 'Although they time and again make reference to "media logic," form and format are their principal concepts,' he observes (Hjarvard 2008b, p. 107). He is right, and of the two stated concepts, 'format' is the most important to Altheide and Snow. 'Form' is there in *Media Logic,* but the authors do not follow this concept further to the understanding of social interaction that is so crucial in Simmel's concept of social form.

They later approached interaction more or less leaving 'form' behind. In *Creating Media Culture* (1983), Snow went to 'format' or rather to the specific 'grammar' guiding the interactions in production of each major mass medium. Snow relates the concepts in his analysis: 'Within each *medium* and for each *format* (type of program or genre), *perspectives*, such as entertainment, are linked with a specific *grammar* resulting in an overall communication *logic*' (p. 13, my emphases). Altheide, in *Media Power* a few years later, explicitly turned from the term 'form' to 'format.' Format offers 'a sense of the underlying interactive order in terms of what is appropriate time, place, and manner' while form with Simmel 'refers to relatively constant patterns of relationships; e.g., dominance-subordination' Altheide argues (1985, p. 13).

This is the crucial point. Social form is constituted through continuous patterns of social interaction. Media logic is a codification of how media formats work; of rules, ways, and regulations in 'the underlying interactive order.' Forms are related to actual interaction, while logic and formats refer to the rules of the game. Media logic could not constitute a form, as Altheide and Snow initially claimed. Neither could the various media, as they also, on some occasions, maintain. At best, they are imprecise. At worst, they risk leading themselves and their readers into a media-deterministic trap.

In his book from 1995, *An Ecology of Communication: Cultural Formats of Control,* David Altheide states clearly that he is not a technological determinist (1995, p. 4). His scholarly focus moves, exactly, towards social interaction.

He observes how social interaction takes place within social contexts where computer-based information and communication technologies play a more and more prominent role alongside television and other established media. Social activities are 'joined with information technology' (Altheide 1995, p. 2). The concept of 'ecology of communication' helps us grasp this. These are the 'all-embracing media' that I laid out in the Introduction to this volume. Altheide, in his book of 1995, turns towards symbolic interactionism, looking for social meanings that are derived through processes of symbolic interaction. As frames and constraints for the interaction, 'formats' are still important. The concept of 'form' has more or less gone, and so has the concept of 'media logic,' although it is not abandoned (Altheide 2004). However, Altheide (1995, pp. 34–35) indicates wider 'cultural logics' (in plural) conceptualized within the ecology of communication. He directs his 'theoretical gaze at the intersection between information technology, communication formats, and meaningful and organized activities and social projects' (Altheide 1995, p. 224).

Stig Hjarvard still sticks to the sweeping concept and concurrent claim of 'media logic.' However, he has made a move similar to Altheide's from the concept of form toward the concept of interaction. Stig Hjarvard's widespread definition of mediatization from 2004 did centre around 'form':

> Mediatization implies a process through which core elements of a social and cultural activity (like work, leisure, play etc.) assume media form. (Hjarvard 2004, p. 48)

Hjarvard's recent definition has become more interactional. Mediatization affects society through the many ways that the media intervene in the social interaction between individuals within a given institution, between institutions, and in society at large. Social interaction consists of communication and action. The media are means of communication (Hjarvard 2008b, p. 120). From this platform, Hjarvard can analyse the concrete ways various media with each their specific characteristics can intervene in social interaction, and even alter interaction. These processes are at the core of mediatization. I regard this approach more constructive and promising for the study of mediatization than the broad generalizations about 'media logic.'

A REREADING

Stig Hjarvard provides a suitable case for a rereading through the lens of social interaction, namely his recent essay on the 'mediatization of religion' (2008e). According to his definition, mediatization, in this case, implies that core elements of religion as a social or cultural activity assume media form. Hjarvard himself facilitates a rereading through social interaction when he adds, 'As a consequence, the activity is, to a greater or lesser degree, performed through interaction with a medium.' However, he keeps his eye on the media logic as he also holds that, as a consequence of religion assuming media form, 'the symbolic content and the structure of the social and cultural activity are influenced by media environments and a media logic, upon which they gradually become more dependent' (Hjarvard 2008d, p. 13).

Hjarvard structures his argument on the three metaphors that Joshua Meyrowitz (1993) introduced to describe the media and their manifestations: media as conduits, media as languages, and media as environments. Mediatization is the process of social change that, in this case, to some extent subsumes religion into the logic of the media, Hjarvard argues. Media as conduits, languages and environments

> ...facilitate changes in the amount, content, and direction of religious messages in society, at the same time they transform religious representations and challenge and replace the authority of the institutionalized religions. Through these processes, religion as a social and cultural activity has become mediatized. (Hjarvard 2008d, p. 14)

As conduits, the media convey a plethora of 'banal' religious expressions; a mix of elements and symbols from folk religion, new age spirituality, and institutional religion alike. Hjarvard analyses these elements as representations, and so they are. However, the banal religious expressions could as well be studied from the perspectives of those who produce and those who consume these representations, that is, the interaction with the texts and symbols that goes on in the production processes as well as in the reception processes. The media logic will then be de-masked and demystified, as one will observe actors and agents in play with the representations. Power relations behind the 'banal' religious expressions will be visible.

As language, Hjarvard observes how television and film, especially, become 'enchanting media' in the postmodern consumer culture. Within this context, there is space for a reenchantment of religion and spirituality in popular-cultural series and stories—contrary to Max Weber's rational prophecy of how the modern world is becoming disenchanted. These new expressions of religion and spirituality are not dependent on the church or other established institutions; they develop within the media themselves. This is part of the media logic, Hjarvard will argue. From a perspective on social interaction, this development could be analysed exactly in terms of the shifting institutional base or frame, with the changing formats and patters of production and reception therein. Focus is on the interactions with the texts from various positions, and the resulting transformation—and mediatization—of the religious/spiritual symbols and their uses.

As environments, the role of the media in relation to religious community and ritual comes to the fore. Hjarvard reminds us of studies that document how collective rituals in late modern societies are performed through the media and how the media themselves shape forms of community that previously would rely on religious organizations. Instead of ascribing the changes to a 'media logic,' one may in concrete ways describe and analyse how these transformations take place. How media interfere in patterns of social interaction will be central.

NEED FOR MIDDLE-RANGE EXPLORATIONS

The concept of mediatization 'makes no claims to more middle-range explorations of actual media forms,' Kirsten Drotner (2008, p. 71) holds. She points out the macro-level approach most mediatization scholars have taken, following on from Habermas' critique of the mediatization of the lifeworld (1987, p. 305). Although the concept of mediatization has been developed more in conceptual and empirical detail by media scholars, Drotner still misses the more concrete take. She acknowledges that Hjarvard offers examples of empirical analyses but finds them 'loosely coupled to his conceptual understanding' (Drotner 2008, p. 71). Since then, Hjarvard has developed his theoretical approach as well as the range of empirical applications (Hjarvard 2008a, 2008b, 2008d). However, challenges to perform more middle-range explorations persist. The sweeping concept of 'media logic' hides, I will argue, the constraints of specific formats and the transformations that are shaped in concrete social interactions and communication processes.

The Swedish media scholar, Kent Asp, who launched the concept of mediatization (or 'medialization') in Scandinavia, was possibly about to sketch a middle-range approach as early as in 1990. He tried to explore and analyse 'the nature of media logic' through the components of media dramaturgy, media format, media routines, and media rationales.

'Media dramaturgy' is considered to be a set of decision-making criteria and judgments that are applied to attract and keep the continued attention of readers, viewers, and listeners. 'Media format' is, as explained by Altheide (1985, p. 13), adaptation to the forms in which the media organize and present information. 'Media routines' are adaptations to the rules and procedures of media practitioners, while 'media rationales' are the strategies, the modus operandi that are followed in the media work (Asp 1990, p. 49). The latter is 'the rationale or logic' of the media work, he states (ibid.). However, these are the more specific work rationales (in plural) and not an overall media logic. It is this concept of a general 'media logic' that Asp helps deconstruct.

IS MEDIA LOGIC A 'LOGIC'?

According to standard dictionaries, the noun 'logic' has two main meanings. 'Logic,' first, is reasoning conducted or assessed according to strict principles of validity. This could be a particular system or codification of the principles of proof and inference, as with Aristotelian logic. It could be the systematic use of symbolic and mathematical techniques to determine the forms of valid deductive argument. Or it could be the quality of being justifiable by reason. Second, 'logic' is a set of principles in the programming of a computer or electronic device so as to perform a specified task *(Oxford American Dictionaries,* Online version) (cf. Sykes 1982, p. 594).

The term 'media logic' as introduced by Altheide and Snow, later to be elaborated by other scholars, has neither of these precise meanings. The media of media logic span more than the technical functioning of computers; they are social media. The reasoning performed in production and reception of communication media is not following a specific system of codification and thought, as hidden in terms like onto**logic**al, phenomeno**logic**al socio**logic**al, dia**logic**al, or method-o**logic**al. Even techno**logic**al is a term that requests stricter principles of validity than 'media logic.'

Media logic is a logic only in the looser sense built on related concepts in a thesaurus. 'Logic' could then relate to terms on agreement (like consistency, uniformity), reasoning (reason, rationality), and necessity (e.g., inevitability, compulsion) (Lloyd 1986). Media logic rather denotes 'practices' and orientation frames in mediatization processes, due to given constraints and 'affordances' (Gibson 1979).

This observation could invite explorations into Pierre Bourdieu's writings. Following the *Outline of a Theory of Practice* (1977) came *The Logic of Practice* (1990). Support for a loose concept of media logic—as practice—could be collected from Bourdieu when he states that practice 'has a logic which is not that of the logician' (1990, p. 86). However, studies into Bourdieu's fields of theory would take us beyond the frame of this chapter. The intention here is rather to follow the traces from Altheide and Snow's conceptualization of 'media logic.'

DOES DIGITALIZATION MAKE A CHANGE?

For David Altheide, digitalization makes a difference to his initial ideas about media logic. In his book from 1995, he takes on board the impact of the computer-based information and communication technologies. As referred to above, this changes his perspective from a general media logic to a social interaction and mediated communication within an 'ecology of communication' (Altheide 1995). When this book was written, the first Web browsers had just been launched; the 'net,' as known through the World Wide Web, was in its infancy. The perspectives on social interaction via internet have not become less significant since—now with specific technologies for 'social networking' (boyd and Ellison 2007).

The developments of the media landscape invite such a change of focus. Some examples and trends:

- Media are becoming more interactive and accessible when it suits the user: internet newspapers are a case in point.
- Contemporary television invites audience participation by SMS and phone-in (Enli 2007).
- Media are becoming 'personal' (Lüders 2007). Internet users may act out a considerable part of their lives on 'social' networking sites.

Winfried Schulz, when he wrote his article to reconstruct mediatization as an analytical concept (2004), did ask 'whether advent of new media might bring an end to mediatization?' He gave three possible answers: First, the 'optimistic,' builds on an idea of direct access communication and self-determination with the internet, where no media logic would operate and create constraints. Second, the 'sceptical' view, observes how new constraints and modes of mediatization rise, and where one has to accommodate to the logic of the *new* media. The third, 'moderate,' approach focuses on convergence processes, where 'old' and 'new' media operate alongside each other with a similar media logic. The mediatization effects of the 'old' media endure in the new. Schulz concludes that the mediatization concept is applicable to all kinds of media.

Schulz does not consider the digitalization of the 'old' media, and he does not discuss the specific characteristics of digitalization. The multimodality that is made possible with the endless combinations of digitized texts, images, sounds, and graphics (Kress and van Leeuwen 2001; Kress 2003) does not support the expression of one overall media logic. It fits the digital media environment more to analyse the mediatization processes through the transforming impact of such mediated communication on patterns of social interaction.

Niels Ole Finnemann (2008) argues that '[n]ew media—whenever they arrive in history—imply extended mediatization.' Internet and digital media create a new epoch. This new media platform differs significantly from the mass media, he argues.

Finnemann criticizes Schulz, Krotz, and Hjarvard for not including the complexities initiated by the new digital media in their writings on mediatization.

To understand mediatization through a general media logic becomes impossible; one has to take into account the specificities of the digital media. The 'logic' of the old media matrix is not sufficient to identify the new dynamics, Finnemann claims.

Media logic—as the logic of presentation and interpretation of messages—develops in the course of interaction between the communicators of a medium, Pekka Isotalus (1998, p. 201) holds. He argues that media logic will always develop. This has been demonstrated with the advent of digital media, which have opened such wide opportunities for social networking and such varied options for multimodal expressions that the general concept of media logic, in my view, has come to an end, unless one makes very specific qualifications about the actual social interactions, constraints, formats, etc. involved in the mediatization processes.

MANAGING WITHOUT MEDIA LOGIC

Chapters in this book other than those I have been concerned with so far demonstrate that it is fully possible to make arguments and analyses about mediatization without applying the concept of 'media logic.' Actually, a majority of the contributors do not relate to the term at all.

Andreas Hepp explicitly avoids 'media logic,' which he considers a linear and overly general concept. Instead, he theorizes on mediatization in the macro perspective on cultural change and differentiation that he applies, with the 'moulding forces' of the media. This, in German 'Prägkraft der Medien,' takes care of the fact that 'media themselves exert a certain "pressure" on the way we communicate' without indicating just one trajectory (or logic) of the media (p. 143). Hepp finds 'Prägkraft' much more open than 'media logic.'

Synne Skjulstad's chapter deals with micro semiotic and textual processes. She leaves 'media logic' aside and states, 'My interest in mediatization is concerned with the textual shaping of symbolic and cultural expressions via a variety of semiotic modes online' (p. 180). Writing about 'interaction design,' she brings the textual aspects of new digital media in direct encounter with the focus on interaction that I have been advocating. The social interaction is also shaped in relation to the textual expressions. Web designers as well as Web users interact with the Web and its multimodal texts in such complex and varied ways that it cannot easily be subsumed under an overall media logic. Interaction design and the uses of interactive web interfaces are forms of communication.

This ties in to Eric Rothenbuhler's chapter on the relations between communicative forms and media logic. As he says, perhaps 'the logic is not in the medium but in the communication' (p. 288).

CONCLUSION

I conclude that it is not viable to speak of an overall media logic; it is necessary to specify how various media capabilities are applied in various patterns of social interactions. It is not that a media logic does not involve social interaction, which, not least, Stig Hjarvard's works make clear. My argument is rather that a focus on a general media logic hides these patterns of interaction.

This is a communication perspective. Social interaction always involves communication. Hence, one has to study how transformations and changes in the mediatization processes take place in communication. Mediatization research should put emphasis on how social and communicative forms are developed when media are taken into use in social interaction.

This applies to both 'old' and 'new' media. However, the 'new' digital tools expand the repertoire of media available for different purposes. It does not make sense to subsume this media variety under a more or less coherent 'media logic.' That's the thinking of the past, the age of mass communication when gatekeepers or editors did indeed control, frame, and format almost all media communication. Such media professionals still do to large extent, and the new digital media also work under constraints. But in media-saturated societies, there is an expanding number of alternative media uses to extend and perform regular social interaction.

Mediatization studies should focus on such practices and develop new concepts and new tools to get hold of how various media-uses shape and change social interaction. Such transformations of interaction practices and patterns may shape new social and communicative forms. Such changes and transformations are at the heart of mediatization phenomena and processes.

All social forms in a media-saturated, high-modern society will be more or less mediatized, that is, at least partly shaped in processes of mediatization. While the conceptualization of mediatization processes is in itself a challenge, as this chapter should demonstrate, it is an empirical task to find out how, and to what extent, modern, technical media intervene in social interaction and social forms.

REFERENCES

Altheide, D. L. (1985). *Media Power*. Beverly Hills: Sage.

Altheide, D. L. (1995). *An Ecology of Communication: Cultural Formats of Control*. New York: Aldine de Gruyter.

Altheide, D. L. (2004). Media logic and political communication. *Political Communication*, 21(3), 293–296.

Altheide, D. L., and Snow, R. P. (1979). *Media Logic*. Beverly Hills: Sage.

Altheide, D. L., and Snow, R. P. (1988). Toward a theory of mediation. In J. A. Anderson (Ed.), *Communication Yearbook* (Vol. 11, pp. 194–223). Newbury Park, CA: Sage.

Altheide, D. L., and Snow, R. P. (1991). *Media Worlds in the Postjournalism Era*. New York: Aldine de Gruyter.

Asp, K. (1990). Medialization, media logic and mediarchy. *Nordicom Review*, 11(2), 47–50.

Bourdieu, P. (1977). *Outline of a Theory of Practice*. Cambridge, UK: Cambridge University Press.

Bourdieu, P. (1990). *The Logic of Practice*. Cambridge, UK: Polity.

boyd, D. M., and Ellison, N. B. (2007). Social network sites: Definition, history and scholarship. *Journal of Computer-Mediated Communication*, 13(1), article 11.

Cottle, S. (2006). *Mediatized Conflict*. Maidenhead: Open University Press.

Couldry, N. (2008). Mediatization or mediation? Alternative understandings of the emergent space of digital storytelling. *New Media & Society*, 10(3), 373–391.

Drotner, K. (2008). Boundaries and bridges: Digital storytelling in education studies and media studies. In K. Lundby (Ed.), *Digital Storytelling, Mediatized Stories: Self-Representations in New Media*. New York: Peter Lang.

Duncan, H. D. (1959). Simmel's image of society. In K. H. Wolff (Ed.), *Georg Simmel, 1858–1918. A Collection of Essays* (pp. 100–118). Columbus: The Ohio State University Press.

Enli, G. (2007). *The Participatory Turn in Broadcast Television. Institutional, Editorial and Textual Challenges and Strategies*. Oslo: Faculty of Humanities, University of Oslo.

Finnemann, N. O. (2008). *The Internet and the Emergence of a New Matrix of Media. Mediatization and the Coevolution of Old and New Media*. Paper presented at the AoIR Internet 9.0, Copenhagen, 16–18 October 2008.

Frisby, D. (1992). *Simmel and Since: Essays on Georg Simmel's Social Theory*. London: Routledge.

Frisby, D. (1994). The foundation of sociology. In D. Frisby (Ed.), *Georg Simmel, Critical Assessments*. Vol. I (pp. 329–346). London: Routledge.

Frisby, D. (2002). *Georg Simmel* (Revised ed.). London: Routledge.

Gibson, J. J. (1979). *The Ecological Approach to Visual Perception*. Boston: Houghton Mifflin.

Giddens, A. (1984). *The Constitution of Society. Outline of the Theory of Structuration*. Cambridge, UK: Polity Press.

Habermas, J. (1987). *The Theory of Communicative Action: Lifeworld and System: A Critique of Functionalist Reason* (T. McCarthy, Trans. Vol. 2). Cambridge, UK: Polity Press.

Hjarvard, S. (2003). *Det selskabelige samfund. Essays om medier mellem mennesker*. Fredriksberg: Samfundslitteratur.

Hjarvard, S. (2004). From bricks to bytes: The mediatization of a global toy industry. In I. Bondebjerg and P. Golding (Eds.), *European Culture and the Media* (pp. 43–63). Bristol, UK: Intellect.

Hjarvard, S. (2007). *Changing Media—Changing Language. The Mediatization of Society and the Spread of English and Medialects*. Paper presented at the International Communication Association 57th Annual Conference, San Francisco, May 24–28, 2007.

Hjarvard, S. (2008a). *En verden af medier. Medialiseringen af politik, sprog, religion og leg*. Fredriksberg: Samfundslitteratur.

Hjarvard, S. (2008b). The mediatization of society. A theory of the media as agents of social and cultural change. *Nordicom Review*, 29(2), 105–134.

Hjarvard, S. (2008c). *Mediatization: Soft Individualism, and Weak Social Ties*. Paper presented at the Mediatization of Religion and Culture, Copenhagen, 20–21 October 2008.

Hjarvard, S. (2008d). The mediatization of religion. A theory of the media as agents of religious change. In S. Hjarvard (Ed.), *The Mediatization of Religion: Enchantment, Media and Popular Culture* (pp. 9–26). Northern Lights. Film & Media Studies Yearbook 6. Bristol, UK: Intellect.

Hjarvard, S. (Ed.). (2008e). *The Mediatization of Religion: Enchantment, Media and Popular Culture.* Northern Lights. Film & Media Studies Yearbook 6. Bristol, UK: Intellect.

Isotalus, P. (1998). Television as a context of performance. *Communications,* 23(2), 189–209.

Kress, G. (2003). *Literacy in the New Media Age.* London: Routledge.

Kress, G., and van Leeuwen, T. (2001). *Multimodal Discourse: The Modes and Media of Contemporary Communication.* London, New York: Arnold.

Lash, S. (2005). *Lebenssoziologie.* Georg Simmel in the Information Age. *Theory, Culture & Society,* 22(3), 1–23.

Levine, D. N. (Ed.). (1971). *Georg Simmel on Individuality and Social Forms.* Chicago: The University of Chicago Press.

Lloyd, S. (Ed.). (1986). *Roget's Thesaurus of English Words and Phrases.* Harlow, Essex: Longman.

Lundby, K. (2008). Introduction: Digital storytelling, mediatized stories. In K. Lundby (Ed.), *Digital Storytelling, Mediatized Stories: Self-Representations in New Media.* New York: Peter Lang.

Lüders, M. (2007). *Being in Mediated Spaces: An Enquiry into Personal Media Practices.* University of Oslo, Oslo.

Mazzoleni, G. (2008). Media Logic. In W. Donsbach (Ed.), *The International Encyclopedia of Communication,* vol. VII (pp. 2930–2932). Malden, MA: Blackwell.

Mazzoleni, G., and Schultz, W. (1999). 'Mediatization' of politics: A challenge for democracy? *Political Communication,* 16, 247–261.

Meyrowitz, J. (1993). Images of media: Hidden ferment—and harmony—in the field. *Journal of Communication,* 43(3), 55–66.

Schulz, W. (2004). Reconstructing mediatization as an analytical concept. *European Journal of Communication,* 19(1), 87–101.

Simmel, G. (1950). The field of sociology. In K. H. Wolff (Ed.), *The Sociology of Georg Simmel* (pp. 3–25). Glencoe, IL: The Free Press.

Simmel, G. (1950 [1910]). Sociability. In D. N. Levine (Ed.), *Georg Simmel on Individuality and Social Forms* (pp. 127–140). Chicago: The University of Chicago Press.

Simmel, G. (1955 [1908]). Conflict (K. H. Wolff and R. Bendix, Trans.). In *Conflict & the Web of Group-Affiliations* (pp. 10–124). New York: The Free Press.

Simmel, G. (1971 [1908]). The problem of sociology. In D. N. Levine (Ed.), *Georg Simmel on Individuality and Social Forms* (pp. 23–35). Chicago: The University of Chicago Press.

Simmel, G. (1978 [1900]). *The Philosophy of Money* (T. Bottomore and D. Frisby, Trans.). London: Routledge.

Snow, R. P. (1983). *Creating Media Culture.* Newbury Park, CA: Sage.

Sykes, J. B. (Ed.). (1982). *The Concise Oxford Dictionary of Current English* (7th ed.). Oxford: Clarendon Press.

Weingartner, R. H. (1959). Form and content in Simmel's philosophy of life. In K. H. Wolff (Ed.), *Georg Simmel, 1858–1918. A Collection of Essays* (pp. 33–60). Columbus: The Ohio State University Press.

Wellman, B. (2003). *Networks for Newbies. Non-technical Introduction to Social Network Analysis:* Centre for Urban & Community Studies, University of Toronto.

Williams, R. (1975). *Television: Technology and Cultural Form.* New York: Schocken Books.

Wolff, K. H. (1950). Introduction. In K. H. Wolff (Ed.), *The Sociology of Georg Simmel.* Glencoe, IL: The Free Press.

CHANGES

CHAPTER SIX

Complexities: The Case OF Religious Cultures

STEWART M. HOOVER

There is little doubt anymore that the evolution of religion and religious cultures goes hand in hand with, rather than alongside, the evolution of secular culture. Thus, one of the major tenets of the traditional notion of secularization—that religion would fade away—has been contradicted by our experience since the mid twentieth century. At the same time that overall trends in Western society (and in the rapidly developing sectors of the Global South) have moved in the direction of increased levels of education, economic prosperity, and social progress, religion has persisted, even flourished.

Important signals of religion's persistence bookended the 1970s. Early in that decade, a newly resurgent conservative religious movement began to make itself known in U.S. politics. This "neo-Evangelicalism," as it was known, arose from the ashes of the fundamentalism that had defined conservative American Protestantism earlier in the twentieth century. A new generation of leaders of that movement realigned its political discourse in new ways, including strategic use of media, unleashing effects on U.S. domestic and foreign policy that are felt to this day. Not least among these effects was the emergence during the second Bush administration of religiously based policy objectives, coinciding with the widespread emergence of ethno-nationalist discourses, tinged with religion, that are today spreading across Europe. Later in the 1970s, an even more portentous event occurred: the Islamic Revolution in Iran. Before that event, it had been relatively easy in Western intellectual, policy, and media circles to dismiss religion's role in global politics. Afterwards, a great soul-searching in those same circles came to the conclusion that religion had reemerged in ways that would be significant for years to come. Today, religion can be seen to influence the way that individuals, groups, movements, and nations define themselves, and to play a role in social and cultural evolution across the globe.

Even more important, though, is the emerging sense that what is going on with religion is integrally related to what is going on with "the media." That is, it can be argued that the religion of late modernity is in many ways a media phenomenon. The two cases above—the emergence of neo-Evangelical politics in the United States and the Islamic Revolution in Iran—are examples of this. What we now call "televangelism" was essential to the emergence of Evangelical politics in the United States. These programs and channels symbolized the political resurgence of the movement at the same time that they came to confront the control that the U.S. religious establishment had previously held over the means of religious communication. Research at the time also showed that these programs helped to legitimize this new form of religion in the minds of publics and elites in the United States and abroad.

Media were also important in the case of the Iranian revolution. It has been shown that the use of "small media," particularly audiocassette recordings, played a vital role in providing direction and solidarity to that movement. In post-revolution Iran, media have continued to be central to the Islamic State, with both formal and sanctioned media and informal and resistive media, continuing to shape the nature of movements and identities among Iranians within the country and among the Iranian diaspora abroad.

These are but two examples among many that can support the claim that, in a general sense at least, attention to "mediatization" is essential to our understanding of the constitution of contemporary religion. It is my purpose here to unpack this situation a bit, based on emergent scholarly literatures in media and religion, on public (and largely mediated) discourses about religion, and on fieldwork among media audiences.

In doing this, my arguments will also address the larger theoretical debates about mediatization so ably addressed elsewhere in this volume. These arguments will, if successful, move in two directions. First, they will help establish the situation of religion as a special and particular case of mediatization. At the same time, they will also help us "look back" at and refine the larger, more general discourses about the nature, extents, and limits of this concept.

RELIGION, RITUAL, AND MEDIA EVENTS

Religion has received a good deal of attention among scholars interested in mediatization. Hjarvard (2008), for instance, has provided a valuable introduction to the question, persuasively arguing that the ways that the media are changing religion are important, even vital, dimensions of contemporary religion. Hjarvard observes that the media can be seen to intervene in a variety of ways with religious institutions, religious and quasi-religious practices, in religious "enchantment," and with religiously-inflected social practices such as public rituals. Through these inquiries, he supports the larger point that mediatization fundamentally changes social institutions, practices, and outcomes. And, as he notes with reference to religion, mediatization does not always flow in a single direction. Sometimes it can be seen to support and encourage traditional religious sensibilities and behaviors; at other times and in other places, it directly confronts religion (as in its contestation with religious institutions over the power to define symbols); and in still other ways, it can be seen to transform the world of "the religious."

In his analysis, Hjarvard further suggests that the question is not only one of what the media "do" to religion as a hermetic, ideal, preexisting reality, but also the ways that social and cultural change are opening the possibility of the media playing a larger role. In a discussion of what he calls "banal religion," for example (p. 12), he suggests that there are a set of sensibilities and practices, emergent in late modernity, that accommodate themselves well to an articulation between the religious and media spheres. This is most obvious, in his view, in the widespread commodification of cultural and social life (p. 16). Markets and commodities and objects define contemporary experience, and religion is not immune to this process, and there are abundant emerging examples of the commodification of religion (many of them mediated) as evidence of this.

Hjarvard's approach integrates and expands some key challenges that have circulated around the larger question of media and religion. For example, it rather directly addresses the literatures on "media rituals" (Carey 1989; Rothenbuhler 1998; Couldry 2004) and "media events" (Dayan and Katz 1992). Each of these has struggled with the category of practice that has been called "civil religion" by sociologists and historians. That is, at the center of arguments about media ritual is the nature and extent of the cross-diffusion of religious and secular authority. The question has become one of whether and under what circumstances the "secular" world of power, politics, civic association, and its attendant meanings, is like "religion." There has been a tendency in these considerations to think that the significance of secular rituals and secular ritual-like events must lie in their nearness in form to some formal or idealized sense of religion. Thus, these large questions of the determinative power of mediated ritual tend to borrow social and cultural legitimacy from the seemingly natural and authentic functions of the idealized religious past. Couldry (2004) suggests that we can move beyond this by recognizing the extent to which mediated rituals constrain and constitute social and cultural life quite without reference to religion. Cottle (2006) notes that media rituals can be seen to readily contest authority and social order as to confirm them, thus any inferred relationship to normative religious truth claims, interests, or sentiments elides relations that are actually incommensurate or even contradictory.

There are really two underlying dimensions here, which are orthogonal with one another. First is the question of whether definitive rituals or events are *properties of whole cultures* or whether they are instead so rooted in *particular structures, movements, or ideas* that they cannot be appropriated beyond. The second dimension is the question of whether they need to be understood as specifically *religious* in some fundamental way, or whether they can also be entirely *secular*. These are important issues, because they condition much of what we must consider in looking at the mediatization of religion. However we qualify or legitimize a given symbolic practice or belief system as being fundamentally about religion, we must be able to distinguish between those things that might look like religion and those things that are, actually, religion.

This is made even more complex, as Hjarvard notes, by the fact that many objects, practices, and settings actually exist on the boundary between "the religious" and "the secular," and that these in fact cross-diffuse each other. It might be noted here that only careful reception analysis can probably parse these differences and distinctions. And the further challenge to consideration of the problem of mediatization rests in the question of whether a given phenomenon is a *mediation of religion* or the *religious (or ritual) inflection of the media*. One thing that theorists of mediatization agree on is that mediatization cannot be simply *instrumental*, but must recognize the general integration of the media into other social spaces.

Thus the mediatization of religion is not a simple matter. Before we can begin to account for it, we must come to terms with some significant conceptual and theoretical challenges. We must try to understand *what is religion* and *what is not*, at the same time that we must be aware of the ways that what might once have been a "bright line" between the religious and secular realms has become porous. And, I might add, we have good reason to expect that the breakdown of this distinction may in fact be one of the effects of mediatization (Hoover 2006). We also need to understand the ways that the implicit power of religion and "religion-like" symbols, practices, and conditions is established in modernity. Does this power, as many contemporary Durkheimians (and indeed, Couldry 2004) argue, derive from the form of ritual and/or its lodgment in social space and social structure, or is there something essentially and necessarily "religious" about these practices and motivations?

Beyond these questions, we must also address issues of location and scale. To what extent are we talking about whole cultures, whole "religions," and whole nations, or are we talking about particular movements, places, identities, and truth claims? We know from contemporary evidence that religious claims and practices can be seen to be persistent and even emergent in all of these ways and on all of these levels (Warner 1992). To what extent does a general theory of "mediatization of religion" need to be applicable across such scales and domains? Or is such a general theory possible or even desirable?

SOURCES OF EVIDENCE

In light of this complexity, it is my purpose here to consider the ways in which media and religion can be seen to interact in contemporary life and in global culture, and to look within these complex relations for evidence of the ways that something new and different is being formed and shaped through this interaction. Furthermore, I will consider the issue of whether we might call this a process or result of "mediatization." The call for studies of mediatization as applied to religion can be said to focus our attention on where these new and different forms of religion are situated, the ways that they interact with the media, and the outcomes of these interactions.

Addressing the question of the mediatization of religion, even in light of the complexities discussed here, in fact requires a broad historical and conceptual overview, looking at the process in the contemporary phenomena and the underlying social dimensions that can help define its extents and limits. Our received histories of religion the West are in fact significant stories about its mediatization.

It has long been held that the Protestant Reformation had its roots in the printing revolution, and that without printing, the Reformation would not have spread in quite the ways it did. The development of the bourgeois public sphere, also a creature of printing and publishing, was accompanied by the emergence of a religious discursive culture that gradually intellectualized, differentiated, and instrumentalized religion. The higher expressions of religious thought, such as the twentieth century development of neoorthodoxy in Western Christianity (and parallel developments in Judaism and Islam) depended on the existence of printed materials and also on hierarchies of discursive authority and on systems and communities of knowledge production (Wuthnow 1989; Eisenstein 1978).

CONCEPTUAL CHALLENGES

Beyond this historical context, there are a set of deeply embedded conceptual challenges to developing a clear understanding of contemporary religion as it might interact with media, become mediated, or even become mediatized. Taken together, these contest the idea that a unitary or general sense of the religious sphere and/or its mediatization is a simple or straightforward matter. The most significant of these are (1) what we do about "essentialist" categories of religion and (2) the problem of commodification and markets.

The problem of essentialism resolves around the fact that we have tended to think of religion as something beyond "the head." What Otto called the "numinous" and Durkheim called "effervescence" continue to define the way we think of religion. Thus there has been a consistent tendency for observers to assume that there is a contradiction between religion *qua* religion and its institutions and structures. This is one of the reasons it has been difficult for us to think of "religion" and "media" at the same time without instrumentalizing one in relation to the other. The typical syllogism is that (1) religion is ancient and "natural," (2) media are modern and "artificial," therefore (3) religion is the larger, more fundamental category, and the relations between them are nothing more than modernity's technological approximation of *true* religion, and thus mediation is only about "influence."

In fact, the situation has always been, and remains, much more complex than that. Today, the way we think of mediatization of religion stems from the centrality of media, media institutions, and media technologies in culture and discourse. This has made it a rather straightforward matter to look at specific relations between the interests of specific historic religions and their presence in "the media." What makes this situation complex is the *integration* of media and religion, something that has been a feature of each all along. For example, the very nature of the so-called "democratic" religious marketplace of the nineteenth-century United States was in its mediation, or mediatization (Hatch 1991; Nord 2004). This religious marketplace has achieved even more powerful expression in the twentieth century. For example, Hendershot (2004) has persuasively demonstrated the extent to which organizations such as Billy Graham Ministries came to constitute and construct mid-century American and—to an extent—European evangelicalism through its extensive practices of mediation and media commodification. This can be seen even more persuasively in the case of the commercial religious marketplace of publishing and music (Borden 2007). At the center of these histories is the sense that these mediated commodities have come to a central place in the construction of Evangelical identities over recent decades (Morgan 1997).

Thus, American protestantism, the movement that has become so determinative of U.S. domestic and foreign policy in the twentieth and twenty-first centuries (and has played a similar but smaller role in Anglophone Canada), is at its base an interaction of traditional "imagined communities" with modernity via a mediation that *represents* but also *constitutes* this movement. This latter—the constitution—is the more telling, important, and perhaps controversial issue.

The question of commodification is even more complex. Against our received notion of the natural constitution of the essentially "religious," religious commodities and the introduction of religion into the commercial marketplace seem contradictory. But, as with mediation, there is an extent to which all religions have always been commodified (Moore 1995). The money changers in the temple, the selling of indulgences, the commercial marketplaces that grow up around and support pilgrimages, and the modern marketplace of religious publishing are but a few examples of this.

Questions of mediation and commodification are important to deal with, because they underlie and support the autonomy of the media marketplace in relation to other social institutions and authorities, particularly the state and religion. A generation ago, Elizabeth Eisenstein (1978) pointed out that the most significance of Gutenberg's revolution was not only in the distribution of books but the establishment and spread of the profession of *the publisher*. As publishing became established as a commercial enterprise, printers needed to depend less on the patronage of the church or the crown. Rooted in their market location, these publishers had the potential to become independent cultural authorities. While it took over a century for commercial printing to become a publishing industry and for that industry to become what we know today as "the media," today that process is nearly complete. This autonomy has forever changed the relations between religion and the state in the West. After the rise of these industries, authorities of all kinds would have to contend with the power of the media to publish (to make public) and therefore to provide a check on the power of state and of religion (Lazarsfeld and Merton 1948).

At the center of my own research is a project that reflects on and studies the current state of media authority and the ways in which its putative practices of mediatization are expressed and experienced in the lives of media audiences in Europe and the United States. It is important to say that while the "authority of the media" is expressed in certain conventionalized ways when we are talking about journalism, the role of what we are calling "mediatization" is more complex, nuanced, and subtle. And at the same time, its effects are far more profound in that they are changing the way that religion and spirituality are experienced and expressed and the roles that they play in global politics and society. The extent of this global geographic reach, combined with the layered and complex way that religion can be seen to be expressed in and mediated by contemporary communications, means that we must look well beyond formal, structural relations for evidence of its effects and implications. I am arguing here that the essential features of the mediatization of religion are found in (1) media autonomy, (2) processes and practices of commodification, and (3) its existence in (and constitution of) a marketplace of religious and spiritual "supply."

CONDITIONS OF MEDIATIZATION

Let us turn to a review of some ways that the mediatization of religion might be conditioned by realities in the worlds of media and religion and the practices of each. First, there is the issue of *reflexivity*. As Giddens (1991) has argued, late-modern, mediated cultures are reflexively self-conscious about the nature of society, culture, and politics, and also about the nature of their own subjectivity. The late-modern taste cultures of irony and postmodernism are one example of this, and the popularity of "fake news" is another. A growing public distrust of authority and of social institutions is another outcome. Reflexivity also explains identities and practices that can seem to contradict traditional, structured ways of understanding the social universe. It is expressed in audience subjectivities that allow them to position themselves as fans at one moment and as ironic critics at another. The media are active in this in that they encourage audiences into such positionalities at the same time that they provide the information that empowers audiences to new, more self-conscious relations to news and politics (cf. Gergen 1996).

This reflexivity then articulates with the complex ways that media audiences exercise autonomy in relation to media messages. While the issue of the autonomy of audiences versus the determination of media messages is far from settled in contemporary media theory (Grossberg 1995; Moores 1993), there is much evidence that audiences are in fact active in the process of media reception. Their autonomy is obviously conditioned by a variety of factors, but the ways that audiences make meaning out of media texts can be as important to the process as the intentions of producers or power of those texts. This situation can be seen across a range of media, but has been shown in the case of specifically religious media and in the case of religious motivations on the part of media audiences (Hoover 2006; Clark 2003).

A second issue is the fact that media practice is necessarily embedded in broader social networks and processes of association. The media are at the center of a cultural economy of information, which in turn is the basis of much of the social and cultural capital on which contemporary social networks and relationships are based. Pierre Bourdieu (1984) has been particularly influential in demonstrating the ways that social relations are maintained through practices of the acquisition and exchange of various kinds of cultural capital. A variety of studies have shown how media-based sources contribute to these processes (cf. Moores 1993;

Gauntlett 2007; Alexander and Jacobs 1998). The idea that contemporary socie-ties suffer from a decline in the resources and practices of association that Robert Putnam calls "social capital" has become persuasive in a number of circles, and the notion that media might in some way contribute positively directly contradicts dominant assumptions in the social capital movement (cf. Putnam 2000). Simply put, it is common there to think of media, particularly television, as associated with declining social capital and civic engagement. Significant to our consider-ations here, it has further been argued that religion is a positive contributor to social capital, and that media in fact detract from the positive or normative role that religion might play (Eberly 2002).

Media scholars, by showing the ways that media are involved in providing resources that Bourdieu might think of as "cultural capital," suggest that the pic-ture is not so clear. Leaving aside for a moment the issue of how "social" and "cultural" capital might be related, it nonetheless bears considering how media-derived cultural resources might support the kinds of association that Putnam and his colleagues see as basic to social capital and civic engagement. Gauntlett and others have shown that media practices and identities actually contribute something to the ways that people interact in daily life. This so-called "water cooler" or "cocktail party" discursive capital is essential to the development and maintenance of social networks, and this kind of capital is largely derived from "the media" (Hoover, Clark, and Alters 2004). Implications for the mediatiza-tion of religion are significant here in that it has also been shown that media-based social relations are important conditions for the construction of religious identities (Hoover 2006).

A third issue has to do with the way that contemporary publics come to under-stand religions, spiritualities, and—more significantly—the religious "other." The media are in fact the primary framing devices and information sources through which the supposed "actual facts" of contemporary life are made public. On the most basic level, this is a question of information and is rooted in journalistic practice and the journalistic functions of the various traditional (and emerging) media. Edward Said's important work on religious understanding and the limits of media framing provides powerful evidence of the ways that the media contrib-ute to knowledge of religions in general, but also to the specific case of under-standings and relations between the Islamic world and "the West" (Said 1997).

This function of the media in relation to religion flows in two directions. First, their position between various religious "objects" on the one hand and audi-ences and publics on the other means that they have a definitive power that acts as a direct confrontation to established religious authorities. The Catholic Church, for example, experienced this in relation to the scandals over sexual abuse by priests that emerged in the early years of the new century. Whereas the Church might have preferred to be able to control access to this kind of information, it was not able to, and this had real impacts on its institutions, nationally and globally.

The second direction that media influence flows is in what publics and audiences know about religions "here" and "there." This role was particularly obvious in the case of the Islamicist critiques of the West surrounding the 9/11 attacks in the United States. There is good evidence that some of the motivation for those attacks derived from a sense of the moral depravity of American culture that was in turn derived from mediated images of the United States and the West more generally widely circulated in the developing world (Hoover 2006). Impressions across the various religious-cultural divides that in part define global politics today are similarly derived from mediations of religion and of religious cultures (Appleby, 2009; Thomas 2008). Thus the mediatization of religion is somehow also rooted in the way that media help frame and represent religion and spirituality. There is also evidence that mediated information about religion and spirituality can contribute to the spread of certain religious and spiritual movements and trends. This has been shown in relation to emerging or "new age" spiritualities and their representation in digital media, but the digital realm seems to be particularly active in this way across a wide range of spiritual and religious domains and movements (Helland 2002; Campbell 2005).

A fourth condition surrounding contemporary media and religion is that there is an extensive and self-conscious "public script" of cultural identity in relation to media (Hoover, Clark, and Alters 2004; cf. Alexander and Jacobs 1998). Long-standing received discourses of "good," "appropriate," and "bad" media are well integrated into social and class sensibilities. These ways of thinking about media are clearly rooted in established cultural value hierarchies. One of the major contributions of the field of British Cultural Studies to our understanding of media was to meet such notions head on, establishing an analytical place for an understanding that different classes articulate with different media that contests implicit normative or formal ideas about which of these media are "good" and which are "bad" and why (Grossberg 1995). And yet, such ideas persist in public discourse and in lay theorizing about the media.

We can relatively easily typify American (U.S. and Canadian) and British households in class, educational, and even religious terms by their media behaviors. But we can also typify them by the ways that they describe themselves as media households. These self-understandings condition identities in important ways and interact significantly with religious and spiritual identities (Hoover 2006). This means that, on some very basic level, the ways that people are "religious" or "spiritual" today are defined by their media "selves"—a clear implication for our evolving theories of mediatization.

Fifth, and related to the issue above, an actual demography of media (as opposed to the attributive "third-person" classification implied in number four) defines and differentiates audiences according to age, gender, sexual preference, ethnicity, and region. Broad-scale mediatization of society and culture must be in some ways rooted in the fact that the media and the practices of media "audience-making" are so integrated into such structural and structured dimensions of social life. There is an extensive literature addressing practices of media reception in each of these areas. These identities are of course important conditions of religious and spiritual practice and possibility in audiences and thus can help define the capacities of the media to make and remake religion and spirituality for these communities.

THE COMPLEXITIES OF MEDIATIZATION

Reflecting on these five dimensions (and I do not mean this list necessarily to be exhaustive), it seems that mediatization would be found in various "geographies." We should not expect it to be unitary along dimensions of either structure or practice. It is clearly conditioned by structural locations of class, age, gender, place, etc. At the same time, dimensions of identity, reception, and meaning-making must play a role. This also means that mediatization's relation to religions and spiritualities cannot be unitary either, but will be differentiated and defined by structural, cultural, and individual conditions and associations as well as by cultural characteristics and practices.

To further complicate matters, we can expect that the mediatization of religion and spirituality is becoming increasingly user generated and user defined. The struggle between religious authorities and "the media" in early stages of the introduction of each new medium could be fought on a certain playing field. Religions thought that they could determine the nature of their own mediation through activities of media production and distribution. Each of the Abrahamic faiths has been through this: The Protestant establishment in the United States and Canada as it encountered the development of film and television, the Vatican as it has responded to bad publicity of various kinds, Rabbinic authorities confronting media cultures rife with antisemitism, the Mullahs in the Islamic Republic of Iran—each has thought that the answer is to control "the message" carried by a unitary media "mainstream." If only the "right" people were in control—it is thought—then the "message" would be fixed. And the approach has often been for these authorities to develop cartel-like arrangements to control the distribution and mediation of their "messages."

In Europe, public broadcasting systems to this day continue to provide airtime to the established religions. A similar system held sway in the United States and Canada until the latter part of the twentieth century. Struggles over such access typify the situation in many parts of the global south as well. In Nigeria, for instance, the emerging tension between Islam and Christianity is increasingly defined by struggles over access to airwaves and newspapers (Griswold 2008). The same can be said for India (Thomas 2008). The implication is that religious authorities—and many adherents—have come to think of the media as a context that plays at least some role in legitimating certain movements, institutions, and truth claims over others. The media, and who is represented where and when in the media, thus have a kind of symbolic power over questions of religious-institutional ascendancy and power. They are vital to religious authority today.

The problem is that contemporary media practice around questions of religion and spirituality is eroding religious authority by redefining where and what "the religious" and "the spiritual" are in media. Today, there are many religious and spiritual messages, and more and more of them are controlled not by authorities of any kind but by the "invisible hand" of the cultural economy. This expanding religious "marketplace" of supply (Hoover 2006; Wolfe 2008) is increasingly mediated and is increasingly involved in the mediatization of religions and spiritualities. New voices in Islamic, Jewish, and Christian youth culture are using the new media to articulate new imbrications of "the religious" through websites, YouTube videos, and blogs. In the process, they are relativizing religion and religious authority. It is important to note that this effect is expressed on two levels. The first is on what we might call a "symbolic" level, where the media sphere has been seen to represent the status of the various religions, and the increasing diffusion of religious voices today subsumes the traditional religions into a context where they are in direct competition with many other, less-established voices. Second, on a more substantive level, this emerging, wide-ranging inventory of religious and spiritual resources carries within it symbols, ideas, and truth claims that directly challenge those of the existing institutions, histories, and doctrines.

This guerilla action is significant, because it takes place against the backdrop of a situation where long ago the structural and practical realities of the mediatized environment have redefined (and elided) boundaries between "the religious" and "the secular" (or "the mediated"). In our work with religious and spiritual identity among media audiences in the United States, we have found that taste cultures around media bear little real relationship to religion in traditional, structural, or institutional terms (Hoover 2006; Hoover, Clark, and Alters 2004).

For example, U.S. Evangelicals' viewing preferences differ little from those of non-Evangelicals. There are class differences and differences by gender, age, and education, but not really by "religion" per se. The major reason for this seems to be the dimension I mentioned above: that of the broad role that the media play in the formation and maintenance of shared social and cultural identities. The media seem to define for their audiences a wider, more commonplace social currency that is mediated and that defines participation in the "common culture." Everyone wants to be part of the common conversation. Few (save the Amish and Fundamentalist Church of Jesus Christ of Latter Day Saints) really *want* to be that *different*, culturally.

This means that there is a powerful engine of social and cultural orientation, rooted in the media, that is at the core of the mediatization of religion. One of the most important dimensions of this engine is in its age demographics. Youth cultures are more mediated and more oriented to mediation and mediatized practice than are their elders. This means that an emergent youth culture of religious and spiritual articulation is emerging "under the radar" of extant arrangements of social, cultural, and religious authority. Both in North America (more so in the case of the United States than Canada), which is more publicly (while unofficially) religious, and in Europe (which is more publicly secularized, but with residues of "official" religion), a global youth culture, rooted in media and in practices of mediatization is arising. This youth culture is one that is less "secularist" in orientation than its forebears and is imbricating, negotiating, and representing new formations of traditional and nontraditional religions and spiritualities. More significantly, perhaps, this youth culture is also active in the contexts of centralized state power such as in China, the theocracies of the Middle East, and Iran.

It is not only youth, though. The mediatization of religion is rooted in the articulation of a range of the sensibilities, contexts, and audiences that make up the complex "glocal" cultural landscape of today. This means that a variety of the boundaries that we have thought to exist between the "religious" and "the secular" broke down long ago and are increasingly problematic. All of this could be an effect of "the media," and thus evidence of an overall, complex, and layered "mediatization."

SOME IMPLICATIONS FOR THEORIES OF MEDIATIZATION

It is clear that to understand the ways that religion and spirituality are being changed by their interactions with the media, we need to look beyond and below the levels where much of the theory building about the mediatization of religion has been articulated. The large questions of the role of mediatization in conditioning the relations of religion to civil society, the state, and national identities, and the way that contemporary, mediatized social life is ritualized and understood in terms of these relations across whole cultures, have drawn much of the attention.

It has been tempting for many observers to look for evidence of mediatization in these large contexts and on large scales. There are good conceptual reasons for starting there. Some of our most powerful and influential sources in social theory (Durkheim and Weber come immediately to mind) have provided fundamental, paradigmatic ways of thinking about religion, religious meanings and motivations, and the religion "object." They have tended to describe an essential role for religion in social and cultural relations and have suggested that its role must necessarily be "mechanical" (to use Durkheim's term) or in other ways essential to the constitution and maintenance of society. Intervening theory making about "secularization" notwithstanding, we today want to at least consider the idea that something as broad and far-reaching as the integration of modern means of communication into culture and society must have some necessary implications for religion. Will the media displace it? Will they make it unnecessary on some level? Will their powers of enchantment displace its effervescence? Will its "works of art" survive the age of its mechanical reproduction (to use a strained a simile)?

Mediatization theory, as it has been applied to religion, has in fact taken a sophisticated and nuanced turn. It has suggested that we can answer these questions empirically, and that we should expect the situation to be complex and to transcend simple questions of instrumental "effects" of media "messages" on religious beliefs and practices. My argument is intended to point to ways in which we must understand both "religion" and "the media" in new ways if we are to make substantive progress in a theory of religious mediatization.

The purpose here has been to point to ways that the situation is more complex, nuanced, and layered. Underlying the various dimensions and conditions discussed here, there are really two claims: First, that in order to understand the contemporary mediatization of religion, we must understand the complexities and nuances of contemporary religion. Second, that this project also demands that we look carefully at the ways that contemporary media, as practiced, direct our attention to places beyond the larger, universal contexts. And, as should be clear, it also seems that many of these dimensions reveal ways that media and religion are articulated to one another in contemporary experience, and thus a clear distinction between "religion" and "the media," and thus how the former is "mediatized" by the latter is difficult to draw.

This argument could be read as a contestation of the whole notion of the mediatization of religion. It is not. Instead, it should be seen as an attempt to broaden and deepen our understanding of how the media are today making something entirely new and different out of religions and spiritualities. It might be argued, in response, that much of the evidence provided here seems to derive from the somewhat particularized, even exceptional, context of the United States and its unique religious culture. There is something to this, but there is also ample evidence that many of the significant trends discussed here can be seen in other national contexts as well, either as part of broader, evolving realities, or as a result of global cross-diffusion of influences from one context to another. There are also some dimensions, particularly in the area of religious authority, that seem in a sense universal, though this of course awaits further empirical or historical test.

This is by no means an exhaustive or systematic assessment of the mediatization of religion. That awaits further work on many fronts by scholars pursuing many projects. But, looking across the issues, trends, and conditions discussed here, it seems we can begin to draw a tentative conclusion about the overall question. That conclusion is that the thesis that the media today are fundamentally changing the nature of religion and spirituality seems to be supported by the evidence. In fact, it seems to be the case that the mediatization of religion has been underway for at least four centuries, and that in a range of complex, subtle, nuanced, and layered ways, it is more advanced and has progressed farther into a variety of social and cultural spaces and levels, than we might have assumed or expected. Much remains to be done to chart its extents and limits, but it is a very promising project.

REFERENCES

Alexander, J., and Jacobs, R. (1998). Mass communication and civil society. In T. Liebes and J. Curran (Eds.). *Media, Ritual and Identity* (pp. 23–41). London: Routledge.

Appleby, R. S. (2009). What can peacebuilders learn from Fundamentalists? In S. M. Hoover and N. Kaneva (Eds.). *Fundmentalisms and the Media*. London: Continuum Press.

Borden, A. (2007). Making money, saving souls: Christian bookstores and the commodification of Christianity. In L. S. Clark (Ed.). *Religion, Media, and the Marketplace* (pp. 67–89). New Brunswick, NJ: Rutgers.

Bourdieu, P. (1984). *Distinction: A Social Critique of the Judgment of Taste.* (Trans. Richard Nice). Cambridge, MA: Harvard University Press.

Campbell, H. (2005). *Exploring Religious Community Online: We Are One on the Network.* London: Peter Lang.

Carey, J. (1989). *Communication as Culture.* Boston: Unwin-Hyman.

Clark, L. S. (2003) *From Angels to Aliens: Teenagers, the Media, and the Supernatural.* New York: Oxford University Press.

Cottle, S. (2006). Mediatized rituals: beyond manufacturing consent. *Media, Culture and Society,* 28(3), 411–432.

Couldry, N. (2004). *Media Rituals.* London: Routledge.

Dayan, D., and E. Katz (1992). *Media Events: The Live Broadcasting of History.* Cambridge: Harvard University Press.

Eberly, D. (2002). *The Soul of Civil Society.* New York: Lexington Books.

Eisenstein, E. (1978). *The Printing Press as an Agent of Change.* Cambridge, UK: Cambridge University Press.

Gauntlett, D. (2007). *Creative Explorations: New Approaches to Identities and Audiences.* London: Routledge.

Gergen, K. (1996). Technology and the self: From the essential to the sublime. In D. Grodin and T. R. Lindlof (Eds.). *Constructing the Self in a Mediated World.* Thousand Oaks, CA: Sage.

Giddens, A. (1991) *Modernity and Self-Identity: Self and Society in the Late Modern Age.* Palo Alto, CA: Stanford University Press.

Griswold, E. (2008). God's country. *Atlantic Monthly,* 30(2), 40–55.

Grossberg, L. (1995). Cultural studies vs. political economy: Is anyone else bored with this debate? *Critical Studies in Mass Communication,* 12, 72–81.

Hatch, N. (1991). *The Democratization of American Christianity.* New Haven, CT: Yale.

Helland, C. (2002). Surfing for salvation. *Religion,* 32(4).

Hendershot, H. (2004). *Shaking the World for Jesus: Media and Conservative Evangelical Culture.* Chicago: University of Chicago Press.

Hjarvard, S. (2008). The mediatization of religion: A theory of the media as agents of religious change. In S. Hjarvard (Ed.). *The Mediatization of Religion: Enchantment, Media and Popular Culture* (pp. 9–26). Northern Lights Film & Media Studies Yearbook 6. Bristol, UK: Intellect.

Hoover, S. M. (2006). *Religion in the Media Age.* London: Routledge.

Hoover, S. M., Clark, L. S. and Alters, D. (with J. Champ and L. Hood) (2004). *Media, Home and Family.* New York: Routledge.

Lazarsfeld, P., and Merton, R. (1948). Mass communication, popular taste, and organized social action. In L. Bryson (Ed.). *Communication of Ideas* (pp. 95–118). New York: Harper & Brothers.

Moore, R. L. (1995). *Selling God: American Religion in the Marketplace of Culture.* Oxford, UK: Oxford University Press.

Moores, S. (1993). *Interpreting Audiences.* London: Sage.

Morgan, D. (1997). *Visual Piety: A History and Theory of Popular Religious Images.* Berkeley: University of California Press.

Nord, D. (2004). *Faith in Reading: Religious Publishing and the Birth of Mass Media in America, 1790–1860.* Oxford, UK: Oxford University Press.

Putnam, R. (2000). *Bowling Alone: The Collapse and Revival of American Community.* New York: Simon & Schuster.

Rothenbuhler, E. (1998) *Ritual Communication: From Everyday Conversation to Mediated Ceremony.* Thousand Oaks, CA: Sage Publications.

Said, E. (1997). *Covering Islam: How the Media and the Experts Determine How We See the Rest of the World.* New York: Vintage Books.

Thomas, P. (2008). *Strong Religion, Zealous Media: Christian Fundamentalism and Media in India.* Newbury Park, CA: Sage.

Warner, R. S. (1993). Work in progress toward a new paradigm for the sociological study of religion in the United States. *American Journal of Sociology,* 98(5), 1044–1093.

Wolfe, A. (2008). "And the winner is…," *Atlantic Monthly,* 30(2), 56–63.

Wuthnow, R. (1989). *Communities of Discourse: Ideology and Social Structure in the Reformation, the Enlightenment and European Socialism.* Cambridge, MA: Harvard University Press.

CHAPTER SEVEN

Differentiation: Mediatization AND Cultural Change

ANDREAS HEPP

POSITIONING MEDIATIZATION: INTRODUCTION

If we consider the present discussion on mediatization, we can identify two positions. First, there is the position whereby the concept of mediatization throws light on a 'media logic' that is active in various social fields. Winfried Schulz, for example, discusses the mediatization of politics in such a frame, understanding as one (and the strongest) aspect of mediatization that 'the actors and organizations of all sectors of society accommodate to the media logic' (Schulz 2004, p. 98).[1] More recently, Stig Hjarvard has discussed mediatization as a 'logic of the media'; that is, 'their organizational, technological, and aesthetic functioning, including the ways in which media allocate material and symbolic resources and work through formal and informal rules' (Hjarvard 2007, p. 3).

The second position is the critique of such a linear view. Maybe most prominent is the critique by Nick Couldry, arguing that all dimensions of society are indeed shaped not only through 'the media,' but also through other acts of appropriation, interpretation, and resistance that are not necessarily media related (Couldry 2003). Taking these reflections, he highlights that 'media-related pressures at work in society...[are] too heterogeneous to be reduced to a single "media logic"' (Couldry 2008, p. 375).

With respect to this discussion, this chapter takes an 'in-between' position. On the one hand, I share all the basic reflections by Nick Couldry, arguing for an approach that emphasizes the power-related, 'dynamic, nonlinear circuit of meaning' (Livingstone 2009) under which Stuart Hall understands any process of media communication (cf. Hall 1997a, b). Moreover, I also share the argument put forward by Nick Couldry that we have to discuss transformations of the media in relation to a 'particular field' (Couldry 2008, p. 377).

But on the other hand, I do not share the general rejection of mediatization theory related to positions like these. In a nutshell, the main argument of this chapter is that we surely have to investigate the mediatization of certain cultural fields carefully in detail and cannot assume a single 'linear media logic.' However, the concept of mediatization becomes useful if we do not relate it to the assumption of one 'media logic' but understand it more generally as a frame for researching the relation between media and cultural change. So while critics of mediatization theories are right in rejecting the linear variants of it, more complex approaches can be helpful for researching on media and cultural change as they offer a more abstract, orientating frame of interpretation.

To make this argument more palpable, I wish to argue as follows: In a first step, I will theorize mediatization as a general approach for researching what I call the 'moulding forces' of the media. Based on this understanding, I then go on to outline a general research frame for an investigation of the mediatization of specific cultural fields. Finally, I conclude by formulating some general considerations for future research on mediatization. So, all in all, this chapter is a theoretical one, trying to formulate an approach on mediatization that is marked by a 'differentiation perspective.' However, it is based on various empirical research in different cultural fields.

THEORIZING MEDIATIZATION:
THE 'MOULDING FORCES' OF THE MEDIA

When theorizing mediatization, one of the most helpful starting points is the understanding of Friedrich Krotz (2007, 2008). The main point for him is to understand 'mediatization'—like 'individualization,' 'globalization,' and 'commercialization'—as 'meta-processes.' A 'meta-process' is not an empirical process in the sense that we can investigate it as—for example—a certain talk or a person crossing the street. Meta-processes are superior theoretical approaches describing long-term processes of change. So a 'meta-process' cannot be researched empirically as a single transformation phenomenon. Notwithstanding, only the formulation of theories of 'meta-processes' allows us to structure the complexity of different empirical data to get a deeper understanding of occurring (long-term) processes of change.

We can best illustrate this with the example of another 'meta-process,' that is, 'individualization.' In the introduction to the volume 'Individualization,' Ulrich Beck and Elisabeth Beck-Gernsheim define this concept as follows:

> The concept of 'individualization' will be developed in this sociological sense of institutionalized individualism. Central institutions of modern society—basic civil, political, and social rights, but also paid employment and the training and mobility necessary for it—are geared to the individual and not to the group. Insofar as basic rights are internalized and everyone wants to or must be economically active to earn their livelihood, the spiral of individualization destroys the given foundation of social coexistence. So—to give a simple definition of individualization—'individualization' means disembedding without reembedding. (Beck and Beck-Gernsheim 2001, p. xxif)

The point of this quote is not just that it demonstrates that individualization is understood 'in a nonlinear mode,' as Scott Lash has written in his foreword to that volume. The main point is rather that, with their approach to individualization, Ulrich Beck and Elisabeth Beck-Gernsheim outline an explanation of the present social change that cannot be proven by any single survey. Rather, we have to understand their theory of individualization as a meta approach that makes it possible to integrate very different results of surveys and qualitative investigations into an overall coherent understanding. This 'meta-process' of 'individualization' is not isolated; so, for example, the quote refers to questions of 'commercialization.' Also, it is in itself contradictory and nonlinear, as it is marked by an unintentional reflexivity.

Without at this point going into further detail on the discussion of 'individualization,' reflecting on this quote permits an understanding of what it actually means to consider 'mediatization' as such a 'meta-process.' Friedrich Krotz outlines the 'meta-process' of mediatization exactly in a comparative manner when he writes:

> By mediatization we mean the historical developments that took and take place as a result of change in (communication) media and the consequences of those changes. If we consider the history of communication through music, or the art of writing, we can describe the history of human beings as a history of newly emerging media and at the same time changing forms of communication. The new media do not, in general, substitute for one another, as has been recognized in communication research since the work of the Austrian researcher Riepel... (Krotz 2008, p. 23)

Basically, we can then argue that mediatization captures the process of an increasing spreading of technical communication media in different social and cultural spheres.

In such a nonspecific understanding, mediatization is certainly related to the theorizing of so-called medium theory, with the distinction among oral cultures, scribal cultures, modern print cultures, and present globalized electronic cultures (Meyrowitz 1995, p. 58; p. Schofield Clark in this volume). Without discussing these arguments of medium theory in detail, one can say that they refer to the idea of an increasing mediatization as not just a linear process of change but as a process with certain tipping points: The specificity of certain media—and thus the thinking of medium theory—is related to the specificity of a certain cultural change.

While this theorizing is an important starting point for an understanding of mediatization in general, it is necessary to theorize the relation of media change and further processes of change in a more complex manner than medium theory does. This is precisely what a theory of mediatization introduces. In a certain sense, mediatization tries to take up the central idea of medium theory that 'media change' and 'cultural change' are interrelated, but tries to theorize this not only in the perspective of the relation from media to cultural change. To do this, a first step is to distinguish between two aspects of mediatization; that is, a quantitative and a qualitative one.

1. Quantitative Aspects of Mediatization

Simply put, the quantitative view of mediatization is marked by the word 'more.' Basically, it is obvious that throughout history the basic number of technological media available to us has increased as well as our different uses of these media. If we focus on this in more detail, we can define mediatization as an ongoing process of the increase of media communication on (a) temporal, (b) spatial and (c) social levels (cf. Krotz 2007).

On the temporal level, the increasing number of technological media is becoming more and more accessible all the time. In the present, television, for example, has no closedown anymore but is an ongoing, never-ending flow of technological mediated communication. The internet makes it possible to surf all the time, and so on.

On the spatial level, we can say that media are more and more accessible across different localities. The telephone, for example, is no longer a media technology related to a certain place of communication, such as the office, private home, or public telephone box. As a personalized mobile phone, it is available virtually across all spaces. The same can be said for television, which as 'public viewing' again has left the private home.

These examples refer already to the social level of mediatization, which means that more and more social contexts are marked by media use. To take a further example for this, computer use is no longer something that is done solely in work contexts. Rather, computer use ranks over the very different social spheres of the private and public, the work time and spare time, and so on.

Reflecting these three aspects of the quantitative perspective on mediatization together, it becomes clear that this perspective encompasses more than a linear process of increase. With the increase of different media in human life in general, we have a synergistic process that brings mediatization additionally forward, for example, in the way cross-media content production is more and more characterized by mediated communication.

Altogether, in a quantitative perspective, it becomes obvious that we are confronted with a long-standing process of spreading media communication that also refers to a qualitative change.

2. Qualitative Aspects of Mediatization

Taking up the ideas of medium theory, we have to focus on the fact that the process of mediatization also comprises qualitative changes in the sense of how the spreading of certain media is related to the specificity of cultural change—or put more simply, as an increase of meaning of media and mediated communication on all levels. In a nutshell, we can capture this qualitative aspect of mediatization if we focus on the interrelation of how technological media 'structure' the way we communicate—how the way we communicate via media is reflected in their technological change.

This consideration refers to Raymond Williams, who has argued that media are both simultaneously 'technology and cultural form' (Williams 1990).[2] *Technology* refers to material procedures and formations that are used in acting—in our case, in communication—to increase its possibilities (cf. Rammert 2007, p. 17). In this sense, 'media of communication' signify 'technological systems with a certain functionality and potential for the spreading of information' (Kubicek 1997, p. 220) as, for example, print. The expression 'media technological change' refers then to the change of these technological systems, which has gained a dynamic impulse by means of digitalization (and the related miniaturization) in recent decades. Thus, we can say that the qualitative aspect of mediatization focuses *also* on the 'material' (Gumbrecht and Pfeiffer 1994) character of media technological change in the sense that media technologies have a 'materialized specificity' that is based on communicative action/practices, and at the same time it structures communicative action/practices.

What we can see here is something I want to call the 'moulding forces' of the media (German: *Prägkraft der Medien*); that is, that media themselves exert a certain 'pressure' on the way we communicate. Television, for example, has the 'pressure' to present ideas in a more linear mode and with a suitable visual presentation. Print, to take another example, makes it possible to develop more complex argumentation, as it can be read more slowly and offers the opportunity for complex ways of structuring text. And the mobile phone, as a last example, makes it possible to stay in ongoing communicative connectivity with a group of people while being on the move—and it exerts a certain 'pressure' to do this. However, all these examples also demonstrate that this is not a direct 'effect' of the 'material structure' of the media but something that only becomes concrete in different ways of mediation; that is, by certain forms of communication. As present forms of symbolic action increasingly integrate technological media, 'communicative change' and 'media change' together form 'mediatization' as a qualitative change and cannot be reduced to each other, for example by arguing that one would determine the other.

Having said this, the concept of the 'moulding forces' of the media holds on the idea that there are different specificities of different media we have to have in focus while researching change. However, these specificities of different media are produced in human acting and without indicating 'one trajectory' (or logic) of the media. So we do not have to focus just effect but *specificity* in multilevel transformation processes.

Relating this back to the three quantitative dimensions of mediatization—the social, spatial and temporal ones—we have to look in detail how the 'moulding forces' of different media become concrete along these various dimensions and in different cultural fields. Such an approach to mediatization offers at the same time a general frame for relating research as well as a starting point for contextualized investigations.

RESEARCHING MEDIATIZATION: CULTURAL FIELDS

When we discuss the question of how to conceptualize research on media and cultural change, the reflections being developed by John B. Thompson in his book, *The Media and Modernity,* are a helpful starting point. Reflecting on the question as to how the media are interrelated with the development of modern societies, Thompson argues as follows:[3]

> If we focus...not on values, attitudes, and beliefs, but rather on symbolic forms and their modes of production and circulation in the social world, then we shall see that, with the advent of modern societies in the late medieval and early modern periods, a systematic cultural transformation began to take hold. By virtue of a series of technical innovations associated with printing and, subsequently, with the electrical codification of information, symbolic forms were produced, reproduced, and circulated on a scale that was unprecedented. Patterns of communication and interaction began to change in profound and irreversible ways. These changes, which comprise what can loosely be

called the 'mediazation of culture,' had a clear institutional basis: namely, the development of media organizations, which first appeared in the second half of the fifteenth
century and have expanded their activities ever since. (Thompson 1995, p. 46)

In my perspective, two arguments in this quote are striking. First, that there is a
'systematic cultural transformation'; that is, we can typify certain patterns along
which cultural change takes place. Second, these patterns should be, for logical
reasons, related to questions of media change. Only therefore we can speak of a
process of 'mediazation of culture.'

Relating these considerations back to the articulation of the state in modernity, Thompson highlights the relevance of the mass media for building up this
new form of economic, political, coercive, and symbolic power. It was the print
media (and later in the twentieth century radio and television as well) on which
the articulation of national identity was based, an identity that first and foremost
made the cohesion of the modern (nation) state possible (Thompson 1995, p. 51).
At this point, his arguments meet with the reflections by others, for example,
Benedict Anderson (1983), Orvar Löfgren (2001), and David Morley (2000). In
a (for sure simplifying) description, the relation between nation state and national
identity can be described as something that had been mediated by the traditional
mass media: newspapers, books, radio, and television. If we ask here for mediatization, that is, the 'moulding forces' of these media, we can at least typify certain
tendencies: On the social level, they addressed the 'mass audience' of a national
population from a 'centre' (and by this helped to construct this 'centre'); on the
spatial level, they reached a national territory (and by this helped to create an
understanding of state borders as borders of the national community); and on the
temporal level, they allowed a more and more speeded-up communication (and
by this an addressing of 'the people' virtually in real time).

If we look in detail, we find additional 'moulding forces' of these 'mass media'
as soon as we focus more on their differences. Of course, print is something different from TV. Nevertheless, we can argue that, up to the middle of the twentieth
century, we had a *tendency* of constructing a territorial national communicative
space by the media.[4] In a certain sense, we can understand this as a certain stage
of 'mediatization of culture' (or in the words of Thompson, of 'mediazation of
culture') that results in something we might call *national-territorial media culture*,
a culture whose primary resources of meaning are accessible through technol-
ogy-based media. By this I do not want to say that all is mediated technically
within these national-territorial media cultures (cf. Hepp and Couldry 2009a).
However, we have a national centering by the media here. But the interrelation
between media and cultural change went further and resulted in something John
Tomlinson has called 'telemediatization' (Tomlinson 2007, p. 94) of culture;

that is, 'the increasing implications of electronic communications and media systems in the constitution of everyday experience.' Based on this, we are nowadays confronted with a much higher multiplicity of different communicative spaces, a process of change we can illustrate with the figure below.

In total, the graph is intended to visualize the main arguments outlined above. Up to the 1950s, the mediatization of culture resulted *in tendency* in the construction of a territorial communicative space and relating national cultures. In the present, we are *in tendency* confronted with a higher pluralisation of mediated communicative spaces that are related to a much higher variability of different cultural context fields such as, for example, the everyday, business, religion, and so forth. The argument here is that this process of change is related to an increasing mediatization along the social, spatial, and temporal dimension. All of them have to be seen in their interrelation to processes of further cultural change, that is, individualization, deterritorialization, and the coming of intermediacy.

1. Social Dimension: Individualization

As mentioned in the beginning of this chapter, we can understand individualization as one dominant meta-process of social change. In the words of Ulrich Beck, this process does not mean only 'the disintegration of previously existing social forms' (class, denomination) but additionally, and based on this, that 'new demands, controls, and constraints are being imposed on individuals' (Beck and Beck-Gernsheim 2001, p. 2). The individual is *urged* to be far more responsible for his or her life while the resources he or she has are not shared equally.

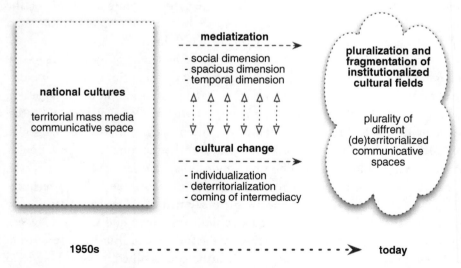

Figure 1: Tendencies of mediatization and cultural change.

If we discuss these processes of individualization, we have to relate them also to the social dimension of mediatization, that is, the spreading of technologically media in different social spheres. For example, within processes of individualization, the media can be understood as an 'instance of orientation.' We can take makeover television shows as an example for this (Ouellette and Hay 2008; Thomas 2009): In shows like 'The Swan' or 'Idol,' the model of individualized lifestyle is brought to the extreme in the sense that the personal story of a willful self-optimization is staged as something usual. These shows can be understood as instances that 'orientate' or 'guide' people in the sense that such an individualized self-optimization is—albeit on a lower level—a regular way of life formation in the present.

Also, we can argue that the media are something like a 'contested market' of the different offerings of individualized societies. With the spreading of the media in very different social spheres, we expect that the different central offerings of the present—fashion, belief, business models, etc.—are communicated via the media. They are the place where these different offerings not only 'compete' in the economic sense of the word but also where the contestation about the 'right way selection' takes place.

If we leave such reflection of the role of pluralized mass media and focus more on digital media of personal communication, we can argue that they have an important role as 'resources for identity bricolage.' Within online chat, for example, it is quite easily possible to negotiate aspects of one's own identity with persons having comparable orientations or interests.

2. Spatial Dimension: Deterritorialization

At the spatial level, we see the spreading of media related to the cultural change of an ongoing process of deterritorialization; that is, an increasing 'loss of the 'natural' relation of culture to geographical and social territories' (García Canclini 1995, p. 229). In a physical respect, deterritorialization is related to different forms of mobility that mark our present cultures (cf. Urry 1999, 2003); for example, the mobility of migrants, of business trips, or of tourism. However, we can also discern a communicative deterritorialization, that is, the uncoupling of communicative spaces from territories as it is related to an increasing global communicative connectivity (cf. Hepp 2008b). Again, we can demonstrate this with some examples.

First of all, the media serve as community-specific identity offerings, not only on the national level but also on the level of deterritorial communities: social movements, fan cultures, religious communities, and diasporas all share the conjuncture that they form networks of communities that transgress different territories translocally and therefore highly relate to technical media of communication for all processes of identity articulation.

Other examples are transnational publics, such as the European public sphere, that are marked by processes of new territorialisation of communication based, however, on a previous transgression of national communicative spaces. While staying segmented nationally (Wessler et al. 2008), they form processes of transcultural understanding.

Finally, we see media aspects of deterritorialization at the level of personal communication. For example, digital media such as e-mail and chat facilitate keeping in touch across different territories of living family and friendship networks.

3. Temporal Dimension: Coming of Intermediacy

If we consider the temporal dimension of the interrelation of mediatization and cultural change and follow the arguments put forward by John Tomlinson (2007), we can detect a 'new coming of intermediacy.' John Tomlinson himself relates this intermediacy *also* to the increasing mediatization of culture, the temporal ubiquitousness of electronic media. For him this is related to a 'culture of instantaneity' (Tomlinson 2007, p. 74), the expectation of rapid delivery, ubiquitous availability, and the instance gratification of desires. Additionally, it is related to a 'sense of directness, of cultural proximity' (ibid.).

If we discuss this in more detail, we can again formulate some examples based on Tomlinson's reflections. First of all, we can argue that media are a kind of 'instance of synchronization,' not only nationally (an argument also developed by John B. Thompson) but also beyond national communicative spaces. Examples of this are outstanding media events (Olympics, disasters, etc.) that 'synchronize,' besides all diversity, certain thematic orientations transculturally (cf. Couldry, Hepp, and Krotz 2009).

Additionally, we can see media as 'founders of cultural proximity,' again not only in the case of 'banal nationalism' (Billig 1995) of the nation state but also in the proximity of the 'telepresence' (Tomlinson 2007, p. 112) of our media communication—for example, in chat rooms. In particular, the mobile phone can be understood as a relevant medium in this regard, as it offers the possibility of a constant personal connectivity. In this sense, it is also appropriated especially by young people, who use the mobile phone and SMS to stay constantly in contact with their peers (cf. Höflich and Rössler 2001).

In all, the different examples have demonstrated (at least this is my hope) that a differentiation of a social, spatial, and temporal dimension of mediatization is helpful, and have illuminated their relation to the cultural changes of individualization, deterritorialization, and coming of intermediacy. Reflecting on this, we open up insight into why, in the present, a *sole* focus on a national-territorial communicative space and a related national culture falls short if we want to understand current media cultures. They are much more complex than such an understanding would indicate, if in a pure form it ever existed. So it seems that the general typification of tendencies of mediatization and cultural change outlined in Figure 1 is a helpful general frame for researching the present interrelation of media and cultural change.

However, at the same time, these arguments appear disaffecting, as one important point in such a general frame remains underexposed, that is, how the 'moulding forces' of the media develop in detail. How does this certain 'pressure of the media' manifest itself? How is it related to which processes of change? If we want to answer questions like these, we have to carry out a further step of concretization, that is, an analysis of the mediatization in specific cultural fields at certain times. We cannot state that the process of mediatization is related to an internal and external pluralisation and fragmentation of culture if at the same time we consider this mediatization as being identical for all different cultural fields.

Using at this point the term 'cultural fields,' my arguments are related to Pierre Bourdieu's (1998) field theory, but not in a direct manner. In a careful discussion of this approach, Nick Couldry (2003) made a number of arguments that rely much more on questions of mediatization than he might have anticipated when formulating them. Discussing Bourdieu's idea that 'journalism' and 'the media' should be considered as one field, Nick Couldry (2003) argues that this approach of Bourdieu falls short, as he does not reflect the special role of this field in relation to others. To do this, it is far more helpful to use another concept of Bourdieu and relate it to the media, that is, the concept of 'meta capital.' Bourdieu has developed this concept to explain the power of the state in relation to other social fields, which is a power related to the circumstance that the state acts directly on the infrastructure of all fields. In the media, Nick Couldry argues, we can discern a comparable 'meta capital,' that is 'a truly dominant concentration of symbolic power ('symbolic power' in the strong sense of a power over the construction of social reality)': 'In highly centralized societies, certain institutions have a specific ability to influence all fields at once' (Couldry 2003, p. 669). In a certain way, here we have an aspect of mediatization in its institutional forms that is a reflection of the media as power-related institutions that put 'pressure' (Couldry 2003, p. 657) on other social fields.

If we transfer these arguments to the thinking about mediatization developed so far, we can argue, on the one hand, that we need a more detailed approach if we want to consider the 'moulding forces' of the media as a general field theory and, on the other hand, that the idea of 'taking a field-specific approach' for the concretization of the social dimension (individualization), spacious dimension (deterritorialization), and temporal dimension (coming of intermediacy) of mediatization is a necessary starting point.

This also calls for a more concrete concept of 'field,' which is why I want to focus on 'cultural context fields' and relate their understanding more to a certain reading of the social constructivism described by Peter L. Berger and Thomas Luckmann (1991, p. 42ff). In their sociology, the concept of institutionalization has a high value. In their perspective, institutionalization takes places if habitualized actions are typecast by types of actors; the result of this are certain institutions, reaching from 'fatherhood' through 'family' to more complex forms like 'school' or 'university.' These forms of institutionalization can be understood as specific, however complex, sets of cultural patterns, marked by multilevel power-relations.

If we do not see these institutions as being isolated but rather as being highly interrelated, we can argue that they articulate certain 'cultural fields.' Therefore, 'cultural fields' in the sense I want to use the term are cultural realms of networked type actions and types of actors, marked by defined power-relations.[5] For example, the field of 'higher education' is not only articulated by the 'university' as an institution but also by 'accreditation agencies,' 'publishing industries,' and so on. My argument at this point is to take a more detailed look at the mediatization of these cultural fields by researching their articulation through various related institutions and power-relations empirically and take a necessary 'radical contextualism' (Ang 1996, p. 66) seriously. If we do this, we begin to get an understanding of how the 'moulding forces' of the media manifest themselves in processes of interrelation with other 'forces'.

CONTEXTUALIZING MEDIATIZATION: TWO EXAMPLES

For such a contextualized approach on mediatisation, I present the following two examples. In the first example, I want to focus on the mediatization of the Catholic World Youth Day, a certain institution that can be understood as characteristic for the change of the 'cultural fields' of different religions. The other example is the mediatization of diasporas, that is, migrant communities on the move. Both examples are based on research published elsewhere; however, here they are systematized in a new way for discussing the matter of researching mediatization in a more general frame.

1. The Mediatization of the Catholic World Youth Day

The Catholic Church's World Youth Day goes back to the year 1985, when it was initiated by Pope Jean Paul II as part of the United Nation's year of youth. Since then, it is celebrated every second or third year, not only as a local event with up to more than 1,000,000 participants, but also as a media event in the hosting country as well as countries with a majority of catholic inhabitants. In these countries, the World Youth Day enables the Catholic Church a media presence it normally has only at Christmas or Easter. Taking the example of 2005, we investigated the mediatization of the Catholic World Youth Day based on various empirical data, in a transcultural comparison of Germany and Italy (cf. Hepp and Krönert 2009). This included interviews with journalists and responsible persons at the Catholic Church; the media coverage in television, newspapers and journals; the 'mediatization *in situ*' (that is, a 'vox-pop' booth in which any visitor to the World Youth Day could speak his or her personal message to radio); and finally twenty-seven interviews we conducted with youth audiences of the media event in Germany and Italy. In a nutshell, our research could demonstrate that the World Youth Day is mediatised, i.e., in its planning, execution, and appropriation, staged as a 'hybrid media event,' integrating moments of 'sacred ceremony,' 'popular pleasure,' and the 'Pope as a symbol' of Catholicism.

These general results can be related to the analytical framework outlined so far. Doing this, we come to the following points:

(a) Individualization. First of all, the conception of the World Youth Day can be related to the individualization of religion (cf. Beck 2008). That means, in the present, religion is increasingly a personal decision for a certain belief, and different religions 'compete' with their orientation offers. The World Youth Day as a media event offers a chance for the Catholic Church to stage its religious offer in a sophisticated way. For this, they developed the format of a 'media church service' that moves patterns into the foreground to secure a staging of the liturgy in a pleasurable way. For this, media experts from television are integrated into the planning of all liturgies and have a 'pole position' during the event itself. However, at the same time, the individualization of religion cannot be monosemized. The example of the 'vox-pop' booth demonstrates that the participating youth use the possibilities they have to communicate the variety of different belief orientations in Catholicism via the media. The same can be said for the internet. We see here a twofold interrelation between mediatization and the institutionalized context field concerning individualization: On the one hand, there is the 'pressure' on the Catholic church to stage itself in a certain media way if it want to position itself as a 'central' belief offer. On the other hand, and in a certain contrast to this, the mass media as well as the internet offer the faithful youth the chance to communicate their variety of individualized faith.

(b) Deterritorialization. For sure, belief communities such as Catholicism have been deterritorial from their beginning, as they define themselves as networks of believers beyond national borders. However, (mass) mediatization offers new ways of staging this community in its deterritoriality. The mediatization first of all makes it necessary to find metaphors for deterritoriality, and again the Catholic Church accepts especially the urge of visual media like television and

press photography for such images and produces (e.g., pictures of the meeting of the Pope with youth dressed in various ethnic clothing). Additionally, the planned integration of youth participants around the world results in pictures of flag-waving youth, again symbolizing the deterritorial character of Catholicism. All this is staged in various communicative spaces of different countries and of various religious groups. Here, mediatization is, on the one hand, again instrumentalized by the Catholic Church as a way of staging its own deterritoriality to the utmost. On the other hand, it means a loss of control over the communication about the 'thickening' (Hepp and Couldry 2009b) of this event in the very different communicative spaces.

(c) Intermediacy. Like any other media event, the World Youth Day is the staging of a wide-ranging intermediacy. More than just the people present at the World Youth Day are integrated in a certain temporally shared experience. Through the (communicative) preparation and postprocessing of the event, as well as the simultaneous staging, the 'deterritorial belief community' of Catholicism (and there especially the youth) is synchronized for a certain moment. *Mediatization* can be understood in this perspective as a simultaneous proximity felt by a group of young Catholics across different countries and addressed on a mediated, Pope-related ceremony at the World Youth Day. Therefore, for the Catholic Church, this also means pressure, that is, the pressure to stage the World Youth Day as a progressing visit of the Pope.

To sum up: We can understand the mediatization of the World Youth Day as an interrelation of 'media moulding-forces' on the Catholic Church to stage itself and its beliefs in a certain way. At the same time, this institution develops a knowledge of 'using' these media possibilities for its own (power) interests, resulting in a 'branding of religion' around the Pope as a kind of 'brand symbol' of Catholicism. However, at the same time, (young) believers accept other forms of mediatization for counter interests. We rather see a mediatization of a struggled cultural field.

2. The Mediatization of Diasporas

The second example I want to present is from our present research on the networking of migrants via various digital media. We are researching this focusing on the Turkish, Russian, and Moroccan diaspora in Germany. In a certain sense, this research can be understood as an investigation of the mediatization of migrant groups. On the quantitative level, it is not surprising to ascertain that digital media are appropriated widely in diasporas. As present research has shown, media in general, and digital media in particular, can be understood as highly important for the processes of articulating diasporic communities, as these media offer the chance for a distinct communicative connectivity that is the foundation of a diasporic articulation across different territories (cf. for digital media, Miller and

Slater 2000; Silverstone and Georgiou 2005; Georgiou 2006; Rydin and Sjöberg 2008). This general estimation is also validated by our own research (cf. Hepp 2008a), while we have to draw clear differences between various diasporic groups. But more interesting is, again, a careful look at the qualitative dimensions of mediatization. As our research is still in progress, we must be careful about formulating general considerations; however, it seems to be possible to typify at least the following points across the different diasporas:

(a) *Individualization.* We also have to understand the diasporas within the 'Western world' in the frame of individualization, inasmuch as we do not have just a process of 'living a certain cultural identity abroad' but, as this process is an ongoing process of articulating a hybrid (i.e., diasporic) cultural identity, a process that can also include a (selective) rediscovery and reimagination of one's own 'origins.' Within this process, television played an important role, as it both offered a communicative link to the 'origin' as well as insight into the live contexts around in the present (cf. Gillespie 1995). With digital media, something new enters that we might call 'individualized networking.' Members of diasporas are 'multinetworked' on an individual basis, that is, a translocal networking within the diaspora group and the country of origin and a more local networking to others (not only migrants) in the place where they live. If we discuss this in the frame of 'media moulding forces,' we can say that, for the young generation, 'individualized integration' means mediated networking both within and across the diaspora.

(b) *Deterritorialization.* By definition, diasporas are deterritorialized, that is, ethnic networks across various territories of different nation states. The Russian diaspora, for example, does not live only in Germany but also in other European countries, and the same can be said for the Turkish and Moroccan ones. Because of this, 'smaller media' (Dayan 1999, p. 22) (letters, family videos, etc.) were always of interest to diasporas as offering the chance to stay in contact within the deterritorial network of diaspora. However, what we now can observe across the different diasporas is a move from the previous 'small media' to digital forms, especially in the case of younger generations. However, if we want to discuss this in the frame of the 'media moulding forces,' it is presently the rather diffuse expectation of being (re)presented digitally as well.

(c) *Intermediacy.* Maybe the most striking point in this cultural context field at the moment is the point of intermediacy. With digital media (and in particular the mobile phone and its 'communicative mobility'), we see the possibility of staying in deep local contact as a migrant family. Many of the persons interviewed by us up to this point indicated (not much different from nonmigrants) that the mobile phone offered the chance of a communicative networking *in situ*, a reassurance in their diasporic community whenever necessary. Again, it is too early to outline here the 'moulding forces' of the (digital) media in detail. However, the interviewed persons talked about a 'pressure' to be connected via the mobile phone.

So maybe we can formulate tentatively, as the research is still in process, that the mediatization of diasporic communities in this context field is related to the intensified communicative connectivity of their members in and across the diaspora while being biographically mobile.

REFLECTING MEDIATIZATION: A DIALECTIC APPROACH

Up to this point, this chapter has been rather a complex argumentation. I started with the position that mediatization theory is right in arguing for a certain 'influence' of the media themselves, but wrong in supposing a general 'media logic.' Doing this, I tried to argue for an understanding of mediatization as an analytical framework that highlights the 'moulding forces' of the media (i.e., the 'pressure' of certain media), but this has to be differentiated when we want to understand the interrelation between media and cultural change. So I have outlined, for the *present change*, a general frame of investigating mediatization especially along three dimensions; that is, the social dimension of individualization, the spatial dimension of deterritorialization, and the temporal dimension of the coming of an intermediacy. In the case of all of these dimensions, we cannot suppose one single general logic of the media, but we have to investigate the concrete interrelation between mediatization and cultural change for certain context fields. While such a contextualized critical analysis is the foundation of an understanding of mediatization (and not general assumptions), this does not mean abandoning the concept of mediatization in total; it offers us a chance to understand media-related changes *across* various context fields while focusing on these fields in their specificity.

In all, I want to argue for a dialectic approach on mediatization: We have to see both the transgressing power of the media across the different context fields as well as across different states and cultures. But at the same time, this does not result in a homology of these fields; rather, it is transformed by the 'inertia' of the institutions within each context field. Only a careful and critical empirical analysis can present such processes in detail. In the best case, mediatization is no more than a concept to link these different detailed studies to a more general analysis of media power within cultural change. But as such, it is highly helpful.

NOTES

1. One can relate this back to the work of David L. Altheide and Robert P. Snow (Altheide and Snow, 1988; Altheide, 2004); see also Kepplinger, 2002, p. 397.

2. In a certain sense, one can say that it is especially the technological aspect of media that is seen as the basis of their 'effect' on culture and society in medium theory.

3. Nick Couldry (2008, p. 379) interprets this quote as a statement against a narrow approach to mediatization, arguing that Thompson 'avoids the term "mediation" because of its broader usage in sociology.' While I share the reflection that Thompson's considerations are addressed against a narrow approach on media effects in processes of cultural change, I understand his use of 'mediazation' in a comparable sense as I use the concept of mediatization, reflecting that the specificity of certain media makes researchable 'moulding forces' in processes of change. In another section of his book, Thompson argues, for example, that there is a 'mediazation of traditions' by certain media: 'Traditions themselves were transformed as the symbolic content of tradition was increasingly inscribed in new media of communication. The mediazation of tradition endowed with a new life: tradition was increasingly freed from the constraints of face-to-face interaction and took on a range of new traits' (Thompson, 1995, p. 180).

4. Of course, these national-territorial communicative spaces had never been totally closed. We can trace processes of media globalization and transcultural communication back to telegraphy and beyond (cf. Mattelart 2003). However, what I want to argue at this point is the overall orientation of media communication to 'national ranges of distribution' and the communicative construction of a 'national centre'—as I have said: a *tendency*.

5. If we relate this use of the term 'cultural field' to Pierre Bourdieu's 'social field,' I argue much more on the level what he calls 'sub-field.' While also, in Bourdieu's thinking, the exact boundaries of fields and sub-fields are more a contingent question for detailed empirical research than a theoretical issue, the risk of his approach is to differentiate social fields on a much too general level to make an appropriate research on processes of mediatization possible.

REFERENCES

Altheide, D. L. (2004). Media logic and political communication. *Political Communication*, 21(3), 293–296.

Altheide, D. L., and Snow, R. P. (1988). Toward a theory of mediation. In J. A. Anderson (Ed.), *Communication Yearbook 11* (pp. 194–223). Newbury Park, CA: Sage.

Anderson, B. (1983). *Imagined Communities: Reflections on the Origins and Spread of Nationalism*. New York: Verso.

Ang, I. (1996). *Living Room Wars: Rethinking Media Audiences for a Postmodern World*. London: Routledge.

Beck, U. (2008). *Der eigene Gott: Von der Friedensfähigkeit und dem Gewaltpotential der Religionen*. Frankfurt a. M., Leipzig: Verlag der Weltreligionen im Insel Verlag.

Beck, U., and Beck-Gernsheim, E. (Eds.) (2001). *Individualization: Institutionalized Individualism and Its Social and Political Consequences*. London: Sage.

Berger, P. L., and Luckmann, T. (1991). *The Social Construction of Reality: A Treatise in the sociology of Knowledge* (Penguin Social Sciences). London: Penguin Books Ltd.

Billig, M. (1995). *Banal Nationalism*. London: Sage.

Bourdieu, P. (1998). *On Television and Journalism*. London: Pluto.

Couldry, N. (2003). Media meta-capital: Extending the range of Bourdieu's field theory. *Theory and Society*, 32(5–6), 653–677.

Couldry, N. (2008). Mediatization or mediation? Alternative understandings of the emergent space of digital storytelling. *New Media & Society*, 10(3), 373–391.

Couldry, N., Hepp, A., and Krotz, F. (Eds.) (2009). *Media Events in a Global Age*. London: Routledge (in press).

Dayan, D. (1999). Media and diasporas. In J. Gripsrud (Ed.), *Television and Common Knowledge* (pp. 18–33). London: Routledge.

García Canclini, N. (1995). *Hybrid Cultures: Strategies for Entering and Leaving Modernity*. Minneapolis: University of Minnesota Press.

Georgiou, M. (2006). *Diaspora, Identity and the Media: Diasporic Transnationalism and Mediated Spatialities*. Cresskill, NJ: Hampton Press.

Gillespie, M. (1995). *Television, Ethnicity and Cultural Change*. London: Routledge.

Gumbrecht, H. U., and Pfeiffer, K. L. (Eds.). (1994). *Materialities of Communication*. Palo Alto, CA: Stanford University Press.

Hall, S. (1997a). The centrality of culture: Notes on the cultural revolutions of our time. In K. Thompson (Ed.), *Media and Cultural Regulation* (pp. 207–238). London: Sage.

Hall, S. (1997b). The Work of Representation. In S. Hall (Ed.), *Representation: Cultural Representations and Signifying Practices* (pp. 13–64). London: Sage.

Hepp, A. (2008a). Communicative mobility after the mobile phone: The appropriation of media technology in diasporic communities. In M. Hartmann, J. R. Höflich, and P. Rössler (Eds.), *After the Mobile Phone? Social Changes and the Development of Mobile Communication* (pp. 131–152). New York: Peter Lang.

Hepp, A. (2008b). Translocal media cultures: Networks of the media and globalisation. In A. Hepp, F. Krotz, S. Moores, and C. Winter (Eds.), *Connectivity, Networks and Flows: Conceptualizing Contemporary Communications* (pp. 33–58). Cresskill, NJ: Hampton Press.

Hepp, A., and Couldry, N. (2009a). What should comparative media research be comparing? Towards a transcultural approach to 'media cultures.' In D. K. Thussu (Ed.), *Internationalizing Media Studies: Impediments and Imperatives* (pp. 42–47). London: Routledge.

Hepp, A., and Couldry, N. (2009b). Media Events in Globalised Media Cultures. In N. Couldry, A. Hepp. F. Krotz (Eds.), *Media Events in a Global Age*. London: Routledge (in press).

Hepp, A., and Krönert, V. (2009). Religious media events: The World Youth Day in Germany. In N. Couldry, A. Hepp, and F. Krotz (Eds.), *Media Events in a Global Age*. London: Routledge (in press).

Hjarvard, S. (2007). *Changing Media, Changing Language. The Mediatization of Society and the Spread of English and Medialects*. Paper presented to the 57th ICA Conference, San Francisco, CA, 23–28 May.

Höflich, J. R., and Rössler, P. (2001). Mobile schriftliche Kommunikation—oder: E-Mail für das Handy. Die Bedeutung elektronischer Kurznachrichten (Short Message Service) am Beispiel jugendlicher Handynutzer. *Medien & Kommunikationswissenschaft*, 49(4), 437–461.

Kepplinger, H. M. (2002). Mediatization of politics. Theory and data. *Journal of Communication*, *2002*, 972–986.

Krotz, F. (1998). Kultur, Kommunikation und die Medien. In U. Saxer (Ed.), *Medien-Kulturkommunikation. Publizistik Sonderheft 2/1998* (pp. 67–85). Opladen: Westdeutscher Verlag.

Krotz, F. (2007). *Mediatisierung: Fallstudien zum Wandel von Kommunikation*. Wiesbaden: Verlag für Sozialwissenschaften.

Krotz, F. (2008). Media connectivity. Concepts, conditions, and consequences. In A. Hepp, F. Krotz, S. Moores, and C. Winter (Eds.), *Network, Connectivity and Flow: Conceptualising Contemporary Communications* (pp. 13–31). New York: Hampton Press.

Kubicek, H. (1997). Das Internet auf dem Weg zum Massenmedium? Ein Versuch, Lehren aus der Geschichte alter und neuer Medien zu ziehen. In R. Werle and C. Lang (Eds.), *Modell Internet?*

Entwicklungsperspektiven neuer Kommunikationsnetze (pp. 213–239). Frankfurt a. M., New York: Campus.

Livingstone, S. (2009). On the mediation of everything. *Journal of Communication*, 59(1), 1–18.

Löfgren, O. (2001). The nation as home or motel? Metaphors of media and belonging. *Sosiologisk Årbok*, 2001(1), 1–34.

Mattelart, A. (2003). *The Information Society: An Introduction*. London: Sage.

Meyrowitz, J. (1995). Medium theory. In D. J. Crowley and D. Mitchell (Eds.), *Communication Theory Today* (pp. 50–77). Cambridge, UK: Polity Press.

Miller, D., and Slater, D. (2000). *The Internet. An Ethnographic Approach*. Oxford, UK: Berg.

Morley, D. (2000). *Home Territories: Media, Mobility and Identity*. London, New York: Routledge.

Ouellette, L., and Hay, J. (2008). Makeover television, governmentality and the good citizen. *Continuum*, 22(4), 471–484.

Rammert, W. (2007). *Technik—Handeln—Wissen. Zu einer pragmatistischen Technik- und Sozialtheorie*. Wiesbaden: Verlag für Sozialwissenschaften.

Rydin, I., and Sjöberg, U. (2008). Internet as a communicative space for identity construction. Among diaspora families in Sweden. In I. Rydin and U. Sjöberg (Eds.), *Mediated Crossroads*. Gothenburg: Nordicom.

Schulz, W. (2004). Reconstructing Mediatization as an Analytical Concept. *European Journal of Communication*, 19(1), 87–101.

Silverstone, R. (1994). *Television and Everyday Life*. London, New York: Routledge.

Silverstone, R., and Georgiou, M. (2005). Editorial introduction: Media and minorities in multicultural Europe. *Journal of Ethnic and Migration Studies*, 31(3), 433–441.

Thomas, T. (2009). 'Lifestyle-TV'—critical attitudes towards 'banal' programming. In S. Van Bauwel and N. Carpentier (Eds.), *Trans-reality Peeping around the Corner: Meta Perspectives on Reality TV* (in press). Lexington, MA: Lexington Books.

Thompson, J. B. (1995). *The Media and Modernity. A Social Theory of the Media*. Cambridge, UK: Cambridge University Press.

Tomlinson, J. (2007). *The Culture of Speed: The Coming of Immediacy*. New Delhi: Sage.

Urry, J. (1999). *Sociology beyond Societies: Mobilities for the Next Century* (International Library of Sociology). London: Routledge.

Urry, J. (2003). *Global Complexity*. Cambridge, UK: Polity Press.

Wessler, H., Peters, B., Brüggemann, M., Kleinen-v. Königslöw, K., and Sifft, S. (2008). *Transnationalization of Public Spheres*. Basingstoke: Palgrave Macmillan.

Williams, R. (1990). *Television: Technology and Cultural Form*. London: Routledge.

CHAPTER EIGHT

Soft Individualism: Media AND THE Changing Social Character

STIG HJARVARD[1]

> The presence of the guiding and approving "others" is a vital element in his whole system of conformity and self-justification. Depriving him of the sociability his character has come to crave will not make him autonomous, but only anomic...If the other-directed man is seeking autonomy, he cannot achieve it alone. He needs friends.
>
> —David Riesman, *The Lonely Crowd*, 1950, p. 327

A recurrent theoretical theme—and key problem—in sociology is how society is possible, that is, how institutions, individuals, and actions connect into a coherent entity. From a bottom-up perspective, the question is how individuals' actions and relations to each other make up the larger social units of society. From a top-down perspective, the question is how the big institutions of society like politics, family, education, and industry (re)produce specific relations between humans and either motivate or force them to act and interpret the world in specific ways that bring the single individual in accordance with the larger society. Max Weber (1904/2001) described how the protestant ethics paved the way for the industrious and self-controlled individual of early capitalism, and Colin Campbell (1987) has demonstrated the importance of romantic sensibility for the spread of consumer culture. With his concept of habitus, Pierre Bourdieu (1998a, 1998c) has tried to transcend the contradiction between the demands of the external and objective social world and the inner and subjective dispositions that guide the action and interpretations of the social actor. Similarly, Anthony Giddens' (1984) structuration theory tries to surpass the traditional dichotomy between macro and micro sociology and explain how social institutions are both reproduced and changed through individual social agents' reflexive use of institutional resources.

In the light of this general sociological theme, the aim of this chapter is to discuss how mediatization processes affect the relationship between the individual and society, with a particular emphasis on how media enable, structure, and change the ways in which individuals acquire normative orientation and enter into social relations with each other. Mediatization may change specific social institutions and phenomena like politics, religion, language, and play in various ways (Strömbäck 2008; Hjarvard 2004a, 2004b, 2008). However, mediatization may also have a more general influence across different social institutions on the ways that social cohesion is reproduced in society at large. At this general level, it will be argued that mediatization stimulates the development of a *soft individualism* that depends on *weak social ties*. The social character proliferating in mediatized and highly modernized societies is characterized neither by a strong, self-dependent individualism nor by strong collectivism in the shape of obedience to powerful organizations or a close-knit family unit. Instead, a paradoxical combination of individualism and sensibility towards the outside world has gained ground. At the same time, strong social ties towards family, school, and workplace experience increased competition from weaker social ties enabled through media network. These developments are at least partly a reflection of the ways in which the formation of the individual's social character—its habitus—has become influenced by extended media networks.

Before entering into the discussion of social character and habitus, let me just briefly specify how I understand the concept of mediatization. Building on the Scandinavian tradition of Asp (1990) and Hernes (1978), mediatization is the process whereby society to an increasing degree is submitted to, or becomes dependent on, the media and their logic. This process is characterized by a duality in that the media have become integrated into the operations of other social institutions (family, work, politics, etc.) while at the same time acquiring the status of a social institution in their own right. Earlier, media were, to a larger degree, in the service of other institutions (like the party press, religious publications, the literary public sphere, etc.) or a cultural institution addressing the society at large and working in the public interest (like public service broadcasting during the period of monopoly). Today, media are increasingly governed by the logic of the media, that is, the institutional and technological modus operandi of the media. This includes the ways in which the media distribute material and symbolic resources (e.g., according to ratings or reading figures) and operate with the help of formal and informal rules (e.g., news criteria). By *media*, we understand technologies that extend the reach of human communication and actions in both time and space. Thus, both older forms of analogue mass media and newer digital and interactive forms of communication are part of the media. Following from this definition, mediatization is not a universal process that characterizes all societies. It is primarily a development that has accelerated in the last years of the twentieth century in modern, highly industrialized, and chiefly Western societies. But through globalization—with which mediatization is heavily intertwined—it spreads to other societies as well.

HABITUS AND SOCIAL CHARACTER

By using the notion of social character and its further developments with the concept of habitus, the aim is furthermore to give the all-pervading discussion of cultural identity a stronger sociological twist. Following newer strands of cultural theory of high or post-modernity, the demise of tradition and rise of self-reflexive subjectivity impels the individual to construct his or her own identity (Beck 1992; Giddens 1991). Under conditions of vast and fast changes due to globalization, urbanization, flexible modes of production, etc., the construction of cultural identity becomes a lifelong process in which the individual may acquire multiple, and to some extent contradictory, identities. There is little doubt that, from the perspective of the individual, the construction of one's own cultural and social identity has become a much more pertinent issue and problem, since identity to a much lesser extent is passed on through traditions or institutions. However, discussions of cultural identity tend to take the individual's subjective experience at face value and correspondingly underestimate the presence of common characteristics of lifestyles within specific social segments of the population. Such discussions may also underestimate the ways in which the cultural and social self-conception of the individual are informed by the cultural and social contexts in which the individual lives. Rethinking the concepts of social character and habitus may provide us with an opportunity to consider the influence of media on cultural and social identity in a way that avoids both the pitfalls of determinism and voluntarism. As such, social character or habitus do not equal social or cultural identity, but they denote the general dispositions by which an individual relates to and interacts with his or her surroundings. Social character and habitus provide a conceptualization of the interface between identity formation and the social and cultural context. Thus, social character and habitus are not meant to replace identity but are concepts that allow us to specify how identity is mediated through social and cultural circumstances, including the media.

The concept of social character has almost disappeared from the vocabulary of modern sociology. However, at an earlier stage, it played an important role in both social theory and empirical analysis. To social psychologist Erich Fromm (1941/1965), who came from the Frankfurt School of critical theory, social character was a key concept. He defined it as *"the essential nucleus of the character structure of most members of a group which has developed as the result of the basic experiences and mode of life common to that group"* (p. 305, emphasis in original). Fromm combined a psychoanalytical understanding of the subject, as influenced by unconscious and biological drives, with a partially Marxist sociology of society's influence on consciousness and behavior. Already, in Sigmund Freud's psychoanalysis, we find a theory of how sexual drives, through suppression and internalization of the norms of parental authority, are channeled into socially acceptable dispositions and actions. Whereas Freud's theory primarily dealt with the psychological aspects of consciousness and subconsciousness, Fromm developed a social psychology in which societal aspects played a more prominent role. Others worked along the same lines, like, for example, Wilhelm Reich (1933/1978), whose study of the mass psychology of fascism also combined psychoanalysis with critical social theory. Another contemporary researcher, Abram Kardiner (1939/1974), was likewise inspired by psychoanalysis and studied the interplay between institutions and "basic personalities" in primitive societies.

Later studies have tried to identify the traits of a national social character. For example, Bellah et al. (1985) have tried to identify the American character and mentality, and Sennett (1998) has given a critical analysis of the ways newer forms of flexible labor may be detrimental to the healthy development of personal character. David Riesman (1950), whose study of the changing American social character we shall return to later, was, contrary to many of his predecessors and contemporaries, not dominated by a psychoanalytical approach. We may describe his work as a combination of social and cultural analysis, as he examined the importance of structural and material developments (population growth, class composition, etc.) by studying the ways these were experienced by individuals and groups. It was the acknowledgment of changing social experiences in the home, the workplace, the city, and the mass media that led him to develop the theory of the other-directed character.

There are several reasons for the disappearance of social character from the agenda of sociology. The cultural "turn" in sociology during the last decades and the rise of social constructivism have put cultural identity on the agenda to the extent that this concept has almost monopolized current thinking of the role of the individual in modern society, including the field of media studies. Thus, the relationship between media, culture, and the individual social agent has become almost synonymous with the interplay between media, culture, and identity. Social character as a concept has, however, not only disappeared because of a recent intellectual trend in sociology or other strands of research, but also because of its internal weaknesses. The notion of social character has had a touch of essentialism by which social character was seen as the innate core of the nation, the authoritarian state, or a primitive society. In this way, the concept lost track of the relational and dynamic aspects between individual and society that it potentially should be able to grasp. In addition, variations and differences were downplayed in the analysis. The early influence from psychoanalysis also contributed to this essentialism, because a few psychoanalytical concepts of sexual and mental dispositions (Oedipus complex, subconscious desires, etc.) came to dominate the perception of how biology, society, and character formation were interconnected. Concurrently with the decline of psychoanalytical theory, the concept of social character lost some of its theoretical underpinnings.

As Meisenhelder (2006) has argued, we may consider Pierre Bourdieu's concept of habitus as the sociological successor to the concept of social character. By habitus, Bourdieu also wants to grasp the fundamental social character of the individual agent's actions and interpretations of his or her position in society. Through habitus, the individual develops a particular lifestyle and set of practices and value orientations that justify the hierarchical position of the individual and make it meaningful. At the same time, habitus informs the individual to think and act appropriately across different social fields. As Bourdieu puts it, "Habitus is this generative and unifying principle which retranslates the intrinsic and relational characteristics of a position into a unitary lifestyle, that is, a unitary set of choices of persons, goods, practices" (p. 8). Lifestyle is built upon a set of classificatory schemata by which the individual makes distinctions within different social fields like politics, food, leisure activities, etc. (Bourdieu 1998a). Habitus does not provide full-fledged interpretations or directions for action in any particular situation. Rather, it consists of a practical, cognitive, and affective as well as bodily disposition that guides interpretation and action.

There is little doubt that Bourdieu's concept of habitus is better equipped to describe the couplings between individual and society than the earlier notion of social character. Habitus allows us to consider how schemata of interpretation and action are intertwined with the structural position of an individual, a particular group, or a social class across a range of social fields. Thus, habitus combines an understanding of social power and class with the specific historical trajectory of a given individual, group, or social class. What is missing in Bourdieu's theoretical framework is a psychological dimension that allows us to understand the interplay between societal development and individual psychology, including emotional and cognitive processes. Furthermore, Bourdieu provides little help concerning the role of modern media in society, including media's influence on habitus and lifestyle formation. His writings on media (Bourdieu 1998b) are unfortunately among his least informed analyzes.

Although Bourdieu's theoretical framework is in many ways more advanced than the concept of social character, I will take my point of departure in Riesman's analysis of the changing social character in the mid-twentieth-century United States. Riesman's general diagnosis of the other-directed social character contains some fruitful insights regarding the role of the media in the construction of habitus. As we shall see, social character in Riesman's analysis points to structural changes at a much more general level than the habitus of specific social classes and groups addresses. Albeit Riesman, in *The Lonely Crowd*, addresses the experiences of the expanding middle class in great detail within a particular historical period, his main argument, nevertheless, concerns the large-scale, indeed epochal, change of character traits in different phases of modernity. And because of the increased mediatization of society, these character traits have proliferated way beyond the specific class and historical period they emerged within. Subsequently, I shall return to the connection between these character traits, habitus, and the media.

FROM GYROSCOPE TO RADAR

Riesman's notion of social character is somewhat similar to Erich Fromm's conception, as he considers social character as the mechanism through which society gets its members to *want* to act in ways they *have* to act as members of society. In continuation of this, he considers social character as a "mode of conformity," that is, the psychological and social dispositions that make an individual or group act in accordance with the demands of a given society and culture. Although this may sound rather deterministic, the argument is not that everybody automatically conforms to the demands of society. As Riesman points out, many people will develop a character that to a lesser degree conforms to societal pressures. But the less the character fits with social context, the larger the psychological and social costs for the individual. Due to this pressure, social character will gradually accommodate the demands of society. But since character is not least formed through childhood and adolescence, the social character of many people will often lag behind the challenges of modern society. Furthermore, Riesman (1969) stresses that conformity is not all there is to social character: "'mode of creativity' is as much a part of it" (p. 6).

Riesman stipulates a typology of three ideal social characters: the traditional, the inner-directed, and the other-directed. The traditional character is governed by shame exercised by the extended family and community in agrarian, traditional society, whereas the inner-directed character is regulated by the feeling of guilt, internalized by the individual through his or her upbringing in industrial, modern society. The other-directed character is not so much regulated by guilt as by a diffuse anxiety for not being recognized and loved by his or her contemporaries. Riesman's argument about the transition from the traditional to the inner-directed character follows along the lines of Max Weber's account of how the spread of a protestant ethics fostered the self-controlled character and work ethos suitable for the early capitalism. Riesman's original contribution lies in his vivid and detailed analysis of the emergence of the other-directed character.

The rapid growth of the consumer society in the mid-twentieth-century United States changed the demands of society on the individual. Expanding consumer opportunities and leisure time created the conditions for a psychology of affluence: the importance of being a hardworking individual was gradually being challenged by the lure of the market to become a good consumer. Whereas the upbringing of the inner-directed character had stressed the need for modesty and good manners, the other-directed character had to enjoy spending money and be able to give grounds for consumer choices. Earlier, work had defined most of the existence, but now life outside the factory and office gained importance. Sociability, dining, sports, and sex not only acquired more time and space but also became topics for discussion and evaluation. In this new cultural environment, the norms of the inner-directed character were of little use, and increasingly the individual had to search in the contemporary world for normative orientation. As Riesman puts it, the tool used by the inner-directed character for social navigation, the *gyroscope*, was gradually replaced by the *radar* of the other-directed character, guiding his or her constant search through the external world for both recognition and normative orientation. The other-directed character is not characterized by a particular lifestyle or norm as such, as these will change over time. The hallmark of the other-directed character is the very disposition to monitor the surroundings through peer groups and media:

> *What is common to all other-directeds is that their contemporaries are the source of direction for the individual—either those known to him or those with whom he is indirectly acquainted, through friends and through mass media. This source is of course "internalized" in the sense that dependence on it for guidance in life is implanted early. The goals towards which the other-directed person strives shift with that guidance: it is only the process of striving itself and the process of paying close attention to the signals from others that remain unaltered throughout life.* (Riesman 1950, p. 22, emphasis in original)

The inner-directed character lived in a class-divided society and often had to uphold his status vis-à-vis persons from other classes (servants, workers, etc.). In contrast, the other-directed character increasingly comes to live surrounded by people of more or less the same social class—the expanding middle class. Concurrently, people are no longer defined solely by class but also by lifestyle. This does not necessarily imply that social divisions become less important, but the competence to read social divisions becomes more sophisticated. As one of many examples, Riesman (1950) suggests that Europeans coming to the United States are likely to think "that salesgirls, society ladies, and movie actresses all dress alike, as compared with the clear status differences of Europe" (p. 74). This is, however, only a superficial similarity. To decode the subtle status differences, the American "must look for small qualitative differences that signify style and status" (p. 74).

In the new urban reality, with millions of people, big offices, and large public institutions, the modern American also has to interact with many more people. Knowledge of fashion, taste, and norms in general become important in this new environment where the boundary between the known and the unknown is no longer as evident as before. Social and organizational skills become imperative if you want to make a career in a modern business, and work acquires, in some sectors, an element of sociability. Quoting Paul Lazarsfeld, Riesman points to a shift in attention from the bank account to the expense account: In a modern organization you should not only work, but also live, feel a sense of community, and be a consumer at meetings, business dinners, and during travel, etc. Work relations get infused with personal relations as the other-directed character puts "into work all the resources of personalization, of glad handling, of which his character is capable, and just because he puts so much energy and effort into work, he reaps the benefit of thinking it important" (Riesman 1950, pp. 310–311).

Many of Riesman's observations are today commonplace, and they have for instance been supported by Joshua Meyrowitz's study (1986) of the rise of a so-called "middle-region" behavioral norm, that is, a performative model, mixing personal and public behavior not least promoted by the media. Inglehart's (1990) study of the spread of post-materialist values in postmodern societies also share similarities with Riesman's argument. When Riesman wrote it, however, he was ahead of his time to such an extent that he was misunderstood. As Riesman himself mentions, his book was received in many quarters as a story of decline, in which the inner-directed hero lost ground to the weak other-directed character, who was way too dependent on the approval and norms of his peer group and the mass media. Such an interpretation does not do justice to Riesman's argument, and the title of the book, *The Lonely Crowd* (which wasn't Riesman's suggestion), bears some of the responsibility for this reception. In general, Riesman is more optimistic than pessimistic about the new social character, just as he is generally positive towards the growth of "new" media like radio, television, recorded music, etc. These foster an increased sociability for the other-directed character, contrary to books and newspapers that drew the inner-directed character away from the group.

Riesman's analysis has its strength in the sweeping overview of cultural change in American society and the cross-disciplinary approach that allows it to discern parallel developments in very different sectors of society. Its strength also points to a weakness. In general, Riesman tries to attribute too many different cultural and social developments to the change in social character. As a consequence, it becomes somewhat unclear how detailed we may be able to specify the new social character. On the one hand, Riesman tends to say that it is basically the urge to monitor the surroundings in order to achieve recognition and normative orientation that makes up the other-directed character (cf. the quotation above). On the other hand, his numerous examples and insightful sense for details suggest a much more elaborate and specified social character. In order to make use of Riesman's character study for our discussion of mediatization, I will choose the narrow definition of the other-directed character. Consequently, the core characteristic of the other-directed character is his or her highly developed sensibility towards an extended network of both persons and media. In other words, we will consider the other-directed disposition as the instrument of character formation rather than the outcome or full-fledged profile of the social character itself.

Riesman's approach has been criticized for not being able to connect the multiplicity of cultural changes reflected by the new social character to more fundamental, macro social phenomena (Meisenhelder 2006). This is correct to the extent that Riesman himself only provides indirect links between social character and macro social explanations like division of labor, urbanization, etc. But this apparent weakness may rightly also be considered the very strength of the argument. Riesman tries to depict how the emerging modern world is experienced in new ways and expands the possibilities for social interaction, and the inner-directed character precisely fails due to the changing modern experience and new modes of interaction. In order to understand the connection between macro and micro social phenomena (i.e., the inner ties between institutions and social actors), we have to consider the structure of both human experience and interactional realms constituted by institutions (including media), since they constitute the connecting node between macro and micro phenomena.

WEAK TIES AND SOCIABILITY

Besides the transformation of social character, Riesman also noticed a change in social relations and forms of interactions. Formerly functional and formal relationships became gradually more personal, and sociability spread to many social spheres as an important mode of interaction. In order to understand these changes in forms of relations and interaction, we shall consider Mark Granovetter's study of weak social ties and Georg Simmel's notion of sociability. In sociology, the distinction between strong and weak social ties is not well defined. In general, the frequency, reciprocity, importance, and duration of interactions between people are considered as indicators of whether the ties between them are strong or weak. Thus, a married couple would usually be an example of people with mutual strong ties, whereas two people standing in a line at a supermarket counter would have very weak or nonexistent social ties to each other. Usually, strong social ties are considered important for the general cohesion of society. But Granovetter (1973) argues that weak social ties are, in some respects, superior to strong social ties, and consequently we can talk about the "strength of weak ties."

Granovetter's original analysis concerned the relationships and flow of information among people looking for a new job. Where you might think that people you are more strongly attached to would provide the best starting point when looking for information, it turned out that weak social ties provided a better flow of information. People with strong social ties to each other may have strong reciprocal commitments but, when it comes to information flow, such relationships tend to circulate already known information. Weak social ties involve less responsibility, but they usually provide the individuals with more and newer information about the world outside—in Granovetter's case, information about available jobs. As regards the spread of information in social networks, Granovetter (1973) concludes, "Whatever is to be diffused can reach a larger number of people, and traverse greater social distance (i.e., path length) when passed through weak ties than strong" (p. 1366).

Granovetter also suggested that social cohesion could benefit from weak social ties. Strong ties within a small group of people may ensure the unity (e.g., in the family or among friends), but weak social ties across such groups are important to keep the larger social unit together. If strong social ties come to dominate, there is a danger of social separation as the information circulating within these groups primarily tends to confirm already existing knowledge and opinions about the external world. This is the problem of the ghetto and the small village community; as strong as they may be internally, they face a gradual decline unless they develop ties to the surrounding society. Social structures consisting only of weak social ties do, of course, also have inherent problems, since both society and the individual need long-lasting and binding commitments. Thus, the question of social cohesion is not a simple choice between strong or weak social ties, but about the overall composition and balance between social relations of different strength and type.

It is exactly this composition and balance between different social relations that the process of mediatization affects. As Schulz (2004) has pointed out, mediatization involves an extension, substitution, amalgamation, and accommodation of face-to-face encounters with mediated encounters. Through these processes, both weak and strong social ties come to be influenced by the affordances of the media. Generally, both mass and interactive media expand the individual's possibilities to monitor the external world and regulate his or her interaction with other persons, real or virtual. Thus, because each individual needs less effort to acquire information about both close and distant surroundings, he or she may not only be able to multiply and intensify distant—and formerly weak—relationships. The information flow within stronger social ties will also intensify and bring these close-knit relationships into much more direct and continuous contact with the external world.

In order to master the growing number of weak social ties, the media support forms of interactions that are suited for such a more casual and less binding relationship. In his historical analysis of broadcasting, Scannell (1996) considers sociability to be one of the key modes of interactions that radio and television promotes. In order to address a mass audience situated at home, radio and subsequent television had to develop forms of communication that suited this particular situation, and sociability proved to be a successful mode of address. Sociability may not, however, be a particular characteristic of broadcast media but a much more general feature of communicative forms promoted by the media (Hjarvard 2005). To a great extent, social network media, like Messenger, Facebook, and LinkedIn, also thrive on sociability as the preferred mode of interaction.

Georg Simmel (1971) accentuates the playful character of sociability, that is, sociability is interaction without any other purpose than the interaction itself. As such, it may be considered a social time-out in which more binding social roles are temporarily suspended. From a utilitarian point of view, it is purposeless, but it nevertheless serves the purpose of making the social company of others enjoyable. We may object to Simmel's interpretation in which he exaggerates the playfulness of sociability. As other modes of interaction, sociability adheres to social norms and expectations that may vary according to culture and social class. Accordingly, there is a world of difference between the sociability of a business dinner, a birthday party in a low-income community, and the rector's annual reception at a university. Joshua Meyrowitz's (1986) diagnosis of the spread of a "middle-region" behavioral norm by electronic media in general and television in particular share many of the same characteristics as Scannell's notion of sociability. Middle-region behavior is, similar to sociability, a balancing act between the private and the public, and between front stage and back stage. With the spread of sociability that balances between the private and the public and at least partially suspends the binding social roles of strong ties, the media both encourage and make possible a continuous monitoring of the wider social environment through weak social ties.

THE MEDIATIZATION OF HABITUS

Three of Riesman's observations concerning the other-directed character seem of special relevance for the construction of habitus in a mediatized society. Firstly, the formation of habitus is to a greater extent shaped through interaction with the *contemporary* society. Secondly, habitus is reproduced through an *intensified monitoring* of an *extended* social environment, and thirdly *recognition* becomes an important regulatory mechanism for development of self-esteem and behavior. Since Riesman wrote about the rise of the other-directed character, the process of mediatization has made interactive media (cell phones, the internet, etc.) much more widespread tools for human interaction in almost all parts of society. At the same time, the media have developed into an important social institution that is governed by its own logic. Consequently, the media intervene in all three of the above-mentioned aspects of habitus formation.

The media produce a continuous representation of our contemporary society that is accessible for everybody in almost all social institutions. Today's political realities, the consumer offers of tomorrow, and the contemporary problems of personal life are all continuously updated and available to the modern individual. The media may also be a source of historical knowledge about the norms and behavior of yesterday, but this will usually be interpreted within a contemporary frame. In a certain sense, humans have of course always lived in their contemporary world, but previously this world was less connected to the wider society. Thus, the possibility of local worlds being out of sync with the development of other parts of society was generally more prevalent in older and less media-saturated society. Concurrent with the proliferation of both mass and interactive media, the individual will increasingly come to live in closer and immediate contact with the wider society. As a consequence, the metabolism between society and individual habitus formation also increases.

The intensified monitoring of an extended social environment is not only stimulated by a concern for general orientation but is also motivated by the increased problematization of all social spheres from politics to sex in high modernity. A growing number of choices and risks makes it imperative for the individual to make decisions. In order to motivate and justify such decisions, knowledge about current norms and trends become important. As Martin Eide and Graham Knight (1999) observe, the media increasingly both problematize and offer solutions to the dispositions of everyday life:

> Far from erasing the troubles and difficulties of everyday life, the growth of knowledge, expertise, and channels of communicating information and help has expanded the scope of problematization, and with it the kind of restless orientation to the lifeworld that modernity ferments. A profusion, and confusion, of new forms and media of help, advice, guidance, and information about the management of self and everyday life continues to develop. (Eide and Knight 1999, p. 526)

Modern journalism is responding to this new social function and has developed new themes and genres to deliver advice to the modern individual about not only politics, but consumer choices, health, child upbringing, etc. As such, the press is not only the fourth estate (i.e., the vigilant watchdog of political power) but also the "fourth service estate" (i.e., the helpful provider of service for the modern individual [Eide 1992]). Through such advice, guidance, and information, the media provide input to the individual's rationalization of his or her norms and practices, that is, the lifestyle of the individual.

It is not only that the individual seeks the media; the media also seek the individual. In a still more commercial media environment, audience maximization has become an important logic of the media, and consequently the media make efforts to comply with the audience's demand for orientation in formats that correspond to the lifestyle of the particular audience in question. The growth of audience and consumer research has greatly increased the knowledge about audiences and their composition in terms of gender, age, income, education, lifestyle, consumer choices, etc. Accordingly, the media will strive to produce content that is in accordance with the lifestyle of attractive segments of the population. Earlier, media were either in service to other institutions addressing a socially defined group according to, for example, political interest (the partisan press), or media were cultural institutions addressing a generalized public promoting a common national culture. Today, the media are less steered by such social interests or common cultural values and are more likely to produce and circulate content in ways that will meet the lifestyle preferences of different segments of the population. Lifestyle magazines, format radio, and cable television are examples of mass media allowing more individualized, lifestyle-based consumption patterns to emerge. But the spread of digital and interactive media has multiplied the ability for media and users to converge around shared lifestyles, that is, practices and representations with a shared value orientation positioned vis-à-vis other media consumption patterns of other groups.

Through segmentation of media products, the media have become more sensitive to differences in audience lifestyles than before. But there are also limits to the extent that media will reflect already existing lifestyles. Whether a given segment of the population will be served by the media—and have its lifestyle represented in magazines, websites, or television programs—depends on the economic attractiveness of the particular segment and other factors such as the size of a particular media market, competitive pressures, generic conventions and trends, etc. Typically, media will try to accommodate several audience segments in one product by putting several lifestyle components into the same product. For instance, the use of focus group research in media organizations often serves to ensure that a new product strikes the right balance between the key target groups of the media in question.

The media are also governed by fashion, that is, a demand for continuous innovation of taste. In order to be read, heard, or seen, not only today but also tomorrow, a media product will have to renew both form and content on a continuous basis. Consequently, it will often be ahead of its audience in terms of lifestyle preferences. The role of guide and advisor for modern individuals also ensures that media content will emphasize the discussion of new developments and trends rather than recycle existing knowledge. However, the intensity and direction of such renewal will, of course, vary according to the particular lifestyle segments that are addressed. Both as a result of market considerations and the requirements of fashion, media not only reflect but also construct lifestyles. As a result, they come to modify the norms and practices that different segments of society are offered as guidance for modern life.

On the whole, we may say that media *socialize taste*, because media products are not only (as all cultural artifacts) positioned within a hierarchical structure of cultural distinctions and cultural capital, they are deliberately developed and tested in order to cultivate specific lifestyle preferences among audiences. As such, they may contribute to a reconfiguration of lifestyle patterns. Media usage patterns will, of course, reflect existing lifestyle differences. But media consumption as a social practice will also inform the renewal of lifestyles and their cultural value vis-à-vis other lifestyles, as media bundle people together in new configurations around cultural objects and practices. For example, during the last decade, lifestyle television concerning interior decorating has very often been dominated by lower-middle-class values. Through these programs, such values are spread to larger parts of the population (Christensen 2008). Contrary to postmodern hypotheses about the disappearing importance of traditional demographic categories (e.g., class, age, gender, and education) as regards social behavior, consumer choice, and media usage (Maffesoli 1996), there is still ample evidence of the relevance of such categories. Also, media usage varies systematically according to, e.g., age, gender, social class, education, and ethnicity (Bennett 2007; Hjarvard 2002b; Roux et al. 2007). However, as also Bourdieu points out, categorical distinctions like class or age may not influence habitus directly but are mediated through the lifestyle of the particular individual and group in question. In a highly modernized society in which institutions and organized interests (parties, unions, churches, etc.) have a less significant position, lifestyle comes to play a more important role as mediator of both cultural and social hierarchies. With media actively linking various networks of audiences around media generated lifestyles, they become part of the reproduction and renewal of cultural and social distinctions in the population.

RECOGNITION THROUGH MEDIA

The media constitute an arena in which the individual may perform, communicate, and act and subsequently acquire recognition. Riesman (1950) did not unfold his notion of recognition, but his basic argument was that the search for recognition plays a more important role for the other-directed character's social integration compared to earlier types of social character. Social theorist Axel Honneth (1996) has developed a distinction between three forms of recognition in modern society that is useful for our discussion. The first type of recognition, *love*, concerns close emotional bonds as between parents and children, husband and wife, and close friendships. From this primary recognition, the individual achieves a fundamental *self-confidence*. The second type of recognition, *respect*, regards the greater society's acknowledgment of the individual's moral accountability, from which follows a set of universal rights as a responsible, legal subject in society. This type of recognition is based on reason and provides the individual with the right to vote, protection against violations from others, etc. From this type of recognition, the individual acquires *self-respect* as an equal person among other fellow citizens. The third type of recognition, *esteem*, is partly emotional, partly rational, but, in contrast to the first two, it is not unconditional. It stems from the recognition by others of the individual's achievements as part of a social group, for example, his or her ability to solve problems in the workplace, be a good neighbor, etc. Through such recognition as a valuable part of cooperative effort and community, the individual achieves *self-esteem*. Each of the three types of recognition belongs primarily to a specific social sphere. Recognition through love takes place in the private sphere, recognition through respect takes place in the public sphere, and recognition through esteem is exercised in the social sphere. Although the first form of recognition may be considered primary, since it is a precondition for humans to develop the ability to enter into mutual relationships with each other, the three forms of recognition are not an order of priority. Obtaining self-confidence, self-respect, and self-esteem are all important for the exercise of individual autonomy. Negatively, Honneth also identifies three types of violations to recognition: violation of the body, the rights, and the ways of life.

Honneth does not himself consider the role of media in relation to processes of recognition. But in view of the mediatization process, the media have come to create a series of new interactional spaces and forms through which recognition may be exercised, and the boundaries among the three forms may become less clear. In a mediatized society, the very representation and visibility of an individual or group may be a valuable recognition, both as a private, public, and social person. Many social network media, such as Facebook, LinkedIn, MySpace, etc., are not only forums for communication and contacts but are also media for recognition of various private, social, and public achievements. As Kaare and Lundby (2008) point out, with the emergence of digital media, new formats for self-representation have become more widespread. Through these self-representations, the individual may authenticate his or her own biographical story and achieve collective recognition of personal identity. Similarly, both fictional and factual mass media products will allow audiences to study the recognition of various individuals, socials groups, and public figures. Newer forms of reality television series are constructed to dramatize the inclusion and expulsion of individuals from a group. Entertainment programs like *Expedition Robinson* and *X Factor* are intense studies in the social play between recognition and violation of the self, both as a private individual, a public figure, and a person belonging to a social group.

As media project sociability as a dominant mode of interaction in many institutional contexts, the media come to influence the ways recognition as love, respect, and esteem are exercised. Because of the partly private, partly public nature of sociability, recognition through the media will often assume a both emotional and rational form. When a private individual or a family presents its profile on the internet and makes friends with others, this private and emotional recognition will also be submitted to a generalized and public notion of what is to be recognized as positive and important personal qualities. When a politician wants to recognize (or violate) a given group's political or social problem (e.g., homeowners' mortgage problems, homosexuals' access to child adoption, etc.), this is not done only through rational deliberation and appropriate legislation. It is usually accompanied by a media performance in which the politician tries to display sympathy and the ability to interact with the type of persons in question (or the very opposite). Thus, rational arguments need emotional performance to prove the authenticity of the public recognition. As regards the third type of recognition, social esteem, we may say that the media have generally expanded the possibilities to obtain such recognition. With increased possibilities to engage in both weaker and stronger social relationships through the media, it not only becomes possible to achieve such recognition through the media, it also requires more work to sustain it.

SOFT INDIVIDUALISM

In the quotation at the very beginning of this chapter, Riesman turns the relationship between individual autonomy and social belonging upside down. The inner-directed character gained his autonomy through a withdrawal or distance from his contemporary world, as he predominantly relied on himself—or, rather, on the normative framework installed in him by parents and other authorities early in life. For the other-directed character, such autonomy is no longer possible, not because he is weaker but because it becomes less helpful to rely on such old normative frameworks. If he tried to do this, he would become not autonomous but merely decoupled from society. Instead, the other-directed character achieves autonomy through the ability to connect to the larger and contemporary social networks. Riesman clearly recognized the media as an important factor in this process, but the mediatization of society has clearly accelerated since Riesman took stock of the mid-twentieth-century United States. As a result, the institutional logic of the media in terms of technology, organization, and aesthetics—in short, the affordances of the media—have come to mold the way people communicate, act, and sustain relationships with each other.

The other-directed character of the present mediatized society is marked by a soft individualism. Modern individuals are increasingly left to produce their own biographies in a society that celebrates everyone's right to be as individual as possible. However, it is a soft form of individualism, since it deviates from earlier forms of individualism in its deep reliance on and sensibility towards the external world. The softness does not imply that the individual is less integrated in society than before. Beck (1992) talks about the institutionalization of the individual biography in order to describe the new forms of dependency between the individual and society when older forms of institutions like class, church, or family become less important to the individual. Accordingly, we may say that the media increasingly provide an important framework in all spheres of society for such an institutionalization of the individual biography. As media become resources for development of lifestyle, moral orientation, and sustaining social relationships, they serve to reproduce and renew the habitus of the individual. Whether we consider this institutionalization of individual biography as negative or positive, as a "mode of conformity," or as a "mode of creativity," is quite another matter. The argument here only points to the integrative function of media. As Riesman noted, the other-directed character needs friends to achieve autonomy. Increasingly, we may add, he also needs the media.

ACKNOWLEDGMENT

1. The author wishes to acknowledge the kind permission of Samfundslitteratur to publish this revised version of chapter six in his book *En verden af medier. Medialiseringen af politik, sprog, religion og leg* [A World of Media. The Mediatization of Politics, Language, Religion, and Play], Copenhagen: Samfundslitteratur, 2008.

REFERENCES

Asp, K. (1990). Medialization, media logic and mediarchy. *Nordicom Review,* 11(2), 47–50.
Bellah, R. N., Madsen, R., Sullivan, W. M., Swidler, A., and Tipton, S. M. (1985). *Habits of the Heart: Individualism and Commitment in American Life.* Berkeley, CA: University of California Press.

Bennett, T., Savage, M., Silva, E., Warde, A., Gayo-Cal, M., and Wright, D. (2006). *Media culture. The Social Organisation of Media Practices in Contemporary Britain.* British Film Institute. Retrieved October 26, 2008, from: http://www.bfi.org.uk/about/pdf/social-org-media-practices.pdf.

Beck, U. (1992). *Risk Society: Towards a New Modernity.* London: Sage.

Bourdieu, P. (1998a). *Distinction: A Social Critique of the Judgement of Taste.* London: Routledge.

Bourdieu, P. (1998b). *On Television.* London: Pluto Press.

Bourdieu, P. (1998c). *Practical Reason: On the Theory of Action.* Cambridge, UK: Polity Press.

Campbell, C. (1987). *The Romantic Ethic and the Spirit of Modern Consumerism.* Oxford, UK: Basil Blackwell.

Christensen, C. L. (2008). Livsstil som tv-underholdning [Lifestyle as TV entertainment]. *MedieKultur,* no. 45, www.mediekultur.dk.

Eide, M. (1992). *Den fjerde servicemakt* [The fourth service estate]. Bergen: Institutt for massekommunikasjon, University of Bergen.

Eide, M., and Knight, G. (1999). Public/private service: Service journalism and the problems of everyday life. *European Journal of Communication,* 14(4), 525–547.

Fromm, E. (1941/1965). *Escape from Freedom.* New York: Avon Books.

Giddens, A. (1984). *The Constitution of Society.* Cambridge, UK: Polity Press.

Giddens, A. (1991). *Modernity and Self-Identity.* Cambridge, UK: Polity Press.

Granovetter, M. (1973). The strength of weak ties. *American Journal of Sociology,* 78(6), 1360–1380.

Hernes, G. (1978). Det mediavridde samfunn [The media-twisted society]. In G. Hernes (Ed.) *Forhandlingsekonomi og blandningsadministrasjon.* Bergen: Universitetsforlaget.

Hjarvard, S. (2002). Seernes reality [The viewers' reality]. *MedieKultur,* 34, 92–109.

Hjarvard, S. (2004a). The globalization of language. How the media contribute to the spread of English and the emergence of medialects. *Nordicom Review,* 1–2, 75–97.

Hjarvard, S. (2004b). From bricks to bytes. The mediatization of a global toy industry. In I. Bondebjerg and P. Golding (Eds.), *European Culture and the Media* (pp. 43–63). Bristol, UK: Intellect Books.

Hjarvard, S. (2005). *Det selskabelige samfund* [A culture of sociability]. Frederiksberg: Samfundslitteratur.

Hjarvard, S. (2008). The mediatization of religion: A theory of the media as agents of religious change. In S. Hjarvard (Ed.), *The Mediatization of Religion: Enchantment, Media and Popular Culture* (pp. 9–26). Northern Lights. Film & Media Studies Yearbook 6. Bristol, UK: Intellect.

Honneth, A. (1996). *The Struggle for Recognition: The Moral Grammar of Social Conflicts.* Cambridge, UK: Polity Press.

Inglehart, R. (1990). *Culture Shift in Advanced Industrial Society.* Princeton, NJ: Princeton University Press.

Kardiner, A. (1939/1974). *The Individual and His Society. The Psychodynamics of Primitive Social Organisation.* Westport, CT: Greenwood Press.

Kaare, B. H., and Lundby, K. (2008). Mediatized lives. Autobiography and assumed authenticity in digital storytelling. In K. Lundby (Ed.), *Digital Storytelling, Mediatized Stories* (pp. 105–122). New York: Peter Lang.

Maffesoli, M. (1996). *The Time of the Tribes.* London: Sage.

Meisenhelder, T. (2006). From character to habitus in sociology. *The Social Science Journal,* 43, 55–66.

Meyrowitz, J. (1986). *No Sense of Place: The Impact of Electronic Media on Social Behavior.* New York: Oxford University Press.

Reich, W. (1933/1978). *The Mass Psychology of Fascism.* London: Penguin.

Riesman, D. (1950). *The Lonely Crowd: A Study of the Changing American Character*. New Haven, CT: Yale University Press.

Riesman, D. (1969). *The Lonely Crowd: A Study of the Changing American Character*, 2nd abridged ed. New Haven, CT: Yale University Press.

Roux, B. L., Rouanet, H., Savage, M., and Warde, A. (2007). *Class and Cultural Division in the UK*. CRESC Working Paper Series, no. 40. Manchester: University of Manchester.

Scannell, P. (1996). *Radio, Television and Modern Life*. Oxford, UK: Blackwell.

Schulz, W. (2004). Reconstructing mediatization as an analytical concept. *European Journal of Communication*, vol. 19(1), 87–101.

Sennett, R. (1998). *The Corrosion of Character: The Personal Consequences of Work in the New Capitalism*. New York: W. W. Norton & Company.

Simmel, G. (1971). Sociability. In G. Simmel (Ed.), *On Individuality and Social Forms*. Chicago: The University of Chicago Press.

Strömbäck, J. (2008). Four phases of mediatization: An analysis of the mediatization of politics. *The International Journal of Press/Politics* 2008, 13, 228–46.

Weber, M. (1904/2001). *The Protestant Ethic and the Spirit of Capitalism*. London: Routledge.

CHAPTER NINE

Dressing Up:
The Mediatization OF
Fashion Online

SYNNE SKJULSTAD[1]

Figure 1: Preparing for the catwalk; a peep behind the scenes. Drawing[2] based on the website of the Italian fashion brand Miu Miu. Here large photographs form the main basis for navigating the website. The navigation is integrated into the textual and informational level of the site.

Source Drawing by Synne Skjulstad

A TEXTUAL VIEW ON MEDIATIZATION[3]

In recent years, the concept of mediatization has been applied to understand the increasing importance of media in a variety of processes of social, cultural, and institutional transformations. My interest in mediatization, however, is concerned with the textual shaping of symbolic and cultural expressions via a variety of semiotic modes online; that is, the shaping and 'fashioning' (Barnard 2004) of the online mediation of fashion within the cultural industries (Lash and Lury 2007; Hesmondhalgh 2007) in advertising and branding on the Web. Couldry suggests that 'mediatization' has as its source '…a notion of replication, the spreading of media forms to spaces of contemporary life that are required to be re-presented through media forms' (2008, p. 376). By way of textual analysis, I examine contemporary, dynamic Web interfaces as culturally framed texts that mediate fashion. I examine how mediatization may be observed as part of textual processes of change in online mediation in actual texts. The mediatization of fashion online, as observed being articulated in these texts, is not primarily marked by replication and remediation (Bolter and Grusin 1999) but also by emergence, variation, movement, shifts, and changes. I approach mediatization as historically anchored (e.g., Gitelman 2006), as facets of fashion have for a long time been closely linked to media. However, as parts of media change, the ways in which fashion is articulated, is mediated, is on the move, and is continuously recut and remarketed, is what I see as central to the mediatization of Web interfaces. The concept of mediatization captures how fashion is spread out and re-presented online and now articulated as multimodal online discourse.

Web advertising is a growing arena for experimentation with different modes of media in online persuasion, especially techniques that are put into play to engage us as consumers (Dallow 2007). More specifically, the term *mediatization* enables us to grasp how what is often referred to as interaction design is articulated textually in an array of Web interfaces for fashion brands. This refers to how Web interfaces become semiotic entities not only at 'surface value' but that signification and semiosis also occur via the navigational systems of websites: a level of websites often not seen as bearing meaning potential.

The websites of fashion companies are the material I use to discuss mediatization in terms of culture, media, and mediation. Here, affective and communicative elements are most important. Style, desire, irony, and allure are at the heart of how fashion is mediated and marketed online. It is not only the attributes of clothes and accessories that are marketed and sold by the companies I focus on; also key is how they 'dress up' online.

In this chapter, I discuss the 'clothing' of fashion sites as a way of further understanding mediatization as a cultural, communicative, and textual construct and, in this case, part of a wider contextualized approach to online adverts in relation to the culture industries. Drawing on Adorno and Horkheimers' critique on the culture industry, Lash and Lury (2007, p. 5) comment on the *global* culture industry: 'If culture industry worked largely through the commodity, global culture industry works through brands.' A season's latest fashions are not only seen in tangible products but also in mediatized articulations of fashion online. Fashion takes the form of brands, and these brands are then marketed and mediatized through persuasive techniques and through a variety of aesthetic ploys so that they are also 'aestheticized' (Welsch 1997). This mediation occurs in magazines, on billboards, and in TV commercials. Increasingly, it also occurs through architecture, interior design, and what Klingmann (2007) refers to as *brandscapes*. At present, such individual means of promoting fashion brands are also often part of wider, integrated, cross-media campaigns and communication (Bechmann Petersen 2007; Dallow 2007). Web advertising often includes elements from different media-specific adverts and mixes these in composite or overarching communication environments (Morrison and Skjulstad, in press).

Taken together, these aspects may be understood from a wider social semiotic view that situates Web advertising and fashion and 'fashions' of Web advertising in a sociocultural perspective on digitally mediated communication. My chapter is part of a wider study into digital advertising and the symbolic, textual, and communicative articulation of persuasive and aesthetic discourses involved in how fashion is marketed and 'mediatized.'[4] Figure 1 marks how both a brand of luxury fashion products and the textual and domain-specific content of its website challenge us to engage in a sociocultural reading of mediatization at a semiotic and symbolic level.

Couldry (2008) differentiates between mediation and mediatization. In the introduction to this volume, Lundy points out that mediatization directs us more directly to the transformative processes that are part of contemporary media and processes of mediation. Mediation and mediatization are undeniably connected but, as I argue, from a communication design perspective, mediatization of fashion online has implications for how fashion in a broader sense is mediated, and now increasingly in digital domains. A communication design view on analysis of Web interfaces places, according to Morrison et al., '...cultural, social, and aesthetic aspects of designing at the centre of digital design where the object of activity is communication' (Morrison et al., in press, p. 27). In contrasting communication design to interaction design, these authors see mediation as central in a communication design research perspective:

> With communication as the focus, however, mediation that is culturally and symbolically framed—and not only interaction—is key to the emergence, exploration, and study of practices of communication design. This is the case for researchers who

analyse text, context, and uses of the digitally designed and mediated. (Morrison et al. [in press], p. 28)

It is within such a framework that I approach mediatization.

Let us revisit the image with which my chapter begins. A hooded mannequin is looking at us. She appears almost doll-like with her flawlessly made up features, porcelain pale skin, and bright red lips. Her head is surrounded by helping hands. They are handling the tools of the trade—curling tongs and hairspray—in the hectic rush of preparation before the Miu Miu fashion show. We are online when we see these images. 'Fashion' is captured not in a glossy magazine fashion photograph but as the main component in the navigational system of a Web interface. Innovation and emergence are central in much of the persuasive online discourse of today's advertising, and new representational techniques come and go online even faster than the seasonal cyclic changes that are central to the fashion industry.

Web interfaces are hard to grasp, both concerning their status as textual objects and how interaction design is articulated as part of such texts. This has to do with relations between 'form' and 'content,' and how structural aspects of Web interfaces such as navigation have 'dressed up' in a complex semiotic outfit. How are we to see navigation as textually manifest in websites? How is form and content in Web interfaces related?

FABRIC OF ANALYSIS

In order to highlight and exemplify how Web navigation is currently being refashioned, I have selected three websites for analysis: the promotional website of the Italian luxury fashion brand Miu Miu, a brand that is part of the Prada Group; the promotional website of the Italian fashion brand Patrizia Pepe; and the Danish Fashion brand Bruuns Bazaar.[5] The websites are rather different in organization and style, but they all share an overall mediatization and aestheticization of the interface, articulated as a navigational system that is inseparable from the 'content' of the sites. As part of being dynamic interfaces, the sites share a variety of kinetic features. However, in the following, I will concentrate on how navigation in these sites have a distinct media form that complicates clear distinctions between 'form' and 'content,' thus accentuating the interface as an integrated site for mediation; one we may see as 'mediatized.'

In the following pages, I place attention on the textual investigations of selected promotional interfaces for fashion brands. I then discuss relations between mediation and mediatization. This is followed by a discussion of Web interfaces and Web navigation as textual sites for mediatization. The relations between media studies and interaction design research are then considered, followed by analysis of the selected interfaces. To close, I take up some implications of a textual view on mediatization.

MEDIATIZATION AND MEDIATION

Relating to my understanding of mediation is a sociocultural view on human meaning-making, or semiosis. Drawing on views from psychology, meaning may be conceived of as being mediated through situated action involving tools and signs (Wertsch 1991; Säljö 2001; Lave and Wenger 1991). In media and communication studies, notions of mediation are discussed within sociological approaches to mediated meaning-making as central to everyday life by, for example, Silverstone (2002). Mediation is also discussed by Bolter and Grusin as remediation (1999). In discussing mediatization and mediation in digital storytelling, a very broad definition of mediation is suggested by Couldry (2008, p. 379) as '...the overall effect of media institutions existing in contemporary societies, the overall difference that media make by being there in our social world.' To more fully understand such processes of meaning-making, there is a need to scrutinize the role of the text in mediation (Fornäs 2000). According to Fornäs:

> Culture is symbolic communication of meaning, with a capacity to bridge or mediate between human beings situated in multidimensional social contexts. This mediation necessarily goes through sensual-textual embodiments of meaning in flows or webs of works, created by signifying practices and appropriated by acts of interpretation, in everyday lifeworlds or in specialised spheres of science and art. (Fornäs 2000, p. 55)

Brought into such a discussion on mediation, the concept of mediatization, importantly, allows us to see interfaces not as only referring to technologies but to textual, cultural, and symbolic mediated expressions in a way that links system and surface in Web interfaces communicatively. The textual embodiments, in this case mediatized Web interfaces, mediate, according to Fornäs (2000), as cultural tools of communication.

Couldry (2008, p. 377) takes up cultural and representational aspects of mediatization: 'Mediatization describes the transformation of many disparate social and cultural processes into forms or formats suitable for media representation.' It is at this level that I approach mediatization within, however, a humanistic framing that draws on social semiotics and that has communication as its main focus. In drawing on social semiotics, I include the term *multimodality* (Kress and van Leeuwen 2001) into my analysis. I do this to highlight the textual complexity and multiple semiotic resources that, in concert, are woven into the fabric of Web interfaces in the online mediation of fashion brands.

Analysis of mediatization at a textual level, anchored in actual texts, enables us to gain a fuller understanding of emerging media-rich and moving interfaces where fashion is also mediated in the navigational system of Web interfaces. Fashion and media have been connected closely for decades. Fashion photography, fashion magazines, and the glam, glitter, and buzz of fashion have deep connections to the media (e.g., Gibbons 2005; Craik 1993; Bright 2005). Music and fashion are widely connected analytically (e.g., Hebdige 1979; McLaughlin 2000), and fashion has, to a high degree, been related to film (e.g., Gaines 2000) and to architecture (e.g., Wigley 1995). However, linkages between fashion, interaction design, and Web interfaces are much less discussed. In online fashion sites, such as Miu Miu, the semiotically charged representation of navigation shows how mediatization of fashion is central to how one may interact with Web interfaces. Web navigation is part of the textual, the communicative, and the semiotically 'dressed up' level of Web interfaces.

MEDIATIZATION AND MULTIMODAL DISCOURSE IN MOVING INTERFACES

There is a need for better linkages between media and communication studies and interaction design research, as these research areas tend to overlap in the digital 'mediascapes' we inhabit. As part of the digitization of media, we find interactive qualities embedded in an array of digital media expressions with which we may interact. Semiotic articulations of interaction design impact on semiosis. This calls for a heightened attention to interaction design as a domain of practice and research that also has to do with communication and semiotics.

The central term taken up in this volume—*mediatization*—provides an important link between processes of the semiotic transformations inherent in media change and micro-level textual analysis of selected multimodal Web interfaces. In particular, Web interfaces as part of online advertising and brand building within the domain of fashion show particularly clearly that interaction design can be articulated multimodally and 'fashionably.'

Writing on brands, institutions, and fashion, Power and Hauge understand brands as:

> The result of a branding process whereby one attempts to charge a product (or a set of products) with ethereal qualities: qualities that primarily function as marketing arguments. A brand's value is thus in the way people end up thinking and feeling about it and the product it is linked with. (Power and Hauge 2008, p. 124)

Processes of mediatization are largely discussed at a macro level in the research discourse on branding (Moor 2003; Arvidsson 2005). How attempts to charge a product with meaning is articulated textually in Web interfaces are seldom given much attention, and few authors carry out textual analysis for discussing these phenomena at a textual level. Relocating the concept of mediatization from wider sociocultural processes that involve media to interaction design as textually manifested in websites, may aid us in explaining how visualized multimodal navigation, as embodied in a variety of Web interfaces, may be seen as a central textual feature in Web communication. Furthermore, it may allow us to see interaction design as a matter of communication and as deeply embedded in branding and advertising online.

Most of the websites of fashion brands are part of an aestheticized advertising discourse where articulations of artful design are at the heart of persuasion. On the Web, fashion is not only seen in the products advertised but also in the way the websites designed for this purpose are composed, or 'fashioned,' as textual expressions. This does not only include colours, images, and alphanumeric text, but also the activities offered to users that are most often experienced through the navigational system of a website. Fashion is therefore not only something we see as instantiated in photographs of embellished snakeskin handbags and pencil skirts, but composed as a means for capturing the visitors' attention and imagination when they traverse a website.

INTERFACES MEDIATIZED

The term 'interface' is not often linked to discussions of mediatization. It is rooted in computer science and has historically been related to both hardware and, at a later point, software. Johndan Johnson-Eilola (2005) reminds us about the changing nature of computing by way of looking at our understanding of interfaces. An interface was initially a set of physical structures that enabled the operators to compute through hard wiring. However, with the onset of the graphical user interface (GUI), the interface has gone through mediatization processes, and wires, plugs, and punch cards have been replaced by seductive images and intricate motion graphics and animation.

Macintosh introduced the GUI to personal computers in the early 1980s (Manovich 2001). Sherry Turkle (1995) describes this shift from command-line interfaces to graphical ones vividly. In her view, the GUI of the Macintosh demarcated a transition from a modernist culture of calculation to a culture of simulation. This refers to how computers were now seen as media that could provide social and cultural experiences. These experiences, according to Brenda Laurel (1993), could be orchestrated by way of approaching interface design through the metaphor of the theatre. As in theatre, all you get is what you see on the stage—in her words, 'The representation is all that is there' (1995, p. 17). In the mediatization of fashion in Web interfaces, the metaphor of the theatre may easily be swapped to that of the catwalk. For example, in the interface of the website of Miu Miu, a fashion show is presented in a series of layered and overlapping photographs. The image below (Figure 2) is based on a screen grab from Miu Miu's website, and it shows how a photograph forms the central component of one selected route through a multilayered and multimodal Web interface. One of the first images we see is a group of press workers filming and photographing on site. However, in a reflexive twist, not a single mannequin or fashion product is visible in the image. The media is represented in Miu Miu's online brand-building to such a degree that they appear as key actors in the spectacle in the online mediation of this brand.

Discussing digital computers, Laurel reflects on the problems of providing a formal definition of an interface that is not only about humans and computers but also takes into account the semiotic level of interfaces: 'The working definition has settled down to a relatively simple one—how humans and computers interact—but it avoids the central issue of what this means in terms of reality and representation' (1995, p. 14). Mediatization is a key term in discussing issues of representation, and the interface above is a media-saturated one in more than one sense.

Figure 2: Drawing based on a screen grab from the website of Miu Miu. The press is presented as main actors. Ironically, not a single mannequin or fashion product is visible in the image, literally bringing the media itself into the interface.

Source Drawing by Synne Skjulstad

In 2001, bridging the humanities and computer science, Lev Manovich discussed the interface as a new media form, central to digital media. With the onset of digital media in the 1990s, as the Web gained momentum and popularity, computers became, according to Manovich, a filter through which all kinds of cultural and artistic production were mediated (2001, p. 64). How this interface is composed textually—as on stage (as suggested by Laurel) is not his main focus. Software is, of course, central to new media in general, but while, for our understanding of interfaces as semiotic constructs, software studies explain underlying qualities of new media, they do not help us to explain or describe how we may see software as mediatized, as multimodal, alluring, and persuasive texts.

DYNAMIC INTERFACES

The World Wide Web is a relatively young medium, and much has happened in the way Web interfaces look and behave since its popular inception in the 1990s. Many of these changes are linked to how navigation is articulated in actual interfaces.

The websites discussed in this chapter share various kinetic features central to the dynamic interfaces often seen in branding sites. Such dynamic interfaces may be said to have the following characteristics (Skjulstad and Morrison 2005, p. 430): They embody kinetic elements independent of a user's actions; they combine a variety of dynamic media; they often occur in the form of one coherent and transversable textual environment where multiple components of the interface are simultaneously visible; in dynamic interfaces, we tend to find dynamic transitions between components of the interface as well as delivery of dynamic data from the system to the interface.

The Web interfaces of Miu Miu, Bruuns Bazaar, and Patrizia Pepe complicate clear distinctions between what we may think of as 'content' and what as 'form,' as these loose categories are increasingly communicatively entwined. They also complicate prevailing distinctions between what we tend to refer to as *interfaces* and what we tend to refer to as *media texts*. The concept of mediatization links navigation to interfaces textually. Navigation has taken on media form to such an extent that the navigation is indistinguishable from what one might refer to as the 'content' of the site. Writing on interaction design, Kolko (2007, p. 78) argues that interaction designers '...are required to balance issues of form with issues of time: interaction occurs in the fourth dimension, and simply tending to aesthetics does not take into account the unfolding experience that a user has with a product.' Navigation in Web interfaces may thus be seen as media expressions where content and form merge into what Löwgren and Stolterman (2004) refer to as a 'dynamic gestalt.' In dynamic gestalts, the sum is more than its parts, and they emerge through time, in use. Drawing on Fornäs (2000) as part of a socio-cultural view on communication design, how the text is articulated, and how it unfolds through time in use, impacts on the communicative experiences of Web users.

AN ENSEMBLE OF MEDIATING RESOURCES

Semiotics is the study of signs, processes of signification, and how this is central to communication. It is a broad research approach to the study of texts and meanings in various situational contexts of culturally meaningful activity. It is at the level of texts and semiosis I approach dynamic multimodal Web Interfaces.

Dynamic websites are often multimodally composed, and this is the case also with navigation. My understanding of the term multimodality is drawn from social semiotics as it is advanced by Gunther Kress and Theo van Leeuwen as part of their theory of communication (2001). They define multimodality as '…the use of several semiotic modes in the design of a semiotic product or event, together with the particular way in which these modes are combined…' (Kress and van Leeuwen 2001, p. 20). Thus, multimodal and dynamic fashion websites are multimodal and multilinear texts that are composed via a medley of semiotic resources that unfold through socially situated use.

A variety of semiotic modes are applied to both produce communicative artefacts and events, as well as for their interpretation. Drawing on Kress and van Leeuwen (2001), communication occurs through articulation and interpretation. Articulation refers to the ways something is being said via digital technology, in this case how a Web interface is composed by way of a range of significations. Interpretation involves how what is articulated is read as part of semiosis.

MEDIA AND INTERACTION DESIGN RESEARCH

The inclusion of the term 'mediatization' into discussions of the semiotic aspects of Web interfaces impacts on our wider understanding of the relationship between the domain of interaction design and media and communication studies—a close but not yet formalized relationship that needs to debated more fully. This is so because the mediatized interaction design central to many fashion sites are articulated through a variety of different semiotic modes such as images, sound, graphics, and animation. As assemblies of semiotic resources, navigation has come to bear meaning and not solely potential for interaction in the strict sense of accessing various parts of a site. However, the textual articulation of interaction design in Web mediation is seldom scrutinized through close textual analysis (Skjulstad 2007b, in press), and the latest 'fashions' of Web design tend to be presented in glossy coffee table books and 'how to' manuals for design practitioners, without accompanying analysis.

REORIENTING INTERACTION DESIGN TOWARDS COMMUNICATION

As part of the wider digitalization of our mediascape, the domain of interaction design is becoming highly relevant for media and communications scholars as digital interfaces are designed for being interacted with. Historically, interaction design has been much more closely linked to computer science, human-computer interaction (HCI), and other domains of design practice and research, than to media and communication studies. Originating in computer science, the term 'interaction design' has been widely applied in the study of HCI. From such a perspective, Preece et al. state, 'By interaction design, we mean *designing interactive products to support people in their everyday and working life*' (2002, p. 6, emphasis in original). However, interaction design is concerned not only with supporting work but is also central for the cultural, symbolic, and textual level of interfaces spanning from the culture industries and art (e.g., Bolter and Gromala 2003) to the branding of fashion online.

From a HCI perspective, Jonas Löwgren and Erik Stolterman (2004) point to interaction design research as primarily relating to academic domains that are concerned with information technology. They do not, however, point to how interaction design is 'mediatized' and relevant also for media and communication studies. Zimmerman et al. (2007, p. 493) point to how the HCI community has struggled to take on board design-related matters as more than '…surface structure or decoration.' I have in another publication pointed to this view on design in HCI as the 'icing of cakes' (Skjulstad 2007a). By icing of cakes, I particularly refer to views that place the communicational potential not in the interwoven fabric of all the multimodal facets of websites, but that separates the semiotic, the expressive, and meaning-laden layers from overall interface design as a merely decorative element without much significance for communication (e.g., Garrett 2003).

Interaction design has been referred to as relating to matters of communication by, among others, Gillian Crampton Smith (2007). She, importantly, gives attention to the communication potentials in the outputs from interaction designers, thus implicitly pointing to digital artefacts as media texts. Interaction design and interface design have been recognized as central to electronic art and as fields of innovation that may inform domains of digital design outside of the art field (Bolter and

Gromala 2003). Morrison and Skjulstad (in press) have analysed the textual level of cross-media interaction design in the branding and advertising of a mobile phone by a leading phone company. However, interaction design has not been much included in research on branding and advertising. *Mediatization* is a key term in linking the multimodal articulation of navigation in Web interfaces to such discourses online. Persuasion is not only in the 'content' of Web interfaces but also embedded in the website as a whole, as a dynamic *gestalt*. This is important—as in the mediation of fashion, Web interfaces are communicative, expressive, and seducing. They are technology based but not perceived primarily as such. There is hence a need to see how Web interfaces act as sites for multimodal and dynamic mediation.

NAVIGATION MEDIATIZED

The websites selected for the following analysis all exemplify ways in which online advertising and brand-building has found its way to Web interface design. Wolfgang Welsch (1997) points to a tendency in contemporary culture to make aesthetic what is not, using processes he refers to as aestheticization. Drawing on Welsch, the scope of aesthetic practice now transcends the domain of art and extends the realm of aesthetics to also include advertising, the internet, architecture, and economy. In such an expanded view of aesthetics, art, and design are now integral to contemporary advertising and branding (Gibbons 2005). In an array of contemporary forms of advertising and branding, aesthetic value is transferred from the outcomes of art and design practice, giving a sense of allure and style to the products being branded (Skjulstad 2007c). Advertising and branding texts now play a seminal role in contemporary culture, partly because of mediatization processes, where objects take on media form. For example, Hjarvard (2004) studied how the toy manufacturer Lego mediatized its product in developing a computer game. The brand expanded its range of products by transforming 'bricks to bytes' in also giving toys media form. However, as part of the mediatization of the fashion industry on the Web, fashion products are now being crafted in materials other than silk and brocade, by way of digital fashion photographs, animations, and videos.

Within media studies, advertising has been discussed as social communication (Leiss et al. 1990) and as persuasive semiosis at the textual and ideological level (e.g., Williamson 1978). However, mediatization processes may be observed within a variety of mediated persuasive texts in digital domains (e.g., Hjarvard 2004; Lash and Lury 2007; Dallow 2007). In his study of the culture industries, Hesmondhalgh (2007) points to how we may see cultural artefacts as texts in a very broad sense. He (2002, p. 12) places texts at the core of the cultural industries: '...they deal with the industrial production and circulation of texts.'

Importantly, neither Hjarvard (2004) nor Hesmondhalgh (2007) carries out close analysis of actual media texts. Less apparent in the research on advertising and branding is attention to persuasive texts where creativity and artistic skill is at the core of mediation. In the selected sites to which I now turn my attention, aestheticized and mediatized navigation is key.

MIU MIU

After many years of a rather bleak Web presence, the fashion brand Miu Miu has recently launched a new website. The website has a vertically organized menu on the left of the screen. When selecting the menu labelled 'the story,' we enter a subsection of the site (Figure 3). In this section, a horizontal row of fashion photographs are arranged against a black background. The images overlap slightly and have different proportions. By selecting an image, by dragging the mouse over

Figure 3: Drawing based on a screen grab of the promotional website of the Italian fashion brand Miu Miu. The lower part of screen shows a section of dynamic text. The overlapping and horizontally organized images serve as the main navigational means.

Source Drawing by Synne Skjulstad

it without clicking, the image and the ones near by it are scaled to larger versions. By clicking on one of them, the image is enlarged and almost fills the screen, as seen in Figure 4. The dynamic menu is the main component in the interface. Such a multimodal representational technique for the navigational system within this section of the site creates a spectacle of colour, textures, and shapes, and juxtaposes a series of fashion images in a dynamic and multilinear montage.

Fashion photography has a complex relationship to the art field and that of the popular culture and the culture industries (Gibbons 2005). In writing on the relationship between art photography and magazines, Bright (2005, p. 134), takes these mediational contexts into account. 'The magazine is not fashion photography's only currency—there are also music videos, lookbooks, catalogues, advertising and catwalk photography. Context is everything with a fashion photograph.' However, Bright does not mention the Web. Fashion photography is now occurring in online domains, as demonstrated by the selected websites. The mediatization of Web interfaces in the mediation of fashion also shows the

Figure 4: Drawing based on a screen grab of the website of Miu Miu. When an image has been selected in the menu, it is not placed as a pop-up image, external to the sites' main interface, but as overlaying the navigational menu and the other elements in the site.

Source Drawing by Synne Skjulstad

need to revisit the fashion photograph closely and examine its new existence online.

The layering (Skjulstad 2007b, in press) of photographs in the interface shows a representational technique often found in dynamic interfaces. By layering elements on top of each other as a navigational and representational feature, screen space is extended drastically. When navigating the images, the screen changes, but these changes are occurring *inside* a defined screen space that is held more or less constant, as opposed to the abruptness of 'jumping' between pages. When selected and enlarged, the photographs overlays the sliding bottom text, as seen in Figure 4.

If looking at the Miu Miu site from a communication design point of view, we do not see websites as code but as complex and rich textual environments. What we encounter is a coherent, multilayered, and multimodal text that moves and may be moved by a user encountering a selection of fashion photographs, which now are digitally mediated and fully integrated into the Web interface. In this section of the site, we do not predominantly encounter a navigational system, but a mediatized online mediation of the brand.

BRUUNS BAZAAR

The Danish fashion brand Bruuns Bazaar presents its novel collections for men and women in a rather detailed way by providing a navigational system that both enables overview and close detail without 'leaving' the dynamic interface, and without breaking the illusion of a coherent screen environment. This is closely related to the integration between the navigation system and its relation to the sharp images of the clothing on models on the catwalk.

The website of Bruuns Bazaar has a horizontal navigational bar located in the top part of the screen. This bar is filled with thumbnails of fashion models wearing clothes from Bruuns Bazaar as they appear on the catwalk during a fashion show. As a user clicks on the images, a prolongation of the sliding navigational thumbnail bar is continued into the screen from right. The length of the navigation bar is thus giving an illusion of exceeding the screen space.

When clicking on a thumbnail's upper, middle, or lower part, a larger version of the selected part of the image fills the screen space. In Figure 5, the upper part of the thumbnail is selected, and a cropped version of the image is shown filling the screen space almost completely. When selecting the middle part of the thumbnail, a detailed view of the middle part (between waist and knee) of the model is shown (Figure 6). When clicking on the lower part of the thumbnail, the models' legs are shown in detail (Figure 7). The full range of media 'content' is

Figure 5: The thumbnails in the upper part of the screen are navigable within image.
Source http://www.bruunsbazaar.com/

on display, and the navigation in this website is presented as an integrated part of Bruuns Bazaar's online 'show.'

In discussing what they refer to as the role of the artist-designer within software, Crampton Smith and Tabor (1996) disagree with the commonly held assumption that content is somehow separate from form: 'Content cannot be perceived without form, and the form of a message affects the content' (1996, p. 43). The semiotic and kinetic qualities in the Bruuns Bazaar site do not only lie in the so-called content but also in the overall composition of the interface as a mediatized space. Here the metaphor of the catwalk is embedded in the navigational menu, where we may study the dressed-up mannequins and their stylish outfits closely. The Bruuns Bazaar site transcends or disrupts notions of Web interfaces as containers into which we may pour 'content.' Writing on digital media, Gunnar Liestøl (2006) sees 'content' as a word empty of content. I find the Bruuns Bazaar site to be demonstrating that such a distinction is unfruitful in textual analysis of multimodal websites. The navigation in the site is as much part of the 'content' as its 'form.'

Through being mediatized, navigation may be seen as a fully integrated part of Web expression at a textual level. As suggested by Manovich (2001) as well as by Gitelman (2006), form and content merge and cannot be seen separately. In a

Figure 6: The thumbnails in the upper part of the screen are navigable within image.

Source http://www.bruunsbazaar.com/

Figure 7: The thumbnails in the upper part of the screen are navigable within image.

Source http://www.bruunsbazaar.com/

view of websites that focuses on communication, interaction design is integral to the shaping of textual expression online.

As Janet Murray (1997) described navigation as having the potential of generating pleasure through the agency offered by the possibilities for moving through intricate textual environments, I see navigation as having taken on media form in dynamic interfaces by application of animation in marking transitions between parts of sites. Pleasure is now not only located in the agency aspect of navigation but in the experientially rich and exuberant navigation offered as a cultural and textual experience. Navigation may be visualized in several ways other than the link convention of underlined words, as once suggested by Jacob Nielsen (2000) in Web usability. Multimodal navigation thus refers to how a variety of communicational resources, such as sound or animation, now might be applied to generate mediatized dynamic transitions between sections of a site, revealing that an important feature in interaction is integrated with the textual level of a site (Skjulstad 2007b).

Bolter and Gromala (2003, p. 11) write on interfaces in electronic art from a media and communication perspective: 'And digital art is all interface, defined entirely by the experience of its viewing or use. That is why digital art can provide such a clear test of the possibilities and constraints of digital design: it fails or succeeds unequivocally on the strength of its interface.' In contemporary multimodal websites such as Miu Miu and Bruuns Bazaar, the interrelation between interfaces and content is so dense that the two are hard to distinguish from one another. Manovich (2001, p. 67) sees this as applying only to electronic art, and asserts that it distinguishes art from design.

However, the concept of multimodal navigation helps to demonstrate that this merger is even more far reaching. In looking at the selected sites, we see navigation as mediatized in displaying the products thess brands offer. As content and interface blend, they morph into complex texts where the interface is mediatized and intertwined with the 'content' in its structuring and textual articulation. Although these mergers are more striking in experimental and 'art' sites, I see many of the same mechanisms fully present within the domain of advertising and branding of fashion as part of the global culture industries. The Miu Miu site is but one example of this, as the sites that shares such features are numerous.

PATRIZIA PEPE

In the website of Patrizia Pepe, a Firenze-based fashion brand, the main navigational menu overlays a grainy and digitally manipulated full-screen video that shows mannequins on the catwalk in a Patrizia Pepe fashion show; choices for further navigation are presented in the form of a three-structure map of the site

Figure 8: Drawing based on a screen grab from the promotional website of the Florence-based fashion brand Patrizia Pepe. Here, the navigational structure is placed on top of full-screen video, showing the navigational options available for a user. The representation of the various sections and choices available for a user is graphically integrated in the main representational interface.

Source Drawing by Synne Skjulstad

and the navigational menu is part of the same screen space of the videos that are central in mediating the products on offer.

The Web interface of the Patrizia Pepe site is shaped as a dynamic single screen environment where there are no abrupt 'jumps' between various interlinked 'pages' (Skjulstad and Morrison 2005). The departure from an underlying 'page metaphor' central to dynamic interfaces tends to be seen in multimodal and dynamic textual environments where transitions between sections of the site are characterized by what Morrison and Eikenes (2008) have referred to as 'transformative motion.' In the concept of transformative motion lies how changes in size, colour, position, and shape over time, central to animation and motion graphics where something changes from one thing to something different, is key in understanding dynamic interfaces.

The grainy quality of the full-screen video in the Patrizia Pepe site connotes a sense of mediatedness, a media aesthetic that works against a sense of direct access to the Patrizia Pepe show as it unfolds. In terms of their theory of remediation, Bolter and Grusin (1999) point to such a representational technique as hypermediacy, the opposite to providing a sense of a direct and immediate, and unmediated mediation. The video in the interface of the Patrizia Pepe site echoes the rasterised quality of a newspaper print, reproducing a sense of media presence.

CONCLUDING REMARKS

The concept of mediatization is a rich one in studying how fashion has a strong multimodal semiotic presence in Web interfaces. In the mediation of fashion online, mediatization brings style, desire, and the extravagant into interface design. As suggested by Ramamurthy (2004, p. 229), 'Within fashion, the ordinary is made to appear extraordinary, and vice versa.' Web navigation in fashion sites has sported stilettos and lipstick, bringing attention to the interface as a reflective and mediational surface (Bolter and Gromala 2003; Bolter and Grusin 1999). However, on such a surface, what you see is not yourself but stylish mannequins, scenes of catwalks, exuberant fabrics, and curling tongs. 'Dressing up,' then, also refers to the mediatized fabric of fashion interfaces. Where a link marker once was a stern underlined blue word (e.g., Nielsen 2000), the representation of links now offer entire colour themes, couture details, and backstage views from fashion shows. Context and content have slipped into the link-node structure of hypertextual mark-up practices. The very materiality of the products advertised is carried over to interfaces by way of large, crisp photographs, animations, and videos. How the Web interface is articulated multimodally has a strong significance for how the brand is mediated on the Web. The 'materials' used in designing navigational menus carry with them significance, just as does the choices of deer leather in Prada bags and black shiny patent leather in a stilettoed shoe.

Textual outcomes of interaction design has not often been analysed in terms of how it may be seen as textually manifest in websites that communicate multimodally. A rather broad understanding of the concept of mediatization may, however, allow us to discuss how the outcomes of interaction design practice can be seen as articulated in multimodal Web interfaces. Interaction design becomes 'mediatized' in Web expression at a textual level. A site's functionality can thus be seen as tightly integrated into its textual character. How the site looks and behaves across links and sections is just as much part of communication as are the texts and images that also constitute the site. In my view, these elements *are* the interface as they unfold multilinearily through use.

Barthes (1977) importantly relocated meaning from the possible intentions of the author to the reader through her or his active involvement with a text. This opens up a plurality of textual meaning that lies in the space between text and the reader's interpretation, situating semiosis *in* and *through* the mediatized interface. In other words, interfaces become multimodal and dynamic sites for socially and culturally situated communication.

In my view, there is no such thing as *the* interface. Instead I see multiple and emerging ones—interfaces that all are communicating differently to different people in a variety of contexts, even within the seducing domain of fashion. The interface of each individual website carries a variety for potential meanings, meanings that may occur through processes of individual actions, but in common spaces. My approach is to view webtexts as examples of media in transition, in which rich and dynamic multi-mediation occurs. Mediatization at a cultural and symbolic and textual level is central to this. Closer attention is needed to the interdisciplinary linkages of media studies and interaction design, domains that meet in multimodal contemporary interfaces in a variety of 'fashions.' Together, these connections allow us to see the overall integrated textual aspects of websites in its full spectrum, as 'dressed up.'

LIST OF SELECTED WEBSITES

http://www.miumiu.com
http://www.bruunsbazaar.com
http://www.patriziapepe.com

ACKNOWLEDGMENTS AND NOTES

1. My thanks to Andrew Morrison and Jon Olav Eikenes for insightful comments and suggestions, without which this text would be a lesser one.
2. While working on this chapter, I originally applied screengrabs from Miu Miu and Patrizia Pepe's website in my chapter. After having written the chapter, I learned that these companies only have the rights for the images applied in their websites for a period of six months. This caused problems for reprinting the selected screengrabs in this volume because Miu Miu and Patrizia Pepe no longer had the copyright of the material. My thanks to Sandra Paoli at Patrizia Pepe for explaining to me the underlying reasons for their strict copyright policy. I apologize for the readers the inconvenience of not being able to see the original screengrabs, as I originally intended would be included in my chapter as images. Finding and contacting all the depicted models and the photographers of/in the images in the websites was too time consuming a task at this late stage of producing the book. I have therefore included my own drawings, so that readers can get an idea of how the websites I discuss looked at the time of writing this chapter. Readers may discover that the actual websites have been

updated and changed at the time this volume is published. I hope this last-minute solution may add an extra layer of meaning to the discussion of 'mediatization.'

3. This essay springs from the results of a Ph.D. program where Web designers' persuasive self-presentations through their portfolios were analysed. This was part of developing an analytical perspective from which experimental Web interfaces could be understood as complex textual entities through close textual analysis. The project resulted in, among other publications, the Ph.D. thesis *Mediational Sites: A Communication Design Perspective on Websites.*

4. This chapter is also a result of the post-doctoral project BRANDO (Branding and Advertising in Digital Domains), where the cross-textual articulations of contemporary practices in aestheticized persuasive communication are scrutinized through close textual analysis.

5. My thanks to Charlotte Mehder at Bruuns Bazaar for letting Peter Lang reprint the screengrabs from the website of Bruuns Bazaar.

REFERENCES

Arvidsson, A. (2005). Brands: A critical perspective. *Journal of Consumer Culture.* 5(2), 235–258.

Barnard, M. (2004). *Fashion as Communication* (2nd ed.). London: Routledge.

Barthes, R. (1977). *Image Music Text.* London: Fontana Press.

Bechmann Petersen, A. (2007). Realizing cross media. In T. Storsul and D. Stuedahl, (Eds.). *Ambivalence Towards Convergence: Digitalization and Media Change* (pp. 57–73). Göteborg: Nordicom.

Bolter, D., and Gromala, D. (2003). *Windows and Mirrors: Interaction Design, Digital Art, and the Myth of Transparency.* Cambridge, MA: The MIT Press.

Bolter, D., and Grusin, R. (1999). *Remediation: Understanding New Media.* Cambridge, MA: The MIT Press.

Bright, S. (2005). *Art Photography Now.* London: Thames & Hudson.

Couldry, N. (2008). Mediatization or mediation? Alternative understandings of the emergent space of digital storytelling. *New Media & Society,* 10(3), 373–391.

Craik, J. (1993). *The Face of Fashion.* London: Routledge.

Crampton Smith, G., and Tabor, P. (1996). The Role of the Artist-Designer. In T. Winograd (Ed.). *Bringing Design to Software* (pp. 37–57). New York: ACM Press.

Crampton Smith, G. (2007). Foreword: What Is Interaction Design? (viii–xix). In B. Moggridge (Ed.). *Designing Interactions.* Cambridge, MA: The MIT Press.

Dallow, P. (2007). Mediatizing the Web: The new modular extensible media. *Journal of Media Practice,* 8(3), 341–358.

Fornäs, J. (2000). The Crucial in Between: The Centrality of Mediation in Cultural Studies. *European Journal of Cultural Studies,* 3(1), 45–65.

Gaines, J. (2000). On wearing the film: Madame Satan (1930) (pp. 159–177). In S. Bruzzi and P. Gibson (Eds.). *Fashion Cultures: Theories, Explorations and Analysis.* London: Routledge.

Garrett, J. (2003). *The Elements of User Experience: User-Centered Design for the Web.* New York: New Riders Publishing.

Gibbons, J. (2005). *Art and Advertising.* London: I. B. Tauris.

Gitelman, L. (2006). *Always Already New: Media, History, and the Data of Culture.* Cambridge, MA: The MIT Press.

Hebdige, D. (1979). *Subculture: The Meaning of Style.* London: Routledge.

Hesmondhalgh, D. (2007). *The Cultural Industries* (2nd ed.). London: Sage.

Hjarvard, S. (2004). From bricks to bytes: The mediatization of a global toy industry (pp. 43–63). In I. Bondebjerg and P. Golding (Eds.). *European Culture and the Media*. Bristol, UK: Intellect Books.

Johnson-Eilola, J. (2005). *Datacloud: Toward a New Theory of Online Work*. Cresskill, NJ: Hampton Press.

Klingmann, A. (2007). *Brandscapes*. Cambridge, MA: The MIT Press.

Kolko, J. (2007). *Thoughts on Interaction Design*. Savannah, GA: Brown Bear.

Kress, G., and van Leeuwen, T. (2001). *Multimodal Discourse: The Modes and Media of Contemporary Communication*. London: Arnold.

Lash, S., and Lury, C. (2007). *Global Culture Industry: The Mediation of Things*. Cambridge, UK: Polity Press.

Laurel, B. (1993). *Computers as Theatre*. Reading, MA: Addison-Wesley.

Lave, J., and Wenger, E. (1991). *Situated Learning: Legitimate Peripheral Participation*. Cambridge, UK: Cambridge University Press.

Leiss, W. Kline, S., and Jhally, S. (1990). *Social Communication in Advertising*. London: Routledge.

Liestøl, G. (2006). Conducting genre convergence for learning. *International Journal of Continuing Engineering Education & Lifelong Learning*, 16(3–4), 255–270.

Löwgren, J., and Stolterman, E. (2004). *Thoughtful Interaction Design: A Design Perspective on Information Technology*. Cambridge, MA: The MIT Press.

Manovich, L. (2001). *The Language of New Media*. Cambridge, MA: The MIT Press.

McLaughlin, N. (2000). Rock, fashion and performativity (pp. 265–285). In S. Bruzzi and P. Gibson (Eds.). *Fashion Cultures: Theories, Explorations and Analysis*. London: Routledge.

Moor, E. (2003). Branded spaces: The scope of 'new marketing.' *Journal of Consumer Culture*. 3(1), 39–60.

Morrison, A., and Eikenes, J. O. (2008). *The times are a-changing in the interface*. Paper presented at International Conference on Multimodality and Learning. Institute of Education: University of London. London, 19–20 June 2008.

Morrison, A., and Skjulstad, S. (in press). Laying eggs in other people's pockets: marketing multiliteracies via mobile technologies. In B. Gentikow, E. Skogseth, and S. Østerud (Eds.). *Literacy—Technology—Cultural Techniques. How Does Communication Technology Mediate Culture?* Cresskill, NJ: Hampton Press.

Morrison, A., Stuedahl, D., Mörtberg, C., Wagner, I., Liestøl, G., and Bratteteig, T. (in press). Analytical perspectives. In I. Wagner, T. Bratteteig, and G. Liestøl (Eds.). *Explorations in Digital Design Research*. Vienna: Springer.

Murray, J. H. (2997). *Hamlet on the Holodeck: The Future of Narrative in Cyberspace*. Cambridge, MA: MIT Press.

Nielsen, J. (2000). *Designing Web Usability*. Indianapolis: New Riders Publishing.

Power, D., and Hauge, A. (2008). No man's brand: Brands, institutions and fashion. *Growth and Change*, 39(1), 123–143.

Preece, J., Rogers, Y., and Sharp, H. (2002). *Interaction Design: Beyond Human-Computer Interaction*. New York: John Wiley & Sons.

Ramamurthy, A. (2004). Spectacle and illusions: Photography and commodity culture (pp. 193–244). In L. Wells (Ed.). *Photography: A Critical Introduction* (3 rd ed.). London: Routledge.

Säljö, R. (2001). *Læring i Praksis* (Learning in Practice). Cappelen Akademisk Forlag: Oslo.

Silverstone, R. (2002). Complicity and collusion in the mediation of everyday life. *New Literary History*, 33(4), 761–780.

Skjulstad, S. (2007a). Clashing constructs in Web design (pp. 81–103). In A. Melberg (Ed.). *Aesthetics at Work.* Oslo: Unipub.

Skjulstad, S. (2007b, in press). What are these? Designers' websites as communication design, In A. Morrison (Ed.). *Inside Multimodal Composition,* Cresskill, NJ: Hampton Press.

Skjulstad, S. (2007c). *Mediational sites: A communication design perspective on websites.* Unpublished doctoral thesis. Dept. of Media and Communication, Oslo: University of Oslo.

Skjulstad, S., and Morrison, A. (2005). Movement in the interface. *Computers and Composition.* 22(4), 413–433.

Turkle, S. (1995). *Life on the Screen: Identity in the Age of the Internet.* New York: Simon & Schuster.

Welsch, W. (1997). *Undoing Aesthetics.* London: Sage.

Wertsch, J. (1991). *Voices of the Mind: A Sociocultural Approach to Mediated Action.* Cambridge, MA: Harvard University Press.

Wigley, M. (1995). *White Walls, Designer Dresses: The Fashioning of Modern Architecture.* Cambridge, MA: The MIT Press.

Williamson, J. (1978). *Decoding Advertisements.* London: Boyars.

Zimmerman, J., Forlizzi, J., and Evenson, S. (2007). *Research through design as a method for interaction design research in HCI.* In Proceedings of the ACM. CHI 2007. San Jose, CA, USA. April 28–May 3, 493–502.

CONSEQUENCES

CHAPTER TEN

Shaping Politics: Mediatization AND Media Interventionism

JESPER STRÖMBÄCK AND FRANK ESSER

McCAIN DEBATING OBAMA[1]

The notion that politics has become mediated (Bennett and Entman 2001; Nimmo and Combs 1983; Silverstone 2007) and mediatized (Cottle 2006; Kepplinger 2002; Mazzoleni and Schulz 1999; Schulz 2004) has gained currency over the last couple of decades. Although these concepts are often used, they are, however, more often referred to than properly defined or thoroughly discussed. Before engaging in our conceptual analysis, let us turn to an example to suggest how the media shape the portrayals and perceptions of political events.

The three televised debates between Senators John McCain and Barack Obama during the 2008 U.S. presidential election campaign took place largely due to the presence of the media and their willingness to broadcast the events. Although political candidates faced off in debates before the advent of mass media, the presence of mass media—not the least, television—increased the potential audience dramatically and gave these events a new quality as major campaign events. The media also turned these debates into national events instead of local events focused primarily on those physically attending the debates. Televised political debates are thus typical examples of "media events" (Dayan and Katz 1992) and "pseudo-events" (Boorstin 1961), set up to suit the demands of the mass media, celebrated as being of major significance, and aimed first and foremost at a distant, imagined although real, audience of mainly passive spectators.

When political debates became televised, their formats successively changed to suit the demands of the media rather than the demands of the contenders or the electorate (Esaiasson and Håkansson 2002; Kraus 2000). This is particularly the case when televised debates have become institutionalized, and political candidates, pragmatically if not theoretically, have no choice but to participate. This is not to say that political candidates and parties do not have a say (Schroeder 2000), but rather that, nowadays, the broadcasting media in many countries have the final say with respect to how the debates are staged, produced, and broadcast.

To those present at the presidential debates between McCain and Obama, the events were unmediated in the sense that they could witness the debates directly. Nevertheless, the media set up the ground rules that the physically present audience had to abide by; for example, they were instructed to be silent during the first and third debates.

For most people, watching in their homes or in public places, the debates were mediated; that is, transmitted by the broadcasting media from the locale of the debates to the audiences wherever they were located. In this sense, and conceptually speaking, mediation should be understood as "a natural, preordained mission of mass media to convey meaning from communicators to their target audiences" (Mazzoleni 2008a, pp. 3047–3048). Politics is thus mediated whenever people experience it through media rather than directly and through their own experiences (Strömbäck 2008).

However, the media did not transmit the debates neutrally. Instead, for several days before the debates, the media speculated about the debates and their importance, thus shaping people's expectations. The candidates and their staffs participated in this "expectation game," but regardless of whether the media were driving the expectation game, the media put their independent mark on it by adding their own speculations and bringing in commentators and pundits to talk about it. Thus, when people sat down to watch the debates and the candidates' performances, their expectations were to a significant degree shaped by the media. The candidates were also aware that the outcome—how the debates finally would be perceived—depended as much on how the media and their commentators interpreted the debates as on any actual or objective reality. They were furthermore aware that their performances would be judged against the media-shaped expectations and that the post-debate analysis might be as important as the debate in itself as to how people perceived who won or came across better. As shown by research on debate effects, the indirect effects, following from the post-debate analysis in the media, might be as important as, or more important than, the direct effects following from a debate in itself (Patterson 1980; Blais and Boyer 1996). Hence, the candidates' target audience was not only, or even primarily, the public at large, but also journalists and media commentators. This arguably had effects on their debate preparations and strategies.

Equally important, during the 2008 debates, the media intervened in various ways. Whether by using split screens, encouraging people to text-message who they think won before the debates were even over, or showing real-time audience responses on the screen during the debates, the end result was that those watching the debates on TV did not see them unfiltered. CNN, for example, chose to continuously track and *show* people's responses to the debates, using real-time response measurements. Instead of transmitting the first debates as neutrally as possible, CNN intervened in a way that inhibited people's opportunity to judge for themselves how the candidates performed. In other words, people saw the debates as the media shaped them, and these media interventions likely affected how the people perceived the candidates and their performances. This is but one example of how modern politics has become not only mediated but also, partly through active and intended media interventionism, increasingly mediatized.

MEDIATION AND MEDIATIZATION

In the literature, the concepts of mediation and mediatization are often used interchangeably to denote approximately the same phenomena and processes. For example, when Altheide and Snow (1988, pp. 196–197) explicate their theory on how "social life is constituted by and through a communication process" and how media logic increasingly shapes the workings and understandings of society, they term this a process of *mediation*, while acknowledging (p. 195) that some prefer the term *mediatization*. Nimmo and Combs (1983) also used the term *mediation* rather than *mediatization* to denote the dynamic processes through which media communication shape and reshape society and our understandings of it. The same is true of Silverstone's recent analysis on the rise of the "Mediapolis" (2007).

The concepts of mediation and mediatization should not, however, be understood as synonymous (Couldry 2008; Hjarvard 2008; Strömbäck 2008). Arguably, *mediation* can be used both to denote a neutral act of transmitting messages through the media and as denoting "the overall effect of media institutions existing in contemporary societies, the overall difference that media make by being there in our social world" (Couldry 2008). However, the essence of mediation as a concept is the rather neutral act of transmitting messages (Mazzoleni 2008a). Using *mediation* to denote both the neutral act of transmitting messages and the active, ever-present, and increased media influence makes the concept less precise and hence less useful.

Mediated communication should therefore primarily be understood as opposed to direct, first-hand, or face-to-face communication, whereas mediated politics primarily should be understood as politics communicated via and experienced through different media (Bennett and Entman 2001; Asp 1986). When politics has become mediated, people depend on the media for information about politics and society in a broad sense of the words, just as politicians and other powerful elites depend on the media for information about people's opinions and trends in society, and for reaching out to people. When politics has become mediated, the media mediate between the citizenry on the one hand, and the institutions involved in government, electoral processes or, more generally, opinion formation, on the other. The media might also mediate between different actors and institutions *within* the governing or political communication system more broadly. Conceptually speaking, the most important aspect related to the mediation of politics is hence whether people, located in various parts of and playing different roles within the political communication system, depend on the media for information and communication with each other (Strömbäck 2008).

In this understanding, the concept of mediated politics is basically a rather static concept. This is not to denigrate it—from a descriptive point of view, it is indeed very important. This is only to suggest that it fails to capture the dynamics of political communication processes and the interrelationships between media and politics and how media influence has increased over time.

Mediatization, in contrast, is an inherently process-oriented concept, focused on how media influence has increased in a number of different respects. Thus, mediatization as a general theory is not focused solely on politics. Rather, mediatization has been conceptualized as being on par with other major societal change processes such as modernization, individualization, and globalization (Hjarvard 2008; Krotz 2007; Mazzoleni 2008b). Mediatization is thus a process affecting all parts of society, either directly or indirectly, albeit to different degrees within or across different societies. As noted by Mazzoleni:

> In brief, the concept of "mediatization of society" indicates an extension of the influence of the media into all societal spheres. Therefore, it is important to see what are the (main) domains that are influenced by the media system (remembering that the media system is both a cultural technology and an economic organization). In broad and general terms, all the main societal domains are affected by the connection between media and society: sex/gender and generational relationships, deviance, control and surveillance, religious and ritual dimensions, power relationships, urban environment and city life, localization and globalization processes, and so on. (Mazzoleni 2008b, p. 3053)

The mediatization of politics is thus part of the more general process of mediatization of and in societies—at least highly developed, post-industrial, and democratic societies. The degree of mediatization might vary, as the degree of modernization, individualization, and globalization also might, but it still affects society—including politics—in numerous and fundamental ways.

MEDIATIZATION AS MEDIA INFLUENCE

At its core, mediatization is a process-oriented concept that is about "changes associated with communication media and their development" (Schulz 2004, p. 88) or, to quote Hjarvard (2008, also 2004), "the process whereby society to an increasing degree is submitted to, or becomes dependent on, the media and their logic." Asp and Esaiasson (1996, pp. 80–81) similarly note that mediatization is a process "in which there is a development toward increasing media influence."

In this context, the media should be understood not only as single operations, formats, or outlets, even though all these aspects are important. The media should rather be understood as an ever-present social and cultural system of production, broadcast, circulation, and dissemination of symbols, signs, messages, meanings, and values. The media should be understood as an institution (Cook 2005). The various media companies, outlets, types, formats, and contents constitute the building blocks of this overall social and cultural system, but the sum is arguably greater than its parts, and the rules and norms that govern the media taken as a whole are often more important than what distinguishes one media company, outlet, type, or format from another (Mazzoleni 2008b; Hjarvard 2008; Altheide and Snow 1979, 1988, 1991; Nimmo and Combs 1983). This is not to say that there are no significant differences among, say, elite newspapers, public service news, and commercial TV news, but rather that the commonalities, from the perspective of mediatization, are more important than the differences.

Stated differently, mediatization means that the media form a system in its own right, *independent* although *interdependent* on other social systems such as the political system (Altheide and Snow 1988; Cook 2005; Hjarvard 2008; Mazzoleni 2008b; Strömbäck 2008). Within this media system, there are hierarchies, with some media being more important in shaping the overall media logic and the configuration of the media system than other media are. For example, during the last decades, television has arguably been the most influential medium. Although some believe that the Internet will change this, thus far, the Internet has not replaced the dominant media and media logic (Schulz 2004), and television still constitutes the most influential medium.

What makes the media so important is not only that they have come to constitute an independent although interdependent social and cultural system in society, but also that the media have become "an omnipresent symbolic environment creating an essential part of the societal definitions of reality," to quote Schulz (2004, p. 93). Hence, the media permeate all spheres of contemporary societies and have become the most important source of information about all matters beyond people's everyday experiences. As noted by Silverstone (2007, p. 5), "The media are becoming environmental." He also notes, "We have become dependent on the media for the conduct of everyday life."

This is a consequence of the notion that people's everyday experiences are heavily shaped by the media, as people react to and interpret phenomena they encounter through the lenses of prior information or schemata (Fiske and Taylor 1991), and as these, to a significant degree, are shaped by information received through various media. Our knowledge or impressions of politicians, political issues, and people or places beyond our own experiences comes primarily from the media. Where would this knowledge otherwise come from? What would we know about John McCain, South Africa, HIV, or any other distant person, place, or issue, were it not for the media and whatever we have learned from various media accounts, ranging from news to documentaries to fictional dramas? In this context, it matters less whether people's understanding is correct in that it corresponds to the actual reality. What matters most is that people base their knowledge, understandings, and opinions on the "fantasy reality" (Nimmo and Combs 1983) or "pseudo-environment" (Lippmann 1997) largely created by the media.

If people are guided by their social constructions or reality, the building blocks of these social constructions are heavily shaped by the media's social constructions. Ample evidence of this can be found in research on the media's ability to influence their audiences through, for example, the processes of agenda setting (McCombs 2004), framing (Iyengar 1991), priming (Iyengar and Kinder 1987), and cultivation (Shanahan and Morgan 1999).

At the same time, a proper understanding of the media's influence requires going beyond theories on their effects on individual perceptions and opinions. These theories depend on a causal logic in which it is possible to make a distinction between dependent and independent variables (Schulz 2004), and they also assume that media effects largely follow from the content of media messages. From the perspective of mediatization theory, the media content cannot, however, be treated as isolated from media formats and media grammar (Altheide and Snow 1979). Furthermore, the omnipresence of the media makes it virtually impossible to separate them from people's everyday life, just as the media cannot be conceived of as being separate from other social, political, or cultural processes. Media effect theories also fail to recognize the reciprocal effects of the media on the subjects and processes of media coverage (Kepplinger 2007), how various social actors beyond "the audience in general" use and are affected by the media (Davis 2007), and how social actors accommodate to the media. This is why

Silverstone's expression that the media have become environmental is enlightening: The environment is always present, and human beings cannot be perceived as being located outside of the environment. Just as birds are dependent on air and fish are dependent on water, the human being lives in and interacts with the environment, and it does not make much sense to ask what the effect of air is on birds, of water on fish, or of environment on the human being. The effects are tremendous and still virtually impossible to isolate and capture.

In other words, if the media permeate and are intertwined with basically all social, cultural, and political processes, and if media content cannot be conceived of as isolated from media formats and grammar, the logic of separating dependent from independent variables is challenged, and the established media effect theories are insufficient for an understanding of the full extent of the media's influence. The media effect theories are important but insufficient. As noted by Schulz (2004, p. 90), "mediatization as a concept both transcends and includes media effects."

This does not mean, however, that it is impossible to get at a greater understanding of the mediatization of society in general or of politics. As suggested by Schulz (2004, pp. 88–90), at least four processes of social change following from the media can be identified: extension, substitution, amalgamation, and accommodation.

First of all, the media *extend* human communication capabilities across both space and time. Second, the media "partly or completely *substitute* social activities and social institutions and thus change their character" (Schulz 2004, p. 88). Things that were previously done in a face-to-face manner or that required physical presence can now be done or experienced through various media. Third, media activities *merge* and mingle with non-media activities or processes, thus becoming an integral part of, and making it all the more difficult to separate the media from, these other activities and processes. Similarly, information gained from media merges and mingles with information gained through interpersonal communication or experiences. As this happens, "the media's definition of reality amalgamates with the social definition of reality." Fourth, as the media become increasingly important, different social actors have to adapt to and alter their behaviors to *accommodate* the media's logic and standards of newsworthiness (Schulz 2004; Strömbäck 2008). In addition to these four processes following from the media, one should add *creation*. Not only do the media create events in the form of texts and programs, the importance of the media makes other social actors *create* events with the main or sole purpose of being covered by the media. This is what Boorstin (1961) refers to as "pseudo-events."

Five crucial social change processes that form part of mediatization and that follow from the media and their influence are thus extension, substitution, amalgamation, accommodation, and creation. These affect society on all levels, from the individual (psychological) to the institutional (sociological). The same is true of media logic, a concept that has already been referred to but that needs to be explicated.

THE CONCEPTS OF MEDIA LOGIC AND POLITICAL LOGIC

Similar to the concepts of mediation and mediatization, media logic is referred to more often than it is properly defined. At the same time, media logic can be conceived of as one important force in the mediatization of society (Mazzoleni 2008c), suggesting that an understanding of media logic is a prerequisite for an understanding of mediatization.

The first to use the concept of media logic was Altheide and Snow (1979, 1988, 1991), and according to their definition:

> Media logic consists of a form of communication; the process through which media present and transmit information. Elements of this form include the various media and the formats used by these media. Format consists, in part, of how material is organized, the style in which it is presented, the focus or emphasis on particular characteristics of behavior, and the grammar of media communication. Format becomes a framework or a perspective that is used to present as well as interpret phenomena. (Altheide and Snow 1979, p. 10)

Although this definition is elusive, media logic can be understood as a particular way of seeing, covering, and interpreting social, cultural, and political phenomena. According to the theory, the various media formats, the production processes and routines, and the media's own need for compelling, attention-grabbing, and dramatic stories shape how the media perceive, cover, and interpret social affairs. In other words, the media have certain formats, processes, and routines, and they need to be competitive in the struggle to capture people's attention. This shapes what the media cover and how they cover it. For example, as a visual medium, television requires good visuals; hence, television news favor stories where there are good or strong visuals (Bucy and Grabe 2007). The media also favor stories that include conflict, as conflict lends itself to more dramatic storytelling (McManus 1994). The media's need for stories that are dramatic and have the potential to capture people's attention might explain their propensity to focus on scandals (Sabato, Stencel, and Lichter 2000) to frame politics as a horse race or strategic game rather than as issues (Patterson 1993; Cappella and Jamieson 1997; Strömbäck and Kaid 2008) and to apply episodic and concrete frames rather than thematic and abstract frames (Iyengar 1991). The growth of the information society turned information scarcity into information surplus (Hernes 1978), creating a need for the media both to reduce information and to turn information into as compelling news stories as possible. Storytelling techniques used to achieve this include simplification, polarization, intensification, personalization, visualization, stereotyping, and particular ways of framing the news (Hernes 1978; Asp 1986; Strömbäck 2000; Esser 2008; Mazzoleni 1987; Patterson 1993). In all these cases, the media content is "molded by a format logic," to quote Altheide and Snow (1988, p. 201), who also note that some important format considerations for events on U.S. network TV news include accessibility, visual quality, drama and action, audience relevance, and thematic encapsulation. Format considerations such as these guide both selection and production of news events and are important for understanding the media's news values and standards of newsworthiness.

While the concept of media logic is important in itself, it also highlights the notion that the media are not guided by logics external to the media themselves. There is one exception, in the sense that media logic is overlapping with that of commercial logic. As most media are run as commercial businesses, media logic both follows from, and is adapted to, commercial logic (Mazzoleni 2008c; Hamilton 2004; McManus 1994). This affects even public service media when they have to compete for audiences with commercial media.

More important, in the context of the mediatization of politics, is that media logic can be conceived of as opposed to political logic (Mazzoleni 1987; Meyer 2002; Strömbäck 2008; Brants and Praag 2006). Although the concept of political logic is less developed than that of media logic, it is crucial for an understanding of how mediatization shapes and reshapes politics.

At the heart of any conceptualization of political logic lies the fact that politics ultimately is about collective and authoritative decision making as well as the implementation of political decisions. This includes the processes of distributing political power; the processes of political deliberation, bargaining, and decision making; the processes of implementing political decisions; and the question of power as it relates to "who gets what, when, and how" (Lasswell 1950). More precisely, political logic consists of at least the following six dimensions (see Lasswell 1950; Meyer 2002; Jones and Baumgartner 2005; Stoker 2006):

- A power allocation dimension: the efforts to, and processes of, distributing and allocating political power through elections or appointments.
- A partisan dimension: the efforts to win partisan advantages, mainly although not exclusively through elections.
- A policy dimension: the efforts to, and processes of, defining problems that require political solutions, and of finding solutions for politically defined problems.

- A deliberation dimension: the efforts to, and processes of, deliberating, building consensus, or compromising between different policy proposals, and of making authoritative decisions.
- An implementation dimension: the efforts to, and processes of, implementing political decisions.
- An accountability dimension: the efforts to, and processes of, monitoring political decision making and implementation, and holding those responsible accountable for their conduct.

While power is an integral and inevitable part of politics, politics is also about policies and programs for solving societal problems that require political decisions, and for reforming society according to various value systems or ideologies. The focus of most political processes is thus on issues; that is, societal problems and suggestions with respect to how these can or should be addressed. Some might argue that power is the ultimate goal, and policy programs and promises are the means to reach that goal (Downs 1957). But others might argue that, while power is the means, being able to enact policies according to their own value system or ideology is the ultimate goal (Sjöblom 1968). The conflict between these two positions will probably never be resolved, but it is important to recognize that politics cannot be reduced to one dimension or to being about either policies or power. Politics is about both power and policies.

More importantly, politics is also about communication, and media communication is an integral part of all the dimensions that form what politics is about. Political actors, located within political institutions, consequently need to take the media into consideration, and the media might independently intervene, in all the processes and along all of the dimensions that form politics. In societies that have become increasingly mediatized, this arguably creates a very real tension and conflicts between media logic and political logic in political communication and governing processes (Mazzoleni 1987; Meyer 2002; Strömbäck 2008; Brants and Praag 2006).

In other words, politics and political communication in a particular society can be governed *mainly* by either media logic or political logic. In the former case, the requirements of the media take center stage and shape the means by which political communication and governing is played out by political actors, covered by the media, and understood by the people. In the latter case, the needs of the political system and political institutions take center stage and shape how political communication is played out, covered, and understood. In the former case, what people find interesting and what is commercially viable for media companies take precedence. In the latter case, what is important for people to know, as interpreted mainly by political actors and institutions, takes precedence. In the former case, media are essentially perceived of as commercial enterprises with no particular obligation apart from catering to the wants and needs of their audiences. In the latter case, media are perceived as political or democratic institutions, with some kind of moral, if not legal, obligation to assist in making democracy work (Croteau and Hoynes 2001; Meyer 2002; Strömbäck 2005; Ferree et al. 2002).

In reality, of course, there are many gray areas between politics and political communication governed by either media logic or political logic. For analytical purposes, the dichotomy is nevertheless helpful, not least because it might allow empirical investigations on the degree to which politics, across time, countries, and political institutions, has become mediatized.

MEDIATIZATION OF POLITICS AS A FOUR-DIMENSIONAL CONCEPT

As suggested by the discussion above, mediatization of politics is a multidimensional concept where at least four separate dimensions can be identified (Strömbäck 2008). The first dimension is concerned with the extent to which the media constitute the most important or dominant source of information and channel of communication. The second dimension is concerned with the media's independence from other social institutions, not least political institutions. Although all institutions, from a social systems perspective, should be perceived of as interdependent, for the media to have an independent impact on other social or political actors or institutions, they have to form an institution or a social system in their own right. The third dimension is concerned with media content—most importantly, news and nonfictional content—and the degree to which media content is governed by media logic or political logic. The fourth dimension focuses on political actors and the degree to which they are governed by media logic or political logic. As political actors are always located within political institutions, this dimension also includes political institutions and how they are governed, although the process of mediatization arguably has less impact on political institutions than on political actors. The four dimensions are depicted as continuums in Figure 1 (Strömbäck 2008).

Taken together and on the aggregate, we believe these dimensions determine the degree to which politics in a particular setting is mediatized. Each dimension could be broken down further into subdimensions, not least to facilitate empirical investigations on how media interventionism along each of the dimensions shapes and reshapes politics and contributes to the mediatization of politics. We will return to this point shortly. Before that, however, some other implications need to be highlighted. First, while the four dimensions of are highly intercorrelated, the breakdown of the concept into separate dimensions might help clarify

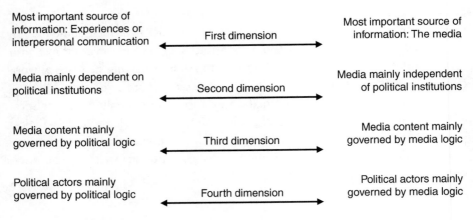

Figure 1: A four-dimensional conceptualization of the mediatization of politics.

the concept and aid in assessments of the degree to which politics in a particular setting is mediatized. Second, as the mediatization of politics should be understood as a process, it should be possible to distinguish between different phases of mediatization (Strömbäck 2008). This does not, however, implicate that the process of mediatization must be linear or unidirectional. It is certainly conceivable that the impact of media logic on political actors, located within political institutions, varies both within and across countries and across time and circumstances. For example, some political actors are more powerful than others in terms of their influence over the political agenda and how the media frame political issues. Hence, some political actors have a greater need to accommodate and adapt to the media logic than others, while the media and media logic have more influence over some political actors and institutions than others. There might also be important differences across countries depending, among other things, on political news cultures (Esser 2008) and on whether they belong to the liberal, the democratic corporatist, or the polarized pluralist model of media and politics (Hallin and Mancini 2004; see below).

In this context, the concept of media interventionism is crucial. As suggested above, it is through media interventionism, intended or inadvertent, that media logic trumps political logic with respect to how the media cover politics. Providing that the first and the second dimensions of mediatization function as prerequisites for the third dimension, and the third dimension as a prerequisite for the fourth dimension, media interventionism helps shape and reshape politics as it is covered by the media, and consequently understood by, the people. But it also affects how political actors actually think and act, and how political processes are played out. As suggested by Cook (2005), Schulz (2004), and others, increasing mediatization forces politicians to adapt to, and even adopt (Strömbäck 2008), media logic and the media's standards of newsworthiness. The end result in such cases is that "politicians may then win the daily battles with the news media, by getting into the news as they wish, but end up losing the war as standards of newsworthiness begin to become prime criteria to evaluate issues, policies, and politics" (Cook 2005, p. 163).

MEDIA INTERVENTIONISM AS CONCEPT AND ENGINE OF MEDIATIZATION

Conceptually speaking, media interventionism refers to a media-centered political reporting style in which, increasingly, journalists and media actors become the stories' main newsmakers rather than politicians or other social actors. It can be interpreted as a professionally motivated behavior by journalists to increase their influence, authority and prestige—and, ultimately, their control over the news content. Its theoretical underpinnings are the concepts of "media intrusion" developed by Davis (1990; see also Baran and Davis 2006, pp. 345–348) and "media's discretionary power" or "journalistic intervention" developed by Blumler and Gurevitch (1995, pp. 86–96; see also Blumler and Gurevitch 2001). To take just one example of media interventionism at work, media interventionism in election campaigns is high when journalists report on politics in their own words, scenarios, and assessments—and when they, for example, grant politicians only limited opportunities to present themselves with their own voices in the news.

Media interventionism refers directly to the third dimension of mediatization and has indirect implications for the fourth dimension. As shown in Figure 1, the third dimension asks whether media content is governed mainly by political logic or media logic. The third dimension thus approaches mediatization from a symbolic interactionist perspective: It asks how political reality is defined and constructed by the news media and, due to increasing mediatization, expects this construction process to be guided by media-specific frames and formats that will influence readers' political worldviews (Mazzoleni and Schulz 1999, pp. 249–252; Johnson-Cartee 2005, pp. 1–41).

To predict the extent to which news organizations will actively format and frame political reality according to autonomous media logic, however, their structural and cultural context needs to be taken into account. The seminal studies by Blumler and Gurevitch (1995, 2001) point at two factors of the *structural environment* that aid journalistic intervention, and hence mediatization along the third dimension, to spread. The first is a political system characterized by weak party organizations, weak party loyalties in the electorate, and weak influence of party ideologies. The second is a media system that is subject to only light state regulation, in which broadcasters are guided less by public service obligations and more by commercial considerations, profit orientations, and competitive market pressures. In addition, Blumler and Gurevitch (1995, 2001) hint at two crucial *cultural factors*. First, they claim that journalistic attitudes toward interventionism thrive in political cultures where public opinion is more cynical and distrustful of political institutions. This is because it creates a climate in which adversarial journalism seems socially acceptable. Second, they argue that it will grow in news cultures that do not consider politicians' statements as intrinsically important, and rather insist that political material should fight its way into news programs on its news value alone, and in consideration of the newsworthiness of competing stories. Aside from structural and cultural influences, Blumler and Gurevitch (1995, 2001) also allude to *professional determinants*. Journalistic intervention is more likely to be triggered by a campaigning industry that exhibits high level of professionalization in their use of media manipulation and news management strategies. On the media side, the level of professionalization is also a factor. Interventionism is more likely to expand in journalistic communities that have achieved a high degree of professional independence and are eager to preserve it against outside interference, and that cherish power-distant role perceptions such as interpreter, critic, watchdog, or entertainer.

On the national level, the media system typology of Hallin and Mancini (2004) leads us to classify the United States as a national news culture whose contextual setting favors the largest degree of journalistic intervention (Blumler and Gurevitch 2001; Strömbäck and Dimitrova 2006). At the other extreme of the spectrum is France, a prototype of the polarized pluralist model of media–politics relations (Hallin and Mancini 2004), where we would expect the least inclination to journalistic intervention. France's history of government-controlled broadcasting hindered the development of a strong and independent journalistic culture and, up to this day, has bred a symbiotic, nonadversarial connivance between journalists and politicians (Chalaby 2005).

These assumptions were recently tested with content analysis of political reporting styles in the United States, France, Germany, and England. It discovered, indeed, evidence of a more interventionist U.S. approach and a noninterventionist French approach (Esser 2008). The degree of interventionism was operationalized as the extent to which journalists grant politicians opportunities in TV news programs to present themselves in their own words (i.e., in their own sound bites). The study found that, over two election cycles, candidate sound bites in campaign news stories were consistently shorter in the United States than in Europe. At the same time that U.S. journalists were found to compress candidates' on-air statements the most, it emerged that U.S. candidates fought by far the most tightly scripted campaigns. This correlation indicates that the more strenuously politicians try to control news coverage, the more journalists resist covering them according to the wishes of politicians, instead reporting something different that gives expression to the journalistic voice. The relationship between assertive news management style and assertive journalistic response (i.e., journalistic intervention) was found to constitute an important dimension of political news cultures. The French news culture appeared as the least independent-minded. French election stories displayed a more passive, yielding reporting style; French election stories were more structured by political logic (and the candidates' policy messages) than by interventionist media logic (that would, at times, be less willing to recycle those messages).

This suggests that the concept of media interventionism is useful and even crucial for a full understanding of how, and through what venues, the media shape news content according to media logic and consequently create strong incentives for political actors to adapt to or adopt media logic and the media's standards of newsworthiness. Or, alternatively, it is important in understanding how media intervene in the dimensions that form part of political logic. This also suggests that, conceptually, mediatization and media interventionism are closely related and can help inform each other, while media interventionism simultaneously can be conceived of as an engine of the mediatization of politics.

CONCLUSION

Both mediatization and media interventionism refer, although not exclusively, to the question of how "political reality" is constructed for the wider public, and the consequences thereof. Both concepts are, furthermore, dynamic and process oriented, which makes them useful for comparisons across time and space. For example, research indicates that news production in the past used to be guided by a higher degree of political logic (serving the needs of political actors, institutions, as well as the democracy as a whole), while today it is more closely linked to a media logic that is driven by media formats and grammar, professional norms and values, and commercial incentives and motives. This suggests increasing media interventionism as well as increasing mediatization; that the concepts are closely related and can inform each other; and how media interventionism works as an engine of the mediatization of politics.

The concept of, and research on, media interventionism are also important, because they suggest how the third dimension of mediatization (media's representation of political reality) can be operationalized and investigated empirically, and how it is connected to the fourth dimension (politicians' publicity strategies) and first dimensions (people's political perceptions). The discussion of interventionism also demonstrates that the second dimension (journalists' professional and institutional autonomy) is an important prerequisite to the entire mediatization process.

It is obvious that linkages to other fields of research, especially to media commercialism, media professionalism, and political public relations, need to be taken into account. For example, commercial motives toward a media-centered reporting style—a reporting style that is guided by media logic rather than political logic—stem to a significant degree from competitive pressures to find attractive, captivating stories. Professional motives toward a media-centered reporting style similarly result from the increasing autonomy of journalists as an occupational group as well as from the increasing autonomy of the news media as a collective institution. This autonomy has led media organizations to become more politically assertive, which has encouraged political actors to professionalize their political public relations and news management. This in turn has created incentives for continued or stronger media interventionism and hence mediatization with respect to both the media content and, at the next stage, political actors and institutions. Thus, there is an interdependent relationship between professionalized political public relations (as a reflexive response to journalistic assertiveness) and media interventionism (as a reflexive response to professionalized political public relations). Both these phenomena are integral parts of the mediatization of politics, further underlining the notion that mediatization research needs to go beyond the classic media effects literature because mediatization is transcending the causal logic of independent and dependent variables.

In other words, the relationships between media and politics are characterized by dynamic interactions and complex interdependencies along various levels and dimensions. As the media have become the most important source of information, and as the media have gained independence from political and other media-external social institutions, media interventionism has become more pronounced, and media content has become increasingly governed by media logic as opposed to political logic. This process creates incentives for political actors and institutions to adapt to the predominance of media logic with respect to the media content, either by increasing their efforts and skills at political public relations and news management or by adopting and internalizing media logic in their own thinking and behavior.

In more and more areas, media logic trumps political logic. Increasingly, the constructions of reality conveyed by the media and shaped by media logic matter more than any actual reality, as it is the only reality to which people have access and thus treat as real. In either case, it is a sign of increasing mediatization of politics.

Ultimately, though, the degree of mediatization and media interventionism is an empirical question. More research is thus clearly needed with respect to, for example, the linkages between mediatization and other theories on political communication and journalism; the antecedents, manifestations, and consequences of media interventionism and mediatization; variations across time and space; what causes these variations; and, ultimately, how and to what extent media shape and reshape politics.

NOTE

1. This chapter was written while Jesper Strömbäck was a visiting professor at the College of Journalism and Communications, University of Florida, under a grant provided by the Sweden-America Foundation. He would thus like to thank the Sweden-America Foundation for this grant and the College of Journalism and Communications for their hospitality.

REFERENCES

Altheide, D. L., and Snow, R. P. (1979). *Media Logic*. Beverly Hills, CA: Sage.

Altheide, D. L., and Snow, R. P. (1988). Toward a Theory of Mediation. In J. A. Anderson (Ed.), *Communication Yearbook 11* (pp. 194–223). Newbury Park, CA: Sage.

Altheide, D. L., and Snow, R. P. (1991). *Media Worlds in the Postjournalism Era*. New York: Aldine de Gruyter.

Asp, K. (1986). *Mäktiga massmedier. Studier i politisk opinionsbildning*. Stockholm: Akademilitteratur.

Asp, K., and Esaiasson, P. (1996). The modernization of Swedish campaigns: Individualization, professionalization, and medialization. In D. L. Swanson and P. Mancini (Eds.), *Politics, Media, and Modern Democracy: An International Study of Innovations in Electoral Campaigning and Their Consequences* (pp. 73–90). Westport, CT: Praeger.

Baran, S. J., and Davis, D. K. (2006). *Mass Communication Theory* (4th ed.). London: Thomson.

Bennett, W. L., and Entman, R. M. (Eds.) (2001). *Mediated Politics. Communication in the Future of Democracy*. Cambridge, UK: Cambridge University Press.

Blais, A., and Boyer, M. M. (1996). Assessing the impact of televised debates: The case of the 1988 Canadian election. *British Journal of Political Science*, 26(2), 143–164.

Blumler, J. G., and Gurevitch, M. (1995). *The Crisis of Public Communication*. London: Routledge.

Blumler, J. G., and Gurevitch, M. (2001). Americanization reconsidered: UK-US campaign communication comparisons across time. In W. L. Bennett and R. M. Entman (Eds.). *Mediated Politics. Communication in the Future of Democracy* (pp. 280–403). Cambridge, UK: Cambridge University Press.

Boorstin, D. J. (1961). *The Image: A Guide to Pseudo-Events in America*. New York: Harper Colophon.

Brants, K., and Praag, van. P. (2006). Signs of media logic. Half a century of political communication in the Netherlands. *Javnost–The Public*, 13(1), 25–40.

Bucy, E. P., and Grabe, M. E. (2007). Taking television seriously: A sound and image bite analysis of presidential campaign coverage, 1992–2004. *Journal of Communication*, 57(4), 652–675.

Cappella, J. N., and Jamieson, K. H. (1997). *Spiral of Cynicism. The Press and the Public Good*. Oxford, UK: Oxford University Press.

Chalaby, J. K. (2005). French political communication in a comparative perspective. *Modern & Contemporary France*, 13(3), 273–290.

Cook, T. E. (2005). *Governing with the News. The News Media as a Political Institution.* 2nd ed. Chicago: University of Chicago Press.

Cottle, S. (2006). *Mediatized Conflict.* Maidenhead: Open University Press.

Couldry, N. (2008). Mediatization or mediation? Alternative understandings of the emergent space of digital storytelling. *New Media & Society,* 10(3), 373–391.

Croteau, D., and Hoynes, W. (2001). *The Business of Media. Corporate Media and the Public Interest.* Thousand Oaks, CA: Pine Forge Press.

Davis, A. (2007). *The Mediation of Power. A Critical Introduction.* London: Routledge.

Davis, K. D. (1990). News and politics. In D. L. Swanson and D. Nimmo (Eds.), *New Directions in Political Communication: A Resource Book* (pp. 147–184). Newbury Park, CA: Sage.

Dayan, D., and Katz, E. (1992). *Media Events. The Live Broadcasting of History.* Cambridge, MA: Harvard University Press.

Downs, A. (1957). *An Economic Theory of Democracy.* New York: Harper & Row.

Esaiasson, P., and Håkansson, N. (2002). *Besked ikväll! Valprogrammen i svensk radio och TV.* Stockholm: Stiftelsen Etermedierna i Sverige.

Esser, F. (2008). Dimensions of political news cultures: Sound bite and image bite news in France, Germany, Great Britain, and the United States. *International Journal of Press/Politics,* 13(4), 401–428.

Ferree, M. M., Gamson, W. A., Gerhards, J. and Rucht, D. (2002). Four models of the public sphere in modern democracies. *Theory and Society,* 31(3), 289–324.

Fiske, S. T., and Taylor, S. E. (1991). *Social Cognition.* 2nd ed. New York: McGraw-Hill.

Hallin, D. C., and Mancini, P. (2004). *Comparing Media Systems. Three Models of Media and Politics.* Cambridge, UK: Cambridge University Press.

Hamilton, J. T. (2004). *All the News That's Fit to Sell: How the Market Transforms Information Into News.* Princeton, NJ: Princeton University Press.

Hernes, G. (1978). Det mediavridde samfunn. In G. Hernes (Ed.), *Forhandlingsøkonomi og blandadministrasjon* (pp. 181–195). Oslo: Universitetsforlaget.

Hjarvard, S. (2004). From Bricks to Bytes: The Mediatization of a Global Toy Industry. In I. Bondebjerg and P. Golding (Eds.), *European Culture and the Media* (pp. 43–63). Bristol, UK: Intellect Books.

Hjarvard, S. (2008). The mediatization of society. A theory of the media as agents of social and cultural change. *Nordicom Review,* 29(2), 105–134.

Iyengar, S. (1991). *Is Anyone Responsible? How Television Frames Political Issues.* Chicago: University of Chicago Press.

Iyengar, S., and Kinder, D. R. (1987). *News that Matters: Television and American Opinion.* Chicago: University of Chicago Press.

Johnson-Cartee, K. (2005). *News Narratives and News Framing: Constructing Political Reality.* Lanham, MD: Rowland & Littlefield.

Jones, B. D., and Baumgartner, F. R. (2005). *The Politics of Attention: How Government Prioritizes Problems.* Chicago: University of Chicago Press.

Kepplinger, H. M. (2002). Mediatization of politics: Theory and data. *Journal of Communication,* 52(4), pp. 972–986.

Kepplinger, H. M. (2007). Reciprocal effects: Toward a theory of mass media effects on decision makers. *Harvard International Journal of Press/Politics,* 12(2): 3–23.

Kraus, S. (2000). *Televised Presidential Debates and Public Policy.* 2nd ed. Mahwah, NJ: Lawrence Erlbaum.

Krotz, F. (2007). The meta-process of "mediatization" as a conceptual frame. *Global Media and Communication,* 3(3), 256–260.

Lasswell, H. D. (1950). *Politics: Who Gets What, When and How.* New York: Peter Smith.

Lippmann, W. (1997). *Public Opinion.* New York: The Free Press.

McCombs, M. (2004). *Setting the Agenda: The Mass Media and Public Opinion.* Cambridge, UK: Polity.

McManus, J. H. (1994). *Market-Driven Journalism: Let the Citizen Beware?* Thousand Oaks, CA: Sage.

Mazzoleni, G. (1987). Media logic and party logic in campaign coverage: The Italian general election of 1983. *European Journal of Communication,* 2(1), 81–103.

Mazzoleni, G. (2008a). Mediatization of politics. In W. Donsbach (Ed.), *The International Encyclopedia of Communication,* vol. VII (pp. 3047–3051). Malden, MA: Blackwell.

Mazzoleni, G. (2008b). Mediatization of society. In W. Donsbach (Ed.), *The International Encyclopedia of Communication,* vol. VII (pp. 3052–3055). Malden, MA: Blackwell.

Mazzoleni, G. (2008c). Media logic. In W. Donsbach (Ed.), *The International Encyclopedia of Communication,* vol. VII (pp. 2930–2932). Malden, MA: Blackwell.

Mazzoleni, G., and Schulz, W. (1999). Mediatization of politics: A challenge for democracy? *Political Communication,* 16(3): 247–261.

Merritt, D. (1998). *Public Journalism and Public Life: Why Telling the News Is Not Enough.* 2nd ed. Mahwah, NJ: Lawrence Erlbaum.

Meyer, T. (2002). *Media Democracy: How the Media Colonize Politics.* Cambridge, UK: Polity.

Nimmo, D., and Combs, J. E. (1983). *Mediated Political Realities.* New York: Longman.

Patterson, T. E. (1980). *The Mass Media Election: How Americans Choose Their President.* New York: Praeger.

Patterson, T. E. (1993). *Out of Order.* New York: Vintage.

Sabato, L. J., Stencel, M., and Lichter, R. S. (2000). *Peepshow—Media and Politics in an Age of Scandal.* Lanham, MD: Rowman & Littlefield.

Schroeder, A. (2000). *Presidential Debates: Forty Years of High-Risk TV.* New York: Columbia University Press.

Schulz, W. (2004). Reconstructing Mediatization as an Analytical Concept. *European Journal of Communication,* 19(1): 87–101.

Shanahan, J., and Morgan, M. (1999). *Television and Its Viewers: Cultivation Theory and Research.* Cambridge, UK: Cambridge University Press.

Silverstone, R. (2007). *Media and Morality: On the Rise of the Mediapolis.* Cambridge, UK: Polity.

Sjöblom, G. (1968). *Party Strategies in a Multiparty System.* Lund: Studentlitteratur.

Stoker, G. (2006). *Why Politics Matters. Making Democracy Work.* New York: Palgrave Macmillan.

Strömbäck, J. (2000). *Makt och medier. Samspelet mellan medborgarna, medierna och de politiska makthavarna.* Lund: Studentlitteratur.

Strömbäck, J. (2005). In search of a standard: Four models of democracy and their normative implications for journalism. *Journalism Studies,* 6(3), 331–345.

Strömbäck, J. (2008). Four phases of mediatization: An analysis of the mediatization of politics. *The International Journal of Press/Politics,* 13(3), 228–246.

Strömbäck, J., and Dimitrova, D. V. (2006). Political and media systems matter: A comparison of election news coverage in Sweden and the United States. *The Harvard International Journal of Press/Politics,* 11(4), 131–147.

Strömbäck, J., and Kaid, L. L. (Eds.) (2008). *Handbook of Election News Coverage Around the World.* New York: Routledge.

CHAPTER ELEVEN

Everyday: Domestication OF Mediatization OR Mediatized Domestication?

MAREN HARTMANN

INTRODUCTION

> It is within the sphere of everyday life that individuals and groups can be agents, able insofar as their resources and the constraints upon them allow, to create and sustain their own life-worlds, their own cultures and values. It is within the sphere of everyday life that the ordinariness of the world is displayed, where minor and often taken-for-granted activities emerge as significant and defining characteristics...And it is in the conduct of everyday life that we can begin to observe and try to understand the salience of information and technologies in humanity's general project of making sense of the world, both private and public. (Silverstone 1995, p. 2)

And it is also within the sphere of everyday life that both domestication and mediatization manifest themselves foremost and at the same time show how they are intertwined and cannot be thought without each other. One claim in this chapter is that it is exactly in the conduct of everyday life that we can begin to observe mediatization processes at work. Another (related) claim is that it is exactly within the everyday that mediatization can also be questioned—on an individual, but also on a theoretical, level. Before engaging with the everyday, though, let us first step back for a moment and return to the rather basic question of the immediate associations that come to mind when we hear the terms *domestication* and *mediatization*.

On a very general level, we immediately know that we are dealing with major societal changes when we look at these concepts. Any '-ation' at the end is a clear reference, especially to the idea of process (sometimes [mis]read as progress).[1] On a more specific level, we are also dealing with associations concerning the actual content of these processes. The 'media' in mediatization is the less problematic on first sight. Mediatization appears to refer to some intensification of media—in yet undefined ways. It could be a quantitative or qualitative increase (as we will see below); the term itself does not yet suggest either. Domestication, however, brings associations from an entirely different context: the house, coupled with the taming of wild animals, that is, a reference to earlier times, when agriculture moved in new directions. It, too, refers to something 'more,' that is, either more domestic or domesticated, but not more of the wilderness.

These intuitive associations tell us a lot. They, first of all, let us ask what kind of intensification exactly is at play in these processes. And they suggest the question of whether this intensification is, at the same time, related to a potentially contradictory tendency: a taming. The above-mentioned everyday life is where domestication and mediatization meet. Next to a—somewhat simple—mediatization of the domestic and/or the everyday, the meeting of the two concepts suggests wider aspects: How far is the mediatization process being tamed? And what would this imply? A few more of the consequences of a potential mediatization of the everyday (and for its theorization in the domestication concept) need to be explored.

In connection with Roger Silverstone's insistence on the importance of the everyday, these are the questions that this contribution sets out to answer. The initial step is an exploration of each of these concepts. The part on mediatization, as we are able to draw on the many other contributions on this book, will remain somewhat brief. It will be followed by a section on domestication. The focus, however, lies on the third part, which offers three aspects of the possible combination of the two concepts: (a) reflections on domestication in the age of mediatization, (b) reflections on the discursive appropriation as a necessary addition to the domestication concept (in the light of mediatization debates), and (c) some initial thoughts on the role of mediation within a 'mediatized domestication' concept. Whether or not (yet another) new term needs to be created to describe this will be the last reflection in this chapter.

MEDIATIZATION—A BRIEF OVERVIEW

Mediatization is, as this book clearly shows, an increasingly used and debated concept, although some theorizations have been around for a few years. As with many such concepts, slight differences in definitions do occur. Knut Lundby has already pointed out in his introduction to this book that a differentiation between *mediatization* and *medialisation* is being made within the German language context, while *mediation*, a prominent term in English, tends not to be used.[2] A clearly defined differentiation between the two, however, remains problematic insofar as different authors state different differences at different moments in time.[3] While much of the differentiation takes place on the linguistic level (a term is too close to another existing term) or refers to historical reasons (see Sonia Livingstone's foreword), another reason for a specific preference can be the basic theoretical framework at play (such as system theoretical approaches tending to use the term *mediatization*).

Here, two major strands can be indentified in the German-language debate around the mediatization concept (the term of choice in this book as well as this chapter). On the one hand, we find mediatization associated with an assumed new structural transformation of the public sphere, based on an increasing inter-dependence of politics and media (hence also the assumed mediatization of polit-ical organizations—see Donges 2008). The interpenetration of the media system with the political system is a key issue in this context, and the emphasis is clearly on public communication, not other forms of communication. A result of this process is the increasing contingency on both sides (Trenz 2006, p. 6). The *media society* concept is often used in connection with this concept, referring to an increasing differentiation in many areas of society that is often linked to develop-ments in the media sphere (e.g., Imhof 2006).[4]

The second strand within the German debate shares the general idea of an increase in the transition from direct communication to indirect, mediated communication forms (cf. Schanze 2002), albeit not necessarily in a linear way (Nick Couldry seems to disagree on the point of linearity implied in the term mediatization—cf. Couldry 2008). This transition, linear or not, brings with it a change in the importance of time, place, and senses for communication pro-cesses. Instead, they are nowadays less clearly based in specific material realms. According to Winfried Schulz (as also outlined by Lundby in his introduction), media allow (a) an extension, (b) a substitution, (c) an amalgamation, and (d) an accommodation. We will return to these aspects in the debate below, since they are crucial anchor points for the relationship to domestication. Overall, Schulz defines mediatization very broadly as something that 'relates to changes associ-ated with communication media and their development' (2004, p. 87) and adds an assessment that sees a problematic development with 'dependencies, con-straints, and exaggerations' (ibid.). This needs to be reassessed at the end of this book—a judgement at this point appears to be too soon.

Friedrich Krotz, in his seminal work on mediatization, is also ambiva-lent about the developments, albeit less clear cut in his assessment. He outlines mediatization as a meta-process. Media are here seen to increasingly shape our social relations and many other (or even most) aspects of our life. This is nonetheless, as this book multiply underlines, not a media-deterministic point of view. Rather, it is the interrelationship between the media and the social that is crucial. Krotz begins his discussion with a differentiation between three forms of mediated communication: (a) mediated dialogical communication, (b) mediated monological communication, and (c) mediated interactive communication (Krotz 2007, p. 17; Hepp and Krotz 2007).[5] The origin of this differentiation is the assumption that face-to-face communication is the basic form of all communication and all other communication forms are modifications of this (which does not imply a value judgement).

Krotz (2007) continues his in-depth analysis of the phenomenon with an emphasis both on the quantitative as well as the qualitative shift that is implied in this meta-process. The latter, however, is the more important and more interesting of the two. Krotz does not simply deliver a brief definition about what mediatization means to him. Instead, he shows a whole range of changes that all relate to the meta-process (and are intertwined as well). He connects this to many existing sociological concepts. His colleague Andreas Hepp and Krotz himself described, in a paper presented at the ICA conference in 2007, that mediatization is the interconnection (or triangle) between media technological change, communicative change, and sociocultural change. This again underlines that this definition of mediatization does not begin with the media change but constructs a rather complex matrix of change and process.[6] The case studies Krotz uses to underline his ideas range from robots (and especially the robotic 'dog' AIBO) to computer games, mobile phones, web chats, and more. Hence mediatization in Krotz' definition is an all-encompassing concept. This makes it rather attractive but also in some ways problematic, because it remains very general (reminding us of Schulz' original definition). The combination with the domestication concept is hence meant to question this generality. It picks up on Krotz' insistence that 'the mediatization meta-process in particular makes it clear that lifeworld-specific communication remains the basis of communication and media in general' (Krotz 2008, p. 28)—hence the lifeworld needs to be analysed in more detail.

DOMESTICATION: THE BASICS

The concept of domestication, first developed in the late 1980s by Roger Silverstone, David Morley, and others (e.g., Morley and Silverstone 1991) and later developed further by Leslie Haddon and other colleagues (see, e.g., Berker, Hartmann, Punie, and Ward 2006; Haddon 2007), is a *media appropriation* concept.

In the first instance, it refers to the micro level of media use (and related perceptions). It describes and analyses the process of 'bringing the media home' both in the concrete as well as in the abstract sense of the word (implying the idea of making it one's own). The domestication concept helps to outline the role of media in people's everyday life in detail, showing the way that media are used for old and new forms of communication and engagement.

When the concept was first developed, it mainly argued against certain reductionisms that had entered both the media and communication studies and the cultural studies field. These concerned a rather functionalistic framework in relation to the notion of audience activities on the one hand. On the other hand, it concerned a concentration on the media text (which left out not only everyday activities but contexts in general, and was even less concerned with the interconnection between the media and the social). Other reductionisms were seen in relation to the complex web of social relations between different people involved in using the media (e.g., a family unit).

To offer an alternative concept, Roger Silverstone, with others, developed the domestication concept. It was the result of the theoretical foundation for a project about the household uses of information and communication technologies (HICT). Working through the idea of ethnographic methods used to study these households (Silverstone, Hirsch, and Morley 1991), and beginning to think of the relationship of media use to consumption (in a wide sense of the word) (e.g., Silverstone and Hirsch 1992), Silverstone in particular eventually named different dimensions of the process of integration of media into these households (and households in general). The emphasis was then on process, that is, on the idea of the media having a life before they enter the household, but continuing to have a 'biography' after they entered (e.g., Silverstone and Haddon 1996). The latter idea was the development of a concept by Igor Kopytoff (1986, p. 64), who had focused on the cultural perspective of the production of commodities, emphasizing that 'commodities must be not only produced materially as things, but also culturally marked as being a certain kind of thing.' Similarly, Silverstone and his colleagues tried to show the specificity of the media as commodities. This was an alternative point of view to many existing ones at the time in the sense that it brought the materiality of the media (back) into the discussion. At the same time, the domestication concept underlines exactly the process of how a medium is made by users into 'a certain kind of thing.'

This 'certain kind of thing' differs for every household unit (and every member therein), it changes over time, and it is situationally different. Hence it is less the domesticated commodity that is being focused on here than the process of domestication and the different power struggles taking place therein. These are captured in the dimensions that Silverstone and colleagues developed to describe the process: commodification (the design and development of the media product, but also its marketing); appropriation (whole process of consumption, but especially the moment when the object enters a household); objectification (the actual usage of the media object, but also its functional and aesthetic placement in the environment); incorporation (the integration of the media technology into the routines of the everyday, i.e., the ways they are used, sometimes also changed); and conversion (the relationship and announcement of the media technology and its use to the outside world) (see also Hartmann 2008a). All of these are located within the household framework, which most of the early domestication work concentrated on (for other developments, see Berker et al. 2006; Haddon 2006).

Silverstone and colleagues also added other theoretical aspects to their concept, which underline the specificity thereof: there is, on the one hand, the double articulation concept (see Hartmann 2006a; Livingstone 2007). Not wanting to enter the detailed discussion once again, the point of mentioning this here is that the double articulation idea (even more than the biography of things mentioned above) reminds us of the specificity of the media as special kinds of commodities and, hence, of appropriation. It simply states that media are (at least!) doubly articulated in the sense of being media in terms of symbolic content as well as media in terms of material objects—or, as Couldry calls it 'as both transmission technology and representational content' (Couldry 2008, p. 375). Objects of consumption they are both.[7] Either aspect brings with it a different setting, both of which, however, need to be looked at in combination (Livingstone 2007, pp. 17–18). Hence the media user is also doubly articulated (ibid.), because he/she is both citizen and consumer within the relationship to media. It implies in principle that media research should equally try to address (at least) both aspects. This, however, has remained problematic thus far. This should not deter us from returning to the basic idea. The therein-expressed tension and challenge, as with the argument here, needs a mediation process. More about this later.

In the same context (of a possible need for mediation), the other main theoretical strand within the domestication framework is the moral economy (e.g., Silverstone, Hirsch, and Morley 1991; Silverstone 1994; Silverstone and Haddon 1996). Just as the formal economy is a very delicate and always-moving structure (as is acutely visible at this moment in 2008), Silverstone and his colleagues announced that households have (or rather are) similarly complex 'economies,' albeit on a moral level. The household and its members, it is assumed, are trying to secure their ontological security and are therein constantly challenged. The media, on the other hand, are one of the most active prospects of the challenge. Hence the moral economy partly serves to adapt to the challenges, partly to protect the household from too radical a change or challenge. The appropriation process is generally characterized by the transition of the media (object) crossing the line between the formal and the moral economy of the household. The values, biographies, and ethics that make up such a moral economy are often protected through a somewhat 'conservative' approach to any new (and doubly articulated!) media object. While this is a never-ending and always principally open process, there are also times of relative stability. At the same time, media provide a challenge (sometimes desired, often not). Television in its mythical character, for example, the focus of much of Silverstone's early work, 'forces us to confront fantasy, the uncanny, desire, perversion, obsession: those so-called troubles of the everyday which are represented and repressed, both, in media texts of one kind or another, and which disturb the thin tissue of what passes for the rational and the normal in modern society' (Silverstone 1999, p. 11).

Again, we are reminded that media are crucial intermediaries, both challenging and often reassuring. At the same time, we are also reminded that the media do not write on an empty slate. Quite the opposite: they are massively embedded within and into existing patterns of thought, routines, etc. Sometimes—despite having maybe been chosen and acquired—they have to fight for a place in someone's life. And sometimes they lose this fight. Silverstone, in the book published recently (and posthumously), takes the idea of the moral even further, claiming that the media construct our moral universe. He argues for a heightened responsibility not only on the media's side (that, too!), but also on the individual level. 'The everyday, hitherto the site of a more or less unreflecting gaze, can, and should, be made more critically aware' (Silverstone 2007, p. 187). The media enables this process (if it does take up the ethical role assumed here), but this needs to be continued elsewhere (with care and hospitality, as Silverstone argues).

Albeit not part of the domestication concept as such, this is a problematic, but not illogical, development of thought from the moral economy onwards. Without wanting to enter the particular discussion around Silverstone's book overall (see, e.g., Dayan 2007), important in the mediatization and domestication context is to stress, just as Silverstone has done, the need to increasingly reflect on the ethical role of the media in current times—exactly because of their multiple articulations—while at the same time to reflect on the individual's responsibilities. This also already addresses some of the criticisms voiced towards the domestication framework that we will turn to now. This will also come back in the later reflections around the notion of mediation.

DOMESTICATION IN THE AGE OF MEDIATIZATION

Above, we have already learned that the domestication concept is facing challenges at the conceptual level (e.g., the ethical questions, but also the question what kinds of articulations we find in media and how this relates to the specificity of appropriation processes). Both theoretically and empirically, recent works have underlined a number of additional points to (re)consider. There is a tendency to think of additional layers for the existing framework. A possible *third articulation*, for example, has been suggested to be part of the articulation processes at work (Hartmann 2006a). This combines not only the object and the symbolic (i.e., the ritual, the flow), but also the content in a more differentiated way. The latter gains a new importance, not least in the light of changing content production and involvement possibilities within the new media.

Irmi Karl, on the other hand, added an additional layer to the *household composition*: the dimension of *sexuality* to the complex web of meaning-making in the domestication process (which sits next to, among others, the question of parenthood, age, education and income, and work location [homeworkers vs. not]). Her work looks specifically at the struggle of identity-work in relation to (again among others) the media that takes place in lesbian and/or women-only households (Karl 2007).

Another focus in terms of those people making up the households is that specific roles have been found to exist. A prominent one in terms of the introduction of new media to existing structures is the *warm expert* (cf. Bakardjieva 2005),[8] the trusted person whom one can rely on for advice and help. In my own research, I found a certain solidarity among users of wireless services in public places—at least as soon as the services broke down (and in terms of sharing the most important resource of all—electricity—cf. Hartmann 2007). Another role for the stranger emerges in public viewing environments, that is, those environments where people come together to watch events on large screens (Hartmann 2008b). Television's move into the public (actually, a return) underlines yet another fissure in the texture of the home and its routines and spaces, especially in the light of more mobile, fluid networks of people, places, and technologies overall. Hence, in this context, we do not find a warm expert, but the other as the *reflective screen* (showing one's sociality) or the *sharing expert*. Mediatization and domestication meet here, especially on the discursive level. Again, I will return to this point.

The move just described relates also to the increasingly porous 'boundary' between home and outside world, as David Morley (himself an early proponent of domestication research [without the label]) explains:

> Under the impact of new technologies and global cultural flows, the home nowadays is not so much a local, particular 'self-enclosed' space, but rather, as Zygmunt Bauman puts it, more and more a 'phantasmagoric' place, as electronic means of communication allow the radical intrusion of what he calls the 'realm of the far' (traditionally, the realm of the strange and potentially troubling) into the 'realm of the near' (the traditional 'safe space' of ontological security). (Morley 2006, p. 23)

Under these circumstances, to establish and/or maintain the moral economy (or several moral economies—see below) is becoming increasingly hard work. This has huge potential as well, but for many people it is first and foremost a challenge. While the boundary was always porous (not least thanks to the media), it now becomes even less detectable. This calls for research both inside the changing households and in many other environments. The household-framework is not gone (and will not disappear—quite the opposite, it, too, has seen a potential increase in media), but it has been challenged in its primacy.

One methodological answer is to take ethnographic methods more seriously. Karl, for example, has actually lived with the people in the households she studied to begin to map their appropriation moves and media uses (Karl, forthcoming). At the same time, she, too, acknowledges that increasing mobilities bring with them the named complexities (see also Höflich and Hartmann 2007). More mobile ethnographic approaches might be part of the answer, that is, the researcher him-/herself might need to acquire a certain mobility in order to adequately follow the person/the media/the situation in question (Hartmann 2006b).

Another point to be reconsidered is the question of how far the domestication framework actually allows the potential for change to be reflected (and detected). Its conservative nature has already been debated (see e.g., Feenberg 1999) as well as partly defended (Silverstone 2006a). Nonetheless, it remains a crucial question, especially in the light of new developments (as well as in terms of Silverstone's later writings). The first step in the rethinking is to take up Eileen Green's idea that it may be more appropriate to think of 'different and at times conflicting moral economies,' rather than *the* moral economy of the household (Green 2001, p. 182)—or, probably, both individual and household moral economies.

Underlying these thoughts is the fundamental question of motivation and attitude to life, because if the ontological security is what we all need to preserve, and, therefore, often defend, then change is a somewhat problematic category. At the same time, change is essential for human development, but it is nonetheless always a threat within the idea of security. In increasingly changing times, the idea of stability needs to be rethought. Not only are there already competing moral economies within one household alone, but, if the home is increasingly an idea that might not be related to household structures anymore (but maybe my laptop or my mobile), the idea of ontological security then becomes a different one. A sense of continuity and order might indeed become more related to the actual objects in question. It might relate to routines other than before (something that features much in my research on Wi-Fi cafes). And the individual programme or site might indeed also gain renewed importance (a Web interface might turn into a sense of belonging—or online social networks turn into the providers of stability). All of this needs to be (and is partly in the process of being) empirically researched. The domestication framework helps to frame it, but it needs further additions. The (dis)trust in the world has changed since those times when television was still dominant. Research on the fragmentation and possible fluidity of identities has pointed in similar directions, and connections to media have frequently been made. 'Being in the world' in relation to others has become increasingly complex—and increasingly mediatized. Just to remind us what 'ontological security' was once defined as might help to underline the complexity of our current undertaking:

> A man may have a sense of his presence in the world as a real, alive, whole, and, in a temporal sense, a continuous person. As such, he can live out into the world and meet others: a world and others experienced as equally real, alive, whole, and continuous. Such a basically ontologically secure person will encounter all the hazards of life...from a centrally firm sense of his own and other people's reality and identity. (Laing 1960, p. 39)

The firm sense of his (or her!) own and other people's reality is something that the domestication process—despite the mediatization of everyday life—wants to secure. It is, however, a difficult battle. And it needs to allow and acknowledge the conflictual without which change is impossible.

Next, we need to add another level of domestication that is less prominent in the original framework: that of discursive domestication. This not only provides another clear link to the mediatization framework, it also offers another explanatory bridge to the necessary update of the framework for the analysis.

DOMESTICATED MEDIATIZATION: THE DISCOURSE

> [T]he main 'effect' media have is their longstanding and increasing interpenetration of different aspects of cultural life by appropriation or domestication of technology-based communication—a process we call mediatization. (Hepp and Krotz 2007, p. 2)

The immediate association of a link between mediatization and domestication is simply that the domestication process shows on the micro level what mediatization provides on the meta level. One related simple assumption would be that mediatization processes clearly enter the domestic and related spheres and that research in this field can illustrate how this takes place: where resistances are, etc. In this sense, domestication would show the processes that Schulz (2004) labelled extension, substitution, and also nowadays, increasingly, amalgation. This, however, would still reduce the rather thought-provoking concept to the mere deliverer of empirical material (albeit in a fairly well-structured manner), a *tool* to show how and where mediatization exists. While domestication research could help to keep a realistic lid on (or offer empirical differentiation for) the mediatization concept, this would reduce it to 'a spanner in the works.' This limitation, however valuable it might be, would not do justice to either of these concepts. Domestication, after all, is meant to show the problematic and dynamic relationship between public and private, between different sets of values, etc., and highlights the role of the media within this process. Mediatization, on the other hand, with its potential (over?)emphasis on change helps to problematize the idea of the media playing a role within everyday life, even where and when they are not used.

Instead, I want to propose here that domestication is a *precondition* for mediatization. This is not to say that domestication is a process with an end that needs to be reached before a state of mediatization can be announced. Instead, I would like to suggest that the engagement with the media that is expressed in the idea of domestication (engagement meaning the whole range of possible encounters, from nonuse to fandom, from imagination to conversion) is necessary for mediatization processes. This claim implies a certain relationship between a more individual level (including groups of diverse sorts), which the domestication process refers to, to a more abstract social level, which the mediatization idea implies. In many ways, then, there is no mediatization without domestication. Or, put differently, domestication is a kind of coping strategy to deal with mediatization—and hence an essential part thereof. But this domestication is not limited to the appropriation processes that have mostly been researched within the domestication framework. Rather, I want to put a renewed emphasis on one aspect that tends to get mentioned only in passing (if at all): the aspect of *imagination*—the domestication dimension that is the least material of all, but which provides an important passage point in the domestication process.

The imagination is the first dimension in the domestication process, since 'commodification necessarily depends on a dimension of imaginative work that potential or actual consumers undertake as they participate, willy-nilly, in the consumption process' (Silverstone and Haddon 1996, p. 63). Imaginative work does not, however, only apply to media technologies that are eventually bought. Quite the opposite: the imaginative work is everywhere—often more so when someone decides not to use a certain media technology. The imaginative work, as suggested here, includes the whole discursive construction around (new) media, their potential societal consequences, the utopian and dystopian debates, etc. These discourses, while an important part of the domestication process, also need to be domesticated. They, too, are integrated into the moral economies—either as reasons for acquisition and use or against; sometimes to justify whole lifestyles, etc. These discursive appropriations take place on many different levels: society overall, organizations, youth cultures, families, individuals, etc. On the societal level, we often get techno-social visions on a large (e.g., information society or information highway) or small (e.g., SecondLife as a commercial 'must') scale. On the more individual level, these appropriations often express themselves in lifestyle choices. An explicit example thereof can be found in television nonuse as an expression of alternative, culturally proactive lifestyles (e.g., Sicking 2000)—which is more differentiated in relation to internet nonuse.

This discursive appropriation is an important aspect of domestication. Hence domestication research has shown, for example, that an understanding that the children's educational needs include computer ownership has often led to its subsequent acquisition.[9] The discursive is increasing thanks to mediatization—and therefore needs to be regarded in the research conducted in the field. It is not meant as a separate part, but simply a renewed emphasis. It is also the link that Andre Jansson (2002) has asked for, between commodification and mediatization, since, as he states, 'mediatization itself generates commodification' (Jansson 2002, p. 16). This is commodification in both Jansson's and the domestication concept's point of view. It is the tension between desire and frustration, and the mythical and metaphoric world constructed to fuel these desires (that have to fail in order for consumption to continue—see Silverstone and Haddon 1996, p. 63). Hence, in a mediatized world, there is more media to consume (both as objects and symbolic content, potentially also individual content) and, at the same time, more consumption on display. Plus, the wider societal discourses tell us about visions beyond the commodity. They show how society overall domesticates the wild—and how society overall is also built on a notion that reflects the tension between old and new that can be found in ontological security. The discursive might in fact be the most 'conservative' of all appropriation dimensions, taking on board social norms and similar limitations.

The double articulation in particular, within which media are meaningful in themselves but also transmit meanings, gets another layer when the discursive is reemphasized. This connects also to Couldry's claim that the media have become the unquestioned centre of society (Couldry 2003) or, slightly less far reaching, a social institution in their own right (Hjarvard, as mentioned in Lundby's introduction). Another important distinction appears to have been made by Stig Hjarvard (chapter 8, this volume) in terms of the differentiation between a direct and an indirect form of mediatization. The indirect, that is, the weaker mediatization form, as Lundby explains in his introduction, is 'when the media and their symbolic world in terms of form, content or organization increasingly influence an existing activity.' This is still a different emphasis from the discursive mentioned here, but it points in the same direction: media itself, but also communication about and around media, is increasingly everywhere. Spaces—discursive or real—without media do become less. This also connects to Schulz' notion of accommodation, that is, the fact that people have to adapt to the media simply because it exists and takes place around them. The perceived inescapability of the media, expressed so well in the mediatization concept, plays out very clearly at this discursive level. Its interplay with the other levels is the most important aspect to be looked at.

Hence, exactly what weak mediatization and accommodation look like and how they are dealt with and translated into and within everyday life, that is, what consequences these processes have for social life, is researched in the traditional domestication field. This is a fundamentally dialectical process, as the double articulation already underlines, or, as Couldry put it:

> '...media' work, and must work, not merely by transmitting discrete textual units for discrete moments of reception, but through a process of environmental transformation which, in turn, transforms the conditions under which any future media can be produced and understood.' (Couldry 2008, p. 380)

This dialectic, this (at least) double articulation, meets once again in the idea of mediation.

MEDIATIZED DOMESTICATION: MEDIATION

> In general, the notion of mediation in the sense of media intervening between ourselves and 'reality' is no more than a metaphor, although it does point to several of the roles played by the media in connecting us to other experience. (McQuail 2005, p. 83)

> Mediation...describes the fundamentally, but unevenly dialectical process in which institutionalized media of communication are involved in the general circulation of symbols in everyday life. (Silverstone 2007, p. 109)

While Denis McQuail does not see mediation as any very specific metaphor, Silverstone uses the term to describe the fundamental changes being discussed in this book. Despite the well-put argument for the term mediatization rather than mediation (see Lundby's introduction) and Krotz' refusal to see mediation as a reference point (2007), I want to return to the concept here as another bridging point. It seems to add a layer that might so far be missing. After all, the mediation idea is much more normative than the mediatization concept and is hence more easily attacked. As such, however, it might also be a highly necessary debate to be had.

But let us, again, begin with defining the core idea. One basic streak therein is that mediation refers to the fact that media help to bring together bits (people, ideas, etc.) that otherwise would be separated by time and space, maybe also by intentions, etc. Silverstone (2002), hence, goes further and claims that mediation is a transformative process in which the meaningfulness and value of things is constructed. Again, we are now moving into the complex arena of ethics. In this sense, we are also moving close to those understandings that refer to the professional mediation, that is, the processes of conciliation, intervention, or negotiation among separated, often conflicted, parties (Livingstone in the foreword to this book). This is sometimes used in courts; increasingly, also, it has become a consultancy job, in which a third party intervenes in a conflict and takes a neutral position, that is, does not take sides, and from there tries to solve the conflict through looking at all aspects and through specific forms of negotiation.

Silverstone described mediation as dialectical, because there is a tension between the producers and the consumers of media, but also because across societies there are uneven possibilities to engage. The dialectics do not necessarily lie with the media as such but with the processes taking place therein. They also, as we have seen, lie in the consumption of media as both texts and objects. Mediation then, is what makes Silverstone's mediapolis 'tick': 'Mediation is a practice in which producers, subjects, and audiences take part, and take part together' (2007, p. 38). It requires active participation in terms of thinking, speaking, listening, and acting (ibid.). This is the necessary process to give life to the ethical stance referred to earlier. In its normativity, it seems to offer the necessary moral antidote to possible anxieties related to processes of mediatization (e.g., Schulz' negative assessment). Taken in this light, mediation is a necessary precondition for mediatization not to go wrong.

However, there remains a slight unease about it all. In many ways, the problematic aspect of the moral economy approach seems to be repeated. Again, ontological security appears to be at the core—now, however, provided by the mediapolis. Both media and its users need to work even harder than before to uphold the basic security standards—without the conflictual and the changeable being at the core of the concern. It is a huge responsibility implied therein. It might be a responsibility that needs to be taken up for mediatization not to become a swear word. Domestication, however, underlines a certain unwillingness to engage as well—it shows many small instances of indeed 'making its one's own,' sometimes in terms of ignoring or not using it. These niches need to remain somehow—coupled, maybe, with a heightened sense of responsibility.

OUTLOOK: SEVERAL TERMS, ONE MEANING?

In the light of the weight of responsibility discussed above, I would like to end on a brief reflection about terminology. I argued above to use the domestication and mediatization concepts in combination; in fact, I have even called one a precondition for the other. Additionally, the argument was that mediatization highlights flaws or lacks in the domestication concept that were already visible, but now get accentuated. One approach to 'update' the domestication framework accordingly was to (re)emphasize (or add) the discursive layer in the domestication approach. This is one of the dialectical bonds between the wider societal stream and those processes taking place in households, in organizations, in specific places or among certain groups, etc. On the other hand, the question of ontological security, moral economies and the mediapolis will need to be addressed in more detail. Only with these additions, it appears, can we think about either a mediated domestication or a domesticated mediatization.

Whether domestication is still an appropriate term for the concept described above has been asked before. But, especially in light of mediatization, this question needs to be continually addressed. What we need to avoid is what Rachel Bowlby claims: 'If a theory gets domesticated, that's the end of it. It becomes like everything else' (2000, p. 306). She goes on to argue that the taming is problematic, but also adds that a certain homeliness could possibly be read more positively: as providing exactly a sense of belonging, niche, playfulness. While she remains ambivalent about domesticating theories, these hints should serve here to remind us that both stability and change are highly ambivalent and problematic. Hence a high moral ground is maybe necessary to keep moving but will never describe the social life 'out there.' The mediatized domestication approach, however, can perhaps illustrate some of the ambivalences in actu and at the same time prevent the mediatization theory from becoming 'domesticated' in Bowlby's sense of the word.

NOTES

1. The same applies to the German terms 'Domestizierung' and 'Mediatisierung,' where the ending '-ierung' is equally used for larger social processes.
2. In the latest edition of *Aviso* (No. 47, October 2008), the information service of the German Communication Association (DGPuK), both sides (mediatization and medialization) are once again promoted and compared to each other.
3. Hence, Thomas Steinmaurer (2003) claims that *mediatization* refers to the technical aspects, while *medialization* refers to the content aspects. Most other authors, however, do not follow this distinction.
4. In contrast to other concepts of society (such as the closely related concepts of network or information societies), the media society concept is characterized primarily by this mediatization process, mostly on the political level (cf. Hartmann, 2005).
5. Schulz (2004) also offers a threefold media differentiation, albeit referring to the functions: (1) the relay or mediation function (the transfer of messages), (2) the semiotic function (the processes of encoding and decoding of meaning), and (3) the economic function (including processes of standardization, commodification, division of labour, profit).

6. Even just the discursive notion of the growing importance and role of media both in our every-day lives and in the world overall is impressive (as the initial thoughts around the terminology underline). These discourses obviously shape practices immensely, but they begin with shaping perceptions.

7. At the same time, it underlines that media are produced, marketed, and in some ways also consumed just as any other product (the culture industry is raising its head, not least in the idea of creative industries). If mediatization is meant to be understood, this qualitative difference remains crucial.

8. James Stewart (2007) added the idea of the 'local expert' to the debate, while Stefan Verhaegh (2007) speaks of the 'warm user.' All point in the same direction.

9. Research also shows that the actual usage later might differ quite a bit from the original aim—again, this is part of a domestication process.

REFERENCES

Bakardjieva, M. (2005). *Internet Society: The Internet in Everyday Life*. London: Sage.

Berker, T., Hartmann, M., Punie, Y., and Ward, K. (Eds.). (2006). *Domestication of Media and Technology*. Maidenhead: Open University Press.

Bowlby, R. (2000). Domestication. In M. McQuillan (Ed.), *Deconstruction* (pp. 304–310). Edinburgh: Edinburgh University Press.

Couldry, N. (2008). Mediatization or mediation? Alternative understandings of the emergent space of digital storytelling. *New Media & Society*, 10(3), 373–391.

Couldry, N. (2003). *Media Rituals: A Critical Approach*. London: Routledge.

Dayan, D. (2007). On morality, distance and the other: Roger Silverstone's media and morality. *International Journal of Communication*, 1, 113–122.

Donges, P. (2008). *Medialisierung politischer Organisationen: Parteien in der Mediengesellschaft*. Wiesbaden: VS Verlag.

Feenberg, A. (1999). *Questioning Technology*. London: Routledge.

Giddens, A. (1997). *Konsequenzen der Moderne*. Frankfurt/M.: Suhrkamp.

Green, E. (2001). Technology, leisure and everyday practices. In E. Green and A. Adam (Eds.), *Virtual Gender—Technology, Consumption and Identity* (pp. 173–188). London: Routledge.

Haddon, L. (2006). Empirical studies using the domestication framework. In T. Berker et al. (Eds.), *Domestication of Media and Technology* (pp. 103–122). Maidenhead: Open University Press.

Haddon, L. (2007). Roger Silverstone's legacies: domestication. *New Media & Society*, 9(1), 25–32.

Hartmann, M. (2005). Der Mythos und seine Metaphern: (Medien-) Gesellschaftliche Leitbilder. In P. Rössler and F. Krotz (Eds.): *Mythen der Mediengesellschaft—The Media Society and Its Myths* (pp. 33–62). Konstanz: UVK.

Hartmann, M. (2006a). The triple articulation of ICTs: Media as technological objects, symbolic environments and individual texts. In T. Berker, M. Hartmann, Y. Punie, and K. Ward (Eds.), *Domestication of Media and Technology* (pp. 80–102). Maidenhead: Open University Press.

Hartmann, M. (2006b). A mobile ethnographic view on (mobile) media usage? In J. R. Höflich and M. Hartmann (Eds.), *Mobile Communication in Everyday Life: Ethnographic Views, Observations and Reflections* (pp. 273–297). Berlin: Frank & Timme.

Hartmann, M. (2007). *Domesticating the Wireless Beast: Wi-Fi Access—Cafe Policies and Cultures*. Unpublished presentation presented at the IAMCR 50th Anniversary Conference, Paris, France; 23–25. July 2007.

Hartmann, M. (2008a). Domestizierung 2.0: Grenzen und Chancen eines Medienaneignungskonzeptes. In C. Winter, A. Hepp, and F. Krotz (Eds.), *Theoriediskussion in der Kommunikationswissenschaft. Band 2: Spezifische Diskussionsfelder* (pp. 401–416). Wiesbaden: VS Verlag.

Hartmann, M. (2008b). Fandom without the trimmings? EURO 2008, public viewing and new kinds of audiences. In N. Carpentier, P. Pruulmann-Vengerfeldt, K. Nordenstreng, M. Hartmann, P. Vihalemm, B. Cammaerts, H. Nieminen, and T. Olsson. (Eds.), *Democracy, Journalism and Technology: New Developments in an Enlarged Europe. The Intellectual Work of the 2008 European Media and Communication Doctoral Summer School* (pp. 255–266). Tartu: University of Tartu Press.

Helle-Valle, J., and Slettemeas, D. (2008). ICTs, domestication and language games: a Wittgensteinian approach to media uses. *New Media & Society.* 10(1), 45–66.

Hepp, A. (2004). *Cultural Studies und Medienanalyse. Eine Einführung.* 2. Auflage. Wiesbaden: VS Verlag.

Hepp, A., and Krotz, F. (2007). *What 'Effect' do Media Have? Mediatization and Processes of Socio-Cultural Change.* Unpublished paper presented at the ICA Conference in San Francisco, May 24–28, 2007.

Höflich, J. R., and Hartmann, M. (2007). Grenzverschiebungen—Mobile Kommunikation im Spannungsfeld von öffentlichen und privaten Sphären. In J. Röser (Ed.) MedienAlltag: Domestizierungsprozesse alter und neuer Medien. (pp. 211–221) Wiesbaden: VS Verlag.

Imhof, K. (2006). Mediengesellschaft und Medialisierung. *Medien & Kommunikationswissenschaft,* 54(2), 191–215.

Jansson, A. (2002). The Mediatization of Consumption. Towards an analytical framework of image culture. *Journal of Consumer Culture,* 2(1), 5–31.

Karl, I. (2007). Domesticating the lesbian?: Queer strategies and technologies of home-making. *M/C Journal,* 10(4). Retrieved 12 Jul. 2008 from <http://journal.media-culture.org.au/0708/06-karl.php>.

Karl, I. (in press). Technology and women's lives: Queering media ethnography. *Reconstruction* 9.1, Fieldwork and Interdisciplinary Research, 2009.

Kopytoff, I. (1986). The cultural biography of things: Commoditization as process. In A. Appadurai (Ed.): *The Social Life of Things: Commodities in Cultural Perspective* (pp. 64–91). Cambridge, UK: Cambridge University Press.

Krotz, F. (1997). Kontexte des Verstehens audiovisueller Kommunikate. In M. Charlton and S. Schneider (Eds.): *Rezeptionsforschung* (pp. 73–89) Opladen: Westdeutscher Verlag.

Krotz, F. (2007). *Mediatisierung: Fallstudien zum Wandel von Kommunikation.* Wiesbaden: VS Verlag für Sozialwissenschaften.

Krotz, F. (2008). Media connectivity: Concepts, conditions and consequences. In A. Hepp, F. Krotz, S. Moores, and C. Winter (Eds.), *Connectivity, Networks and Flows. Conceptualizing Contemporary Communications* (pp. 13–32). Cresskill, NJ: Hampton Press.

Laing, D. (1960). *The Divided Self: An Existential Study in Sanity and Madness.* London: Penguin.

Livingstone, S. (2007). On the material and the symbolic: Silverstone's double articulation of research traditions in New Media Studies. *New Media & Society.* 9(1), 16–24.

McQuail, D. (2005). *Mass Communication Theory.* 5th ed. London: Sage.

Morley, D., and Silverstone, R. (1991). Communication and context: ethnographic perspectives on the media audience. In K. B. Jensen and N. Jankowski (Eds.): *A Handbook of Qualitative Methodologies.* London: Routledge (pp. 149–162).

Schanze, H. (2002). Medialisierung. In H. Schanze: *Metzler Lexikon Medientheorie—Medienwissenschaft. Ansätze—Personen—Grundbegriffe* (p. 199). Stuttgart: Metzler.

Schulz, W. (2004). Reconstructing mediatization as an analytical concept. *European Journal of Communication*, 19(1), 87–101.

Sicking, P. (2000). *Leben ohne Fernsehen*. Wiesbaden: DUV.

Silverstone, R. (1993). *Domesticating the Revolution: Information and Communication Technologies and Everyday Life*. Unpublished conference PICT National Conference, Kenilworth, UK, May 1993.

Silverstone, R. (1994). *Television and Everyday Life*. London: Routledge.

Silverstone, R. (2002). Complicity and collusion in the mediation of everyday life. *New Literary History*, 33, 745–764.

Silverstone, R. (2006a). Domesticating domestication. Reflections on the life of a concept. In T. Berker, M. Hartmann, Y. Punie, and K. Ward (Eds.): *Domestication of Media and Technology* (pp. 229–248). Maidenhead: Open University Press.

Silverstone, R. (2006b). *Media and Morality: On the Rise of the Mediapolis*. Cambridge, UK: Polity.

Silverstone, R., and Haddon, L. (1996). Design and the domestication of information and communication technologies: Technical change and everyday life. In R. Mansell and R. Silverstone (Eds.): *Communication by Design. The Politics of Information and Communication Technologies* (pp. 44–74). Oxford, UK: Oxford University Press.

Silverstone, R., Hirsch, E., and Morley, D. (1991). Listening to a long conversation: An ethnographic approach to the study of information and communication technologies in the home. *Cultural Studies: Theorizing Politics, Politicising Theory*, 5(2), 204–227.

Silverstone, R., and Hirsch, E. (Eds.) (1992). *Consuming Technologies: Media and Information in Domestic Spaces*. London: Routledge.

Steinmaurer, T. (2003). Medienentwicklung und gesellschaftlicher Wandel. In Behmer, Markus et al. (Eds.): *Medienentwicklung und gesellschaftlicher Wandel: Beiträge zu einer theoretischen und empirischen Herausforderung* (pp. 103–120). Wiesbaden: VS Verlag.

Stewart, J. (2007). Local experts in the domestication of information and communication technologies. *Information, Communication & Society*, 10(4), 547–569.

Trenz, H.-J. (2006). *Mediatization and Democratization in the EU*. ARENA Working Paper No. 14, http://www.arena.uio.no (accessed 20/09/2008).

Verhaegh, S. (2007). From simple customer to warm user; Or, who cares about the maintenance of community innovations? *Observatorio (OBS*)*, 1(3), 155–184.

CHAPTER TWELVE

Mobile Belongings: Texturation AND Stratification IN Mediatization Processes

ANDRÉ JANSSON

In this chapter, I am interested in the social interplay between two ambiguous forces of modern society: mobility and mediatization. More specifically, I am interested in what these forces do to people's senses of belonging and continuity. The impact of both mobility and mediatization is somehow dualistic in this regard—on the one hand providing vivid resources for identity work and the accumulation of social capital, on the other hand threatening to invoke rupture and dissonance to the lifeworld. This ambiguity stems not only from the complexity of the processes as such—there is a plethora of different mobilities and mediatizations—but also from the multifaceted and situated nature of people's senses of belonging. The not-so-long-ago predominant understanding of home and belonging as a matter of roots, stability, and place-making, stemming from phenomenology and humanist geography, has been rightly challenged by a more post-structural and nomadic view of the home as an open-ended process of becoming. However, the latter has also shown a tendency to slip into metaphysics, morally condemning people's widespread and enduring resistance to mobility and (mediatized) social renewal (see Cresswell 2006, Ch. 2). Even though it would seem fair to hold that we are witnessing a society becoming more globalized and, in some respects, even cosmopolitan, the point I want to elaborate in this chapter is that we must also empirically reassess the significance of *social durability* within this development. To balance the post-structural argument that change and flux also occur through repetition (Deleuze 1994), we must keep in mind the opposite perspective: (a) that continuity and reproduction reside within, through and behind seemingly ephemeral mobilities, flows, and mediations, and (b) that certain parts of society and certain regions of our private lifeworlds are little affected by mobility and mediatization.

The triangular relationship between mobility, mediatization, and belonging can be studied within a broad range of contexts and from many different angles. The first objective of this chapter, then, is to develop a theoretical framework for analysing *the mediatization of belonging*. Merging theoretical perspectives from Pierre Bourdieu, Henri Lefebvre, and Gaston Bachelard, I will pay particular attention to the (re)productive interplay between material and social belongings, pointing to how the distinctive inclusion and exclusion of media texts and technologies operate through more durable structures of taste (Bourdieu), texture (Lefebvre), and imagination (Bachelard).

My second aim is to clarify what happens to the mediatization of belonging *under mobile life conditions*. This aim will be fulfilled through an abductive analysis of first-hand ethnographic data, gathered in spring 2008 among a group of Swedish expatriate professionals working within the development sector in Nicaragua. As Shaun Moores (2006) has recently argued, the case of (trans) migration is of particular interest if we want to reach a deeper, more phenomenological understanding of people's mediatized spaces of belonging. This is precisely because this kind of mobility infuses a potential disturbance of the lifeworld; a rupture in the processes of mediation. Exploring the balance between such transitions and the above-mentioned structures of durability, I will put forward two key conclusions from my fieldwork:

1. Cultural capital, as embodied through taste and expressed, for instance, through media use, attains a disembedding and re-embedding function and thus operates as a mobility resource.
2. The appropriations and uses of new online media among cosmopolitan expatriates may entertain intimate bonds at a distance but also reinforce the social and cultural distinctions generated by global mobility.

TASTE, IMAGINATION, AND TEXTURE:
CONTINUITIES OF SOCIAL AND MATERIAL BELONGINGS

The concept of belonging can be understood in at least two different ways, suggesting two different relationships between self and environment. On the one hand, we may speak of belonging as an experience of *community* and *integration*. In order to establish a sense of personal continuity, a biography of the self, the individual must be recognized simultaneously as a unique social being and as part of a larger social context, whether a family, a workplace, or nation-state. In this view, the individual's sense of belonging stems from the interplay between expressive practices and the recognition gained from the social world. As asserted by phenomenologists such as Schutz and Luckmann (1973) and social psychologists such as Giddens (1991), socialization is thus largely based on signifying practices, that is, *cultural praxis*, through which people come to identify with those with whom they feel they have 'something in common.'

On the other hand, we may understand belonging in terms of *possession*. Belongings are the things we own (albeit not always in a strictly economic sense), notably the material goods that give shape and substance to our everyday environments and social performances. When discussing what makes people feel 'at home' in the world, the copresence of (or links to) familiar people *and* objects is frequently mentioned (e.g., Seamon 1979; Morley 2001; Novicka 2007). The material grounding of everyday life, whether it is a stable home-place, a *Heimat*, or a constellation of mobile properties, is important not only as an expressive stage but also as a memory bank for the life biography and as a secure harbour for nonreflective activity. Through our routinized everyday practices, these secure material environments extend beyond the realm of our personal belongings (typically thought of as the home-place), forming a regionalized material geography of the lifeworld—understood as the taken-for-granted space of everyday life—linking the private domain to the public, and thus opening our lives to the plural spaces of wider social interaction (e.g., Goffman 1959, 1971; Schutz and Luckmann 1973).

Belonging is thus not one thing but many—especially in modern societies marked by the 'pluralization of lifeworlds' (Berger et al. 1973). Every individual's sense of belonging is founded on a conglomerate of different social and material identifications and varies over time depending on his or her life trajectory. What all senses of belonging have in common, however, is that they emerge through an interplay between the social and the material realm. This interplay, as noted above, is mediated through culture. To pin down the 'essence' of any sense of belonging, I would like to combine Gaston Bachelard's notion of *resonance*, taken from his book *The Poetics of Space* ([1957] 1969), with Pierre Bourdieu's ([1979] 1984) theory of cultural *taste*. The sense of belonging can then be defined as *the experience of cultural resonance between the social and the material realms of belonging; and what governs the production of resonance is the embodied cultural predispositions of taste.*

The cultural logic of identifying social and material properties has been brilliantly expressed in Bourdieu's work, such as in this extract from *Distinction*:

> *The system of matching properties, which includes people*—one speaks of a 'well-matched couple,' and friends like to say they have the same tastes—is organized by taste, a system of classificatory schemes which may only very partially become conscious although, as one rises in the social hierarchy, lifestyle is increasingly a matter of what Weber calls the 'stylization of life.' ... *Taste is the practical operator of the transmutation of things into distinct and distinctive signs,* of continuous distributions into discontinuous oppositions; it raises the differences inscribed in the physical order of bodies to the symbolic order of significant distinctions. (Bourdieu [1979] 1984, pp. 174–175, emphasis added)

Bourdieu's view of taste as an organizing principle of 'matching properties' holds that within the cultural realm there is basically no difference between people and objects—all things are transmuted into signs. Whether people feel at ease with the sociomaterial constellations of their lifeworld depends on whether they can identify with these people and objects. This is not to say that the sense of belonging always requires the precise 'sharing of tastes,' but that there has to be an overarching *sensed* and *felt* meaningful relationship, a resonance, between the various properties of the lifeworld. The stronger ties an individual establishes to social and material properties, the more significant these properties become to the overarching sense of resonance. In the same manner, the loss of resonance expresses itself for instance when people 'grow apart' or feel an urge to move, cutting the ties, as an effect of the social alteration of lifeworlds and tastes.

In Bachelard's discussions of resonance, we are taken on a journey through the emotions and imaginations that tie people to their domestic home—here understood both as the symbol and the material container of people's sense of belonging. Familiar objects in the domestic environment are loaded with sedimented meanings, attached to both general mythologies and private experiences—the entrance door, the kitchen table, the bed—the stuff that not only provides practical affordances but also constitutes a haven for our most private memories, imaginations, and fantasies. Through our *material imagination,* mundane physical objects are also immersed with metaphorical, poetic qualities, which may drive our practical desires, whether it has to do with everyday domestic consumption or with a longing for home of the past (cf. Lane 2006). According to Bachelard, our attachment to places and their material properties grows stronger through our practical involvement in the production of these places. This view also corresponds to Bourdieu's notion of taste as an embodied principle reproduced through praxis rather than a cognitive scheme (see also Hennion 2007). In a wonderful essay, Bachelard (1961) traces this condition even to the mundane act of turning on the light, arguing that electric light can never provide the same sense of place attachment, nor the same kind of poetic imagination, as the light from a fireplace or an oil lamp. While the production of the former is based merely on a switching procedure, the latter requires practical work, entertainment, and personal involvement in the midst of day-to-day life. Hence, if we follow Bachelard, strong senses of resonance involve acts of imagination and creativity. Thus they can be contrasted to alienation (the experience of being estranged from the production of one's own lifeworld) as well as to dissonance (the experience of a lifeworld in conflict).

The maintenance of personal structures of taste and imagination, I argue, is a significant source for the continuity of a sense of belonging. These structures guide people to environments and practices through which they can develop bonds to people and objects and, by extension, generate a sense of cultural resonance. But there is one additional component that must be added, and that is the *textures* produced through the above-mentioned sociomaterial processes. By texture, a concept borrowed from Henri Lefebvre's ([1974] 1991) *The Production of Space*, I mean the 'communicative fabric of space'—the cultural-material weave that *binds* together and gives a certain *feel* to a space or region (for an extensive discussion, see Jansson 2006, 2007a). Texture is something through which cultural praxis materializes according to regular rhythms (daily routines, seasons, traditions, etc.) into something deeply felt (the fabric of communication), bypassing the realm of semiotics, and also something through which the material fabric of space communicates with us. It is through the regular (re)production of familiar textures, that is, texturation, that *spaces of belonging* and cultural resonance take form (Figure 1). These spaces are not necessarily confined to certain places, however, but must also provide connections to the surrounding world and may sometimes be more or less detached from material geographies (cf. Morley 2000, 2001; Wise 2000; Moores 2004).

Textures are relatively durable structures whose stability is a product of two things. Firstly, textures are social constructs inseparable from the intersubjectivity and taken-for-grantedness of the lifeworld. Textures are already in place when we are born, and through the invisible hand of *habitus* (Bourdieu, [1979] 1984, Ch. 3), we get socialized into how to interpret, evaluate, and make use of them. Secondly, textures evolve and endure through cultural-material *sedimentation*—the repetition of communicative and spatial practices in relation to material and cultural infrastructures. All together, this means that texture is inherent to all spatial and communicative practices—these practices are both *textured* (through textural affordances and scripts) and *texturing* (through textural enactment and articulation). The power of texturation is typically experienced when certain infrastructures break down and our intended practices are no longer possible to perform, or

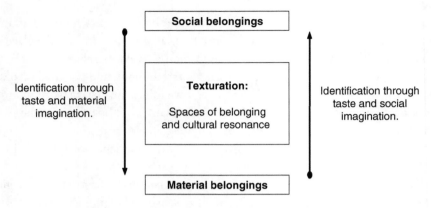

Figure 1: The process of texturation as the production of spaces of belonging.

when we come as foreigners to a new spatial setting and do not understand how to get around or behave. Such experiences of dissonance or alienation point to the fact that while textures are certainly a site of mutuality, trust, and belonging, they also, simultaneously, operate as a cultural-material mechanism for social *exclusion* and *stratification*.

This discussion brings us to the crossroads of Bourdieu's and Lefebvre's critical views of *social space*. What these thinkers have in common are (a) a view of *space as a processual realm of social and cultural struggle* and (b) a view of *communication as a structured practice that (re)produces social space as a cultural-material formation*. Lefebvre ([1974] 1991) has used the term 'texture' to describe how spatial practices leave their marks in space and are successively turned into what he calls 'reticular patterns'—material traces and arrangements that 'embody the "values" assigned to particular routes' (ibid. p. 118). Lefebvre also argues that texture is both an enabling structure and an obstacle to spatial practice. It is possible for human subjects to act outside of textures or to break the rules, but most of the time textures determine spatial practices, which in turn 'embody a signifying practice even if they cannot be reduced to such a practice' (ibid. p. 57). This is indeed a cultural materialist view of spatial production, depicting how imagination and taste are always implied or embedded in spatial practice and material structures. This is also what Bourdieu argues when he describes how people, objects, and activities enter into social systems of classification. Understood as a social realm, it is thus not only the materiality of space that prohibits the realization of certain activities, but even more so the codes of classification that sometimes exclude entire social groups—such as foreigners, outsiders, and the poor—from making use of textures in a meaningful way.

The cultural-materialist framework outlined here can be seen as a possible answer to Morley's (2001, p. 426) call for a 'materialist' version of media and cultural studies. As we will see, this perspective helps us integrating a spatial phenomenology of global media and communication, as outlined by, for instance, Jörg Dürrschmidt (2000) and Shaun Moores (2004, 2006), with a structural critique of the stratified landscape of power in which mediatization and mobility occur (cf. Lundby's argument in the introduction to this book).

MAINTAINING AND RENEWING THE LIFEWORLD: MEDIATIZATION AND MOBILITY

To borrow the terminology of Harold A. Innis ([1951] 1964), it seems relevant to argue that the dominant ideologies of modern media development have sustained space-biased communication rather than time-biased, reinforcing more far-ranging patterns of connectivity and more liquid patterns of interaction (e.g., Castells, [1996] 2000; Mattelart, [1996] 2000). At the same time, however, one must not lose sight of what James Carey (1989) famously termed the ritual uses of media, and their stabilizing power to bind time and to anchor and reembed personal senses of belonging in a localized texture (see also Rothenbuhler 1998; Larsen and Tufte 2003). Similarly, John Tomlinson (1999) has argued that it is problematic to believe that people in general are becoming more cosmopolitan or deterritorialized only because they may have access to a wider range of communication media. Tomlinson encourages us to also consider the other viewpoint: that many new media, and perhaps especially mobile ones, operate as 'technologies of the hearth' (Tomlinson 2001; Morley 2007, Ch. 7). For instance, mobile telephones and chat platforms are more often used for entertaining close family bonds and friendships, also within narrow geographies, than for extending social networks to other contexts or parts of the globe. To echo Robert Putnam (2001), new media are thus primarily used for sustaining *bonding* social capital, preserving the cultural resonance within the lifeworld, instead of acquiring *bridging* social capital; that is, to make new acquaintances in new contexts and thus renewing the constellation of the lifeworld.

This observation leads to two diverging views of the mediatization of texture and belonging. On the one hand, it might be described as a process of increasingly plural and floating spaces of belonging. On the other hand, it might be described as a process of increasing resources for reproducing the stability and coherence of the home-place and other 'care structures' (such as media space itself). The point to make here, however, is that mediatization does not conform to any one of these opposite views. Rather, it affects society in a plethora of ways along this hypothetical continuum, largely following the preexisting stratifications of society. This is exactly what Doreen Massey (1991) has pointed out in her discussion of how late modern geometries of communication and mobility reproduce power geometries, where the control of flows and connectivities belongs to those who are already in control of economic and cultural capital.

Still, this picture of mediatized global stratification and sociocultural reproduction must not lead us to simplified categorizations of individuals as either 'locals' or 'cosmopolitans,' even though such divisions make sense on a structural level (Hannerz 1990). Instead, if we consider the role of media technologies and texts within the model presented in Figure 1, we may address how these ambiguities and tension fields are spelled out, on a more practical level, as inherent dynamics of texturation as such. Beginning at the bottom of the figure, we can see that communications media are in themselves material belongings. As material belongings, they hold a double function. As concrete expressions of taste, they say something about who we are. They also provide links, or routes, to other spaces and contexts (cf. Jansson 2001). These other spaces, and the people occupying them, are often familiar to us. But sometimes they are more utopian in character, offering what Kevin Hetherington (1998, Ch. 5) discusses in terms of significant 'elsewheres.' Such 'elsewheres' may, for instance, represent alternative tastes, lifestyles, and ethical holdings, and they are important sites to which our social and material imaginations can escape (see also May 1996). Even though most experimental impulses may never be realized, a general openness towards 'the other,' a willingness to bridge cultural gaps, may lead to a gradual alteration of textures. At the same time, however, inasmuch as the media may accelerate the potential redisposition of tastes and imaginations, another likely outcome is a growing sense of dissonance and unease, a loss of belonging, and a willingness to break from the life conditions at hand.

To some extent, every individual must handle these kinds of ambivalences—the push and pull between repetition and change and among dreams, possibilities, and restrictions. Mediatization means that a growing number of such 'decisions' (whether consciously or not) are influenced by mediated experiences. This is to say that, in modern society, textures are necessarily becoming increasingly mediatized. If we disconnected ourselves, we would also lose our sense of belonging, finding ourselves in a state of what geographer Edward Relph (1976), in an illustrative (but highly conservative and media-critical) manner, once termed 'existential outsideness' (see also Moores 2006). On the other hand, and just as important a point, textures, tastes, and the imaginative quest for cultural resonance function as protective filters, sheltering the (inter)subjective lifeworld from too-rapid changes or ruptures. As media ethnographic research showed a long time ago, media texts and technologies can make their way into everyday life only if they *fit texture*: they must pertain to an accessible time and space, amalgamate with other social practices and their rhythms and contribute to the cultural resonance between the material and social realms of belonging. In this context, there seem to be particularly interesting points of correspondence between the idea of cultural resonance I suggest here and Roger Silverstone's understanding of how the appropriation of new media is negotiated through the *moral economy of the household* (see Silverstone et al. 1992).

But what happens to these processes and experiences under mobile life conditions? At the outset, if we understand by *mobility* the geographical relocation of people, it seems to imply almost by definition a potential rupture or threat to the sense of belonging as well as to the composition of textures. Moving to another place means that the conditions of everyday life change and that the sense of continuity must be regained. However, one can raise two main objections to such a general claim. Firstly, it would be wrong to depart from a conception of belonging as rooted in one single place and clearly bounded textures. As several recent studies have pointed out, in most mobile groups—and particularly among those known as 'commuters,' 'the international business elite,' 'global nomads,' 'mobile families,' etc.—a sense of belonging can be established through the practices of mobility itself, whether long or short distance. Spaces of belonging may then consist of particular patterns of place attachments and the repetition of time-space paths (e.g., Sager 2006; Mascheroni 2007; Gustafson, forthcoming). These movements are in themselves to be understood as part of texturation.

Secondly, people's understandings of home and belonging evolve significantly in and through their experiences of what it is to go away. This means that many forms of travel, notably leisure tourism, do not threaten the textures of day-to-day life but merely provide the traveller with some 'time-out.' This refers to a liminoid state of temporary (anti-)routines, involving exceptional media habits, that by and large contradict the structures of ordinary life (Urry 2002; Banim et al. 2002; Jansson 2007b). Under such mobile circumstances, cultural resonance may still be achieved as long as the individual feels secure in the social crowd (e.g., travelling with friends) (see Heimtun 2007) or gains exceptional experiences that are somehow valuable to his or her personal life biography (see Hetherington 1998)—and, perhaps most importantly, feels secure in the prospect of returning home.

Migration, however, is something very different from tourism and various forms of travelling lifestyles. Although the structures of taste and imagination are assets that can be brought along on the journey, as well as certain material belongings such as mobile media technologies, there will always be a textural rupture. The local neighbourhood, the private house or apartment and, most often, friends and family are left in the place of origin. This calls for new textures to take shape in order to compensate for what has been lost; a process that, in turn, might disturb the relevance of tastes and imaginations. Under such circumstances (which are especially problematic in cases of involuntary migration), the media can often help compensate for the loosened sense of belonging and security, enabling daily routines to be continued (such as watching a TV series or reading the newspaper) and close bonds to be maintained through online interaction (e.g., Morley 2000). Nevertheless, most migrants will also find that old routines make less sense when implemented in a new local environment. What works in one place cannot be pasted onto another. Place still matters and, as we will see, this classical statement also holds true under highly mediatized and cosmopolitan conditions.

THE CASE OF EXPATRIATE PROFESSIONALS

Studying expatriate groups can bring information about how people handle social renewal in general and what particular significance the media have for maintaining and reestablishing a sense of belonging. But one must also keep in mind that the conditions among expatriate professionals are different from many other migrants or transmigrants.

Firstly, these people are engaged in *a voluntary form of mobility*, normally related to a specific organization or company, which means that there are good conditions for solving issues of dwelling and social services as well as for becoming socially integrated through one's workplace. Secondly, expatriates live abroad for a *measured amount of time*, normally knowing that they have a home and a job to return to in their country of origin. Thirdly, as opposed to people engaged in longer periods of global travelling, who take up temporary jobs in order to finance further travelling and leisure activities, the mobility of expatriate professionals is less experimental, foremost tied to *career opportunities or other kinds of competence related incitements*. This, in turn, and fourthly, means that the expatriates' time abroad is normally tied to one particular location in which more or less *permanent living conditions* have to be established.

These conditions together position the 'expatriate lifestyle' somewhere in-between global tourism and permanent migration, suggesting that the key to an understanding of the complexity of temporary foreign residence is to regard it as an *exceptional* and *hybrid* condition. While the expatriate period marks a substantial time-space of a person's life biography, it is also put 'within brackets' as a sacralized period during which professional tasks and ordinary daily routines blend with more or less extraordinary experiences, notably cultural encounters and events. The exact composition of this mix, furthermore, varies significantly between groups, depending on work, location, personal interests, and so on.

The group under study here consists of *six interviewees* who share the following characteristics:

- They are Swedish citizens living and working in the city of Managua, Nicaragua.
- They work for nongovernmental organizations (NGOs) within the development sector, which means that they are in close contact with, on the one hand, Nicaraguan everyday society, spending significant amounts of time in 'the field' meeting local interest groups and inhabitants, and, on the other hand, the networks of the 'global civil society' (cf. Kaldor 2003).
- They are all well educated, in possession of large amounts of cultural capital but moderate amounts of economic capital, due to the nature of their organizations. The latter condition is, of course, highly relative: the persons interviewed earn little money compared to many other professional Westerners in transitional societies (for instance, those within the diplomatic sector) but are among the more affluent by Nicaraguan standards, affording a lifestyle and material standard corresponding to life in Sweden.
- They all speak the local language, Spanish, and are thus able to interact with local citizens with few restraints.
- All interviewees have previous experiences of living, working, and studying abroad. Some of the interviewees may even be called transmigrants, working on a contract that is just one in a sequence. Together, their work experiences cover much of the developing world, including Central, East, and South Asia, East Africa, and South America.

In sum, the persons I have interviewed compose a group that very much looks like the *cosmopolitan ideal type*, whether we apply Ulf Hannerz' (1990) well-known definition of a cosmopolitan ethos; apply Terhi Rantanen's (2005, Ch. 6) more inclusive understanding of (mediated) cosmopolitan experiences; or regard their entrepreneurial life trajectories as expressions of an overarching cosmopolitan social condition (Beck 2000).

The fieldwork I have carried out consists of a combination of ethnographic observations and interviews. I spent altogether four months in Managua, during a period similar to a sabbatical, while my wife worked for a Swedish development organization operating in Central America. This means that I lived in a sort of 'expatriate community,' sharing much of everyday life with other people in similar situations, and could get an inside view of the issues I wanted to study. When selecting my informants, I wanted to reach a good demographic variation while keeping the above-mentioned criteria constant. The selection contains three men and three women in various family situations in the age span of twenty-five to fifty-five years. They live in ordinary houses or apartments in different parts of Managua. Most interviews were conducted in domestic settings in Managua and lasted for 90 to 120 minutes. All names that figure in this text are fictive.

CULTURAL CAPITAL AS A MOBILITY RESOURCE

As a cultural researcher among cosmopolitan Swedes in Nicaragua, I soon realized that cultural capital provides an unmistakable resource for the establishment of a sense of belonging. While nationality indeed works as a resource for getting integrated within the expatriate community (in this case largely revolving around the Nordic national embassies and the school for Nordic children), cultural capital enables the individual to identify social contexts that resonate with his or her taste, more or less regardless of national identity. One of my interviewees, Erik, a man in his fifties who has lived in different developing countries during most of his grown-up life, states that he has actually maintained pretty much the same lifestyle regardless of country and city—a lifestyle he self-ironically describes as 'middle-class with cultural inclinations.' His cultural consumption has been fairly constant, which means that this aspect of his identity is even accentuated in a city like Managua, with a relatively small cultural scene:

> **Erik:** I think this is a social phenomenon, a social cement one may say. Regardless of whether one goes to the theater or to the cinema, one always meets somebody one knows here, because it's the same little circle that goes. That is perhaps also an attraction with Managua that, due to this smallness, one becomes part of this intellectual upper-middle-class élite, which are those who frequent these places, such as cultural events.

Cultural capital can thus be regarded as a 'disembedding mechanism,' embodied through taste and lifestyle, which transcends many other cultural boundaries. While cultural capital is indeed less exact and less measurable than the disembedding abstract systems that Anthony Giddens (1991) originally refers to (such as expert systems, and standardized technological infrastructures), it is indeed a resource that can be exchanged and reinvested through mobility. In fact, while cultural capital operates as a disembedding mobility resource, mobility itself, and in particular the kind of global mobility discussed here, is an asset that easily mutates into cultural capital. An important link between mobility and cultural capital, in turn, is the bridging social capital discussed by Putnam (2001)—related to the fact that cultural capital in its more elaborated form involves a reflexive interest in other cultures, and that mobility is a way of gaining valuable cross-cultural experiences and contacts. In cosmopolitan circles, the combination of cultural capital and global experiences is thus the most significant status marker and perhaps the single most important factor for maintaining a sense of belonging when moving to a new place.

This means that cultural capital not only disembeds, it also *re-embeds*. While, as a comparison, a U.S. blockbuster movie or a global television format may have a cross-cultural potential, as they appeal to a broad audience, they do not hold the same distinctiveness as, for instance, exhibitions and live theatre or music performances, and they do not provide access to any particular localized social community.

The process of re-embedding is not without its complications, however. Erik describes that much of his everyday texture has remained more or less the same: He reads the newspaper every morning, watches a current affairs programme every Sunday, and uses public media in the same way as he used to do when living in Sweden. But these patterns of use need to be localized. Like all informants in my sample, Erik stresses that, in spite of all the new affordances that come with the internet, after a while abroad, it does not make much sense to read a Swedish newspaper or watch a Swedish current affairs programme online. The sense of cultural resonance is successively lost, which, for one thing, means that it gets hard to comprehend and evaluate the discussions in the media, which then become just 'empty words.' Furthermore, it means that the media practice itself loses its ritual value when remediated and exported to a texture in which the natural connection between social and material belongings is lost. Erik mentions how several times he has podcasted two Swedish current affairs radio programmes that he, in Sweden, 'slavishly listens to,' but always is disappointed. Two hours of listening in Sweden while still in bed on Sunday mornings felt too short but, when podcasting the same programmes from his Nicaraguan home, 'two hours feels too darn long.'

In the interview with Jens, a father in his thirties who is now on his third longer stay abroad, we find a somehow different approach, albeit still an expression of cultural capital. While Jens holds that the practical relevance of Swedish media shrinks when living abroad, he also stresses that there are good political reasons to follow the public debate in Sweden. Social change on a global scale, he argues, is dependent on actions not primarily in poor countries but more significantly in the affluent world, such as in Sweden. His interest in the Swedish debate is thus channelled to a great extent through his cosmopolitan outlook and engagement in the global civil society. In the case of Jens, the unity of cultural capital and global experiences leads to a highly independent media selection:

Jens: I follow several Swedish blogs on a daily basis. They give me an impression of how people I identify with are reasoning...I know what kinds of persons they are, and by listening to what they say, who are in Sweden, I can hear and read between the lines what the political atmosphere is like in Sweden. It gives me more than reading dry newspaper articles.

This quote points to how media rituals must gain cultural resonance in order to materialize and become part of an everyday texture. Jens turns on his computer immediately when arriving at his office—the same thing every day, except when he is travelling in the more remote areas of the country. Reading political blogs becomes a ritualized way of gaining a type of information that, at the same time, entertains his taste and his social imagination of Swedish society, and tells him what goes on in the minds of people like him.

MEDIATIZATION AND THE GLOBALIZATION OF SOCIOCULTURAL DISTINCTIONS

Speaking of a 'cosmopolitan taste' is of course using a harsh generalization. Still, there is an interesting shared logic to the ways in which my informants handle new technologies, a logic that can be specified through the seemingly contradictory concepts of *antimaterialism* and *openness*. While the expressions of antimaterialism can be related to cultural capital, as shown in Bourdieu's original studies, openness has to do with the strong global orientation and the willingness to make use of technological tools that might sustain mobility. In other words, I here consider cosmopolitanism as an ethos emerging through the synergetic exchanges between cultural capital and global mobility. All my interviews show evidence of this balance; new media are regarded as necessities for a travelling lifestyle, while also kept at a minimum and handled in a manner that stresses *independence* and *control*. Erik describes how he has indeed set up a Facebook account but also realizes that this form of interaction gives him a negative sense of losing control: 'Facebook takes away some of the good things with digital media—that I control my filters.' Similarly, Sofia, a woman in her thirties, was engaged in Facebook in summer 2007, 'when everybody else was,' and found it a good way of maintaining contacts all over the world. But, as she got more and more tired of the amount of unwanted material she received, she began monitoring various filters and eventually lost interest in the whole platform.

New media technologies are thus welcome so long as they do not steal time or energy. While Erik is the only person who maintains an interest in media technologies as such, due to the nature of his work, the others try to avoid 'too many functions.' It is also obvious that private media are predominantly used as devices for networking, locally as well as globally, and rarely for entertainment purposes.

As told by, for instance, Stina, a younger woman conducting an internship, who does not even want to have a TV set in her home, amusements are located to the public realm. The mobile phone, which she bought after three days in the new country, is used for coordinating these public events:

> **Stina:** Locally, I'm texting quite a lot, like 'what happens this week?' 'going to the movies?'—as a coordination tool...I don't have a camera in the phone. At home [in Sweden], I have the simplest model—as long as I can send SMS and make phone calls, I'm happy. And that's exactly what I have here, too. That's enough.

Stina's description once again shows how preestablished sociomaterial media textures are partly brought along to the new environment, providing a sense of continuity, but are also reshaped in order to fit local conditions. This refers, in particular, to the mobile telephone, which stands out as the single most important tool for becoming integrated in the new social environment.

Contacts with Sweden and the rest of the world, on the other hand, are maintained by means of the computer: e-mail, chat, and (video) phone. As such, the computer attains an important bridging function, since it enables people to actually 'take the step.' Knowing that friends and family are just a phone call away, and that access is unlimited, even audiovisual, makes it easier to imagine an expatriate lifestyle. This potential is primarily expressed among the younger interviewees, whose trajectories as cosmopolitans are still at a relatively early stage—cosmopolitanism is clearly a 'learning process' (see Thompson and Tambyah 1999). Nevertheless, global contacts become increasingly sporadic during the course of a stay and largely turn into an imagined rather than interactive community:

> **Sofia:** Primarily, you want to feel that it's easy to contact one another...But the continuous communication gets more spread out the longer you are away. After a while, you get immersed into this new world, and then it becomes less important to communicate everything...But as soon as someone has been here, then the communication starts over again and they remember things and wonder, and 'now I can see you there,' and 'are you by the computer there and there,' and 'in that room by the banana trees,' and so on...

Clearly, under these circumstances, the durability maintained by the media is just as much a matter of imagination and a sense of security as it is about actual interaction. In some cases, interaction is even expressed as tiresome, due to the loosening sense of mutual identification. We are here eloquently reminded of Carey's (1989) and Rothenbuhler's (1998) arguments that the cultural meaning of the media is largely located beyond the content of the communication itself, related above all to the social interaction and communion it produces and is produced through. Similarly, in his account of the relationship between 'social networks, travel, and talk' John Urry (2003) points to the significance of 'meetingness.' This means that mediated communication to only a limited extent replaces direct interaction and rather reproduces the need for such meetings—and thus generates more mobility. As Sofia's story shows, this idea also makes sense the other way around: direct face-to-face experiences (e.g., having visitors) stimulate further contact and thus hold a key role for sustaining social continuity.

My interviewees in various ways express an acceptance of the distance from Sweden and the fact that media are no full substitute for close bonds. Sofia states that, since she knows that she will go back to Sweden again, she even prefers to 'keep the worlds apart.' However, it is not only Nicaragua and other geographical locations that are kept apart. More interesting is that the combined patterns of mobility and mediated connectivity generate a successive gap, a sociocultural distinction, between what we may loosely term 'locals' and 'cosmopolitans.' Among the expatriates, there is a shared experience of losing contact with people who are less mobile. The creation of such a distinction is not actively chosen, however, but rather appears like a product, a gradually reembodied habitus, evoking feelings of dissonance as the individual realizes that he or she can no longer identify with old friends. This experience is most clearly expressed among the younger interviewees, who most distinctly have put their time abroad within brackets as a time-out. When they also realize that their friends back home have put the expatriate period within brackets and show little interest in their new experiences, a rift emerges. This becomes especially obvious when visiting or returning to Sweden.

> **Stina:** The interest has been very shallow among many of my friends. Especially among those who haven't been part of the communication [MSN, mail, Skype]— shallow interest. Perhaps a simple question of 'how it was'—and it's not easy to summarize six months or a whole year in a developing country in a few sentences. I can feel that there is no understanding...and they haven't done much to get that understanding...Especially among people who have travelled and been away for longer periods, then the understanding is much bigger, and there you find a common ground that others cannot understand.

The rift between 'locals' and 'cosmopolitans' is an expression of a weakening cultural resonance. The bottom line of this process is the discrepancy in terms of mobility and global experiences. But it is also a process that the mediatized geometries of communication reinforce rather than solve. During the expatriate period, much of the global communication seems to occur with other people on the move rather than with people in the home country (if we overlook communication with professional contacts based in Sweden). New media thus contribute in a significant way to the establishment of networks and communities of mobile professionals, feeding a cosmopolitan sense of belonging and resonance. At the extreme point, which is most clearly expressed in the interview with Lars, who is also the oldest in my selection, the mediatization of belonging is no longer separable from the mediatization of mobility.

CONCLUDING REMARKS

Introducing a cultural-materialist view of mediatization, I have in this chapter examined what the combined forces of mediatization and mobility do to people's senses of belonging. In particular, I have emphasized the role of durable structures of taste, imagination, and texture, which together govern the amalgamation of material and social belongings. I have empirically shown that these are both enabling and sheltering structures, providing a balance between continuity and change among people on the move. Through the cultural-materialist perspective, I argue, the analysis of mediatization can find a bridge between phenomenological studies of mediatized spaces of belonging and structural studies of global geometries of communication (including both media and mobility). Here, I also want to stress the enduring relevance of Pierre Bourdieu's cultural sociology. While Bourdieu's model of social space is indeed problematized in times of globalization, mediatization, and mobility, when value structures are breaking loose from sociomaterial stratifications and territories, the basic logic on which Bourdieu's analyses are founded are also relevant on a global scale. It might be fruitfully combined with, for instance, Doreen Massey's notion of power geometries. I would even argue, with support from my empirical findings, that the social influence of mediatization and mobility in some respects broadens the scope of Bourdieu's theory. As shown in this chapter, for instance, the symbiotic possession of cultural capital and global mobility explains the complexity of cosmopolitan spaces of belonging—spaces that simultaneously rely on mediated connectivity and provide a distinctive shelter from the maelstroms of mediatization.

REFERENCES

Bachelard, G. ([1957] 1969). *The Poetics of Space*. Boston: Beacon Press.

Bachelard, G. (1961). *La Flamme d'une Chandelle*. Paris: PUF/Collection.

Banim, M., Guy, A., and Gillen, K. (2002). *Escaping the Everyday? Women's Clothing on Holiday*. The Open University: Everyday Cultures Working Paper, No. 6.

Beck, U. (2000). The cosmopolitan condition. *British Journal of Sociology*, 51(1), 79–105.

Berger, P., Berger, B., and Kellner, H. (1973). *The Homeless Mind: Modernization and Consciousness*. New York: Vintage Books.

Bourdieu, P. ([1979] 1984). *Distinction: A Social Critique of the Judgement of Taste*. London: Routledge.

Carey, J. W. (1989). *Communication as Culture: Essays on Media and Society*. New York: Routledge.

Castells, M. (1996/2000). *The Rise of the Network Society (The Information Age: Economy, Society and Culture, Vol. 1)*. 2 nd ed. Oxford, UK: Blackwell.

Cresswell, T. (2006). *On the Move: Mobility in the Modern Western World*. London: Routledge.

Deleuze, G. (1994). *Difference and Repetition*. New York: Columbia University Press.

Dürrschmidt, J. (2000). *Everyday Lives in the Global City: The Delinking of Locale and Milieu*. London: Routledge.

Giddens, A. (1991). *Modernity and Self-Identity: Self and Society in the Late Modern Age*. Cambridge, UK: Polity Press.

Goffman, E. (1959). *The Presentation of Self in Everyday Life*. London: Penguin.

Goffman, E. (1971). *Relations in the Public: Micro-studies of the Public Order*. New York: HarperCollins.

Gustafson, P. Mobility and territorial belonging. *Environment and Behaviour* (in press).

Hannerz, U. (1990). Cosmopolitans and locals in a world culture. *Theory, Culture and Society*, 7(2): 237–51.

Heimtun, B. (2007). Depathologizing the tourist syndrome: Tourism as social capital production. *Tourist Studies*, 7(3), 271–93.

Hennion, A. (2007). Those things that hold us together: Taste and sociology. *Cultural Sociology*, 1(1), 97–114.

Hetherington, K. (1998). *Expressions of Identity: Space, Performance, Politics*. London: Sage.

Innis, H. A. ([1951] 1964). *The Bias of Communication*. Toronto: Toronto University Press.

Jansson, A. (2001). Contested meanings: Audience studies and the concept of cultural identity. In Kivikuru, U. (Ed.) *Contesting the Frontiers: Media and Dimensions of Identity*. Göteborg: Nordicom.

Jansson, A. (2006). Textural analysis: Materialising media space. In J. Falkheimer and A. Jansson (Eds.) *Geographies of Communication*. Göteborg: Nordicom.

Jansson, A. (2007a). Texture: A key concept for communication geography. *European Journal of Cultural Studies*, 10(2), 185–202.

Jansson, A. (2007b). A sense of tourism: New media and the dialectic of encapsulation/decapsulation. *Tourist Studies*, 7(1), 5–24.

Kaldor, M. (2003). *Global Civil Society: An Answer to War*. Cambridge, UK: Polity Press.

Lane, J. F. (2006). Towards a poetics of consumerism: Gaston Bachelard's 'material imagination' and narratives of post-war modernisation. *French Cultural Studies*, 17(1), 19–34.

Larsen, B. S., and Tufte, T. (2003). Rituals in the modern world: Applying the concept of ritual in media ethnography. In D. Murphy and M. M. Kraidy (Eds.) *Global Media Studies*. New York: Routledge.

Lefebvre, H. ([1974] 1991). *The Production of Space*. Oxford, UK: Blackwell.

Mascheroni, G. (2007). Global nomads' network and mobile sociality: Exploring new media uses on the move. *Information, Communication & Society*, 10(4), 527–44.

Massey, D. (1991). A global sense of place. *Marxism Today*, June 1991, 24–29.

Mattelart, A. (1996/2000). *Networking the World 1794–2000*. Minneapolis: University of Minnesota Press.

May, J. (1996). A little taste of something more exotic: The imaginative geographies of everyday life. *Geography*, (81)1, 57–64.

Moores, S. (2004). The doubling of place: Electronic media time-space arrangements, and social relationships. In N. Couldry and A. McCarthy (Eds.) *Mediaspace: Place, Scale and Culture in a Media Age*. London: Routledge.

Moores, S. (2006). Media uses and everyday environmental experiences: A positive critique of phenomenological geography. *Participations*, 3(2).

Morley, D. (2000). *Home Territories: Media, Mobility and Identity*. London: Routledge.

Morley, D. (2001). Belongings: Place, space and identity in a mediated world. *European Journal of Cultural Studies*, 4(4), 425–48.

Morley, D. (2007). *Media, Modernity and Technology: The Geography of the New*. London: Routledge.

Novicka, M. (2007). Mobile locations: Construction of home in a group of mobile transnational professionals. *Global Networks*, 7(1), 69–86.

Putnam, R. D. (2001). *Bowling Alone: The Collapse and Revival of American Community*. New York: Simon & Schuster.

Rantanen, T. (2005). *The Media and Globalization*. London: Sage.

Relph, E. (1976). *Place and Placelessness*. London: Pion.

Rothenbuhler, E. W. (1998). *Ritual Communication: From Everyday Conversation to Mediated Ceremony*. Thousand Oaks, CA: Sage.

Sager, T. (2006). Freedom as mobility: Implications of the distinction between actual and potential travelling. *Mobilities*, 1, 465–88.

Schutz, A., and Luckmann, T. (1973). *The Structures of the Life-World*. Evanston, IL: Northwestern University Press.

Seamon, D. (1979). *A Geography of the Lifeworld: Movement, Rest and Encounter*. New York: St Martin's Press.

Silverstone, R., Hirsch, E., and Morley, D. (1992). Information and communication technologies and the moral economy of the household. In R. Silverstone and E. Hirsch (Eds.) *Consuming Technologies: Media and Information in Domestic Spaces*. London: Routledge.

Thompson, C. J., and Tambyah, S. K. (1999). Trying to be cosmopolitan. *Journal of Consumer Research*, 26, 214–41.

Tomlinson, J. (1999). *Globalization and Culture*. Cambridge, UK: Polity Press.

Tomlinson, J. (2001). *Instant Access: Some Cultural Implications of 'Globalising' Technologies*. University of Copenhagen: Global Media Cultures Working Paper No. 13.

Urry, J. (2002). *The Tourist Gaze*, 2nd ed. London: Sage.

Urry, J. (2003). Social networks, travel and talk. *British Journal of Sociology*, 54(2), 155–75.

Wise, J. M. (2000). Home: Territory and identity. *Cultural Studies*, 14(2), 295–310.

CHAPTER THIRTEEN

Social Inequalities: (Re)production through Mediatized Individualism

TANJA THOMAS

MEDIA IN THE CONTEXT OF INDIVIDUALIZATION AND INDIVIDUALIZATION DISCOURSE

> They are ashamed, they don't want to, they can't. Apparently, wretched poverty exists especially in areas where transfers are not taken advantage of. Junkies don't go to the welfare office; they don't apply as "clients" at employment agencies. The poverty report calls this miserable existence "self-imposed isolation…" It is a life of "indifferent uniformity," which does not see the benefit of a welfare career—the offer of dignity by the welfare state—and fails to see a meaning despite transfers. More redistribution would not even reach those isolated. …The welfare state did not fail these poor, since they don't even take advantage of it. But maybe others failed—the family, neighborhood, relatives or the community. In fact, is it impossible that poverty and misery exist without anyone failing? (Hank 2008)

Journalist Rainer Hank was quoted with these words in an online article of the daily newspaper *Frankfurter Allgemeine Zeitung (FAZ, translated)*. It was published on May 26, 2008, under the title "Gut, dass wir die Armen haben" (We're Lucky to Have the Poor) and refers to the publication of the poverty report of the German government on May 18, 2008. This report was repeatedly called "alarming," among other things, by the online version of the *Spiegel* magazine, which explains: "According to the report, 13 percent of German citizens are poor; they net less than 781 euros. A further 13 percent are kept from poverty only by government support. The gap between the rich and the poor is growing—the middle class is shrinking" (*Der Spiegel*, May 19, 2008, translated).

Rainer Hank's quote precedes this article because it refers to several aspects that are relevant for the sociological individualization discussion and at the same time points to the mediatized portrayal of individualization processes.

His reaction to the poverty report expresses contemporary ideas of individualization processes—for instance, by talking about becoming a "client" of employment agencies, by using the term "self-imposed isolation" from social communities, or by assigning responsibility (e.g., "they don't take advantage of it.")

Therefore, on a discoursive-symbolic level, the 'isolated' are committed to 'self-control' and 'self-responsibility' as well, regardless of their position in the structure of social inequalities. Furthermore, the short extract alludes to the fact that acceptance is regulated politically (e.g., "offer of dignity by the welfare state"). This leads to the question of whether the conditions of social inequality should also be regulated. However, *Frankfurter Allgemeine Zeitung* suggests privatization as a solution (refer to the comment in the quotation about the potential failure of family, neighborhood, relatives). In any case, the state is not held accountable for conditions of distress ("Is it impossible that poverty and misery exist without anyone failing?"), although it needs to be mentioned that releasing the state from responsibility should not be misinterpreted as a decrease in social control but something that leads to changed forms of social control.

Based on this recent example, I will first look back on the individualization debate, which began in the mid 1980s following Ulrich Beck's respected theses. Today it continues with varying emphases, and even Beck has changed his position in the meantime, referring to developments that are touched upon in the aforementioned quote.

Then, still in view of Hank's quote, I will argue why this chapter suggests a fundamental analytical distinction for studying the phenomenon of 'individualization': Distinguishing between a social-structural and a discoursive level demonstrates the relevance of mediatized communicative practices; the experiencing, interpreting, and processing of individualization processes is characterized and structured, among other factors, by the media.

The introductory example clearly asks for a contemporary notion of individualization. I will develop a concept of individualization that underlines the importance of mediatization processes for an adequate analysis of its own processes. The media convey knowledge: thus the aforementioned quote about the poverty report exemplifies how responsibility for the allocation of opportunities is assigned via order semantics. Closely linked to this is the—mediatized—conveyance of fundamental social ideas about responsibility and capacity to act in times of high unemployment, dismantling of the welfare state, stock market crashes, and financial crises.

Underpinned by this, the article suggests a notion of media culture and mediatization, which is embedded in communication studies as well as social theory. Moreover, links between mediatization and individualization processes are exemplified. Finally, the last part sketches challenges for further research.

THE "MODERNIZATION OF MODERN SOCIETY": "THE END OF THE INDIVIDUAL" OR "INDIVIDUALIZATION WITHOUT END"?

Individualization has long been characterized as a "process of the increasing, irreversible release of society members from traditional commitments and stereotyping forces, which gives them greater freedom of choice and autonomy," as Axel Honneth (2002, p. 141, translated) states in reference to Émile Durkheim.

However, considering Georg Simmel, Honneth points out that the sociological diagnosis 'individualization' carries an innate precarious ambivalence, since the pluralization of roles, commitments, and belonging is not automatically linked with an increase in individuality, individual autonomy, or freedom of the subjects.

Markus Schroer (2001) identified three traditions in the history of theory, which evaluate the individualization process differently: The first tradition bundles works that understand the rising attribution of 'individuality' by education, administration, and the culture industry as a process of disciplining, which results in a conformist 'individualism.' Studies of the second paradigm interpret functional pluralization as an opportunity to increase individuality, which releases the ability for reflexive, self-responsible life conduct. The third school of thought considers the process a double-edged development of emancipation from traditional commitments underpinned by an increase in conformity (Honneth, 2002, referring to Schroer, 2001).

Therefore, it remains unclear whether the individualization surge stated by Beck adds up to better opportunities for an autonomous life or hinders these. One often finds the simplified opposition of two prognoses: one that proclaims the "end of the individual," and one that heralds an "individualization without end" (Brose and Hildenbrand 1988).

The thesis of the "end of the individual" invokes data and insight that evidence the continued impact of the most important structural factors: class, gender, ethnicity, and age assign unequal life opportunities and paths of life. Faced with the power of unequal living conditions and the obvious influence of social structures and biography-relevant institutions, the fight for autonomous life practices seems—using the words of Pierre Bourdieu (1990)—an expression of "biographic illusion." Bourdieu furthers states that the "end of the individual" is hidden under the veil of an ideologically expected self-dramatization. In fact, Gabriele Wagner (2004) argues, "Tschaka Tschaka"—shouts of a motivation trainer do not turn employees into "labor entrepreneurs" (Voß and Pongratz 1998). And cosmetic surgeries in reality TV formats like *The Swan* do not turn "chicks into swans," as the daily newspaper *taz (die tageszeitung)* cynically writes. (And even if they looked the part, referring to Bourdieu, their capital would only increase for a specific milieu.) On the contrary: in addition to the damage of structural failure, those willing to work on the self are burdened, according to Wagner (2004, p. 8, translated), with the shame of being "weak-spirited chicks" and "losers," when "outbreaks of confidence find their end at the insurmountable boundaries of the social structuring of biographies."

Compared to this, the thesis of "individualization without end" does not fundamentally question the validity of the sociostructural framing of biographies, but its works are widely optimistic and focus on the potentially broadened space for the construction of biographies.

However, the assessments of individualization processes are currently deteriorating, as the much-quoted works by Ulrich Beck and Elisabeth Beck-Gernsheim illustrate—especially when considered in chronological order. In their opinion, individualization first means "release" of actors from traditional social forms, specifically "first the dissolution and then the replacement of industrial-societal life forms by others, in which the individuals have to create, stage, and cobble together their own biographies" (Beck and Beck-Gernsheim 1993, p. 179, translated).

When social and societal structures are separated from their positions in time and space as well as their social-historical contexts, the individuals are confronted with the challenges of a "reflexive life conduct" (Voß 1991; Jurczyk and Rerrich 1993). Beck initially marks this change with the shift from normal biographies to "choice biographies" (Beck 1986, p. 217). Under the conditions of competitive economies, these then change into "risk, even tightrope biographies," as he points out later, together with Elisabeth Beck-Gernsheim (Beck and Beck-Gernsheim 1994, p. 13).

This is due to the fact that the single subject is societally positioned as individual actor and director of its own biography. Thus they conclude that "individualization does not result from the free decisions of individuals. Individualization is a force, albeit a paradox one, to construct, create, and stage not only one's own biography, but also of integration and networks, all under changing preferences, decisions and life stages" (Beck and Beck-Gernsheim 1993, p. 179).

In retrospective of the Keynesian crisis and the cutback in welfare intervention forms, Lemke (2000, p. 39) introduced the thesis that leader capacities are shifting away from the state and towards "responsible" and "rational" individuals. Thus he deciphers the "retreat of the state" as a governing technique and demonstrates that it will not lead to a lack of state regulation and control competencies but can be seen as a reorganization or restructuring of governing techniques. In this notion, social security and its reform are attached to the request to bear one's own life risks and to organize one's connection with society independently and responsibly.

Axel Honneth and Martin Hartmann also identify an increased pressure to conform, resulting from the neoliberal restructuring of the capitalist economic system. They assert that before, individualization could be interpreted as a clear proliferation of individual autonomy, while, in the context of the new organization forms of capitalism, it morphs into unreasonable demands, disciplining, and insecurities, which amount to the effect of societal desolidarization (Hartmann and Honneth 2004, p. 10).

Ulrich Beck's newer society diagnoses sound bleak as well. In view of the new regulation for granting unemployment pay in Germany in 2005, he stated, "The society of more held the state responsible, the society of less looks to the individual, releases it to the limits of its possibilities" (Beck 2005, p. 15, translated). Then he concludes, "This might be a new governing strategy. It is not based on the principle of welfare and paternalism, but on self-responsibility and self-attribution of mistakes, even…the principle of voluntary self-amputation: one has the choice what to cut. Self-fulfillment means: everybody is the master of one's own adaptation to the less."

Individualization—and to me this is the point—is no longer considered a process that leads to an increase in autonomy. Individualization becomes a normative source for social acceptance processes—and mediatization processes, as I will discuss in the following, contribute to this.

INDIVIDUALIZATION PROCESSES IN MEDIA CULTURES: BASIC ANALYTICAL DISTINCTIONS

In order to expand the previous theoretical remarks to include the importance of the media and processes of mediatization, I suggest an analytical distinction, which again is supported by the quote in the beginning.

Studies about individualization processes will benefit from an analytical distinction between a socio-structural level (on which individualization can be understood as differentiation of life [conduct] forms and circumstances) and a level of cultural codes and discourses (which questions whether the individuals are responsible for their action competencies and consequences or whether social influences should be considered) (Berger 1997, p. 81; referring to Wagner 2004, p. 27).

Therefore, one level perceives individualization as ongoing social differentiation, while the other studies the societally changing, cultural-symbolic, and structural positioning of subjects, which demands self-control, self-responsibility, and self-surveillance (Wagner 2004, p. 28). Thus individualization is reconstructed as a specific mode of socialization, which links two aspects and does not overlook that structural restrictions based on social positioning cannot be easily overruled.

Hans-Ernst Schiller (2005, p. 8) is another author who picks up the interrelation of these two aspects: an analysis that refers to the objective circumstances of life calls for a real-life dimension on the one hand and a normative dimension on the other, which claims that the value of the individual has increased in societal reality. Schiller coins the term "individualism"[1] for this societal-normative dimension and defines the invocation of individuality in the sense of independence, self-responsibility, and creativity of the singular subject as central ideas.

It seems that this perspective bears great potential for the analysis of media communication, since it explicitly considers tensions between the ongoing inequalities of opportunities, the opening of social spaces to individual biographic projects, and the shift of attributions, which assign the individual more and more responsibility for the success of societal integration.

Underpinned by this, and following Wohlrab-Sahr (1997), I recommend conceptualizing individualization as a mode of socialization, which requires self-control, self-surveillance, and self-responsibility from the subjects. The individuals' positions within the structural network of social inequality, their unequal opportunities and options for action are disregarded, while at the same time they are differently prepared, able or willing to react.

On the cultural-symbolic level, according to Beck, the changing circumstances of life generate a "form of conscience"—and I would like to add a form of practice to that—as a collective phenomenon. That means it is not about a singular, subjective conscience but about a societally generated, socially implied, and culturally dominant reading of how one's life can be shaped (Wagner 2004, p. 37).

The thesis is that this and other socially dominant readings of the self and the world cannot be appropriately captured and understood without an understanding of media cultures and processes of mediatization. Therefore, I will first suggest notions of media culture and mediatization in the following.

INDIVIDUALIZATION IN THE CONTEXT OF MEDIA CULTURE AND MEDIATIZATION

Meanwhile, the fact that the media support the social organization and structuring of the everyday is accepted common ground in communication, media, and cultural as well as (media)sociological studies: TV, for instance, transforms the public, structures attention and emotion, conveys agendas and perspectives, creates an order of things, and helps to avoid conflicts—but it can also serve as a means to mark the "others;" it can be a characteristic of status and roles as well as a battleground for individual rights and independence (refer to Weiß 2003, for a summary). Thus it is involved in the (re)production of social relations and concepts. However, Hannelore Bublitz's claim (2005) that, in times of globalization and media culture, society is not produced through a social synthesis but a mass cultural one, remains rightly contended. Nick Couldry even vividly warns against "mediacentrism" when he writes:

> At the very least, this means defining the object of media studies as the consequences of media for the social world. But if our aim is to understand as clearly as possible the *consequences* of media for the social world, than it cannot be valid to *assume* in advance what we want to find out: so it must be wrong (and this is why mediacentrism is a fallacy) to assume that media are more consequential than other institutions that structure the social world (economic, material, spatial, and so on). (Couldry 2006, p. 12, emphasis in original)

The notions of "media culture" and "mediatization" that I will introduce as concepts in the following do not support mediacentrism. But "media culture"—as Hickethier argues for instance—is a productive conception, which helps to frame the culture forming aspects in and of the media, conceptualize culture as produced by the media, and study the media dimensions of culture (Hickethier 2003, p. 455). Or in other words, the media are not only "mediators" (agencies) and monitoring authorities (critique), but also a created part of culture (Hickethier 2003, p. 440).

I want to emphasize that I am not suggesting an opposition but an integration of media and culture. To render this relationship more precisely, the concepts of media and culture need to be explained. Culture is not possible without the media, as Pias et al. (1999, p. 8) state in their Kursbuch Medienkultur (Media Culture Coursebook). They say we should pay less attention to whether culture is defined, for instance, as the entirety of big signifying symbolisms, as a system to disseminate values and norms, as a daily empirically reproduced frame for communications and relations, or as a production framework in higher and lower tiers of the art and entertainment industry. We should agree that there are no media, at least not in a substantial and historically stable sense. Instead, the search for a common frame for the different notions of the media should focus on the fact that the media achieve their status as scientific, that is, systematizable object by putting what they save, process, and convey under conditions that they produce or are themselves (Pias et al. 1999, p. 10).

Tying in with this recommendation, I suggest a notion of media that is shaped by communication studies. Following Friedrich Krotz, I understand media as something

> ...that modifies and changes communication, can be differentiated, and leads to the emergence of new forms of interaction and communication. Thus the media are—to put it bluntly—staging machines on the one hand, since they provide communication content, and experience spaces on the other hand, since they are used, received, and acquired. (Krotz 2003, p. 23, translated)

These two perspectives on the media are mediated by a third one, since the media also have to be understood and analyzed as regulated social and culturally active institutions in society (Krotz 2007, p. 89f).

This perspective enables us to understand changing media offers, without assuming causality, as developments that accompany changing social conditions like relationships and everyday experiences. In addition, changing media offers coincide with different social competencies, which emerge in self-socialization when using media-related communication and can be updated and reproduced in everyday practices.

Therefore, media actions are not the consequences of technological preconditions but are embedded in social contexts and practices and gain their significance and value from them.

Underpinned by this, the beginning and end of a (media)culture analysis might be the simplified question of *how* we do what we do. To even pose this question, we assume that options for action are available for the existing "conditions," meaning historical, societal, and cultural circumstances (Lindner 2004, p. 11).

Thus culture is described as procedural events, which include a symbolic as well as an action dimension. In this context, the work of cultural studies scholars reminds us that not only the processes of inclusion in hegemonic cultures need to be analyzed, but also the active contention with cultural forms, the processes of making, negotiating, fabricating, and staging, which produce culture today. A procedural notion of media culture is particularly important for that.

Friedrich Krotz and I have suggested elsewhere (2008, p. 28) that media cultures be considered actualizations of mediatized cultural practices at specific points in time and in specific societal constellations. Hence, mediatization is a general shift of societal as well as individual communication practices on different levels, which utilize new and changing media potentials, plus all related consequences for the everyday life, knowledge, identity, and relationships of people as well as for culture and society (Krotz 2005). The present-day process of mediatization is affected by the ubiquity of the media, their contents, and further symbolic practices of the people. It can be framed as a growing entanglement of the media with the everyday and communication, as a process of banalizing the use of the media and their contents, and as an increase in orientation functions based on an increasing complexity of personal media environments (Krotz 2007).

MEDIATIZED INDIVIDUALIZATION: INVOCATIONS OF INDIVIDUALITY AND PRACTICES OF USING IT

Underpinned by this, I want to exemplify how individuality is currently mediatized, that is, framed by media offers and media use and treated with the help of mediatized communicative and cultural practices. I will then formulate several orientation points for analyzing mediatized individualization processes.

"You know what you want. We have the program for it" was an advertising slogan for Premiere, a German pay-TV channel, a few years back. This slogan demonstrates that neither programming nor the viewers' TV use are based on the criteria of balance or plurality, but rather on the certain knowledge of (own) preferences. Hereby, the access mode and the idea of individualized preferences and needs are interrelated—on the one hand, individualized subjects rationalize and justify the access mode of the new programming and provide its inner logic and objectives; on the other hand, they actualize their individuality via the access mode (Stauff 2005, p. 277).

This invocation of individuality, which contemporary TV picks up and uses, is an important characteristic of the contemporary telemedial communication process. A myriad of discourses, techniques, and practices invoke, produce, and reproduce individuality as an important factor of televisual mechanisms and as a specific relation to the self and the world (cf. Stauff 2005, p. 278).

Back in 1995, Georg Soeffner titled an article of his collection "Die Ordnung der Rituale" (The Order of Rituals) with "Wählen als Freizeitgestaltung" (Voting as Free Time Activity). With this he reminds us of certain German TV shows, similar to many others produced in Western countries. He recalls *Wünsch dir was (Make a Wish)* with Dietmar Schönherr und Vivi Bach as an early form of a show with "audience voting" for the candidate at the beginning of the 1970s; shows like *Pro & Contra*, chart shows, voting via applause, postal vote—or later, more modern—via TED (Tele Dialog).

Soeffner theorizes that the act of voting itself, the decision about others in relaxing, media-staged game situations, produces pleasure: it compensates the viewer, who now becomes a decision maker and master of taste, for his usual inconspicuousness (Soeffner 1995, p. 175).

In addition, it alludes to what Eggo Müller (2005, p. 10) felicitously called the service discourse of commercialized TV, which calls for the right of the "consuming citizen" and "mature consumer" and initiates, processes, advocates for, or even actualizes, the viewers' seemingly individual interests and wishes. Obviously, this has a political economic downside, which currently becomes evident in the cross-media marketing of reality TV formats.

I have discussed various versions of the media staging of general freedom of choice, often combined with a revitalization of the myth about individual success and the call for motivation and self-responsibility. Examples are the German adaptations of internationally marketed casting shows like *DSDS* (*Deutschland sucht den Superstar*) or *Popstars*, surgery shows like *The Swan* or *Spieglein, Spieglein*, or makeover shows like *Das Model und der Freak* (cf. Thomas 2009). They invoke "individuality" in the mode of self-disciplining and at the same time enforce deindividualization with the help of normalization processes and pressure to conform. What these shows acknowledge is the *will* to change and "self-actualization," as illustrated by the host's mottos: Detlef D. Soost, jury member of the German version of *Popstars*, tells his candidates, "You have to burn." Heidi Klum, host of *Germany's Next Top Model*, explains her basic rules in her book, *Body of Knowledge: 8 Rules of Model Behavior (to Help You Take Off on the Runway of Life)*. One of the most important ones: "You have to want it, baby."

Some newer works study TV genres as part of a complex (neoliberal) power technology and consider the "prominence" that one can temporarily achieve in reality TV as a new mode of subjectification and a "neoliberal form of self-technique" (Sauer 2001, p. 165; also refer to Bratich 2006; Hay and Ouellette 2008). In summary (and simplified), these works show how models of acceptable "normal" subjectivity are staged and how a desirable treatment of the self is portrayed. They emphasize that the media are involved in the (re)production of a subjectification regime, which corresponds with neoliberal paradigms like "self-responsibility" and "self-attribution" in times of high unemployment and precarious employment.

This is not to say that an experience of self-empowerment is impossible. When candidates of the surgery show *The Swan* are lead in front of a mirror after several operations and motivational coachings, they might become, if not swans, at least blackbirds or finches. Although that might sound sloppy, it is a serious statement if one considers the notion of subjects it is based upon, and if one does not infer action practices from objectives, as is often practiced following Foucault and governmentality studies.

In addition, several studies diagnose a "proliferation of a confession culture." Günter Burkart (2006), for instance, looks into online communication and emphasizes that the rise of personal websites cannot be understood without referring to individualization processes.

Eva Illouz (2006) studies self-presentations on online dating websites. She assumes that the internet continues public stagings of the self using a psychology jargon of the kind that companies, support groups, and talk shows have developed (cf. Illouz 2006, p. 160). Using dating and "romance on the Web" as examples, she describes how the economy of attention changes with the quantity of communication opportunities and offers, and how this influences the self-marketing of subjects. Even though the presentation on the Web could be manipulated in many different ways, she insists that language-based self-presentations tend to be uniform and reificated, based on the fact the people treat themselves and others as language categories and take the abstract term for being the real thing (Illouz 2006, p. 125). Following Adorno, Illouz recognizes that—for instance during the daily encounter with fake consumption goods—cynical feelings dominate because there is a force to do something even though one sees through it (Illouz 2006, p. 133).

Peter Mühlbauer (2007) views internet platforms like MySpace in a similar way and polemicizes that they are evidence for a hyper-exhibitionism and a hyper-conformism, and in that regard they can be compared to casting shows.

I believe that this discussion about the invocation of individuality in mediatized communicative processes would benefit from a more systemized analysis, using Friedrich Krotz's differentiation: interpersonal via media, with media (in production and reception), or interactive processes, for instance with artificial intelligence (Krotz 2008, p. 50).

INDIVIDUALIZATION PROCESSES IN MEDIA CULTURES: POTENTIAL AND CHALLENGES

These observations about the link between individualization and mediatization lead to my questions and requests, which challenge media and communication studies and refer to integration and disintegration processes in media cultures.

I am particularly interested in the gap between the cultural symbolic positioning of the subject on the one hand and structural restrictions and institutional dependencies on the other. Sociological studies tell us that individualization depends on gender, milieu, and class, and on the level of subjective biographic meaning and order structures. Discussions about media discourses and media actions should include this differentiation as well.

The dynamics of social structure produce a myriad of experiences and make it difficult to develop a lifelong milieu conscience. This fundamentally challenges the real-life relevance of structural categories and may lead to an individualized reading of social inequality, transforming in into "spaces for opportunities." It would be interesting to do empirical research on whether and how media communication enforces, frames, or discourages these processes.

Individualization calls for more active integration—which also means that individuals have to create their own contexts for their role commitments.

These integration requirements have everyday consequences, which a special research team in Munich has analyzed utilizing a concept of "everyday life conduct" dating back to Weber. The question is how the subjects "cope with it all," since it is the single person who has to juggle life spheres that are competing and only partially conveyed by social life conduct. Günter Voß, Werner Holly, and Klaus Boehnke studied the role of the media in these processes in projects like "Neue Medien im Alltag" (New Media and the Everyday) (2000).

Furthermore, I want to argue for an expansion of the "life conduct" concept to include one more dimension: The media also offer models of life conduct—action-orienting values and desirable lives on the one hand, and on the other, action patterns with symbolic meaning, which enable communication with other actors during social interactions (Otte 2005, p. 452).

On a higher level, one could ask how the media are involved in fragmenting society and at the same time holding it together. A classic sociological answer would refer to religion, nation, and in some cases maybe democratic republicanism, which facilitate integration by translating societal norms and values into the identities of subjects. Media and communication sociology would add the question of whether individualization and integration processes are modified in a mediatized communicative socialization and whether a mediatization of acceptance brings about "new" instruments of societal integration. This is an aspect of individualization and media culture that would certainly benefit from the social theoretically based know-how of communication studies.

NOTE

1. Castel (2000, p. 404 and p. 408, translated) likewise writes about a "negative individualism," which demands from the singular subject that they "choose, decide, invent tricks and take care of not drowning."

REFERENCES

Beck, U. (2005, Feb. 3). Die Gesellschaft des Weniger. Arbeitslosigkeit, Hartz IV: ein Land steigt ab. *Süddeutsche Zeitung*, 15.

Beck, U. (1986). *Risikogesellschaft. Auf dem Weg in eine andere Moderne*. Frankfurt/Main: Suhrkamp.

Beck, U., and Beck-Gernsheim, E. (1993). Nicht Autonomie, sondern Bastelbiographie. Anmerkungen zur Individualisierungsdiskussion am Beispiel des Aufsatzes von Günter Burkart. *Zeitschrift für Soziologie*, 22, 178–187.

Beck, U., and Beck-Gernsheim, E. (1994). Individualisierung in modernen Gesellschaften—Perspektiven und Kontroversen einer subjektorientierten Soziologie. In U. Beck and E. Beck-Gernsheim (Eds.), *Riskante Freiheiten. Individualisierung in modernen Gesellschaften* (pp. 10–42). Frankfurt/Main: Suhrkamp.

Berger, P. A. (1997). Individualisierung und sozialstrukturelle Dynamik. In U. Beck and P. Sopp (Eds.), *Individualisierung und Integration. Neue Konfliktlinien und neuer Integrationsmodus?* (pp. 81–95). Opladen: Leske & Budrich.

Bourdieu, P. (1990). Die biographische Illusion. *Bios*, 3, 75–81.

Bratich, J. Z. (2006). Nothing is left alone for too long. Reality programming and control society subjects. *Journal of Communication Inquiry*, 1, 65–83.

Brose, H. G., and Hildenbrand, B. (1988). *Vom Ende des Individuums zur Individualität ohne Ende.* Opladen: Leske + Budrich.

Bublitz, H. (2005). In Zerstreuung organisiert. Paradoxien und Phantasmen der Massenkultur. Bielefeld: transcript.

Burkart, G. (Ed.). (2006). *Die Ausweitung der Bekenntniskultur—neue Formen der Selbstthematisierung?* Wiesbaden: VS.

Castel, R. (2000). *Die Metamorphosen der sozialen Frage. Eine Chronik der Lohnarbeit.* Konstanz: UVK.

Couldry, N. (2006). *Listening Beyond the Echoes. Media, Ethics, and Agency in an Uncertain World.* Boulder, CO: Paradigm.

Hank, R. (2008, May 26). Gut, dass wir die Armen haben. *Frankfurter Allgemeine Zeitung Online.* Retrieved September, 23, 2008 from http://www.faz.net/s/Rub0E9EEF84AC1E4A389 A8DC6C23161FE44/Doc~E7A9C294987AA42779E21ECE43F46A05C~ATpl~Ecommon~ Scontent.html.

Hartmann, M., and Honneth, A. (2004). Paradoxien des Kapitalismus. Ein Untersuchungsprogramm. *Berliner Debatte Initial*, 15, 1–17.

Hay, J., and Ouellette, L. (2007). *Guidelines for Living: Television and the Government of Everyday Life.* Cambridge, MA: Blackwell.

Hickethier, K. (2003). Medienkultur. In G. Bentele, H.-B. Brosius and O. Jarren, Otfried (Eds.), *Öffentliche Kommunikation. Handbuch Kommunikations- und Medienwissenschaft* (pp. 435–457). Wiesbaden: Westdeutscher Verlag.

Honneth, A. (2002). Organisierte Selbstverwirklichung. Paradoxien der Individualisierung. In A. Honneth (Ed.), *Befreiung aus der Mündigkeit. Paradoxien des gegenwärtigen Kapitalismus* (pp. 141–158). Frankfurt/Main, New York: Campus.

Illouz, E. (2006). *Gefühle in Zeiten des Kapitalismus.* Frankfurt/Main: Suhrkamp.

Jurczyk, K., and Rerrich, M. S. (1993). *Die Arbeit des Alltags. Beiträge zu einer Soziologie der Alltäglichen Lebensführung.* Freiburg in Breisgau: Lambertus.

Krotz, F. (2001). *Die Mediatisierung kommunikativen Handelns. Der Wandel von Alltag und sozialen Beziehungen, Kultur und Gesellschaft durch die Medien.* Wiesbaden: Westdeutscher Verlag.

Krotz, F. (2003). Zivilisationsprozess und Mediatisierung. Zum Zusammenhang von Medien-und Gesellschaftswandel. In M. Behmer, F. Krotz, R. Stöber, and C. Winter (Eds.), *Medienentwicklung und gesellschaftlicher Wandel. Beiträge zu einer theoretischen und empirischen Herausforderung* (pp. 15–38). Wiesbaden: Westdeutscher Verlag.

Krotz, F. (2005). Handlungstheorien. In L. Mikos and C. Wegener (Eds.), *Qualitative Medienforschung. Ein Handbuch* (pp. 40–49). Konstanz: UVK.

Krotz, F. (2007). *Mediatisierung. Fallstudien zum Wandel von Kommunikation.* Wiesbaden: VS.

Krotz, F. (2008). Kultureller und gesellschaftlicher Wandel im Kontext des Wandels von Medien und Kommunikation. In T. Thomas (Ed.), *Medienkultur und soziales Handeln.* (pp. 43–62). Wiesbaden: VS.

Lemke, T. (2000). Neoliberalismus, Staat und Selbsttechnologien. Ein kritischer Überblick über die governmentality studies. *Politische Vierteljahresschrift*, 41, 31–47.

Lindner, R. (2004). Introduction. In L. Musner (Ed.), *Kultur als Textur des Sozialen. Essays zum Stand der Kulturwissenschaften* (pp. 11–13). Wien: Löcker.

Mühlbauer, P. (2007). Hyperangepasstheit und Hyperexhibitionismus. Sind Castingshows und MySpace verwandte Phänomene? Retrieved September, 27, 2008 from http://www.heise.de/tp/r4/artikel/25/25222/1.html.

Müller, E. (2005). Performativ, transformativ, interaktiv. *Montage/AV*, 14 (1), 137–154. Retrieved May, 4, 2007 from http://www.let.uu.nl/~Eggo.Mueller/personal/onderzoek/performativ_transformativ_interaktiv_2005.pdf.

Otte, G. (2005). Entwicklung und Test einer integrativen Typologie der Lebensführung für die Bundesrepublik Deutschland. *Zeitschrift für Soziologie*, 34, 442–467.

Pias, C., Vogl, J., Engell, L., Fahle, O., and Neitzel, J. (Eds.) (1999). *Kursbuch Medienkultur. Die maßgeblichen Theorien von Brecht bis Baudrillard*. Stuttgart: DVA.

Sauer, B. (2001). Die serielle Zivilgesellschaft. Vom Einbruch der Politik in das Echtmenschenfernsehen. In E. Flicker (Ed.): *Wissenschaft fährt "Taxi Orange." Befunde zur österreichischen Reality-TV-Show* (pp. 155–173). Wien: Promedia.

Schiller, H.-E. (2005). *Individualismus. Zur Kritischen Theorie der Individualisierung*. Retrieved May, 7th, 2007 from URL: http://www.rote-ruhr-uni.com/texte/schiller_individualismus.pdf.

Schroer, M. (2001). *Das Individuum der Gesellschaft*. Franfurt/Main: Suhrkamp.

Soeffner, H.-G. (1995). Die Inszenierung von Gesellschaft—Wählen als Freizeitgestaltung. In H.-G. Soeffner (Ed.), *Die Ordnung der Rituale* (pp. 157–176). Frankfurt/Main: Suhrkamp.

Spiegel (2008). Verschwinden der Mittelschicht. Alarmierender Armutsbericht entfacht Steuerstreit (2008, May 19). *Der Spiegel Online*. Retrieved from http://www.spiegel.de/politik/deutschland/0,1518,554023,00.html.

Stauff, M. (2005). *Das neue Fernsehen. Machteffekte einer heterogenen Kulturtechnologie*. Münster: Lit.

Thomas, T., and Krotz, F. (2008). Medienkultur und Soziales Handeln. Begriffsarbeiten zur Theorieentwicklung. In Thomas, T. (Ed.). *Medienkultur und soziales Handeln*. (pp. 17–42). Wiesbaden: VS.

Thomas, T. (2009). "Lifestyle-TV"—Critical attitudes towards banal programming. In N. Carpentier and S. van Bauwel (Eds.) *Trans-reality Television. The Transgression of Reality, Genre, Politics and Audience in Reality TV*. Lexington, MA: Lexington Books, in preparation.

Voß, G. G., and Pongratz, H. J. (1998). Der Arbeitskraftunternehmer. Eine neue Grundform der Ware Arbeitskraft. *Kölner Zeitschrift für Soziologie und Sozialpsychologie*, 50, 131–158.

Voß, G. G., Holly, W., and Boehnke, K. (Eds.) (2000). *Neue Medien im Alltag: Begriffsbestimmungen eines interdisziplinären Forschungsfeldes*. Opladen: Leske & Budrich.

Voß, G. G. (1991): *Lebensführung als Arbeit. Über die Autonomie der Person im Alltag der Gesellschaft*. Stuttgart: Enke.

Wagner, G. (2004). *Anerkennung und Individualisierung*. Konstanz: UVK.

Weiß, R. (2003). Alltagskultur. In H.-O. Hügel (Ed.), *Handbuch Populäre Kultur* (pp. 23–32). Stuttgart/Weimar: Metzler.

Wohlrab-Sahr, M. (1997). Individualisierung: Differenzierungsprozeß und Zurechnungsmodus. In U. Beck and P. Sopp (Eds.), *Individualisierung und Integration. Neue Konfliktlinien und neuer Integrationsmodus?* (pp. 23–36). Opladen: Leske & Budrich.

CHAPTER FOURTEEN

Continuities: Communicative Form AND Institutionalization

ERIC W. ROTHENBUHLER

In this chapter, I offer a series of observations about mediatization, the phenomenon and our attempts to theorize it, while giving relatively equal treatment to two contrary themes. We need to view mediatization in terms of theoretical continuity, recognizing what it has in common with communication in general and a long history of social activities being organized around systems of communication. We also, though, need to view mediatization in terms of the specificity of each case; we need to address the particular heterogeneity of the process in each different set of historical, social, and institutional circumstances. I will close with an idea to rectify these two contrary intellectual needs, a proposal for a theoretical perspective that recognizes the continuity of mediatization and its institutional particularities.

COMMUNICATIVE FORMS

In the days I was working on this chapter, I was lucky to visit the Danish National Museum in Copenhagen. They have a display of pre-Bronze Age burial stones (if I remember correctly), each painted with a long stick-figure arm and hand reaching straight up the stone with four horizontal lines painted just beyond its grasp. Somehow these figures arrested my attention; they seemed powerfully poignant, but I could not say one confident word about what they meant. Why four lines? Why was that motif repeated? Was the hand reaching or receiving? Did we see its palm or its back? I couldn't say; and yet it spoke to me. I saw a primitive expression of human spirit, of reaching, of desire, of creative imagination. And I imagined a teacher and a pupil: You do it this way, four short lines like this; otherwise it isn't right. Repeated across different stones found in different places, this figure represented communication about communication, the coordination of expressive social action around ideas of the right way to express something. As such it was a communicative form: a shape, a structure that could carry its own meaning, independent of who made it, because it was based in and expressive of communication about communication.

Every museum and every consideration of what is called human prehistory includes attention to such ancient and indecipherable markings on stones. Inscrutable though they may be, all of us, expert and lay alike, recognize them immediately as signs, as marks that somebody left to be read, even if we cannot read them. We recognize them as evidence of human will, thought, imagination, expression, and labor—and the desire to connect, to relate, to account for oneself to someone else.

Peirce's definition of a sign as something that stands for something it is not, in some situation, for somebody, for some purpose, emphasizes that no one left those marks accidentally. They appear in the same form on multiple stones in multiple places because someone must have been practicing, teaching, professing, preaching, or whatever were the ancient equivalents. Someone was saying to him or herself or to a student or their clan mates or neighbors, this is the right way to do it. Someone must have been recognized as doing it well and therefore been asked to do it more often or when it was more important. Maybe many people scratched these signs into the dirt, but only some invested the labor of leaving their marks in stones. While they scratched and painted at the stone, someone else hunted and gathered. Necessarily, some of their communication was organized by reference to that communication: You paint; I will hunt.

It is useful to think about mediatization in continuity with this deep history of humans leaving signs for others to read and organizing their social interactions around that. Today we have an industrialized technology of communication. Like all of its forebears, it is communicatively organized around the production of communication. That reflectiveness generates centers of gravity in fields of creative intelligence, attention, and interpretation that appear as repeatable forms of communication—that stick figure arm and hand reaching for the four horizontal bars, the pyramid form of the newspaper story, or the formula narrative of the situation comedy.

MEDIATIZATION: PHENOMENON AND CONCEPT

I take *mediatization* as a name for the process by which activities of various social spheres come to be conducted under the influence of the media, with the media, through the media, or by the logic of the media. The idea resonates because examples come so readily to mind. From family life to politics to globalization, the sense that the world is in transition is widespread, and communication scholars, politicians, public commentators, and lay observers alike see that the media, conceived broadly, are key participants if not the very infrastructure of those changes. We can all think of examples to add to those already reviewed by Hjarvard (2008), Schulz (2004), and the other chapters of this book.

Politics, business, education, art, and religion are conducted with attention to the needs and internal logics of the media, because their success has come to depend on media. Family life, friendship, and leisure are increasingly mediated too, conducted with cell phones, texting, e-mail, the internet, and personal digital devices. These diverse examples can be considered importantly similar to the extent there is some structuring logic of the media so that anything conducted with it, through it, or under its influence shares some attributes and is distinct in those same ways from activities conducted separately and differently from the media.

These shifts and changes in our social world have received wide notice, and many scholars have offered concepts to address them. The mediatization literature has attempted to organize this work under a single heading, but it has generated considerable debate over terms and logic, as reviewed elsewhere in this book. Here I want to emphasize points of commonality among these different conceptualizations and related terms of theory. Mediation, media logic, media forms, mediazation, medialization, mediatization: despite the differences in detail, most of these words are used to address a related cluster of concerns, even if not with the same emphases.

While acknowledging that both mediatization and mediation are useful concepts, for example, Couldry (2008) criticizes the use of mediatization to theorize social change, because it is the more linear, directional one. He says mediatization implies that once there were natural social processes and then the media changed them. Rather than mediatization as a conception of a linear, unidirectional, predictably causal process, he prefers Silverstone's concept of mediation for an open-ended and dialectical process of less-predictable social change.

On the one hand, it does seem the concept of mediatization depends on an idea that there are preexisting, if not natural, processes independent of the media and then the media do something to them. On the other hand, none of the key works on the topic propose any such simple thing in those explicit terms. Mediatization is taken to address a complex social process, more observable at the level of institutional, collective, and macro-social trends than it is predictable at the level of individual interactions, like urbanization, modernization, or individualization. It is supposed to vary across institutional spheres, social settings, and historical periods. Some scholars of mediatization suppose its logic depends on the media being a condition of social action, an environment to which actors respond—and this is more or less in line with Silverstone's concept of "mediation."

In his last major work, Silverstone (2007) was reaching for another set of metaphors. He said "the media are becoming environmental...We have become dependent on the media for the conduct of everyday life. They have become the sine qua non of the quotidian" (p. 5). He subtitles his book "On the Rise of the Mediapolis." The term *media worlds* has some currency, and I use it to convey the idea that media are something we live inside as much as they are technologies we use for expression, information, influence, and entertainment. A decade ago, George Gerbner helped found a cultural environment movement, arguing for more systematic attention to the role of the media in building the cultural world in which we live. Innis's (1951, 1972) theoretical history of the relations between information technologies and the shapes of the cultures that depend on them, and the media ecology perspective influenced by his work (reviewed by Schofield Clark, this book) can be read as intellectual associates of this project as well. Simmel's concept of social form, as reviewed by Lundby (this book), is another important precursor, and many others could be named from any of the traditions of philosophy, social theory, anthropology, or cultural history that emphasize issues of form. It is form, after all, that is at the heart of the mediatization discussion: do media have a distinct form and the capacity to impose it on or replicate it through other social activities, processes, and institutions?

If we take mediatization as a topic, a research question, or a perspective rather than a specific theory, then we can benefit from this wide range of conceptual associations among the works of these and other scholars and avoid the need to debate the details. In this perspective, mediatization, or whatever you prefer to call it, is a term for drawing attention to how social activities begin to change in the presence of the media; it is a useful way to draw attention to a certain class of media consequences; it is a topic to investigate rather than a prediction or a knowledge claim. Then the more specific theoretical claims of some of these authors can be used as heuristics to generate research questions or tentative explanations. This approach also has the advantage of expecting differences across historical and social settings, technological and economic configurations, institutional structures, and political systems.

INVESTIGATING MEDIATIZATION

How should mediatization be investigated? There seems only one answer: historical and comparative studies. How else could we know that something has been altered, is being done differently in interaction with the media, than through historical study? How else could we know it is the media and not something else that produced that historical change other than through comparative study?

The very idea of mediatization arises in historical thinking, and Hjarvard (2008), Schulz (2004), and others are explicit on this point. They see mediatization as a concept for major social change on the order of urbanization, industrialization, or individualization. Historical examples are as easy to think of as are contemporary ones.

The media have been major participants, if not the sole cause of permanent change, in several spheres of social life. No one can imagine that politics will ever again be conducted as it was before television, and the Democratic campaign in the 2008 American Presidential election has demonstrated the differences in process, organization, and substantive appeal made possible when campaign strategies are adjusted to the interconnected logic of the internet. Educational institutions and practices have adjusted to the needs and habits of generations of children raised on succeeding generations of media. The development and change of American musical culture has been dependent on its media and media businesses, from the beginnings of the sheet music trade in the nineteenth century through the development of a record business for diverse popular styles in the 1920s and on to the contest between CD sales and digital downloading today (e.g., Katz 2004; Kenney, 1999; Millard, 1995). The social presence and cultural influence of American music all over the world is another testimony to the mediatization of that cultural sphere. How else did it get there? How else could it have had its influence? Lynd and Lynd (1929) and Willey and Rice (1933) documented the changes in leisure and family life produced in the 1920s in America by what Lynd and Lynd called "those space binding leisure time inventions imported from without"—the phonograph, radio, cinema, newspaper, magazine, and automobile.

Despite the ready examples, historical and comparative inquiry always yields surprises. As Hallin and Mancini (2004) point out, "Comparing U.S. and Italian TV news in the early 1980s, familiar patterns of news construction, which we had to some extent assumed were the natural form of TV news, were revealed to us as products of a particular system" (p. 2). Similarly, they cite Bendix's work demonstrating that what we tend to think of as "the" process of urbanization has worked out very differently in India and other non-Western states. On the other hand, they point out that comparative analysis can provoke generalizations where we had thought we were observing particular processes. They offer the example of the increasingly skeptical tone of journalism toward political leaders in the last few decades. In the United States, this tends to be talked about as a post-Vietnam, post-Watergate phenomenon. Nevertheless, they say that comparative analysis shows that the same trend appears in most of the Western democracies.

DIFFERENTIATION

One set of crucial questions for conceptualizing mediatization involves institutional differentiation. To the extent mediatization is conceived as a process by which previously independent social activities come to be dependent on the media and shaped by the media's own institutional needs, we must first conceive the media as themselves independent and differentiated systems. We have to have an answer to how that would happen historically, to what would be the mechanisms to produce and sustain that differentiation.

This is most obvious and easiest to understand in regard to the press and politics. It is only in the presence of something we can reasonably call an independent press that it makes sense to talk about the press influencing government or politics; it is only after that influence is large and important that we would expect to see something we could call mediatization, as the conduct of government and politics begins to be adapted to the needs of the press.

Differentiation is a central issue for social systems theorists, and it is no accident that Parsons, Luhmann, and Alexander have each written on the differentiation of the media as an independent institutional system. Hjarvard (2008) points out that media scholars tend to be suspicious of such social system schemes, but he recognizes the necessity of the issue for theorizing mediatization and offers an adaptation in the form of an open-ended heuristic. Hjarvard's design identifies historical periods of dominance for three configurations of institutional character defined by dominant logic, media system, and purposes and objectives. He distinguishes periods when the media were fully dependent on other institutions, expressed their views, and served their needs; periods when their operational independence was supported within the larger system; and periods when they were fully independent and sufficiently influential that other institutional spheres adjust their activities to fit the needs of the media.

The question of differentiation, like mediatization, is also usually addressed within a national system or on the basis of a few convenient examples of national comparisons. Hjarvard's scheme, for example, is worked out in reference to Danish and Northern European political media and would have to be adjusted in obvious ways to fit other national settings. Interestingly, Hallin and Mancini (2004) point out that the differentiation *between* national media systems "is clearly diminishing; whether that process of convergence will stop at a certain point or continue until national differentiation becomes irrelevant we cannot yet know" (p. 13). This is important to the discussion of mediatization because (a) to the extent the differentiation of media from other institutional systems within nation states depends on some process of unfolding inherent characteristics of media technologies, media work, or media institutions, we should expect media systems in different countries to grow more alike. And (b) if one part of the logic of media is to connect and to replicate, then we should expect the media systems of different countries to connect with each other and to repeat each other's materials more readily and more often as they become more differentiated within their own country and more similar internationally—and that, in turn, would lead to yet more differentiation from other institutions. The first of these points addresses evidence of the media-logic form of mediatization. The second raises the possibility of mediatization as a worldwide process.

MEDIA LOGIC AND INSTITUTIONAL SPECIFICITY

But what of this idea of media logic? It is a most inviting idea that there may be some inward nature, inherent logic, structure, or technological form to a medium, so that its uses systematically, even if slowly and incrementally, tend toward one set of social outcomes. This was Innis's logic in his discussions of media bias and such of his claims as that the printing press produced the industrial revolution (Innis 1951). But if so, why did it not produce the industrial revolution in China or Korea, where moveable type was known before Gutenberg's invention?

The Protestant Reformation would appear an excellent example of mediatization. It was a major social-historical change that depended on a medium: the printing of large numbers of Bibles in vernacular, as well as other books and news of the movement. It changed the shape and practice of religion—re-formed it—to include media: reading, preaching, and singing. Thinking with Innis, it is tempting to imagine an inner logic of the printing press so that it "wants" to make more copies and find more readers. It is tempting to imagine that this inner logic replicated itself in the spreading Reformation movement and then in the new Evangelical forms of Protestantism.

If that was all the result of the unfolding of some inward logic of writing or books or printing, though, then why do the three great religions of the book have such different relations with the printed word? Why do Judaism, Christianity, and Islam (and the different sects within them) promote such different relations between their adherents and their texts?

Despite the ready examples of apparently permanent social change wrought by the media, it is equally easy to identify examples when the apparent effects of the media have failed to obtain, or where the effects of "the same" medium appear to be very different in different settings. If there is some inherent logic or technological form to radio broadcasting, why was it designed and operated so differently in the United States and Europe and with such different results? Why does commercial broadcasting today still appear so different from noncommercial broadcasting? Is it because the logic of commerce or advertising is more influential than the logic of the medium? But why were the form, audience, and social consequences of commercial radio in the United States so different in the network era and after the rise of formatted radio in the 1950s? Why does the visuality of the medium work out differently in television and film? Why do French film, Hollywood film, Hong Kong film, and Bollywood film look so different and travel the world so differently?

These examples illustrate the heterogeneity of media forms in different historical, social, and institutional settings; it could appear there is no hope for concepts that assume a stable, inner nature of each medium. Let us try another approach, though. No one can imagine Innis was completely wrong, for example, to point out that paper-based systems of communication were more portable and thus more conducive to trade and empire than were orality, stone, clay, or parchment. Similarly, it seems right, somehow, even if general and abstract, when Innis identifies an affinity among the printing press, the factory, and a culture that values trade, that measures value in number of copies sold. Surely it also seems right, even if general and abstract, to think there is an affinity between the ways in which politics are conducted differently today, via and under the influence of television, and the characteristic structures, processes, logic, or systemic needs of the television institution. Having pointed to the affinity, of course, we also imagine it is part of the explanation, that the inner logic of the media form has influenced the social activities conducted with its aid. To handle the heterogeneity of the results, though, we need to add consideration of at least two other structuring elements.

Every one of the media we consider has systems of financing and organizing its work, and those systems will have powerful structuring logics of their own. For profit and not-for-profit, income from admissions, consumer sales, patronage, or advertising, government versus private patronage, each system of financing is a powerful shaper of media work and media products. Whatever might be the inner logic of television, for example, it will be modulated by a given system of finance. These issues need to be considered at a lower level of detail as well, in terms of inter-industry and intra-industry competition and strategy, and in terms of industrial and organizational structure, occupational careers, and work routines.

The production of culture literature is a useful guide on these issues (see Peterson 1990, 1994, 1997, for example).

If we might think of finance and organizational issues as external to communication and culture, then we also need to address a set of structuring elements that arise internally. Every instance of communication implies a mode of address to its audience or interlocutor and appears in a socially recognizable form with semiotic and pragmatic structure. Cultural artifacts and performances are structured as narratives of various types, genres, styles, and modes. Similarly, any medium of communication and any system of finance is going to be deployed socially for some communicative purpose: expression, influence, narration, connecting, announcing, relating, networking, etc. The list can be proliferated, but the point is clear enough: We cannot account for either the variance or the stability of media forms without attention to their social nature as communicative and cultural forms.

If we address the logic of the medium, the system of financing and organizing its production and reception, and the structures and processes of its communicative and cultural forms, all three simultaneously, we will have a rough model of the process of institutionalization as it applies to media of communication and culture. With such a model we might find, for example, that we actually can account for the similarities and the differences among radio, television, and film in France, the United States, and Hong Kong. Mediatization, then, will be the name for a very general process, a topic of research that will show it to work out differently in different institutional, social, and historical circumstances.

CONTINUITY

However varied its results may be, though, mediatization can also be understood as a larger, more elaborate version of the basic human process of communication. Mediatization may appear in distinct and varied forms tied to particular institutional structures, dominant technologies, and cultural systems, but it is not different in kind from the basic process of communication everywhere, in all its forms and contexts.

We know ourselves and others, we connect, relate, and account via the forms and processes of communication—and all communication is always, already mediated. In this sense, mediatization is not a new phenomenon but a fundamental of communication. The mediatization of religion has been the focus of some interesting research, for example (reviewed by Hoover, this book), but from this point of view, religion was always, already "mediatized," though we did not call it that. A religious ceremony, for example, is a carefully constructed social event in which the gathering and arrangement of people, and speech, gesture, posture, clothing, architecture, music, icon, image, and decoration are all according to conventional form. Religious experience is produced in interaction with, and thus under the influence of, these media forms. From this point of view, in terms of their status as media of communication and the capacity of their forms and formats to shape experience, print, radio, television, and the internet are not so different from speech, gesture, posture, and the rest.

It is worthwhile to emphasize this continuity in order to avoid the too simple view of mediatization that Couldry (2008) criticized. From the point of view of general communication theory, it is a mistake to imagine that religion is an autonomous activity and that media are external phenomena. If the starting point of our thinking is that religion is something that operates by its own rules in its own spheres and the media are something other, technologies or institutions in an outside environment, operating by their own rules, then the next step will be to conceive of the relation between media and religion in terms of media doing something to religion or introducing changes into it.

This thinking derives from a prior, more widespread tendency to think of the media as representing some kind of unnatural communication, but we need to rid ourselves of that unhelpful presumption. All communication is via media, starting with speech and gesture, continuing through writing, and on to the elaborate systems of twentieth-century industries of printing, broadcasting, and the internet. From this point of view, the carefully coded speech, gesture, posture, clothing, architecture, music, iconography, statuary, and decoration of a religious service are part of the same continuum of media we see in the rest of the worlds of communication. From this point of view, media are not inherently something outside religions that threaten to do something to them, but the very tools of the conduct of religion.

Of course, some media may be outside threats to some religions in some situations. This requires historical investigations of specific cases, the study of institutions and practices, as introduced in the previous section. Why did some religions become comfortably centered on a book? How do some use the television more successfully than others? Is there an elective affinity between evangelism and television analogous to the affinity Weber (1905/1976) found between capitalism and Calvinism?

Whatever the particularities those historical and institutional studies lead us to consider, we must remember the continuities as well. There could be no elective affinities, there could be no religions of the book, unless the intersection of the two phenomena is in a human, communicating actor. Mediatization is possible because of the striving, human actor, reaching for communicative connection in this world, putting this together with that, taking some thing to stand for something it is not, in some situation, for some purpose.

All imaginable forms and instances of communication are structured by four requirements. There must be some element of the internal world of the social actor, of ideas, feelings, meanings, emotions, identifications, and so on. These must be externalized, given material form in an external world where they can be observed, encountered, and engaged by others. That material, external form must be in the shape of collective systems so that it can be read by the other, it must participate in semiotic code, genre, narrative, icon, ritual, or other recognizable, shared, collective form. That collective form must be expressive of and interpretable as individual meaning. All communication is structured by these four simultaneously necessary aspects: internal-ideal, external-material, individual, and collective. Identifying these produces an inherently sociological communication theory (Rothenbuhler 1987, 1993; Shepherd and Rothenbuhler 1991) that follows Alexander's (1982–83) structure of theoretical logic.

In the present context, the point is that all communication must be in shared and shareable forms, media, and modes. This is mediatization. Therefore, all communication is always, already mediatized.

RECTIFICATION

How can we rectify these intellectual tensions? How can we deal with our theoretical knowledge that mediatization is just a modern, industrialized version of communication in general, and our sense as citizens and social observers that things really are different now and rapidly getting more different? How can we use our knowledge of theoretical continuity and study the interesting and important particularity and variance in the institutional histories of media, politics, religion, and other institutional spheres? I have two proposals.

On the one hand, we can treat it as a fairly straightforward problem of method and level of analysis. All we need to do is manage to study institutional histories while thinking about more general analytic continuity. The details of each case can illustrate the range of possibilities that specific instances of the general phenomenon might take. This is another aspect of the advantages of thinking of mediatization as a topic of research rather than a specific theory. This approach involves more, though, than a simple trick of level of analysis. Making our work historically realistic requires some moderation of the ambitious generality of the theory, too.

The historical and comparative study of mediatization becomes relevant because of the institutional differentiation and growing systemic importance of the media, as Hjarvard (2008) in particular has been careful to address. In other words, while the theory might point to general continuities, we nevertheless do recognize differences. We can show how the practice and experience of religion has always and will always depend on media, in a general communication theory sense, and nevertheless recognize that the historical religions and media have become institutionally differentiated and specified. Each has its own institutional structure, process, public identity, and social expectations. Analogously, some media have institutional structures playing identifiable roles in public life, and others do not. We can identify the theoretical continuities among print, broadcasting, and internet on the one hand, and speech, gesture, and posture on the other, and still recognize that there are industries of the one and not of the other.

So that is one suggestion for rectifying a theory of continuity and awareness of differences: pursue theoretically informed historical studies and let our knowledge of history temper the generality, abstractness, and ambition of our theories. The second suggestion is a shift in the theoretical perspective on mediatization itself.

The strong form of the media logic argument is both the most intriguing and the most troublesome approach to mediatization. The idea that there is some inherent structuring logic of a medium that unfolds or replicates in use so that anything conducted with it, through it, or under its influence shares some key attributes with the medium and is distinct in those same ways from the same activities conducted without the medium, generates powerful and intriguing hypotheses. Yet, as discussed above, it is at least as easy to think of exceptions as to identify the patterns.

Perhaps the logic is not in the medium but in the communication. Perhaps the inner logic of the medium as such, its technological nature, is not the most important influence. As a technology, each medium offers constraints and possibilities; there are things that are more difficult to do and those that are easier. What gets done is still a social choice shaped at least as much by its social situation as by the medium as such. The printing press may "want" to reproduce large numbers of copies, but it cannot and will not do so unless there is a social use for large numbers of copies. It is the cultural value placed on the Bible, a rising cultural interest in individual study and knowledge, and a sense of a new religious movement that led to the Bible being printed in large numbers—not the wants of the printing press.

Communication, as discussed above, is structured by the connection of internal-ideal and external-material, individual and collective. The inner logic of communication in action, then, requires the use of form and a network of self-referencing, other-referencing, and context referencing. Communication is replete with signs connecting the communicator and the communicated as well as semiotic references forward and back in the flow of communication, connecting elements in the sequence of signs, and references to the context, purpose, audience or addressee, and more. Acts, performances, texts, and objects of communication are tied to their actors and situations through a variety of self-referential signs—self-referential, in this case, meaning that the communication refers to itself. It is, then, communication about communication, and all communication requires such.

Self-reference is the first condition for the capacity of systems to self-organize. If communication is always self-referential, then it is always ready to become a self-organizing system. If communication is a system for generating possibilities, such as the system of a language generates uncountable possibilities for statements, then self-organizing systems within it would appear as relatively stable forms against an otherwise always changing, always varied background. These forms would be identifiable patterns of communication that get repeated, that attract attention to themselves, that offer something like semiotic centers of gravity, and that are relatively isolated from their environment of other possibilities. Imagine the teacher and student painting those stick figure arms and outstretched hands on those ancient stones: "Here, be careful, you do it like this." Imagine the rookie newspaper reporter watching the veteran editor rework a text into classic pyramid form. If communication is a generator of social forms through its self-referencing, self-organizing nature, we should expect larger amounts of more complex communication to generate more forms of greater complexity.

The media industries tend to be catalysts of communication. MacDougald (1941), for example, found that more songs became bigger hits for shorter periods of time after radio than before. In the 1950s, after Top 40 and other programming formulas were designed around playing short lists of the most popular songs repeatedly through the day, the popular music charts showed even more rapid turnover with yet more songs becoming hits for even less time. Pool (1983) showed that media can push communicative trends in all possible directions, generating more of even opposing tendencies. He found that the telephone, for example, had been associated with both greater concentration of population and its greater diffusion. The telephone, combined with the elevator and other electrical technologies, allowed greater concentration of business and personnel in city centers, in more densely packed blocks of taller buildings. Combined with electrical streetcars and the automobile, though, it also allowed greater diffusion of the at-home population into city suburbs. The telegraph in its day, and the computer in ours, increased both the speed of movement and the complexity of organization of train cars and shares of stock alike (Beniger 1986).

Generalizations are risky, but in the spirit of conceptual speculation, if communication is a generator of forms, and the media are catalysts of communication, we should expect the media to be super-generators of forms. To the extent mediatization is the process of re-forming the activities of one sphere according to the needs, structures, processes, logics, or interests of media institutions, it is, then, such an activity of generating forms. On the one hand, we can recognize the continuity of communication; mediatization is the latest, largest, most complex example of the ancient process of painting signs on rocks. On the other hand, we can recognize what began to genuinely change in the twentieth century and seems to be accelerating now, as technology and industrialization have superheated the process.

If we expect communication to generate forms, and communicative forms to operate as self-steering, self-preserving systems (Rothenbuhler, in press), and media industries to radically catalyze the process, then we should expect reorganization of media systems and their relations with other institutions increasingly around those forms. Self-organizing systems are expected to gain degrees of closure and relative autonomy from their environment as self-reference and self-steering replace environmental monitoring. This can develop by degrees, but it will cross a threshold at some point. A long history of steady growth in size, complexity, and accumulating change in media industries and the other institutions with which they interact could reach such a point and reorganize relatively quickly. The communicative productions of the media and the communicative interactions around those productions—interactions among personnel within the media and between the media and other institutions—would become more clearly structured in reference to more recognizable media forms. The rise of mediatization, as we have come to theorize it, may depend on the radical growth in communication about communication.

SUMMARY AND CONCLUSION

Mediatization is an interesting idea with several provocative conceptual associations; indeed, any theorizing about social, cultural, symbolic, communicative, or media forms could be relevant to the topic. It is a timely idea, resonating with the widespread sense among citizens and social observers alike that our worlds are changing rapidly and that media industries and media technologies are playing a central role in that. It pulls our thinking in two contrary directions, though. On the one hand, we are tempted to see mediatization in terms of theoretical and historical continuity, as another example of communication in general and the long steady growth of social structures in size and complexity. On the other hand, the concept does seem to organize our attention to a phenomenon that appears genuinely new and seems to work differently in its different settings. These intellectual tensions can be rectified by seeing mediatization as a product of catalyzing communication as such. Communication generates forms around which further communication organizes. Media accelerate that process in frequency, size, and complexity.

REFERENCES

Alexander, J. C. (1982–83). *Theoretical Logic in Sociology* (four volumes). Berkeley, CA: University of California Press.

Beniger, J. R. (1946). *The Control Revolution: Technological and Economic Origins of the Information Society*. Cambridge, MA: Harvard University Press.

Couldry, N. (2008). Mediatization or mediation? Alternative understandings of the emergent space of digital storytelling. *New Media & Society*, 10, 373–391.

Hallin, D. C., and Mancini, P. (2004). *Comparing Media Systems: Three Models of Media and Politics*. Cambridge, UK: Cambridge University Press.

Hjarvard, S. (2008). The mediatization of society. A theory of the media as agents of social and cultural change. *Nordicom Review*, 29(2), 105–134.

Innis, H. A. (1951). *The Bias of Communication*. Toronto: University of Toronto Press.

Innis, H. A. (1972). *Empire and Communication*. Toronto: University of Toronto Press.

Katz, M. (2004). *Capturing Sound: How Technology Has Changed Music*. Berkeley, CA: University of California Press.

Kenney, W. H. (1999). *Recorded Music in American Life: The Phonograph and Popular Memory, 1890–1945*. New York: Oxford University Press.

Lynd, R. S., and Lynd, H. M. (1929). *Middletown: A Study in American Culture*. New York: Harcourt Brace.

MacDougald, D. (1941). The popular music industry. In P. F. Lazarsfeld and F. N. Stanton (Eds.), *Radio Research 1941* (pp. 65–109). New York: Duell, Pearce and Sloan.

Millard, A. (1995). *America on Record: A History of Recorded Sound*. New York: Cambridge University Press.

Peterson, R. A. (1990). Why 1955? Explaining the advent of rock music. *Popular Music*, 9, 97–116.

Peterson, R. A. (1994). Culture studies through the production perspective. In D. Crane (Ed.), *The Sociology of Culture: Emerging Theoretical Perspectives* (pp. 163–190). Oxford, UK: Blackwell.

Peterson, R. A. (1997). *Creating Country Music: Fabricating Authenticity*. Chicago: University of Chicago Press.

Pool, I. de Sola. (1983). *Forecasting the Telephone: A Retrospective Technology Assessment of the Telephone*. Norwood, NJ: Ablex.

Rothenbuhler, E. W. (1987). Neofunctionalism for mass communication theory. In M. Gurevitch and M. R. Levy (Eds.), *Mass Communication Review Yearbook*, Volume 6 (pp. 67–85). Newbury Park: Sage.

Rothenbuhler, E. W. (1993). Argument for a Durkheimian theory of the communicative. *Journal of Communication*, 43 (Summer), 158–163.

Rothenbuhler, E. W. (in press). From media events to ritual to communicative form. In N. Couldry, A. Hepp, and F. Krotz (Eds.), *Media Events in a Global Age*. London: Routledge.

Schulz, W. (2004). Reconstructing mediatization as an analytical concept. *European Journal of Communication*, 19, 87–101.

Shepherd, G. J., and Rothenbuhler, E. W. (1991). A synthetic perspective on goals and discourse. In K. Tracy (Ed.), *Understanding Face-to-Face Interaction: Issues Linking Goals and Discourse* (pp. 189–203). Hillsdale, NJ: Lawrence Erlbaum Associates.

Silverstone, R. (2007). *Media and Morality: On the Rise of the Mediapolis.* Cambridge, UK: Polity Press.

Weber, M. (1976). *The Protestant Ethic and the Spirit of Capitalism* (T. Parsons, trans.). New York: Scribner's Sons (originally 1905).

Willey, M., and Rice, S. (1933). *Communication Agencies and Social Life.* New York: McGraw-Hill.

Conclusion:
Consensus AND Conflict[1]

KNUT LUNDBY

This book has laid important theoretical groundwork in how an interdisciplinary collection of scholars is working with ideas of mediatization. Further steps would include more empirical studies to examine these claims as well as reviews of previous research that might be argued as falling within a framework of mediatization, whether or not the author originally envisioned his or her work as such.

AN OVERALL PERSPECTIVE

The unity of this book, I claim, is to be found in an overall perspective on mediatization. The discussion is theoretical, trying to connect macro- (sociological) theory with micro- and middle-range theories and analyses. The book also composes a comprehensive picture of mediatization across specific fields or institutions such as politics, religion, and everyday life. By this, the book tries to grasp general developments and processes. This collection takes an inclusive approach to mediatization without homogenizing. It is open to local aspects of mediatization (the micro- and field-specific) without becoming provincial.

There certainly is a need for more empirical analyses of mediatization processes while, at the same time, the necessity to qualify the theoretical underpinnings of such studies. Theoretical considerations, as in this volume, help clarify the role of the media and make studies of their impact more adequate. Without a solid theoretical framework, specific case or field studies of mediatization may be superficial. As Krotz concludes at the end of his chapter, 'all empirical research makes sense only if we are able to develop adequate theoretical approaches and bind them together with the existing theories into a close network of academic knowledge. This is what mediatization could be helpful for' (p. 37).

A VARIETY OF EMPIRICAL STUDIES

A variety of examples of solid and relevant empirical research on mediatization have already been undertaken. Although this volume includes a chapter on the mediatization of politics (Chapter 10), it aims to develop dimensions of the concept of mediatization as applied in the domain of politics rather than offering actual studies of how mediatization of politics is played out. However, such studies exist. The theoretical understanding of mediatization had one of its offspring in studies and observations of how the media transformed politics (Asp 1990; Mazzoleni and Schultz 1999) although postmodern theorists were first (cf. the introduction to this book).

There were early empirical studies, for example Fairclough's analysis of the 'order of mediatized political discourse,' with a case study of a BBC current affairs programme. He looked at repertoires of voices, discourses, and genres, and the shifting configurations of articulations that they entered into. He also considered mediatized political discourse as, itself, an 'arena of intersection and tension between the orders of discourse of professional politics and the media' (Fairclough 1995, p. 197).

There are studies of the communication of science. Peter Weingart illustrates mediatization (he uses 'medialization') through three cases: in prepublication of scientific discoveries in the media, with scientists that become media stars, and with the intertwining of scientific, political, and media discourses in the climate change debate (Weingart 1998). Esa Väliverronen studies mediatization of the biotechnology debate. Modern biotechnology with the prospects and threats of gene therapies meets most of the criteria for a good news story, he holds, and the media interfere and transform the issues at stake (Väliverronen 2001).

Throughout this book, there have been several references to religion. Again, this has been to illustrate and underpin the general theoretical arguments about mediatization. By contrast, a collection on the mediatization of religion offers a variety of empirical studies on enchantment, media, and popular culture (Hjarvard 2008c). They range from the American reality television series *Lost* (Clark 2008) to 'banal' religious representations in Danish media (Hjarvard 2008b), just to mention two scholars who are represented in this volume.

Hjarvard has also studied the mediatization of language, arguing that mediatization has increasingly become an independent vehicle of linguistic change through the media's widespread use of English and through the development of 'medialects.' These are the variations and changes in language and language use induced by the media (Hjarvard 2007, 2008a).

The Danish toy manufacturer LEGO is the core case in studies of the mediatization of toys and the global toy industry. LEGO developed figures and series that draw upon media fiction to produce new fictional stories in the play with these bricks and designs. There is a move from 'bricks to bytes' in LEGO computer games. 'LEGO toys increasingly invite play in which storytelling is the crucial activity and narratives about the play are promoted through a whole range of media platforms' (Hjarvard 2004, p. 59, 2008a).

CONSENSUS: MEDIATIZATION OF THE USUAL

In its theoretical explorations, this collection concentrates on mediatization of the habitual or usual, of everyday life and of regular institutional practices in high modern, media-saturated societies. This implies a focus on consensus in line with a ritual view of communication directed toward the maintenance of society (Carey 1989, p. 18). However, in mediatization customary social fields and practices are transformed through the deep involvement with the media, as explained in the various chapters of this book. Mediatization is a concept with which to grasp such media and societal changes, as Krotz underlines in his chapter. Schrott and other contributors then unfold the various dimensions or 'mechanism' of mediatization to get hold of the more specific changes.

Mediatization is treated on various levels in this book.

Krotz introduces mediatization as a historical and long-term meta-process alongside globalization, individualization, and commercialization. Hepp refers to differentiation and cultural changes on this level of civilization or macro analysis, although he becomes somewhat more specific.

Individualization as a meta-process resonates to the level of individual participation in high modern society. Thomas shows how individuality is mediatized. She develops a concept of individualization that underlines the importance of mediatization. Individualization is, today, a source for social acceptance, a mode of socialization. Mediatized communicative and cultural practices contribute to this.

This is a matter of lifestyles, which is at the core of Hjarvard's analysis of 'media and the changing social character.' With Riesman's notion of social character and its further developments with Bourdieu's concept of habitus, Hjarvard contributes to the discussions on cultural identity. There is a mediatization of habitus. The media intervene in all aspects of habitus formation. He finds that the 'other-directed character of the present mediatized society is marked by a soft individualism' (p. 175).

This makes an imprint on everyday life. Hartmann claims that it is exactly in the conduct of everyday life that we can begin to observe mediatization processes at work. It is also within the everyday that mediatization can be questioned: Hartmann regards domestication as a precondition for mediatization. The concept of domestication refers to the micro-level of media use (and related perceptions). It helps to outline in detail the role of media in people's everyday life.

Everyday life is becoming more mobile. Jansson is interested in 'the social interplay between two ambiguous forces of modern society: mobility and mediatization' (p. 243). More specifically, he is interested in what these forces do to people's senses of belonging and continuity. He develops a theoretical framework for analysing 'the mediatization of belonging.'

This ties in with Lundby's proposal to direct the interest in a certain 'media logic' towards studies of changing social relations in the mediatization processes. All social forms in a media-saturated, high modern, society will be more or less mediatized. It is an empirical task to find out how, and to what extent, modern, technical media intervene in social interaction and social forms.

This applies to the institutional level as well. To select a few cases on this level that are analysed in the book:

In the shaping of politics, Strömbäck and Esser hold, mediatization means that the media form a system in its own right independent of as well as interdependent on the political system. In this context, they find the concept of media interventionism to be crucial.

In education, media are both a cultural element outside the institution and a technical element within the educational context. Friesen and Hug argue that the practices and institutions of education need to be understood in a frame of reference that is 'mediatic,' that is, shaped by the transformative power of the media.

The fashion industry is analysed by Skjulstad as this institution 'goes online.'

She examines how mediatization may be observed as part of textual processes of change in online fashion presentations. Emergence, variation, movement, shifts, and changes mark the mediatization of fashion online. The concept of mediatization 'captures how fashion is spread out and re-presented online and now articulated as multimodal online discourse,' Skjulstad (p. 180) observes.

Several of the chapters in this book move at the level of macro cultural-historical changes without moving into meta-processes:

Hoover analyses religious cultures. His emphasis is on contemporary complexities following long historical transformations since the Protestant Reformation and the concurrent introduction of printing technology. He argues that, in order to grasp the contemporary mediatization of religion, we must understand the complexities and nuances of contemporary religion as well as of contemporary media. It will be clear, Hoover says, that 'media and religion are articulated to one another in contemporary experience, and thus a clear distinction between "religion," and "the media," and thus how the former is "mediatized" by the latter, is difficult to draw' (p. 136).

In his chapter on mediatization and cultural change, Hepp discusses the 'moulding forces' of the media in relation to individualization, deterritorialization, and the intermediacy that could be experienced when the media bridge time and space. With this general differentiation in mind, Hepp advises us to look in detail at how the 'moulding forces' of different media are played out in different cultural fields.

The influence of media technology is then obvious, as Clark points out when she discusses 'media ecology' in relation to mediatization theories. However, she warns against collapsing the concepts of 'medium' and 'technologies' as Marshall McLuhan did. She observes the social construction of technology, following Raymond Williams. He argued that technologies 'were not merely artifacts but were also embodiments of knowledge and skillful practices that are required for the use of any tools or machines,' Clark writes (p. 92) paraphrasing Williams.

Rothenbuhler balances the focus on the transforming power of 'the media' by building his argument from continuities and from communication: 'We know ourselves and others, we connect, relate, and account via the forms and processes of communication—and all communication is always, already mediated. In this sense, mediatization is not a new phenomenon but a fundamental of communication' (p. 285).

Rothenbuhler argues that we need to get rid of the widespread tendency to think of the media as representing some kind of unnatural communication. Other contributors in this collection, among them Krotz, also underline that mediatization has to be understood in a communication perspective. Krotz even holds that the mediatization concept 'defines communication as the core activity of human beings' (p. 31).

This does not imply, however, that there is just consensus: mediatization processes largely follow the preexisting stratifications of society, as Jansson reminds us. The 'control of flows and connectivities belongs to those who are already in control of economic and cultural capital,' he argues (p. 250). Thomas observes the production and reproduction of social inequalities through mediatized individualism. The media, she writes, 'support the social organization and structuring of the everyday...but it can also serve as a means to mark the "others," it can be a characteristic of status and roles as well as a battleground for individual rights and independence' (pp. 268–269). Livingstone states it succinctly in the foreword: The concept of mediatization allows us to rethink questions of media power.

CONFLICT: MEDIATIZATION OF WAR AND CRISIS

The said 'usual' uses of media may well involve conflicts and contradictions. However, they are usually resolved through negotiations and regulated procedures. At unusual times, the media may be part of war, crisis, and violence. Then mediatization may be a matter of not just life but also of death. After all, such 'unusual' and conflictual uses are more usual or frequent than we may want to admit.

War has become mediatized. This is not just a matter of war journalism but of an intricate relationship between the media and the military shaping the image of war. This has, of course, impact on the public's ongoing perception of war (Hoskins 2004). However, there is also a 'mediatization of memory' operating when wars are commemorated and renarrativized, not least in television (Hoskins 2007). The 'virtual' Gulf War in 1991 reached a peak in 'representations of mediatized warfare' (Deer 2007, p. 6). Television is also instrumental in mediatizing the global 'war on terror' (Cottle 2006b) as television coverage becomes a part of terrorist plans.

Reviewing a series of books 'on the mediatization of war,' Denis McQuail recognizes that the media have become more involved in issues of war and peace. 'In the case of the last Iraq war, the apparatus of deception was visible to the world from the beginning even in the mainstream media of the United States, for those who cared enough to see.' But the media, he adds, 'are not the main source of the problem' (McQuail 2006, p. 118).

Although not the source, the way war and other serious global crises are reported and shaped through mediatizing techniques (Cottle 2008a) may make a significant difference to the outcome and change the course of the event. The same goes for the global humanitarianism trying to comfort the wounds of war. The major aid agencies play with the 'media logic' and seek to 'brand' themselves in the media (Cottle and Nolan 2007). Trying to get their messages across in today's global communication environment, the aid management organizations are involved in the relations of communicative power that inform and shape the mediatization of humanitarian crisis (Cottle 2008b).

War and crisis are not treated specifically in this book. There is no separate theory for the mediatization of conflicts. However, when the scope turns empirical, there are specific areas of war and crisis to cover, as indicated above.

CONFLICT AND SOCIAL PERFORMANCE

The above is reflecting a general 'mediatized conflict' perspective as laid out by Simon Cottle (2006a). A notion of social performance is applied within the conflict perspective. Mediatized conflicts invite elaborate forms of social performance and social drama. Victor Turner (1974, pp. 78–79) did link social conflict with social drama. Jeffrey Alexander and Ronald Jacobs (1998) observed how media events (Dayan and Katz 1992) could develop into mediated social drama. Their case was the beating of the black Rodney King by white Los Angeles police in 1991 that was filmed and put on local television. Cottle further developed the concept of 'mediatized public crisis' with a case study of the racist murder of Stephen Lawrence in Britain in 1993 (Cottle 2005; 2006a, pp. 61–72). In a recent piece on reporting demonstrations, Cottle claims that the cultural turn in contemporary social theory prompts researchers to engage in qualitative studies of mediated dramaturgy, performance, and spectacular dimensions of such events (Cottle 2008c, p. 866).

This cultural turn, more than any others, refers to the work of Jeffrey Alexander and his colleagues. In the collection on *Social Performance* (Alexander, Giesen, and Mast 2006), Alexander explains his 'cultural pragmatics' as positioned between texts and practices in the study of meaning. His argument is 'that the materiality of practices should be replaced by the more multidimensional concept of performances' (Alexander 2006, p. 29). This argument draws upon the general notion of 'symbolic action' (Alexander and Mast 2006).

Alexander's approach opens doors to mediated communication and to processes of mediatization. However, his interest is basically in cultural and social theory. Other cultural and social theorists go more directly to the media—most prominent perhaps being John B. Thompson. In his analysis of *Ideology and Modern Culture* (1990), he outlines the 'mediazation of modern culture'—where the circulation of symbolic forms become increasingly mediated by the media industries. In *The Media and Modernity* (1995), Thompson further elaborates how this 'mediazation' has transformed the production and circulation of symbolic forms since the introduction of printing in the late fifteenth century (p. 46), and how the 'mediazation' has transformed traditions. The 'uprooting of traditions did not starve them of sustenance. On the contrary, it prepared the way for them to be extended and renewed by being reembedding in new contexts and remoored to spatial units that exceeded the bounds of face-to-face interaction' (Thompson 1995, p. 180).

War and conflicts intensify the mediatization processes. However, there is nothing new: social performance was introduced into the mediatization discourse when the Norwegian sociologist Gudmund Hernes introduced the media dramaturgy techniques in the 'media-twisted society' (Hernes 1977; Asp 1990).

MORAL OF MEDIATIZATION—OR MEDIATION?

War and conflicts also intensify the ethical and moral challenges of mediatization. Major crises make the political importance of mediatization processes more visible.

Lilie Chouliararki takes her readers right into hardship. She writes about *The Spectatorship of Suffering* (2006), drawing attention to the relation between mediatization and pressing humanitarian, global, concerns. Instead of the pessimistic view on mediatization (or 'mediation,' as she prefers) with Baudrillard's post-structuralist and Habermas' critical approaches, Chouliararki views mediation as moral education. She advocates 'the critical analysis of mediation as a symbolic technology of power, which endows spectators with conditional freedom—the option to be agents on the world we watch on television but always within the historical divisions of global power in which broadcasting already operates' (Chouliaraki 2008, p. 847).

The 'ethics of mediation' is a central thread in debates about the future of politics on a global scale, Nick Couldry states in his book, *Listening Beyond the Echoes: Media, Ethics, and Agency in an Uncertain World*. 'Researching those ethics must encompass the major inequalities in the ability of different nations, groups, and individuals to be heard through the world's media system,' he continues (Couldry 2006, pp. 96–97).

Roger Silverstone, in his last book, raises issues on *Media and Morality*. He reminds us that mediation is 'uneven' because 'the power to work with, or against, the dominant or deeply entrenched meanings that the media provide is unevenly distributed across and within society' (Silverstone 2007, p. 109). Daniel Dayan, in a review, finds that Silverstone's moral approach 'tends to do exactly what he accused the media of doing. It quietly divides others into big others (treated as such), and smaller others (dissolved altogether, or treated as if they were just an extension of "me")' (Dayan 2007, p. 120). The moral obligations rest with everyone.

Chouliararki (2006), Couldry (2008), and Silverstone (2007) prefer the word 'mediation' and not 'mediatization.' However, as noted in my introduction, 'mediation' for Silverstone and his colleagues has the same transforming capabilities as 'mediatization' throughout this book.

Hartmann, a long-term affiliate of Silverstone, writes in her chapter herein how he 'claims that mediation is a transformative process in which the meaningfulness and value of things is constructed' (pp. 237–238). Hartmann observes that, again, 'we are now moving into the complex arena of ethics' (p. 238). However, she feels a slight unease about this moral economy approach. She sees 'a responsibility that needs to be taken up for mediatization not to become a swear word' (p. 238).

Chouliaraki observes the multimodality of mediation ('difference within the semiotic') and the multifunctionality of mediation ('difference outside the semiotic') (Chouliaraki 2006, pp. 70–96). These aspects imply the kind of transformations that, in this book, rest with the term *mediatization*. However, when she pleads for mediation as moral education (Chouliaraki 2008), the transformations must not be such that the challenge to ethical action is distorted or removed.

The relation between 'mediatization' and 'mediation,' as discussed in the foreword and introduction, then returns as an issue. Several contributors comment on this distinction throughout the book. Hartmann, after all, finds the mediation idea as developed by Silverstone, to be 'much more normative' than the mediatization concept (p. 237). Mediation requires active participation in terms of thinking, speaking, listening, and acting (Silverstone 2007, p. 38). 'This is the necessary process to give life to the ethical stance referred to earlier. In its normativity, it seems to offer the necessary moral antidote to possible anxieties related to processes of mediatization (e.g., Schulz' negative assessment). Taken in this light, mediation is a necessary precondition for mediatization not to go wrong,' Hartmann (p. 238) holds.

However, the views are divided. According to Strömbäck and Esser, using mediation to 'denote both the neutral act of transmitting messages and the active, ever-present, and increased media influence makes the concept less precise and hence less useful.' To them, 'the essence of mediation' is 'the rather neutral act of transmitting messages,' while 'mediatization,' in contrast, 'is an inherently process-oriented concept, focused on how media influence has increased in a number of different respects...Mediatization has been conceptualized as being on par with other major societal change processes such as modernization, individualization, and globalization...Mediatization is thus a process affecting all parts of society, either directly or indirectly, albeit to different degrees within or across different societies' (p. 208).

Clark's comment (p. 93) on how those in cultural studies think about the process of mediation as constitutive of reality opens a key point of divergence between mediatization and mediation theories. It lays the foundation for mediation's interest in the role of human agency in both creating and using technologies, she holds. To overemphasize technology apart from human agency may lead to technological determinism. However, mediation approaches may emphasize human agency to such an extent that it under-examines technologies. Clark finds that 'mediatization' covers the ways in which technologies and humans together co-create realities and hence jointly contribute to social change.

This identification of mediatization processes from below is, after all, a point well made, especially as Sonia Livingstone, in the foreword, already grasped it from above, when she wrote that mediatization 'refers to the meta-process by which everyday practices and social relations are historically shaped by mediating technologies and media organizations.'

NOTE AND ACKNOWLEDGMENT

1. I am grateful to Lynn Schofield Clark and Stig Hjarvard for support and suggestions for my work with this concluding chapter. I also thank the anonymous final reviewer for the challenge to make such a final statement.

REFERENCES

Alexander, J. C. (2006). Cultural pragmatics: Social performance between ritual and strategy. In J. C. Alexander, B. Giesen, and J. L. Mast (Eds.), *Social Performance: Symbolic Action, Cultural Pragmatics, and Ritual* (pp. 29–90). Cambridge, UK: Cambridge University Press.

Alexander, J. C., Giesen, B., and Mast, J. L. (Eds.). (2006). *Social Performance: Symbolic Action, Cultural Pragmatics, and Ritual*. Cambridge, UK: Cambridge University Press.

Alexander, J. C., and Jacobs, R. N. (1998). Mass communication, ritual and civil society. In T. Liebes and J. Curran (Eds.), *Media, Ritual and Identity* (pp. 23–41). London: Routledge.

Alexander, J. C., and Mast, J. L. (2006). Introduction: Symbolic action in theory and practice: The cultural pragmatics of symbolic action. In J. C. Alexander, B. Giesen, and J. L. Mast (Eds.), *Social Performance: Symbolic Action, Cultural Pragmatics, and Ritual* (pp. 1–28). Cambridge, UK: Cambridge University Press.

Asp, K. (1990). Medialization, media logic and mediarchy. *Nordicom Review*, 11(2), 47–50.

Carey, J. W. (1989). *Communication as Culture. Essays on Media and Society*. Boston: Unwin Hyman.

Chouliaraki, L. (2006). *The Spectatorship of Suffering*. London: Sage.

Chouliaraki, L. (2008). The media as moral education: Mediation and action. *Media, Culture & Society*, 30(6), 831–852.

Clark, L. S. (2008). Religion, philosophy, and convergence culture online: ABC's "Lost" as a study of the processes of mediatization. In S. Hjarvard (Ed.), *The Mediatization of Religion: Enchantment, Media and Popular Culture* (pp. 143–163). Northern Lights. Film & Media Studies Yearbook 6. Bristol: Intellect.

Cottle, S. (2005). Mediatized public crisis and civil society renewal: The racist murder of Stephen Lawrence. *Crime Media Culture*, 1(1), 49–71.

Cottle, S. (2006a). *Mediatized Conflict*. Maidenhead: Open University Press.

Cottle, S. (2006b). Mediatizing the global war on terror: Television's public eye. In A. P. Kavoori and T. Fraley (Eds.), *Media, Terrorism and Theory: A Reader*. Oxford, UK: Rowman and Littlefield.

Cottle, S. (2008a). *Global Crisis Reporting*. Maidenhead, Berkshire: Open University Press/ McGraw-Hill.

Cottle, S. (2008b). *Humanitarian NGOs, News Media and Relations of Communicative Power in the Global Age*. Paper presented at the The Mediatisation of Humanitarian Crisis, POLISMedia, LSE, London, 13 November 2008.

Cottle, S. (2008c). Reporting demonstrations: The changing media politics of dissent. *Media, Culture & Society*, 30(6), 853–872.

Cottle, S., and Nolan, D. (2007). Global humanitarianism and the changing aid-media field. "Everyone was dying for footage." *Journalism Studies*, 8(6), 862–878.

Couldry, N. (2006). *Listening Beyond the Echoes. Media, Ethics, and Agency in an Uncertain World.* Boulder, CO: Paradigm Publishers.

Couldry, N. (2008). Mediatization or mediation? Alternative understandings of the emergent space of digital storytelling. *New Media & Society*, 10(3), 373–391.

Dayan, D. (2007). On morality, distance and the other. Roger Silverstone's "Media and morality." *International Journal of Communication*, 1, 113–122.

Dayan, D., and Katz, E. (1992). *Media Events: The Live Broadcasting of History.* Cambridge, MA: Harvard University Press.

Deer, P. (2007). Introduction: The ends of war and the limits of war culture. *Social Text*, 25(2), 1–11.

Fairclough, N. (1995). *Media Discourse.* London: Edward Arnold.

Hernes, G. (1977). Det media-vridde samfunn. *Samtiden*, 86(1), 1–14.

Hjarvard, S. (2004). From bricks to bytes: The mediatization of a global toy industry. In I. Bondebjerg and P. Golding (Eds.), *European Culture and the Media* (pp. 43–63). Bristol, UK: Intellect.

Hjarvard, S. (2007). *Changing Media—Changing Language. The Mediatization of Society and the Spread of English and Medialects.* Paper presented at the International Communication Association 57th Annual Conference, San Francisco, May 24–28, 2007.

Hjarvard, S. (2008a). *En verden af medier. Medialiseringen af politik, sprog, religion og leg.* Fredriksberg: Samfundslitteratur.

Hjarvard, S. (2008b). The mediatization of religion. A theory of the media as agents of religious change. In S. Hjarvard (Ed.), *The Mediatization of Religion: Enchantment, Media and Popular Culture* (pp. 9–26). Northern Lights. Film & Media Studies Yearbook 6. Bristol, UK: Intellect.

Hjarvard, S. (Ed.). (2008c). *The Mediatization of Religion: Enchantment, Media and Popular Culture.* Northern Lights. Film & Media Studies Yearbook 6. Bristol, UK: Intellect.

Hoskins, A. (2004). *Televising War: From Vietnam to Iraq.* London: Continuum.

Hoskins, A. (2007). Ghost in the machine: Television and wars' past(s). In S. Maltby and R. Keeble (Eds.), *Communicating War: Memory, Media and Military* (pp. 18–28). Bury St Edmunds, Suffolk: Arima Publishing.

Mazzoleni, G., and Schultz, W. (1999). "Mediatization" of politics: A challenge for democracy? *Political Communication*, 16, 247–261.

McQuail, D. (2006). On the mediatization of war. *The International Communication Gazette*, 68(2), 107–118.

Silverstone, R. (2007). *Media and Morality: On the Rise of the Mediapolis.* Cambridge, UK: Polity Press.

Thompson, J. B. (1990). *Ideology and Modern Culture. Critical Social Theory in the Era of Mass Communication.* Oxford, UK: Polity Press.

Thompson, J. B. (1995). *The Media and Modernity.* Oxford, UK: Polity Press.

Turner, V. (1974). *Dramas, Fields, and Metaphors: Symbolic Action in Human Society.* Ithaca, NY: Cornell University Press.

Väliverronen, E. (2001). From mediation to mediatization. The new politics of communicating science and biotechnology. In U. Kivikuru and T. Savolainen (Eds.), *The Politics of Public Issues* (pp. 157–177). Helsinki: Department of Communication, University of Helsinki.

Weingart, P. (1998). Science and the media. *Research Policy*, 27(8), 869–879.

Index

academic learning model, 72
accommodation, 236–7
actor-network theory, 94–5, 97
advertising, 180, 181, 190–1
agency, 95
Alexander, Jeffrey, 299
Altheide, David, 8, 103, 104, 106–8, 110–11, 113–15, 207, 213
American character, 162
American musical culture, 281, 289
Anderson, Benedict, 145
Annie Hall (1977), 85–6
antimaterialism, 256
Aristotle, 63
Asp, Kent, 12, 113
audience, 52, 130, 210
    demographics, 133
    mass, 145
    maximization, 171
Augustine, St., 63
Auslander, Philip, 7
autonomy, 10, 129, 130, 173, 174–5, 220, 265, 267, 290
average consumers, 79

Bachelard, Gaston, 244–7
banal nationalism, 148
Baudrillard, Jean, 10, 13, 14, 96
Beck, Ulrich, 141, 146, 264, 266, 267
Beck-Gernsheim, Elisabeth, 141, 266
behavior, individual, 49–50
behavioral norms, 166, 169, 170
belonging(s)
    concept of, 244–5
    mediatization of, 244
    social and material, 244–9
    spaces of, 247, 251
Beniger, James, 97
Benjamon, Walter, 10
Berger, Peter, 24, 29, 150
biographies, 266
blogs, 77, 79
Blumenberg, Hans, 80
Blumler, Jay G., 45
Bourdieu, Pierre, 22, 33–5, 114, 149, 159–60, 163, 244, 246, 266
Bowlby, Rachel, 239
branding, 184–5, 190–1
brandscapes, 181

British Cultural Studies, 132
broadcast media, 67–8, 169
Bruuns Bazaar, 182, 187, 193–6
Bublitz, Hannelore, 269
Burkart, Günter, 272

Campbell, Colin, 159
capital, 33–4
    cultural, 130, 131, 244, 254–6
    meta, 149
    social, 130, 131, 249
capitalism, 159, 267
Carey, James, 28, 29, 93, 249
Cassirer, Ernst, 63, 66, 67, 81
casting shows, 272
Catholic Church, 131–2, 150–2
Catholic World Youth Day, 150–2
causality, 94, 95
cell phones *see* mobile phones
chat, 77, 147, 148, 249
Chicago school, 106
childhood, 75
children, socialization of, 22–3, 36, 58
choice biographies, 266
Chouliararki, Lillie, 300, 301
Christianity, 134
cinema, 21
civilization, 35
civil religion, 125
Clark, Lynn Schofield, 14, 85, 297
CNN, 207
Coleman, James, 10, 49
commercial culture, 79
commercialization, 5, 25
commercial logic, 8
commodification, 129, 236
common culture, 135
communication, 27, 288–9
    as basic practice, 25
    ecology of, 111
    face-to-face, 23, 24, 30, 31, 208
    mediated, 1, 2, 23–4, 30–2, 208,
        227, 228
    non-mediated, 30
    personal, 147

    public, 52
    understanding, 28–31
communication media, 2, 5, 23
communicative forms, 277–80
community, 245
computer games, 21, 31
computers, 27
conduits, 7, 112
confession culture, 272
Confessions (Augustine), 63
conflict, 7, 104, 109, 212, 238, 293, 298–9
consensus, 295–8
consumer culture, 159
consumer research, 171
consumer society, 165
consumption, 7
contemporary society, 170
content, and form, 107, 108–9
context, 52
contingencies, 52–3
continuity, 244, 245, 285–7
control, 256
The Control Revolution (Beniger), 97
cosmopolitan ideal type, 253
cosmopolitans, 257
Cottle, Simon, 7, 12, 106, 299
Couldry, Nick, 12–13, 105, 139, 140, 149,
    180, 183, 236, 269, 286, 300
crisis, 298
crisis of control, 97
critical theory, 162
cultural capital, 33–4, 130, 131, 244, 254–6
cultural change, 2
    deterritorialization, 147–8
    mediatization and, 139–54, 297
cultural context fields, 149–50
cultural identity, 132, 135, 161, 296
cultural industries, 1
cultural logic, 8, 111
cultural materialism, 248–9
cultural praxis, 245
cultural proximity, 148
cultural reality, 24
cultural resonance, 250–1, 256
cultural studies, media ecology and, 93–7

cultural tradition, 89–90
cultural turn, 299
culture, 29
  commercial, 79
  common, 135
  concept of, 28
  confession, 272
  consumer, 159
  global, 181
  media, 268–71
  mediatization of, 3
  participatory, 78–9
  print, 75, 77
  religious, 123–37
  youth, 134, 135
culture industry, 181, 190
cybernetics, 94–6, 98
"The Cyborg Manifesto" (Haraway), 94

Dayan, Daniel, 7
demographics, 133, 172
Derrida, Jacques, 68
determinism, 68, 88, 91–3, 97, 161
deterritorialization, 147–8, 151–3
dialectic approach, to mediatization, 154
diasporas, 152054
differentiation, 282–3
diffusion of innovations, 27
digital divides, 22
digitalization, 114–16
direct mediatization, 5
discursive turn, 67
disenchantment, 112
Distinction (Bourdieu), 246
domesticated mediatization, 234–7
domestication
  concept of, 228–31
  mediation and, 237–8
  mediatization and, 225–39
  process, 235–7
  terminology, 238–9
domestication theory, 25
double articulation, 237
Drotner, Kirsten, 6, 113
dualism, 35

Durkheim, Émile, 265
dynamic gestalts, 188, 190
dynamic interfaces, 188–9
dynamic websites, 188

ecology of communication, 111
An Ecology of Communication (Altheid), 110–11
education
  after mediatic turn, 77–80
  mediatic turn and, 70–7, 80–1
Eide, Martin, 170
Eisenstein, Elizabeth, 10, 129
Elias, Norbert, 22, 35–6
Ellul, Jacques, 96
elsewheres, 250
empathy, 30
empirical studies, 45–6, 113, 294–5
enchantment, 125
encoding/decoding communication model, 29–30
entertainment, 1
environments, 7
epistemology, 66
essentialism, 128
Esser, Frank, 6, 15, 101, 102, 104, 205
esteem, 173
ethics of mediation, 300–2
Evangelicalism, 128, 134–5, 281
Evangelical politics, 124, 128–9
everyday life, 225, 295–8
  see also domestication
expatriates, 244, 252–4, 257
Expedition Robinson, 174
experiential reality, 14

Facebook, 77, 169, 173
face-to-face communication, 23, 24, 30, 31, 208
Fairclough, N., 294
fake news, 130
fallacies, 86
family, 22
fantasy reality, 210
fascism, 162

fashion, 171–2
  brands, 181
  media and, 184
  mediatization of online, 179–99, 296
fashion photography, 192–3
field theory, 149
figurations, 35–6, 37
film, 112, 284
fine arts, 13–14
Finnemann, Niels Ole, 115–16
form, 106–10
format, 106–8, 110
forms of sociation, 108
Fornäs, Johan., 183
Foucault, Michel, 67
fourth estate, 171
framing, 9, 79, 80, 131
France, media-politics relations in, 218–29
Frankfurt School, 162
Freud, Sigmund, 162
Friesen, Norm, 14, 63, 296
Fromm, Erich, 162, 164

gaming, mediated, 1
Georg Simmel on Individuality and Social Forms (Levine), 109
Gerbner, George, 280
German-language scholarship, 64, 65, 71–2, 75, 227
German literary theory, 64
German literature, 43
gestalts, 188, 190
Giddens, Anthony, 160, 254
global culture, 181
globalization, 5, 25, 27–8, 161, 256–9
global politics, 129–30, 132
Goffman, Erving, 30
Graber, Doris, 57–8
grammar, 110, 210–11
Granovetter, Mark, 167–8
graphical user interface (GUI), 185
Green, Eileen, 233
guilt, 164–5
Gurevitch, Michael, 45
Gutenberg, 10

Gutenberg Galaxy (McLuhan), 89
gyroscope, 165

Habermas, Juergen, 4–5, 22, 23, 29, 33, 65
habits, 36
habitus, 33–6, 159–60, 247, 295–6
  mediatization of, 169–72
  social character and, 161–4
Hall, Stuart, 29, 140
Hank, Rainer, 263–4
Hannerz, Ulf, 253
Haraway, Donna, 94, 96
Hartmann, Maren, 15, 225, 267, 296, 300
Harvey, Olivia, 94
Havelock, Eric, 90
Hepp, Andreas, 15, 105, 116, 139, 297
Hernes, Gudmund, 10, 12, 299
Hetherington, Kevin, 250
Hickethier, Knuth, 66
Hjarvard, Stig, 5–8, 10, 12–15, 101, 102, 104–6, 110–13, 124–6, 139, 159, 190, 281
Hoggart, Richard, 89
home, 251
Honneth, Axel, 173, 265, 267
Hoover, Stewart M., 15, 123, 296–7
household, moral economy of, 230–1, 233, 251
household behaviors, 132
household composition, 232
household uses of information and communication technologies (HICT), 229–31
Hug, Theo, 14, 63, 296
human-computer interaction (HCI), 189
human development, 75
humanitarianism, 298
human/technology interface, 94
Hume, David, 96

identity
  cultural, 132, 135, 161, 296
  religious, 132
identity constructions, 7
Illouz, Eva, 272

imagination, 235, 246–7, 250
impression management, 55
independence, 256
indirect mediatization, 5
individual, end of the, 265–7
individual behavior, 49–50
individual decision making, 170–1
individualism, 49, 268
   mediatized, 263–74
   soft, 160, 174–5
individuality, 271–3
individualization, 5, 25, 27, 141, 146–7,
   151, 153, 295
   in context of media culture and
      mediatization, 268–71
   media and changing, 263–5
   processes, in media cultures, 267–8
   without end, 265–7
industrial revolution, 281
information and communication
   technologies (ICTs), 65, 73
information revolution, 97
information society, 212–13
inner-directed character, 164, 165–6
Innis, Harold, 2, 23, 89–91, 249, 280, 281
innovations, diffusion of, 27
institutionalization, 48–9, 51, 53, 150
institutional perspective, 5
institutional specificity, 283–5
institutions, 41–2, 51
   competing, 53
   educational, 74–7
   political, 215, 216
   social, 215
instructional media, 71, 73
integration, 245
interaction design, 116, 184–5, 188–90, 198
interactive media, 37, 64, 170
interfaces
   dynamic, 188–9
   mediatized, 185–7
   Web, 180–8, 190–1
intermediacy, 148, 152–4
internet, 1, 21, 27, 31, 77, 209
intranets, 2

Iran, Islamic Revolution in see Islamic
   Revolution
irony, 130
Islam, 134
Islamic Revolution, 123–4
Isotalus, Pekka, 116

Jacobs, Ronald, 299
Jameson, Frederic, 13–14
Jansson, André, 15, 236, 243
Jenkins, Henry, 78–9
Johnson-Eilola, Johndan, 185
journalism, 149, 170–1, 282
journalistic intervention, 217–19

Kant, Immanuel, 66
Kardiner, Abram, 162
Karl, Irmi, 232
Katz, Elihu, 7
King, Rodney, 299
Klum, Heidi, 272
Knight, Graham, 170
knowledge, 7
Krämer, Sybille, 65, 68
Kress, Gunther, 188
Krotz, Friedrich, 5, 10, 12, 14, 21, 70, 105,
   140–1, 227–8, 270, 294, 295

language(s), 7, 11–12, 67, 295
Lash, Scott, 2, 110, 141
Latin America, 3
Latour, Bruno, 94
Laurel, Brenda, 185, 186
Lawrence, Stephen, 299
laws, 36
Lazarsfeld, Paul, 166
learning, 7, 34–5
Leavis, Frank R., 89
Lefebvre, Henri, 244, 247, 248
LEGO, 190, 295
leisure activities, 1–2
Lepsius, Rainer, 51
Levine, Donald, 109
life conduct, 274
lifestyle preferences, 171–2, 295–6

lifeworlds, 4, 65, 249–52
linearity, 105–6, 227
linguistic turn, 67
LinkedIn, 169, 173
Linvingstone, Sonia, 11
Lister, Martin, 93–4
live broadcasting, 7
Livingstone, Sonia, 301–2
locals, 257
Löfgren, Orvar, 145
logic, 114
    commercial, 8
    cultural, 8, 111
    media, 7–9
    political, 212–15, 220
    technological, 8
    see also media logic
The Lonely Crowd (Riesman), 164, 166
Louw, Eric, 55
love, 173
Luckmann, Thomas, 24, 29, 150
Lundby, Knut, 14, 101, 227, 293, 296

Macintosh computers, 185
manners, 36
Manovich, Lev, 187
Marcinkowski, Frank, 44
Margreiter, Reinhard, 66, 69
Martín-Barbero, Jesús, 3, 4
Marvin, Carolyn, 93
Marx, Karl, 95–6
Marxist sociology, 162
mass audience, 145
mass communication sciences, 43
Massey, Doreen, 249–50, 257
mass media, 3, 42, 46–8, 145, 162
mass psychology, 162
material belongings, 244–9, 250
    see also belonging(s)
material imagination, 246, 250
Mazzoleni, Gianpietro, 4, 6, 8, 208
McCain, John, 205–7
McLuhan, Marshall, 2, 10, 63–4, 67, 76, 77,
    86–7, 89–91, 93, 95–6, 98, 297
McQuail, Denis, 7, 237, 298

Mead, George Herbert, 22, 24, 29, 30
The Mechanical Bride (McLuhan), 89
media, 5, 23, 160–1
    all-embracing, 1–2, 111
    broadcast, 67–8, 169
    as center of society, 236
    changing social character and, 159–75
    communicational practices associated
        with, 27
    definition of, 5
    individualization and, 263–5
    instructional, 71, 73
    interaction design research and, 188–9
    interactive, 37, 64, 170
    mass, 3, 145
    modernity and, 3
    moulding forces of, 140–4, 145, 149
    new, 115, 117, 249, 257
    news, 1, 9, 212–13, 216–19, 281–2
    print, 67
    recognition through, 172–4
    small, 124
    social institutions and, 22–3
    socialization and, 58
    social network, 77, 169, 173
    technical, 1
The Media and Modernity (Thompson), 10,
    144–5
media appropriation, 228, 230–1
media audiences, 130, 133
media authority, 129
media bias, 281
media-centered reporting, 220
mediacentrism, 269
media change, 142
media culture, 268–71
media development, as nonsubstitutional, 26
media didactics, 73
media dramaturgy, 113
media dynamics, 69
media ecology, 3, 69–70, 74, 86–7, 297
    cultural studies' objections to, 93–7
    definition of, 87–91
    mediatization and, 98
media effects, 9, 41–2, 47–8, 66, 210–11

media environment, 27
media events, 7, 125, 148, 205–6
media formats, 8, 210–11, 212
media forms, heterogeneity of, 284
media framing, 131
media grammar, 210–11
media influence, 209–12
media intrusion, 217
media interventionism, 216–20
media literacy, 70–1, 73, 76–7
mediality, 63–4, 69–70
medialization, 63–4, 69–70, 227
media logic, 7–9, 12, 13, 25, 26, 45, 47, 48,
    51, 101–17, 139, 288
    coherency of, 103–5
    concept of, 212–15
    digitalization and, 114–16
    as form or format, 106–8
    impact on public communication, 52
    institutionalization of, 42, 48–9
    institutional specificity and, 283–5
    linearity and, 105–6
    as logic, 114
    managing without, 116
    middle-range explorations and, 113
    political logic and, 220
    social interaction and, 110–13
media mass, 46–8
media organizations, 2, 48
media pedagogy, 71–3
media producers, 9
media rituals, 125–6
media routines, 113
media saturation, 2–4
mediascapes, 184
media society concept, 227
media studies, 86, 95, 162, 190
media system, 217–18
mediated communication, 23–4, 30–2, 208,
    227, 228
mediated gaming, 1
mediated reality, 14
media texts, 187
mediatic turn, 63–81
    education after, 77–80

education and, 70–7, 80–1
    introduction to, 64
    philosophy of, 66–8
    sociology of, 64–6
mediation, 3, 12–13, 25–6, 183–4, 207–9,
    227, 237–8, 280, 301
mediatization, 1–4, 63–4, 69–70
    alternative definition of, 46–8
    of belonging, 244
    concept of, 21–37, 44–5, 160, 279–80
    contextualizing, 150–4
    cultural change and, 139–54, 297
    definition of, 111
    dialectic approach to, 154
    of diasporas, 152–4
    dimensions of, 50–5
    direct vs. indirect, 5
    domestication of, 225–39
    of fashion online, 179–99, 296
    as framework for empirical work, 31–2
    of habitus, 169–72
    historical perspective on, 9–11
    institutional perspective on, 5
    investigating, 281–2
    of language, 295
    linguistics of, 11–12, 25–6, 227
    on macro level, 49–50
    mechanism of, 48–9
    media ecology and, 87, 98
    as media influence, 209–12
    media interventionism and, 216–19
    mediation and, 12–13, 183–4, 207–9,
        237–8, 301
    of memory, 298
    as meta-process, 24–5, 27–8, 31,
        140–1, 295
    middle-range explorations and, 113
    mobility and, 243–59
    moral of, 300–2
    overview of, 226–8
    perspective on, 293–4
    of politics, 6, 45–6, 55–7, 205–21,
        281, 296
    positioning, 139–40
    qualitative aspects of, 143–4

quantitative aspects of, 142–3, 144
relevance of, 42
of religion, 6–7, 111–13, 123–37, 288, 294, 296–7
remediation and, 13–14
researching, 42–6, 144–50
of society, 4–6
textual view on, 180–2
theoretical relations, 33–7
theorizing, 140–4
underlying assumptions, 23–8
of the usual, 295–8
in various fields of activity, 6–7
of war and crisis, 7, 298, 299
mediatization theory, 32
Mediatized Conflict (Cottle), 106
mediatized individualism, 263–74
media worlds, 280
Medienpädagogik, 71–3, 76–7
medium of communication, 90–3
medium theorists, 2–3
medium theory, 2–3, 12, 28, 142, 143
membership, 37
memory, 298
Messenger, 169
meta capital, 149
metaphors, 89
meta-processes, 5, 10, 24–5, 27–8, 31, 140–1, 295
Meyrowitz, Joshua, 6–7, 28, 112, 166, 169
middle-range approach, 113
middle-region, of behavioral norms, 166, 169
migration, 244, 251–2
Miu Miu, 182, 186, 187, 191–3
mobile phones, 21, 36–7, 144, 148, 249
mobility, 296
    cultural capital and, 254–6
    expatriates and, 252–4
    mediatization and, 243–59
    voluntary, 252
modernity, 2, 3, 5, 10
modernization, 265–7
Molenda, Michael, 71
Mollenhauer, Klaus, 75, 76
Moores, Shaun, 244

moral economy, 230–1, 233, 251
morality, 300–2
Moring, Tom, 6
Morley, David, 145, 228, 232–3
Mühlbauer, Peter, 273
Müller, Eggo, 271
multimedia, 71
multimodality, 13, 115, 183, 188, 301
multimodal navigation, 196
Murray, Janet, 196
music, 21, 281, 289
Mykkänen, Juri, 6
MySpace, 173

nationalism, 148
national social character, 162
national-territorial media culture, 145
negative feedback, 95, 97
neo-Evangelicalism, 123, 124, 128, 281
neo-institutionalism, 51
new age movement, 132
new media, 115, 117, 249, 257
news media, 1, 9, 212–13, 216–19, 281–2
New York University, 91
Nielsen, Jacob, 196
Nigeria, 134
9/11 attacks, 132
Noelle-Neumann, Elisabeth, 49
non-mediated communication, 30
norms, 36

Obama, Barack, 205–7
Ong, Walter, 89, 90–1, 98
online chat, 147, 148, 249
online communities, 37
ontological security, 233, 239
openness, 256
Orality and Literacy (Ong), 90
other-directed character, 162, 164–5, 167, 169–70, 174–5

Park, Robert, 106, 108–9
Parsons, Talcott, 28
participatory cultures, 78–9
Patrizia Pepe, 182, 187, 196–8

pedagogy
after mediatic turn, 77–80
mediatic turn and, 70–7
peer groups, 22
personal communication, 147
personal continuity, 245
personal identity, 173–4
personality formation, 35–6
Peters, John Durham, 97
philosophy, of mediatic turn, 66–8
The Philosophy of Money (Simmel), 109
Poetics (Aristotle), 63
The Poetics of Space (Bachelard), 245
political actors, 214, 215, 216, 220
political communication, 51
political institutions, 215, 216
political logic, 102, 212–15, 220
political reality, 219
political system, 217
politicians, constructed celebrity of, 55,
56, 57
politics, 2, 6, 31
ethics of mediation and, 300
global, 129–30, 132
media influence in, 209–12
mediatization of, 45–6, 55–7, 205–21,
281, 296
power and, 213–14
positive feedback, 95
possession, 245
Postman, Neil, 69, 74–5, 76, 77, 87–9,
91–2, 98
post-modernity, 2, 13–14, 130, 161, 166
power, 52
politics and, 213–14
symbolic, 33–4
power geometries, 249–50, 257
power structures, 9
presentation, 48
presidential debates, 205–7
press, 170–1
print, 143–4, 145
print culture, 75, 77
printing press, 7, 10, 281
print literacy, 75–6

print media, 67
privatization, 264
The Production of Space (Lefebvre), 247
protestant ethics, 159, 165
Protestant Reformation, 127, 281, 296–7
pseudo-environment, 210
pseudo-events, 211
psychoanalysis, 162, 163
psychogenesis, 35–6
psychology of affluence, 165
public broadcasting systems, 134
public communication, 52
public scripts, 132
public viewing environments, 232
publishers, 129
publishing, 129
Putnam, Robert, 131, 249

qualitative aspects, of mediatization, 143–4
quantitative aspects, of mediatization,
142–3, 144

radar, 165
radio, 76, 169, 283
Rantanen, Terhi, 253
rational choice theory, 49–50
rationality criteria, 50, 51, 52
reality
experiential, 14
political, 219
social, 24
social constructions of, 210
reality television, 36, 174, 266, 272, 294
fantasy, 210
recognition, through media, 172–4
rectification, 287–90
re-embedding process, 255
reference groups, 37
reflexive screen, 232
reflexivity, 130, 141
Reich, Wilhelm, 162
religion, 2, 96, 281
airtime for, 134
civil, 125
commodification of, 129

conceptual challenges, 127–30
individualization of, 151
mediatization of, 6–7, 111–13, 288, 294, 296–7
role of, 136
social capital and, 131
religious authorities, 131–2, 134
religious cultures, 123–37
religious identities, 132
religious "other", 131–2
Relph, Edward, 250
remediation, 13–14, 180, 198
resonance, 245, 246–7, 250–1, 256
respect, 173
Riesman, David, 15, 159, 162, 164–7, 172–4
rituals
    media, 125–6
    religious, 125
Rogers, Everett, 27
Rothenbuhler, Eric, 15, 101, 116, 277, 297
rules, 36
Rusch, Gebhard, 65

Said, Edward, 131
sanctions, 52
Sapir-Whorf hypothesis, 29
Schiller, Hans-Ernst, 268
schools, 22, 74–7
Schroer, Markus, 265
Schrott, Andrea, 14, 41, 101, 102, 104
Schuetz, Alfred, 24, 29, 37
Schulz, Winfried, 10–11, 44, 105, 115, 139, 211, 227, 236–7
secularization, 123, 125, 126, 136
self-confidence, 173
self-control, 264, 268
self-empowerment, 272
self-esteem, 170, 173
self-optimization, 147
self-organizing systems, 289
self-reference, 289
self-representation, 173–4
self-respect, 173
self-responsibility, 264, 268, 272
self-socialization, 36

semiotic modes, 188–9
sexuality, 232
sharing expert, 232
Shibutani, Tamotsu, 37
signs, 278
Silverstone, Roger, 3–4, 12, 225, 226, 228–31, 237–8, 280, 300
Simmel, Georg, 101, 106, 107, 108–10, 167, 169, 265
Simon, Herbert, 10
Skjulstad, Synne, 15, 116, 179
small media, 124
Smith, Gilliam Crampton, 189
Snow, Robert P., 8, 103, 106, 107–8, 110, 207, 213
sociability, 109, 167–9, 174
social acceptance, 58
social action, 94
social actors, 160, 210
social belongings, 244–9
social capital, 34, 130, 131, 249
social change, 2, 11, 58, 91, 97
social character, 295
    formation of, 164
    habitus and, 161–4
    inner-directed, 164, 165–6
    media and changing, 159–75
    national, 162
    other-directed, 164–5, 167, 169–70, 174–5
    Riesman on, 164–7
    traditional, 164
    types of, 164–6
social conformity, 49
social construction of technology school, 92–3, 94, 95
social constructions, 210
social constructivism, 150, 162
social cooperation, 30
social dimension, of mediatization, 146–7
social divisions, 165–6
social durability, 243
social exclusion, 248
social forms, 108–10
social identity, 135, 161

social inequality, 264, 265–6
social institutions, 159, 160, 215
social interaction, 2, 110–13, 116
socialization, 36, 58, 245
social level, of mediatization, 142–3
social movements, 3
social network media, 77, 169, 173
social networks, 130–1
social performance, 299
social psychology, 162
social reality, 24
social space, 248
social stratification, 248
social ties, weak, 160, 167–9
sociation, 108–9
societal media effects, 41–2
societal structures, 41–2
society, 29
    consumer, 165
    contemporary, 170
    individual and, 160–75
    media, 227
    media as center of, 236
    media-saturated, 1–2
    mediatization of, 4–6, 209–11
    modernization of, 265–7
    social units of, 159
sociocultural distinctions, 256–9
sociogenesis, 35
sociological communication theory, 287
sociology, 158–60
    Marxist, 162
    of mediatic turn, 64–6
Soeffner, Georg, 271
soft individualism, 160, 174–5
Sonesson, Göran, 65
Soost, Detlef D., 272
spaces of belonging, 247, 251
spatial dimension, of mediatization, 147–8
spin doctoring, 55, 56, 57
spiral of silence, 41
spiritualism, 96–7
spirituality
    mediatization of, 123–37
    see also religion

spiritual movements, 132
sports, 2
Steinmaurer, Thomas, 43
Stolow, Jeremy, 96, 97
storytelling techniques, 213
Strauss, Anselm, 37
Strömbäck, Jesper, 6, 12, 15, 101, 102, 104, 205
structural environment, 217
structuration theory, 160
student academic learning model, 72
subjectivity, 161
superegos, 36
symbolic capital, 34
symbolic forms, 3
symbolic power, 33–4
symbolic violence, 34

tabloid press, 6
tastes, 172, 246, 247, 250
technical media, 1
technological determinism, 88, 91–3
technological logic, 8
technology, 25, 67, 92–3, 143
telegrams, 26–7
telegraph, 93, 96–7, 289
telemediatization, 145–6
telephone, 289
telepresence, 148
televangelism, 124
television, 21, 36, 76, 112, 143, 145, 169, 209, 231, 269
    politics and, 45–6
    presidential debates on, 205–7
Television (Williams), 109
television news, 212, 213
temporal dimension, of mediatization, 148
terminology, 11–12, 25–6, 227, 238–9
terrorist attacks, 132
texting, 77
textures, 247–8, 249, 251–2
theatre, 185–6
theoretical relations, 33–7
Theory of Civilization (Elias), 35–6
Theory of Communicative Action (Habermas), 4

Thomas, Tanja, 15, 263
Thompson, John B., 3, 10, 12, 144–5, 148, 299
Tomlinson, John, 145, 148, 249
tourism, 7, 251
traditional character, 164
transformations, 3, 5, 9–11, 13, 96, 105, 113, 117, 145, 183, 301
translation, 11–12
transmigration, 244, 251–2
travel, 251
trends, 172
Turkle, Sherry, 185

Understanding Media (McLuhan), 89
United States
    neo-Evangelicalism in, 123, 124, 128–9
    news culture in, 218–19, 281–2
urbanization, 161
Urry, John, 257

Väliverronen, Esa, 294
van Leeuwen, Theo, 188
voluntarism, 161

Wagner, Gabriele, 266
war, mediatization of, 7, 298, 299
warm expert, 232
weak social ties, 160, 167–9
Web 2.0, 77, 78, 79
Web advertising, 180, 181
Web browsers, 115
Weber, Max, 9, 112, 159, 165, 286
Web interfaces, 180–8, 190–1
Web navigation, 182–3, 190–1, 193–8
Weingart, Peter, 294
Wellman, Barry, 106
Welsch, Wolgang, 190
Wikis, 79
Williams, Raymond, 28, 29, 87, 88, 89, 92–3, 95, 109, 143
work ethos, 165
World Wide Web (WWW), 69, 115, 188–9

X Factor, 174

youth culture, 134, 135

About the Editor

KNUT LUNDBY is Professor of Media Studies in the Department of Media and Communication at the University of Oslo, Norway. He holds a Dr.philos. degree in sociology from the University of Oslo. He was the founding director of the interdisciplinary research centre InterMedia at the University of Oslo, focusing on design, communication, and learning in digital environments. He is the director of the Mediatized Stories project and edited *Digital Storytelling, Mediatized Stories: Self-representations in New Media* (Peter Lang, 2008).